NEW LABOR
IN NEW YORK

NEW LABOR IN NEW YORK

Precarious Workers and the
Future of the Labor Movement

**Edited by Ruth Milkman
and Ed Ott**

ILR Press

An imprint of
CORNELL UNIVERSITY PRESS   ITHACA AND LONDON

First published 2014 by Cornell University Press
First printing, Cornell Paperbacks, 2014

Printed in the United States of America

Library of Congress Cataloging-in-Publication Data

New labor in New York : Precarious workers and the future of the labor movement / edited by Ruth Milkman and Ed Ott.
    pages cm
  Includes bibliographical references and index.
   ISBN 978-0-8014-5283-3 (cloth : alk. paper)
   ISBN 978-0-8014-7937-3 (pbk. : alk. paper)
1. Precarious employment—New York (State)—New York.   2. Labor unions—Organizing—New York (State)—New York.   3. Labor movement—New York (State)—New York.   I. Milkman, Ruth, 1954– editor of compilation.
II. Ott, Ed, editor of compilation.

  HD5858.U6N49 2014
  331.8809747'1—dc23

                                                          2013032650

Cloth printing   10 9 8 7 6 5 4 3 2 1
Paperback printing 10 9 8 7 6 5 4 3 2 1

Contents

Preface and Acknowledgments

Ruth Milkman and Ed Ott

This book is the culmination of a long process of collective effort. It began in early 2011, when we decided to coteach a seminar in the Sociology program at the City University of New York (CUNY) Graduate Center entitled "Toward a New Labor Movement: Community-Based Organizations, Unions, and Worker Centers in New York City." To enroll in the course, interested students were required to make a commitment to conduct in-depth fieldwork and to write a case study of an organizing campaign or group, with the understanding that we would eventually try to publish an edited volume like this one. We were extremely fortunate to attract an extraordinary group of PhD students from various departments at the Graduate Center, as well as a few from the Labor Studies masters' program at CUNY's Joseph S. Murphy Institute for Worker Education and Labor Studies, where both of us are on the faculty.

We then began a collective intellectual and political journey, reading a series of key texts on work and labor, as well as on ethnographic and participatory research methods. The group had lively and often passionate discussions from the outset, and meanwhile each participant plunged into the field. Some of the students were already connected to the campaigns or organizations they were writing about; in other cases we facilitated the necessary connections. On the whole, all the organizations and individuals with whom we partnered were highly cooperative and welcoming—although, not surprisingly, we did occasionally encounter situations where organizers or staffers were concerned about revealing information that they would prefer to keep private. Happily those situations were all amicably resolved. We were only sorry that we were not able to include more campaigns and organizations in the project, due to limited resources and capacity.

The students shared progress reports with one another toward the end of the spring 2011 semester, and wrote preliminary drafts of their case studies at that stage as well. The two of us provided detailed feedback on all the drafts, and met with each student individually to discuss next steps. Over the summer, the fieldwork continued, and the group decided to extend the course into a second semester (fall 2011). This time each class session focused on one of the case studies, along with key texts that had influenced each one. All the students had by now revised their earlier drafts, which were then circulated to the entire group; everyone produced written comments on these drafts, which were posted on the course website prior to each weekly meeting. In that second semester, we had intense oral discussions of each case. Each student then rewrote her or his paper once more, and at the end of the semester the two of us again offered detailed feedback. Regrettably, two of the students who participated in the course—Andres Leon, who was part of the spring 2011 course, and Dominique Nisperos, who was involved both semesters—were ultimately unable to complete their projects due to time constraints, but both contributed significantly to the collective discussions and we thank them for that.

Although situated in a university, this project is not typical academic research. From the outset, it involved a collaborative partnership between our research team and the social actors who are the focus of the analysis. Our goal was to produce academically rigorous research and analysis, but also to produce contributions that would be valuable to the organizers and activists involved in the campaigns and groups whose efforts we documented, and by the labor movement more generally, both in New York City and around the country. CUNY is an extraordinarily hospitable environment for this kind of project; both the Graduate Center and the Murphy Institute attract many students who are committed to publicly engaged scholarship, so we could not have found a better institutional setting for this effort.

We were extremely privileged to obtain financial support for the project from the Ford Foundation through the Labor-Community Collaborative. We thank Katherine McFate and Hector Cordero-Guzman, both of whom were at the Foundation when we first began searching for funding, for their guidance and support and for helping orient us to the Foundation. We are especially grateful to Ford Project Officer Laine Romero-Alston for providing funding for the Collaborative, which in turn supported this effort under the leadership of Amy Sugimori and later Lucia Gomez-Jimenez.

Thanks to this funding, we were able to provide infrastructural support for the project. We thank Shoshana Seid-Green and Miguel Cervante for their excellent interview transcriptions. In addition, CUNY graduate student and statistical analyst Laura Braslow supported us by analyzing data from the American Community Survey and the Current Population Survey as needed to inform the case studies. And Dao X. Tran did a meticulous job of formatting the final text of the volume.

The financial support from Ford and the Collaborative also enabled us to organize a public conference at the Murphy Institute on March 9–10, 2012, which attracted over two hundred people and generated important discussions of the project as a whole as well as enriching each of the case studies. Critically important to this process was the presence of leaders from the various campaigns and organizations whose work the papers documented. We are grateful to the Murphy Institute staff, especially Anita Palathingal, Karen Judd, Pamela Whitefield, Nelly Benavides, and Eloiza Morales for their logistical support for the event, and also to CUNY graduate student David Frank, who assisted us with registration. Harmony Goldberg, also a chapter author, skillfully constructed and helped manage the conference website.

By this point, all the students had revised their papers once again, in response to our comments from the end of the fall 2011 semester, and about a month before the conference we posted the resulting drafts on a password-protected website accessible to registered participants. The cases were not formally presented at the conference, although everyone present had access to them through the website.

At the gathering itself, we divided the cases into four groups, each of which was the focus of a two-hour conference session. Each session featured an expert commentator—Dan Clawson, Dorothy Sue Cobble, Jennifer Gordon, and Dorian Warren played this role magnificently. They provided rich and thoughtful feedback on the papers and the larger project, both orally and subsequently in writing. They each presented short summaries of the papers in their sessions, and then offered constructively critical comments on each, followed by open discussion with the audience. The conference also featured an introductory presentation from Ruth Milkman and closing remarks from Ed Ott, which became the basis for the introduction and afterword, respectively, included in this volume.

We encouraged the organizers and staffers who had partnered with the researchers to provide feedback on the papers at every stage of the project, and many did so in the form of detailed comments on the conference papers and presentations. In addition, we thank Allen Hunter, Rebecca Givan, and Julie Rivchin Ulmet, each of whom attended the conference and then took the time and trouble to send us written comments on the project and selected cases. Taking all this into account, all the papers were revised once again following the conference; after that came additional feedback from us, followed by further rewriting and editing—finally generating the chapters collected in these pages. Ruth Milkman was privileged to spend the 2012–13 academic year as a fellow at Harvard's Radcliffe Institute, which provided an ideal setting in which to complete this labor-intensive process and to draft the book's introduction.

Frances Benson, our editor at Cornell University Press, was enthusiastic about this project from the outset and we are deeply grateful for her support and her patience during the long process of putting this volume together. We thank as well the anonymous reviewer for the press, as well as the entire press production team.

NEW LABOR
IN NEW YORK

INTRODUCTION

Toward a New Labor Movement?
Organizing New York City's Precariat

Ruth Milkman

"Our basic system of workplace representation is failing to meet the needs of America's workers," Richard Trumka, president of the American Federation of Labor–Congress of Industrial Organizations (AFL-CIO), declared in March 2013, in an unusually candid acknowledgement of the deep crisis facing U.S. unions in the twenty-first century. "The AFL-CIO's door has to be—and will be—open to any worker or group of workers who wants to organize and build power in the workplace," he added. "Our institutions, our unions will experiment, will adapt to this new age" (Trumka 2013). Although Trumka used the future tense, the AFL-CIO had already begun to follow this path when he uttered these words. In recent years the federation has entered into a series of partnerships with community-based organizations representing domestic workers and day laborers—groups that have almost never had access to union membership. And in October 2011 the AFL-CIO issued a national charter to the Taxi Workers Alliance Organizing Committee (TWAOC)—despite the fact that taxi drivers are not legally "employees" and therefore lack collective bargaining rights under U.S. labor law (Massey 2011c).

The TWAOC is an outgrowth of the New York Taxi Workers Alliance (TWA), one of the many community-based groups, known as "worker centers" (Fine 2006), that have sprung up around the United States in recent decades to organize and advocate for low-wage and marginalized workers, most of them—like the vast majority of New York City taxi drivers—immigrants. Some centers focus on sectors that traditional unions have almost never tried to organize, like domestic work or day labor; others on industries that were once highly organized but from which unions have nearly disappeared, like restaurants or garment manufacturing; still others recruit "independent contractors" like taxi drivers who are unprotected by most labor and employment laws because they are legally classified as self-employed.

This book includes thirteen case studies of recent efforts by both unions and worker centers to organize the unorganized in the New York City metropolitan area. Home to some of the first U.S. worker centers and to thirty-seven of the 214 that exist nationwide at this writing, New York has the single largest concentration of this new form of labor organizing.[1] In recent years, as part 4 of this volume documents, New York also has become a launching pad for efforts to expand the scale of worker centers by building national organizations, such as the TWAOC. However, most worker centers, in New York and elsewhere, remain locally based and modest in size—especially relative to labor unions, which despite decades of decline still had over fourteen million dues-paying members nationwide in 2012 (Hirsch and Macpherson 2013).

Worker centers are the primary alternative organizational form that has emerged alongside traditional unions with a focus on organizing the new "precariat" that has burgeoned in the United States and other advanced industrial economies in recent decades. Precarious workers, as the term suggests, typically have no employment security and most are excluded from the legal protections that the organized labor movement struggled to achieve for the proletariat over the past century (Standing 2011, 8; Vosko 2010, 2). Instead the precariat is embedded in what Kalleberg (2011, 83) describes as "market-mediated" or "open" employment relations, with "relatively weak labor market institutions, standards and regulations." Although the term "precariat" is new, the work arrangements it refers to are hardly without historical precedent: in many cases they parallel older forms of labor exploitation that were widespread in the United States prior to the New Deal reforms of the 1930s.[2]

The worker center movement, which itself echoes pre–New Deal forms of labor organizing in some respects, took shape in the 1990s. It was a response to the growth of the precariat in the 1970s and 1980s, on the one hand, and to the rapid deunionization that marked those same decades, on the other. Although some worker centers actually were launched or funded by traditional unions, most labor leaders greeted the rise of these new organizations with deep skepticism, and in some cases with outright hostility. For their part, worker center leaders often looked askance at traditional unions, which they considered anachronistic and poorly equipped to meet the needs of the marginal, precarious workers they sought to organize. Thus, as Janice Fine put it, what might have been "a marriage made in heaven" was instead "more of a mismatch" (Fine 2007, 336).

Over time, however, as U.S. union membership continued to decline and the number of worker centers grew steadily—from only four in 1992, to 137 in 2003, and then to over two hundred by 2013 (Fine 2011, 607, 615; personal correspondence with Fine)—this mutual hostility began to soften. Union leaders increasingly were confronting the growth of precarious labor arrangements within their own traditional jurisdictions, and gradually came to appreciate the utility of the innovative organizing tactics and strategies the centers had developed. At the same time, as several of the chapters in this volume illustrate, many worker center leaders developed a more positive view of traditional unions as they struggled to build durable organizations. Starting on the West Coast (Milkman 2010), a process of rapprochement between unions and worker centers began to unfold, which by the 2010s had spread to the national level.

New York is the most highly unionized large city in the United States, with union density (the proportion of wage and salary workers who are union members) roughly double the national average (Milkman and Braslow 2012). As such it is the nation's premier example of what Rich Yeselson (2013, 79–80) calls "fortress unionism," a metropolitan region where high union density also sustains a labor-liberal political bulwark. But New York is also marked by higher levels of income inequality than any other large U.S. city, and it is home to a large and growing precariat. The chapters that follow, each of which is based on original research and participant observation, document and analyze the recent efforts of several New York-based worker centers and union-community partnerships to organize this expanding segment of the workforce. Taken together, these case studies offer a richly detailed portrait of the new labor movement in New York City, as well as several recent efforts to expand that movement from the local to the national scale.

Labor's Crisis

Obituaries for the U.S. labor movement have been a perennial in both academic and journalistic commentary since the 1970s, when declining union membership first attracted widespread attention. Indeed, union density has been in free fall for decades. By 2012, only 11.2 percent of U.S. wage and salary workers, and 6.6 percent of those in the private sector, were union members. As recently as 1973 the figures were 24.0 percent and 24.2 percent, respectively (Hirsch and Macpherson 2012)—already far below the mid-1950s peak of about 33 percent.[3] In the public sector, union density remains much higher (35.9% in 2012), and has been relatively stable over recent decades, even as the gap between public and private sector unionization rates has widened steadily.

Arguably the power and influence of organized labor has been reduced even more than these data suggest, especially in the private sector. In the 1950s and 1960s many nonunion private-sector employers routinely matched union wages and working conditions, hoping to preempt unionization; in recent years that dynamic has been reversed, as nonunion competition drives down compensation and standards among the few remaining unionized firms. As a result, unions that won improvements in pay and working conditions for their members in the past increasingly have been forced to surrender them in contract "givebacks." Since the 1970s, moreover, large-scale strikes—historically the most effective expression of union power and leverage—have become conspicuous mainly by their absence, as figure I.1 shows. In contrast, lockouts have become more common, and the few large strikes that do occur are often defensive actions provoked by employers seeking to win large-scale concessions from once-powerful unions, typically leaving workers defeated and demoralized.

Although some commentators have called for a revival of strikes as a means to rebuild the U.S. labor movement (for example, Burns 2011), this seems highly unlikely in the absence of a major shift in the nation's legal regime, which currently allows employers to "permanently replace" workers who go on strike over economic issues and imposes crippling penalties on traditional unions that violate the many legal restrictions on strike activity. Although recent demonstration strikes in the fast food industry and at Walmart have attracted significant attention and public support, these have been brief and relatively small-scale events. Moreover, these actions were led by worker centers and other community-based organizations, which are not bound by the same laws as unions and thus can more easily engage in strikes and other forms of direct action. Indeed legal constraints on traditional unions dating back to the 1947 Taft-Hartley Act are one of the key drivers of the decades-long decline in union density and power (Yeselson 2013).

Moreover, as many commentators have pointed out (for example, Fletcher and Gapasin 2008; Early 2011), some of organized labor's wounds are self-inflicted. Factionalism and internal divisions within the movement, along with bureaucratic inertia and missteps by individual union leaders, have contributed to labor's decline, although their effects are difficult to measure systematically. Globalization and technological change have had an impact as well, especially in the manufacturing sector—historically a key union stronghold. But these factors constitute at best a partial explanation for the dismal plight of organized labor in the United States. The fact that unionization has fallen as sharply in place-bound industries such as construction and hospitality as in the footloose manufacturing sector already suggests the limits of globalization-centered explanations. Moreover, some of the unions that are regularly pilloried by critics as overly bureaucratic and "top-down"—notably the giant Service Employees International

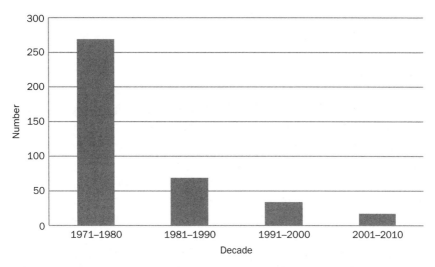

FIGURE I.1 **Average annual major work stoppages involving 1,000 or more workers, by decade, United States, 1971–2010.**

Data from U.S. Bureau of Labor Statistics, "Major Work Stoppages in 2010," press release, February 8, 2011, http://www.bls.gov/news.release/archives/wkstp_02082011.pdf.

Union (SEIU)—are among the few that have managed to expand their membership in recent decades, defying the larger downward trend in union density.

The primary source of labor's crisis is neither the movement's internal problems nor the deleterious effects of the twin processes of deindustrialization and outsourcing, but rather the broader logic of neoliberal economic restructuring that took root in the 1970s. From the outset, the neoliberal agenda included explicit efforts to weaken or eliminate unions, which for its proponents represent an unacceptable form of interference in the labor market. Other core elements of neoliberalism—deregulation (especially in former union strongholds such as transportation and communication), privatization (which often involves shifting jobs from the unionized public sector to nonunion private-sector firms) and more recently, austerity policies—have had less direct but equally devastating effects on workers and their unions.

By the late twentieth century, for most private-sector employers in the United States, unionization was simply anathema, viewed as a source of economic inefficiency and "adversarialism." Except in a few "legacy" industries where unions retained a foothold, the industrial relations departments that once were standard in large U.S. corporations had long since been replaced by human resources departments, for whose staffers "avoiding" unionization was a central preoccupation (Kochan, Katz, and McKersie 1987). With assistance from the burgeoning cadre of professional labor consultants, virtually any employer eager to prevent or eliminate unionization could manage to do so, systematically circumventing the 1935 National Labor Relations Act (NLRA), the New Deal legislation that guaranteed U.S. workers' rights to union representation and collective bargaining (Logan 2006; Lafer 2007), which remains the law of the land.

Meanwhile, new business strategies designed to shift market risks from employers to subcontractors, or to individual workers themselves, stimulated rapid growth in nonstandard, precarious forms of labor. The relatively stable employment model on which midcentury unionism had been predicated was dismantled systematically, as companies redoubled their efforts to cut labor costs in the face of deregulation, which fostered new forms of cutthroat competition, or simply to boost profits or to please stockholders in the context of an increasingly financialized economy. Sweatshop labor—nearly extinguished in the heyday of the New Deal order—soon resurfaced. At the same time this era spawned a vast population of "independent contractors," many of whom performed tasks previously done by ordinary wage and salary workers. They ranged across many industries and occupations, from blue-collar jobs such as truck and taxi driving to highly skilled information technology and other professional fields.

These developments steadily reduced the share of the labor force covered by the NLRA as well as by the 1938 Fair Labor Standards Act (FLSA), which sets minimum wages and regulates hours, overtime, and working conditions for "employees" in most industries.[4] Independent contractors are excluded from coverage under both these core statutes, and also lack access to employer-provided health insurance, paid vacation and sick days, pensions, and other benefits. Most part-time, temporary, and other nonstandard workers—all categories that have expanded dramatically in recent decades—also are denied access to such employer-provided benefits, although these latter groups generally are covered by the NLRA and FLSA.

Along with the lawful strategies employers have adopted to circumvent the bedrock labor protections established during the New Deal era, illegal practices that are explicitly banned by the NLRA and FLSA have become increasingly prevalent, further undercutting the varieties of unionism that took hold in the 1930s and flourished in the mid-twentieth century. For example, the number of workers fired for attempting to organize—a blatant violation of the NLRA— grew ninefold between 1950 and 1990 (Meyerson 2012, 24); such firings took place in 34 percent of a representative sample of 1,004 union organizing campaigns conducted between 1999 and 2003 (Bronfenbrenner 2009). In addition, violations of minimum wage laws, overtime pay requirements, and other labor standards first established by the FLSA have become commonplace in recent years, especially in the low-wage labor market (Bernhardt et al. 2009).

Rapid growth in the 1980s and 1990s in the ranks of unauthorized immigrant workers—a population disproportionately vulnerable to labor and employment law violations and often fearful of seeking redress through legal channels (despite the fact that nearly all the provisions of both the NLRA and FLSA cover all employees, regardless of immigration status)—has exacerbated these trends. Increasingly, however, U.S. citizens or authorized immigrants—especially new labor market entrants—are joining the precariat as well.

Starting in the late 1980s, alarmed by these developments and hoping to reverse the continuing decline in union density, labor organizers in some U.S. unions began to experiment with new tactics and strategies. One effective approach that was widely adopted in this period was to demand direct employer recognition of newly organized workers, to avoid the pitfalls of the increasingly treacherous NLRA representation election process. At the same time, forward-looking unions began to recruit a new generation of organizers and staffers, many with experience in other social movements, who helped to infuse the labor movement with new ideas (Voss and Sherman 2000). In this period some unions also launched efforts to organize precarious low-wage immigrant workers, including the unauthorized, and soon falsified the widespread assumption that such workers were "unorganizable" (Milkman 2006).

These initiatives culminated in John Sweeney's 1995 election to the presidency of the AFL-CIO, and his rallying call to "organize the unorganized," which sparked widespread hopes of labor movement revitalization. Indeed, this effort led to many creative organizing campaigns involving a range of innovative strategies and tactics (see Corrigan, Luff, and McCartin 2013). As a result, the decline in union density did slow briefly in the late 1990s, but that respite proved short lived, and membership losses continued to hemorrhage in the new century. In 2005, after their hotly debated proposal to restructure the AFL-CIO was rejected, SEIU and a few other large unions that had been especially aggressive in organizing during the previous decade formed a rival labor union federation, Change to Win. The breakaway group envisioned launching large-scale campaigns in place-bound industries such as services, hotels, trucking, and construction. However, this effort failed to achieve its own targets, much less to ignite the major labor upsurge some of its founders had hoped for, and soon the split became yet another symbol of organized labor's disarray.

Although all these developments preceded the 2008 financial crisis and the Great Recession, the surge in unemployment and other forms of severe economic distress associated with the downturn only made matters worse for workers and organized labor. In the aftermath of the financial crisis, moreover, unions faced renewed attacks on the political front. Despite sharply diminished membership, in the late twentieth and early twenty-first centuries, the labor movement had managed to retain considerable political influence, largely through their ongoing campaign contributions and get-out-the-vote efforts on behalf of labor's Democratic allies (Dark 1999). As private-sector unions continued to shrink, however, these political activities were forced to rely more heavily on resources from public-sector unions, which remained intact.

That in turn led conservative strategists in groups such as the American Legislative Exchange Council (ALEC), funded by major corporate interests, to focus their attention on undermining public-sector unions. In 2011, with guidance from ALEC, Republican governors in Wisconsin and several other Midwestern states launched coordinated campaigns to pass laws eliminating or limiting collective bargaining rights for public-sector workers. That effort ultimately succeeded in Wisconsin, despite the massive grassroots protests that it provoked, as well as in Indiana (Nichols 2011). Public sector union density in both states declined precipitously, from 50.3 percent in 2011 to 37.4 percent in 2012 in Wisconsin, and from 28.3 to 22.8 percent in Indiana (Hirsch and Macpherson 2013).

Adding further to labor's political woes, in 2012 Republican elected officials in Indiana and Michigan moved—once again with assistance from conservative political groups—to secure passage of "right to work" laws in their states (Confessore and Davey 2012). Such laws—widespread in the South and in parts of the West but never previously enacted in the Midwest, which had been a bastion of industrial unionism in the mid-twentieth century—prohibit labor-management contract clauses that require union-represented workers to pay union dues.

These defeats not only led to still further erosion of union density but also deeply resonated as attacks on iconic landmarks of U.S. labor history. Wisconsin had been the very first state to pass legislation authorizing public-sector collective bargaining in 1959, and Michigan was the site of the massive General Motors strike that had galvanized the original upsurge of industrial unionism in the 1930s. That such sacred territories were now vulnerable to successful right-wing attacks deeply demoralized what remained of the organized labor movement, which was still recovering from the failure of its campaign to win labor law reform at the federal level a few years earlier. Even under the relatively labor-friendly Obama administration and with Democratic majorities in both houses of Congress, that effort had ended in ignominious defeat and was abandoned in 2010.

Faced with this bleak situation, the labor movement became increasingly open to alternatives to its traditional repertoire of strategies and tactics in the twenty-first century. In what journalist Harold Meyerson (2011) aptly termed a "Hail Mary pass," unions began to scale up their efforts at community-based organizing. The AFL-CIO's Working America program, launched in 2003, has recruited over three million working people, none of whom are union members, to support labor-friendly political candidates; it already has had a significant impact on recent elections (Meyerson 2012; Dean 2012). And in 2011, the giant SEIU launched its Fight for a Fair Economy (FFE) campaign, mounting door-to-door canvas operations in communities of color in seventeen cities across the nation, with a political and community-organizing agenda in mind. (Turner, this volume, documents the New York City FFE campaign in detail.) Although SEIU was in far better shape than most other large unions, its leaders began to speak openly about what they saw as the futility of continuing to pursue traditional union organizing in the face of the escalating attacks on organized labor.

As the downward spiral continued, organized labor began to reach out to other social movements—including the meteoric Occupy Wall Street movement, which won extensive union support in New York and elsewhere soon after it emerged in the fall of 2011. In addition, labor has become a leading ally of the immigrant rights movement in recent years. The dramatic 2000 shift in the AFL-CIO's official policy, definitively renouncing support for immigration restriction and embracing immigrant worker organizing, was initially promoted by the SEIU and the other unions that later left to form Change to Win. But even among those unions that remained in the AFL-CIO, the massive immigrant rights protest demonstrations that erupted nationwide in the spring of 2006 eliminated any lingering doubts about the "organizability" of immigrants. Those marches also helped inspire labor's growing support for worker centers—most of which focus on low-wage immigrants, and which have close ties to the larger immigrant rights movement. Increasingly, as Trumka's 2013 speech (cited above) implied, union leaders have come to view these alternative forms of organization as helping to lay the groundwork for future revival. As the labor movement increasingly turns away from the now-broken system created in the New Deal era, which employers unilaterally abandoned decades ago, it is also returning to its own historical roots, reviving an older strategic repertoire that U.S. unions widely practiced in the early twentieth century (Cobble 1991a, 1997).

New York City Labor, Old and New

In the middle of the twentieth century, when U.S. labor was at its peak, union density in New York was only slightly higher than in the nation as a whole (Troy 1957). In the decades that followed, however, the gap widened dramatically. As Figure I.2 shows, in 2011–12, in both the public and private sectors, New York City's union density was approximately twice the national level. At that time there were about 735,000 union members in the five boroughs, and density was

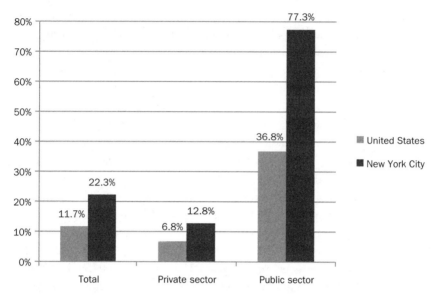

FIGURE I.2   **Union density, by sector, United States and New York City, 2011–12.**

Data from Milkman and Braslow 2012 (U.S. Current Population Survey, Outgoing Rotation Group). Percentages shown include the eighteen months from January 2011 to June 2012.

higher in New York than in any other major U.S. metropolis. New York remains a labor-friendly city, a rare bright spot in the national firmament, still relatively insulated from the desperate crisis that organized labor faces in most of the United States.

In the Progressive and New Deal eras, its strong and politically powerful private-sector unions played a crucial role in helping to shape New York City's social-democratic political culture. They also contributed to an institutional infrastructure that provided affordable housing, public transportation, and other social benefits on a scale that, as historian Joshua Freeman (2000) argues, set the city apart from the rest of the United States. Since the mid-1970s fiscal crisis and the restructuring that followed, however, this cultural and institutional legacy has been severely eroded, and growing inequality has increasingly isolated New York's union members from the city's larger working-class population.

As many commentators have pointed out (most recently Western and Rosenfeld 2011), declining private-sector unionization since the mid-1970s accounts for a large proportion of the recent growth in U.S. earnings inequality. Paradoxically, however, twenty-first-century New York has not only the highest level of union density but also the highest level of income inequality among the nation's large cities. In part this is due to the huge concentration of financial–industry employees whose salaries have skyrocketed in recent decades (most of whom have substantial unearned income as well). Moreover, even if the decline has been modest relative to that in the nation as a whole, private-sector union density in New York City is much lower today than in the past: as recently as 1986, it was 25.3 percent, nearly twice the level a quarter century later (see figure I.2). Although the private-sector decline began long before the Great Recession, it accelerated after 2007 (Milkman and Braslow 2012). By contrast, public-sector union density in New York City has been stable in recent decades, and actually rose slightly after 2007, despite the downturn. Indeed, at this writing the gap between public- and private-sector unionization rates in the city is at a record high.

Job growth in New York has been highly polarized in recent years, with rapid expansion in low-wage service industries such as hospitality and retail (Petro 2011; Abel and Deitz 2012), alongside steady growth in professional, managerial, and technical jobs. Income inequality parallels this pattern, as rising incomes at the top end combined with stagnant or declining incomes at the bottom to produce a pattern of sharp income polarization (Fiscal Policy Institute 2012). The city's unionized workers are part of a shrinking middle class: they have lost ground relative to top earners, but are highly privileged relative to low-wage workers, growing numbers of whom have become part of the new precariat. Although union members make up nearly one-fourth of the overall New York City labor force, they comprise only about one-eighth of the private sector, and are at growing risk of political isolation as nonunion low-wage work continues to expand. As Bhairavi Desai, executive director of the New York TWA, warned, "Unless we lift the floor, the ceiling is going to collapse" (Greenhouse 2008b).

The city's workforce has also been transformed by the wave of new immigration from Latin America, Asia, Africa, and the Caribbean that followed the passage of the Immigration and Nationality Act of 1965, which lifted previous restrictions on immigration to the United States from the global South. As a result, New York has returned to its historic role as an immigrant gateway city. Many of the less-skilled newcomers have joined the emerging precariat, finding jobs as domestic workers, in restaurant kitchens, in garment sweatshops, on nonunion construction sites, as taxi drivers, and in other low-wage jobs. Over time, however, immigrants have also moved into the unionized sector of the city's labor market. As figure I.3 shows, by 2011–12, in New York City, foreign-born workers who had arrived in the United States before 1990 had a *higher* unionization rate than their U.S.-born counterparts. Unionization rates were much lower among more recent immigrants, however, especially those who arrived in the United States in the 2000s. Indeed, this is the group most often found in low-wage, precarious employment.

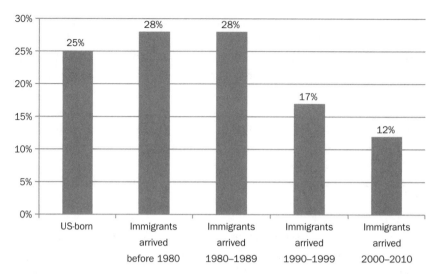

FIGURE I.3   **New York City unionization rates, by nativity and date of arrival in the States, 2011–2012.**

Data from Milkman and Braslow 2012 (U.S. Current Population Survey, Outgoing Rotation Group). Percentages shown include the eighteen months from January 2011 to June 2012.

Recent immigrants are overrepresented in several occupational groups that are explicitly excluded from coverage under labor and employment laws such as the FLSA and NLRA—for example, street vendors, domestic workers, and taxi drivers—all of which have expanded in recent decades (see Dunn, Goldberg, and Gaus, all in this volume). Foreign-born workers also make up a substantial share of the low-wage workforce in the city's burgeoning retail and restaurant industries, where precarity assumes a different form: most jobs *are* covered by the FLSA and NLRA, yet workers are nevertheless often paid less than the legal minimum wage and other violations are widespread (Shapiro, this volume; Brady, this volume; Bernhardt, Polson, and DeFilippis 2010).

In other sectors, legal violations are less widespread, but access to employment security or the ability to earn a living wage is blocked by other means. For example, in many frontline retail jobs, as recent research has documented, employers' scheduling practices severely limit the number and predictability of hours (Ikeler, this volume; Luce and Fujita 2012; Lambert and Henly 2010). Such jobs employ more female than male workers, including a substantial number of immigrants but many U.S.-born workers as well.

Yet another rapidly growing component of the city's precariat is composed of highly-educated professional and technical workers who are freelancers or employed on short-term contracts. In contrast to earlier generations of workers in similar occupations, and despite their high level of skill and education, many of these middle-strata workers find it difficult to secure full-time or full-year work, and most lack access to health insurance, paid vacations, sick leave, and other benefits (King, this volume).

The Emergence of Worker Centers in New York

Perhaps because the deunionization process that undermined labor's strength in so many other parts of the nation was far slower in New York, few of the city's union leaders were concerned about the new forms of precarious work when they first began to appear on the horizon in the 1970s and 1980s. A notable exception was the International Ladies' Garment Workers Union (ILGWU), which launched a "Campaign for Justice" in the late 1980s that in many ways prefigured the worker center movement that would flourish in later years. Unlike most of its New York-based counterparts at the time, the garment workers union already faced a life-threatening crisis in the wake of the massive global outsourcing of clothing production, and immigrants in nonunion sweatshops accounted for a growing share of the garment factory jobs that remained in New York City. As its historical base collapsed, the ILGWU embarked on a bold experiment, establishing two community-based centers in New York (along with three more in other parts of the country) oriented toward recent immigrants employed in the burgeoning nonunion sector of the garment industry. In creating these centers, the ILGWU self-consciously invoked its own history of building community-based "social unionism" among Jewish and Italian garment workers in the early twentieth century. Once again it began to offer nonunion immigrants English classes, skills training, and immigration counseling in the new centers (Hermanson 1993).[5]

Almost a decade earlier, in 1979, a group of Chinese immigrant worker-activists had founded the Chinese Staff and Workers' Association (CSWA) in New York's Chinatown, the very first worker center established in New York and among the first in the nation. Some of CSWA's founders had been involved in union organizing efforts with the Hotel Employees and Restaurant Employees (HERE), but they were frustrated by the union's bureaucratic practices and its lack of attention to the needs of Chinese immigrant restaurant workers. Seeking an alternative approach, they established a community-based organization that aimed to serve the specific needs of immigrant workers. Unlike the ILGWU centers, CSWA was entirely independent of the traditional labor movement, supported instead by foundation grants and membership dues. As one commentator noted, "CSWA was critical of the framework of traditional trade unionism, including its business nature, its racist and anti-immigrant tradition, its tendency of compromising, its increasing reliance on legislatures and electoral politics, and its narrow focus on economic gains rather than the development of its members" (Chen 2003; see also Kwong 1994).

CSWA established a labor rights clinic to help workers facing employment law violations such as nonpayment of wages, a chronic problem confronting immigrants employed in the city's garment and restaurant industries alike. From the start, the group encouraged workers themselves to take an active role in addressing such problems, urging them to collaborate with others facing similar issues, rather than simply receiving services from lawyers and other experts. Rank-and-file leadership development and collective action were also central aims of the organization. And despite the fact that its founders were highly critical of traditional unions, CSWA succeeded in winning recognition for an independent restaurant workers' union in several Chinatown establishments. However, that achievement proved short-lived as skyrocketing real estate values and rising rents drove the newly unionized restaurants out of business (Chen 2003).

The next major worker center initiative launched in the New York City area was the Long Island–based Workplace Project, which attorney Jennifer Gordon founded in 1992. Although it focused on Central American rather than Chinese immigrant workers, most of whom were day laborers and domestic workers rather than factory or restaurant workers, in most other respects it was similar to CSWA. From the outset, the Workplace Project's primary focus was on unpaid wages and other violations of employment law, and like CSWA it explicitly rejected the mainstream labor union tradition in favor of an organizing approach that emphasized rank-and-file worker empowerment and leadership development. The Workplace Project, again like CSWA, also took pains to avoid becoming a legal or social service provision agency that treated workers as "clients" rather than empowering them to organize collectively on their own behalf. To this end, in order to receive services from Workplace Project lawyers, workers were required to attend a series of classes on workers' rights (Gordon 2005).

These early initiatives defined the template of the worker centers that later multiplied in New York City and elsewhere in the nation starting in the 1990s. Indeed, many of those centers have acknowledged that they were directly inspired by and modeled after the Workplace Project or CWSA, or both (Fine 2006, 284n3). Apart from the ILGWU's Campaign for Justice, none of the early New York centers were union sponsored, although that would change in the 2000s. Whereas by the 1980s the ILGWU already faced the type of survival-threatening crisis that, as Kim Voss and Rachel Sherman (2000) have shown, often leads unions toward radical strategic innovation, such crises confronted relatively few unions in New York City at that time. Most of the city's unionized workers were employed in place-bound industries such as the construction trades, hospitality, health care, utilities, and the public sector. New York never had many of the large-scale factories that had given rise to the large CIO unions in the 1930s, and thus was much less affected—apart from the garment industry and a few other small-scale manufacturing industries—by the massive deindustrialization of the 1970s and 1980s (Freeman 2000). Indeed, that was one reason that union density remained higher in New York than in many other U.S. cities.[6] Unions did lose ground in New York City's retail and restaurant sectors (Ikeler, this volume) as well as in manufacturing, but otherwise the city's labor movement remained largely intact—a highly exceptional case of a city largely insulated from the devastation facing unions across the nation.

Nevertheless, in the late 1990s, a few New York local unions launched efforts to organize the emerging precariat by more traditional means. In 1996, a local affiliate of the national Laborers Union, whose leadership had made immigrant organizing a priority in reaction to the challenges it faced in other parts of the country, ran a successful campaign in New York among low-wage asbestos removal workers—most of whom were unauthorized Latino immigrants recruited through labor brokers, who faced a variety of abuses (Kieffer and Ness 1999). The next year, a New York local of the Union of Needletrades, Industrial, and Textile Employees (UNITE), a successor to the ILGWU (which had merged with the Amalgamated Clothing and Textile Workers in 1995), launched a union drive among Mexican immigrants employed in small delicatessens and greengrocers in an effort to recruit in new sectors, as its historic base in garment manufacturing continued to shrink (Ness 2005). Two other union drives in this period among the emerging precariat involved African immigrant grocery delivery workers and South Asian livery car drivers. As independent contractors, both these groups were excluded from the NLRA and FLSA, but in both sectors workers organized on their own, later attracting support from established local unions—the United Food and Commercial Workers (UFCW) and the International Association of Machinists and Aerospace Workers (IAM), respectively (Ness 2005).

Apart from these campaigns, all of which found it extremely difficult to establish durable organizations, most of the city's established unions took little interest in recruiting New York's growing precariat in the 1990s. However, that decade gave rise to a burst of activity on the part of newly established worker centers in New York, including several of the organizations profiled in this book. The Taxi Workers Alliance, which would later become part of the national TWAOC, dates from the early 1990s (Gaus, this volume); the Freelancers Union was founded in 1995 (King, this volume); Domestic Workers United (DWU), although officially founded in 2000, built on predecessor organizations created in the 1990s (Goldberg, this volume); and Make the Road New York was founded in 1997 (McAlevey, this volume). Min Kwon's predecessor organization, the Young Korean Service and Education Center, dates back even earlier, to 1984; like CSWA it focuses on a single ethnic group. Although it was originally a traditional social service agency, in the 1990s it began the transition to a worker center (McQuade, this volume).

None of these groups were union-sponsored; on the contrary—like CSWA and the Workplace Project—they deliberately set out to create alternatives to traditional unions, which their leaders saw as ill-suited to the needs of the new precariat. Drawing on the template created by the Workplace Project and CSWA, they focused on grassroots organizing among low-wage workers (apart from the Freelancers, whose main base was college-educated professionals from the start) and leadership development programs, while also offering legal services and social and educational opportunities. Although committed to popular education and empowerment for the workers they recruited, the centers were professionally led and staffed by advocates—often lawyers or college-educated staffers with other types of specialized training.

The centers have perfected the science of filing back pay claims and pursuing complaints about other employment law violations with government regulatory agencies; many also initiated successful lawsuits over violations, often winning millions of dollars in settlements. Some have also focused on winning new forms of social protection from the state, such as paid sick days and living wage laws (Broxmeyer and Michaels, this volume).[7] Framing their campaigns as struggles for social and economic justice, they construct compelling narratives that include the voices of workers themselves, skillfully attracting public and media attention to the plight of the new precariat. They build alliances with consumers and other key community actors, including elected officials and faith leaders, and exert material and moral leverage over employers, who they often "name and shame" into making concessions. They conduct strategic research to identify vulnerabilities in the power structure and generate public pressure on lawmakers to win passage of legislative and regulatory reforms. Many of their members are immigrants, and they also regularly engage in immigrant rights advocacy.

The worker centers, despite a limited resource base and small staffs, have proven highly successful at these efforts. Their strategic repertoire is strikingly different from that of traditional labor organizations. They do not aim to establish ongoing collective bargaining relationships with employers. Nor do they have the capacity to mount large-scale popular mobilizations. Instead they deploy their limited resources to maximum effect by focusing on staff-driven research, media outreach, and legal and political campaigns to win immediate concessions from employers and to win new protective legislation. Although they often aim to recruit workers as members, the centers often find it difficult to sustain long-term relationships once the immediate need for legal or other services has been met.

Historical Antecedents

Although they also draw on newer traditions, like the popular education methods of Paulo Freire (1970; see also Horton and Freire 1990), worker centers in some respects echo the organizational forms that emerged in the early twentieth century among southern and eastern European immigrants, an earlier wave of precarious workers. Settlement houses and labor reform groups such as the Women's Trade Union League flourished in the Progressive Era, exposing sweatshops and employer abuses, lobbying for protective legislation, providing educational and social services to immigrant workers, and assisting their efforts to unionize. Although their structure and goals differ from today's worker centers in some respects, these groups too often relied on philanthropic support and were staffed by highly educated elites. In that era, labor unions—which then represented about the same proportion of U.S. workers as in the early twenty-first century (Freeman 1998)—lacked the institutional infrastructure later provided by the NLRA; but those, like the ILGWU, that actively recruited low-wage immigrants relied on a broad strategic repertoire that include many features of today's community-based organizing.

However, by the early twenty-first century this earlier history had been largely obliterated from public memory. When the worker centers first began to expand in New York and elsewhere in the 1990s, few trade unionists recognized the parallels to earlier forms of organizing, nor did they see the centers as serious contenders for rebuilding the labor movement's waning power. To many labor leaders, worker centers appear as weak organizations with limited resources, lacking any ability to build or maintain a large membership base. Janice Fine has insightfully summarized the salient differences in culture and structure between worker centers and unions:

> Worker centers are non-bureaucratic, grass-roots organizations with small budgets, loose membership structures, improvisational cultures and strategies that are funded by foundation grants . . . the inverse of prototypical American unions. . . .
>
> Unions are often alienated by workers centers' non-connection to industry and employer, broad and blunt internal organizational structures, loose membership bases, and ad hoc and reactive organizational ways of operating.

> Ideologically, some unions are annoyed by some centers' anti-capitalist rhetoric and are perplexed by their tendency to focus on the distant horizon as opposed to shorter-term political, policy and industry organizing goals. (Fine 2007, 341)

Fine also pointed out that in most cities, including New York, worker centers are "under-networked," working in relative isolation from one another (Fine 2006, 226, 240), and sometimes even competing directly for funding.

Indeed, in the 1990s, in the absence of union support, most worker centers relied primarily on foundation grants, although some (for example, the Taxi Workers Alliance) also had significant income from membership dues and contributions. Indeed, one factor that helps explain why more worker centers were established in the New York metropolitan area than in any other part of the country is the city's uniquely thick concentration of philanthropic institutions. New York is also home to a disproportionately high supply of attorneys, which is relevant here as well, since most worker centers provide extensive legal services to members and often initiate lawsuits involving violations of employment law.[8] But unlike Los Angeles, for example, where in the 1990s there was extensive synergy and strategic convergence between worker centers and key local unions that were experimenting with new organizing strategies and recruiting thousands of immigrants (Milkman 2010), in New York there was little contact between the centers and the established unions, and considerable skepticism—on both sides. That would gradually change, however, in the twenty-first century.

A Marriage of Old and New Labor?

Some commentators argue that worker centers represent an inherently limited form of organization. The most incisive and comprehensive critique along these lines is that of a sympathetic insider, Steve Jenkins, a former staff member of Make the Road New York, among the city's most successful worker centers (McAlevey, this volume). He points out that although worker centers have often successfully organized to bring employers who illegally violated minimum wage regulations and other basic standards into compliance, they are not in a position to go further than this: "unlike union campaigns, where workers can potentially demand higher wages, vacation days, and health insurance, these types of worker-center campaigns are advocacy campaigns primarily confined to remedying illegal practices" (Jenkins 2002, 69). He also maintains that despite their dedication to empowering ordinary workers, in practice worker centers rely on "professionals such as lawyers and social workers [who] *mobilize elite institutions* such as government agencies, foundations, media or courts to help clients achieve the change they are seeking. . . . However, the changes that can be achieved are limited to those that are palatable to elite decision-makers" (Jenkins 2002, 61, 72).

Other commentators, similarly, have highlighted the perils of dependence on foundation support for advocates of radical social change (Smith 2007; Wolch 1990), and this is indeed one of the primary dilemmas confronting worker centers as they seek to scale up their efforts. Jenkins's comparative reference point is labor unions, which as he notes are funded by membership dues and thus not beholden to elites. He recognizes that worker centers have what he calls "advocacy power," enabling them to name and shame abusive employers, and to lift up workers' own voices and include them in public policy debates. But he argues that the centers lack the "social power" that unions historically have been able to wield by organizing members to withhold their labor and thus disrupt capitalist production.

Jenkins's thesis about the limited power of worker centers is compelling, but his comparison to labor unions—at least under current conditions—is less persuasive. He fails to acknowledge that unions themselves face a variety of formidable legal and institutional constraints in the twenty-first-century United States.[9] Although strikes were indeed a key vehicle of labor unions' social power in the past, they have been rendered increasingly ineffective and indeed have virtually disappeared from the United States in recent years. The new political-economic order that has in effect replaced the New Deal—notwithstanding the fact that laws such as the FLSA and NLRA are still on the books—has undermined organized labor's traditional strategic repertoire in other respects as well (Piven and Cloward 2000).

Moreover, the ability of mainstream U.S. unions to pursue a radical agenda is severely constrained by their relationship to the established legal system, which restricts the types of activities in which they can participate. As Stephen Lerner (2011a) argues, "Unions with hundreds of millions in assets and collective bargaining agreements covering millions of workers won't risk their treasuries and contracts by engaging in large-scale sit-ins, occupations and other forms of nonviolent civil disobedience." Unions have far greater financial and staff resources than worker centers do, but, Lerner notes, they are "just big enough—and just connected enough to the political and economic power structure—to be constrained from leading the kinds of activities that are needed" (Lerner 2011a, 9–10). Moreover, worker centers have greater room for maneuver as they are not covered by labor laws restricting unions from engaging in secondary boycotts and various forms of direct action.

As union density and power continued their relentless decline into the twenty-first century, leaders and activists in the organized labor movement became increasingly interested in exploring alternatives to traditional union strategies, and the achievements of the worker centers began to capture their attention. The centers had educated thousands of workers directly about their rights, won significant concessions from employers, won new protective legislation and improved enforcement, and won the hearts and minds of many ordinary citizens. At a time when labor unions were increasingly ignored, and even demonized, in the mainstream media, the worker centers had proven themselves highly effective at directing public and media attention to employer abuses of immigrants and other low-wage workers.

Starting around the turn of the twenty-first century, a few key New York unions—HERE, SEIU, and the UFCW, as well as its affiliate, the Retail, Wholesale and Department Store Union (RWDSU), all of which had experience collaborating with worker centers in other parts of the country—began to seriously experiment with their own efforts at this new form of organizing. Three of the organizations profiled in this book began as union-sponsored initiatives, all launched after the year 2000. The Restaurant Opportunities Center (ROC), created by an HERE local in the aftermath of the September 11, 2001 attacks, went on to mount a series of successful campaigns targeting employers who had violated existing minimum wage laws and other labor standards, winning millions of dollars in back pay (Brady, this volume). With a somewhat different focus, in 2002 the SEIU building services local union, in partnership with two other New York unions and two community organizations, founded the New York Civic Participation Project (also known as La Fuente). The main aim was to promote immigrant union members' civic and political involvement (McFarland, this volume). And in 2005, partnering with a community-based organization, RWDSU launched the Retail Action Project (Ikeler, this volume). RWDSU also launched several union drives among precarious workers in the retail sector, among other efforts targeting nonunion grocery stores in Brooklyn, again in partnership with community-based organizations (Shapiro, this volume).

In New York and nationally, union interest in immigrant organizing further increased in the aftermath of the massive immigrant rights protests that swept the nation in the spring of 2006. That November, the New York City Central Labor Council, whose executive director was then Ed Ott (coeditor of this book), invited the TWA to join the Council, a move with no precedent in recent memory and one that prefigured the national AFL-CIO's issuance of a federal charter for the TWAOC five years later. Ott also encouraged the city's labor movement to support DWU, the Freelancers Union, and other fledgling worker centers that were organizing and advocating on behalf of the city's rapidly growing precariat (Greenhouse 2008b). Although Ott stepped down from the Central Labor Council soon afterward, New York unions increasingly supported worker center campaigns in the years that followed. For example, the unions threw their political support behind worker center campaigns for protective legislation, such as the Domestic Workers' Bill of Rights and the New York Wage Theft Prevention Act, both of which were enacted by the New York Legislature in 2010.

Although they initially had been doubtful about the viability of collective bargaining for the workers they organized, worker center leaders have become much more open to traditional unionism in recent years. This change developed along with the centers' aspirations to expand in scale, to build more durable organizations, and to be financially independent rather than continuing to rely on philanthropic foundations for support. This new openness and the centers' efforts to scale up from local to national organizations—as documented in the chapters in this book on ROC, DWU, and TWA (Brady, Goldberg, and Gaus, respectively, this volume; see also Cordero-Guzmán, Izvanăriu, and Narro 2013)—have led them into more extensive partnerships with organized labor, especially at the national level. "Worker centers are movements in search of institutions," the AFL-CIO's Ana Avendaño recently commented. "And our unions are often institutions in search of movements" (Eidelson 2013, 16).

Recent initiatives such as the AFL-CIO's national TWAOC charter have nurtured the growing ties between unions and worker centers around the country. In New York, some local unions recently have engaged in the highest form of flattery, adopting the worker centers' strategic and tactical playbook in renewed efforts to recruit low-wage immigrant workers and other members of the new precariat into union ranks. One example, documented in the next chapter of this book, is the unionization drive that the UFCW launched in the summer of 2011 at a Target department store on Long Island with a workforce dominated by Caribbean immigrants (Becker, this volume). Other recent examples include a successful 2012 RWDSU campaign to unionize car-wash workers in Queens (Semple 2012), and a series of one-day strikes at New York fast food outlets organized by the community-based organization New York Communities for Change, with support from SEIU (Greenhouse 2012b).

Further fueling the growing interest in new organizing strategies among traditional unionists in New York was the Occupy Wall Street movement, which large numbers of New York City union leaders and members alike (and their counterparts around the country) enthusiastically supported. Although tensions and conflicts between Occupy and the traditional unions periodically surfaced, organized labor's support for the occupation was reciprocated by an infusion of new energy and involvement by Occupy activists in local union struggles (Lewis and Luce 2012). This led to increased recognition among union leaders that they had something to learn from other social movements and thus further encouraged the formation and deepening of active union partnerships with worker centers and other community-based organizations like those documented in this volume (see the chapters by Shapiro, Broxmeyer and Michaels, and Turner).

To date, these collaborative efforts are small in scale and their sustainability has not yet been fully tested. But they do suggest the possibility that a marriage between traditional unions and worker centers may yet be consummated, at least in relatively labor-friendly environments such as that of New York City. To be sure, this May-to-December relationship, one in which the partners have vastly unequal resources, is at serious risk of devolution into what Frege, Heery, and Turner (2004) call a "vanguard coalition," in which case excessive union domination could easily render it a barren marriage. But if both partners can manage to retain sufficient independence, such a marriage of convenience might yet prove fruitful, multiplying the capacities of unions and worker centers alike to confront the formidable challenges presented by the growth of the new precariat, and incubating a generation of new labor activists and new labor movement organizational forms.

Part I

IMMIGRANT UNION ORGANIZING AND UNION-COMMUNITY PARTNERSHIPS

1

TAKING AIM AT TARGET

*West Indian Immigrant Workers Confront the
Difficulties of Big-Box Organizing*

Benjamin Becker

On June 17, 2011, a Target store in Valley Stream, New York, became the first to go to a union election in over twenty years. There are over seventeen hundred Target stores across the United States, employing 355,000 workers, but none of these stores are unionized. The election in Valley Stream did not alter this record: workers voted 137–85 (out of 260 eligible voters) against union representation. The union vying for the workers' vote was United Food and Commercial Workers (UFCW) Local 1500, which represents nineteen thousand workers—primarily in chain grocery stores—in the New York City metropolitan area.[1] After nearly a year of legal wrangling, the National Labor Relations Board (NLRB) ruled in 2012 that Target had illegally intimidated its employees, throwing out the election results and setting the stage for a new vote. At the time of this writing, it is unclear how and if such an election will take place; after the first election and prior to the NLRB decision, Target announced a six-month closure of the store—ostensibly for renovations—which displaced and dispersed the existing employees.

Valley Stream is just outside New York City, but the majority of Target's workforce lives in the West Indian neighborhoods of nearby Queens. The campaign involved three main worker-leaders—Tashawna Green, and two other workers named Aaron and Sophia, all of whom are Jamaican immigrants.[2] Nearly the entire prounion worker organizing committee, numbering around fifteen to twenty people, came from Jamaica and Guyana, with a few from Haiti and St. Kitts. Although exact data on the ethnic and national composition of the workforce is not publicly accessible, the committee appeared to be roughly representative of the store. Committee meetings often had a bilingual dimension: workers spoke with one another in Patois before turning back to address the union staff in English.

That a group of West Indian immigrant workers would bring the first big-box retail store in recent memory to a union election is less surprising than it may appear. Immigrants often bring their own political experiences, conceptions of justice, and community identities to bear on U.S. labor struggles. And in New York City, West Indian immigrant workers have a high rate of unionization (Milkman and Braslow 2011). In Jamaica, Sophia had been a schoolteacher and a union member, and she had been politically active there as well. Aaron credited his prolabor views to the Jamaican education system, which gave him an appreciation of social movements, history, and politics more generally. Green, only twenty-one years old, explained that her mother "[knew] everything about unions" from her years in Jamaica and had raised her with prolabor beliefs. Other committee members cited positive experiences with labor unions in New York City—especially SEIU-1199 and AFSCME-DC37, which represent home health care and public-sector workers, respectively.[3]

Until recently, much of organized labor viewed immigrants as a threat to hard-won labor standards, and supported exclusionary measures in both immigration policy and hiring practices. That has decisively changed since the 1990s, and today the labor movement officially embraces immigration reform and encourages the unionization of unorganized immigrants. Many unionists, however, still cling to the view that immigrants are less likely to join union organizing campaigns because of their fears of reprisals and deportation. Even the mass immigrant rights marches of 2006 have not fully dislodged this once-conventional wisdom.

There is no doubt that immigrants face additional economic and legal risks in labor struggles, and that employers have often invited raids by immigration authorities during NLRB election campaigns (Compa 2000). But many labor commentators and scholars have argued that despite these significant challenges, immigrant workers may be *easier* to organize than U.S.-born workers. Many immigrants are familiar and comfortable with labor unions because of experiences in their home countries. Most important, immigrant workers' social networks—relied on for daily survival and in particular for finding jobs—facilitate the construction of solidarity that is a critical element in unionization efforts (Ness 2005; Milkman 2006).

These dynamics were present in the Valley Stream Target campaign, although they proved insufficient to produce a union victory. This chapter explores the reasons, highlighting three key obstacles to unionization that proved decisive. For one, the campaign was unable to bridge the divide in the store's workforce between older first-generation West Indian immigrants, on one side, and younger second-generation and U.S.-born workers, on the other. These two groups had different attitudes about their jobs and about unions, a difference reinforced by the fact that they tended to work on different shifts, with older workers much more likely to be working at night. As the Target campaign proceeded, the union proved unable to recruit organizing committee leaders among the day-shift workers. This problem was linked to the campaign's second obstacle: the union's divided priorities between its broader retail strategy and its Valley Stream organizing efforts. Despite devoting considerable resources to the Valley Stream campaign, UFCW Local 1500 approached it as an offensive tactic in the context of a broader *defensive* strategy to protect local unionized grocery chains from being undercut by big-box retailers. The strategy largely relies on public and political pressure against nonunion retailers to either extract concessions or block their entry into unionized areas. In the case of Valley Stream, this strategy appears to have shaped key union decisions—how soon to file for an election and whether to proceed with a vote—that made a victory considerably less likely. Even after five weeks of frequent house visits from twelve full-time union organizers, a week before the election around one-third of the workers had not been successfully contacted. Finally, the third obstacle the campaign faced was management's intransigent opposition to the union. Target ran a fairly conventional antiunion campaign—in other words, an extremely hostile and aggressive one—that frequently crossed the lines into illegality. The NLRB's subsequent ruling against Target, and the company's decision to close the store and disperse its employees, confirmed this observable pattern of unscrupulous behavior.

Although this campaign did not result in unionization, it did lay bare the company's illegal actions, puncturing its carefully cultivated public image and resulting in an NLRB order to change its policy regarding on-site union solicitation activities. Combined with the lessons learned by organizers and workers alike, these effects of the campaign may improve the prospects of union victory in future big-box organizing.

The Making of the Campaign

Local 1500's top priority in recent years has been to service its sizeable membership in the grocery chain stores, and to protect them from nonunion competitors such as Whole Foods and Walmart. Target had not been the subject of a sustained UFCW campaign; however, the Valley Stream campaign was not initiated by organizers who clandestinely signed up workers or infiltrated the store. Instead, the workers came to the union, eager to organize.[4]

Although the Valley Stream workers had their fair share of horror stories, it is unlikely that the overall treatment of employees there was exceptionally bad in comparison to other Target facilities. Rather, a particular confluence of employer actions, broadly perceived as unjust, led the workers to start talking union. The cliché that "the boss is the best organizer" was confirmed as a group of particularly disliked managers became a lightning rod for anger and frustration. The workers' primary grievances had to do with respect (as in most union campaigns), racism, favoritism, and inconsistent scheduling.

In respect to scheduling, many Target workers were upset by the labor "flexibility" regime that is now widely used in the retail sector (Lambert 2008). This involves constant modification of workers' schedules and shifts in relation to the ebb and flow of consumer traffic and sales, measured in real time. On this basis, frontline managers often reduce even "full-time" workers' scheduled hours and then call, e-mail, or text them to "fill in" on an ad hoc basis. Retailers also increasingly engage in "workloading," a practice that involves reducing workers' hours to zero for long stretches of time if sales are low. This forces those affected to choose between applying for unemployment insurance and looking for work elsewhere, or remaining officially on the payroll with the hope that they will be called in later. In addition to avoiding overtime costs, this system cuts the benefits expenses for retail employers, who typically determine health insurance eligibility based on hours worked. The result is not only to "blur conventional distinctions between standard and non-standard employment" but also to radically shift the burden of market instability onto workers and their families (Lambert 2008).

Union contracts obstruct or weaken this precarious labor regime in some settings, but it has generally become the norm throughout the U.S. retail sector. Indeed, because of the cutthroat competition characteristic of the industry, non-union stores and union stores often have similar starting pay rates. But union contracts usually include established pay scales and raises; unlike at Target and Walmart, a full-time floor-level worker with a few years in a unionized store can earn something that approximates a "living wage."[5] Additional benefits that may result from unionization are: more regularized work schedules, greater access to health insurance, promotion based on seniority rather than favoritism, grievance procedures, the possibility of transfers between stores, and the ability to challenge arbitrary reviews and rulings without jeopardizing job security.[6]

Target had fully adopted this flexibility regime even before the Great Recession, but it became particularly frustrating for the workers in the Valley Stream store after 2008. Managers responded to complaints about reduced hours by pointing to the economic crisis—but then continued to hire new workers. But the economic crisis undoubtedly was a factor. By further enlarging the pool of available workers, and limiting the options of existing employees, it gave the corporation even more latitude than before to restructure its scheduling policies. In addition, Target's sales revenues and share prices took a noticeable hit in the recession, along with other retailers targeting its "middle-income" clientele. As a result, Target began to aggressively shift its retail model in the direction of Walmart, emphasizing low prices and expanding its grocery offerings. At the same time, it adopted a more aggressive scheduling regime with the goal of whittling away excess labor costs.

Target employees claim they were hired in full-time positions, and were gradually scaled back. Although Vice President of Labor Relations Jim Rowader claimed it was "simply not true" that workers wanted to work more hours than they were offered, Tashawna Green, twenty-one, one of the leaders of the workers' committee, had her hours scaled back from 20 to 30 hours per week to 8 to 15 hours per week—the equivalent of a 50 percent pay cut (Spencer 2011). Green also received a humiliating eight-cent-per-hour raise, which, given her reduced hours, amounted to only one extra dollar on her paycheck. Other workers, such as Charmaine Brown, thirty-six, received no raise whatsoever, stuck at $8 per hour even after several years of service; her hours had been drastically cut as well. Adding insult to injury, only employees who worked at least 32 hours per week qualified for health insurance and other benefits; the dramatic reduction in hours meant that fewer made this cut after 2008.

Many Target workers, like low-income workers everywhere, rely on publicly provided social services to augment their wages. These workers must carefully steer between the Scylla and Charybdis of their low-wage work on one side, and several government bureaucracies on the other: If their income level goes up just past a particular threshold, they risk losing their eligibility for food stamps and other vital programs. But retail jobs like Target pay so little—far below a "living wage"—that receiving full-time hours there would not nearly cover the lost food stamps, Medicaid, and housing subsidies.

This subject made union organizers uneasy because it potentially undermined their focus on restoring diminished hours. Although workers would prefer to have a living-wage job than to deal with the web of government bureaucracies, what if unionization added hours but failed to deliver a significant enough wage increase to make up for the lost government services? It is impossible to know the extent to which such concerns influenced the votes of Target Valley Stream workers—if at all—but this dilemma is one likely to emerge in future union drives in the low-wage retail sector.

Members of the workers' committee, many of whom were recipients of food stamps and other government services, were more forthright on the subject and had a straightforward solution: higher wages. They argued that they worked hard, wanted to work more, generated profits for their employer, and ought to be compensated adequately. A sixty-two-year-old committee member and Jamaican immigrant poignantly asked, "We work—why should we have to go to welfare?"[7] Some attributed their outrage against this system to their backgrounds in Jamaica, where no comparable welfare system exists and workers are therefore entirely dependent on wages. Challenging the conservative caricature of "welfare"—that it creates dependency and laziness—these workers pointed out the fundamental injustice of the welfare–minimum wage trap and placed the responsibility on Target to provide sustainable long-term employment, from which they could provide for their children and send them to college. The union, they hoped, would help win the respect and economic stability they deserved.

In the Valley Stream store, a well-respected employee in the Human Resources department known as "Ms. Monica" had previously mediated some of these grievances. She had been a unionist in her native Jamaica before immigrating to the United States and took a keen interest in workers' lives, often going the extra mile to allow them to take leaves, qualify for social services, and avoid arbitrary reviews. When a union had probed the Valley Stream store a few years earlier, Aaron (a backroom bicycle assembler and leading member of the workers' committee) remembered Ms. Monica saying, "You don't need a union—I'll be your union." For Aaron and others, she had in fact played this role in the store, serving as a buffer against management. But in February 2011, after fourteen years of service, Ms. Monica was suddenly fired for "bad performance." She subsequently filed an age and sex discrimination lawsuit that the company appeared eager to settle.

Her firing sparked outrage among some Target employees, who believed Ms. Monica had been dismissed because of her proworker sympathies. April, a mother of six who worked in overnight logistics, knocking down and replacing shelves, was shocked that Target would "do that to my auntie"; she compared it to a husband divorcing an older wife for a younger woman. For Aaron, it meant that the workers would have no buffer against management. Union organizers made much of this during the campaign, pointing out that since any manager can be fired, not even the friendliest one can substitute for a union.[8]

Aaron also linked Ms. Monica's firing to the sentiments of Lisa, the store manager of Dominican background who allegedly stated, "There are too many Jamaicans working here." Lisa had already earned the enmity of overnight workers over a similar issue. Because there are no customers—or in Target lingo, "guests"—in the store during the graveyard shift, workers had often listened to West Indian music while they worked, until Lisa forced them to stop. She had also insisted that the overnight workers tuck in their shirts while cleaning, lugging around heavy packages, restocking shelves, and so forth, which further enraged them. Several workers viewed these new policies in the context of Lisa's alleged anti-Jamaican remarks.[9] Workers also were critical of Matt, a white supervisor and recent college graduate who reportedly bragged about his family's Southern "redneck" roots. Many perceived him not only as a racist but as someone who showed favoritism toward particular workers. There were complaints that he badgered workers he disliked, and that he intentionally changed workers' schedules so he could later write them up.[10]

The firing of Ms. Monica played an important role in connecting the Valley Stream workers with UFCW Local 1500. But because of the union's national focus on Walmart and the resources required for a new battle against Target, it was initially reluctant to mount an organizing campaign. Warning that it would be an "uphill battle," they asked the workers to show their seriousness by soliciting union authorization cards from their coworkers. The next day, Aaron had sixteen union cards in hand; within a few weeks, a handful of devoted workers had signed up 120 of the store's 260 "team members."[11]

The 46 percent of the workers who signed up surpassed the necessary 30 percent to file for an election with the National Labor Relations Board. But it fell far short of the 70–80 percent that unions usually aim for before filing if their goal is to seriously contend for victory in an election that will occur several weeks later. A company's antiunion campaigning often whittles away 20 to 30 percent of the initial card signers. This is precisely what took place in the Valley Stream case, with the final number of "yes" votes coming in 30 percent lower than the number of signed authorization cards.

Except for the graveyard shift, the store was not a true "hot shop," a workplace spilling over with anger and grievances among workers that leads to strong support for unionization. To build prounion sentiment throughout the store would have required an investment of far more time and effort on the part of the organizers to identify leaders across the various shifts and departments and recruit them to lead the workers' committee. Instead, the union filed for the election with the 120 cards they had in hand after only a month of organizing, and immediately moved into election campaigning mode over the next six weeks.

Why had they filed with so few cards? The lead organizers at Local 1500 asserted it was at the insistence of the workers, who feared that the company had caught wind of the campaign, and knew that there would be an influx of new part-time hires for the summer months.[12] As will be discussed below, the quick filing also jibed with the union's overall media and political strategy.

Despite the eagerness of the workers' committee, and the significant resources devoted to the campaign by the union, the decision to file so soon rapidly brought all the challenges of the campaign to the surface. These included (1) the limited representativeness of the organizing committee, which accurately reflected the workforce in terms of ethnicity and nativity, but not generationally or by shift; (2) tension with the union's broader defensive strategy against big-box retail; and (3) the structural advantages that the company had over the union in controlling the terms of the conversation, particularly under the pressure of the impending vote. In the rest of this chapter, I explore all three of these issues in detail.

The Workers' Committee: Not Fully Representative

The most viable path to successfully organizing the Valley Stream Target workers would have been to draw on the personal networks and connections of the committee of prounion workers. Indeed, a small but dedicated group occasionally accompanied staff organizers on home visits. As the organizers themselves acknowledged, these workers were highly effective in relating to their coworkers, helping them express their grievances, reminding them of past injustices, and combating the company's presentation of the union as an outside "third party." In home visits, union organizers stressed to undecided workers that the union had come to Valley Stream at the behest of other Target workers like themselves; they were there to help workers form their own organization.[13]

The core of prounion workers maintained a high level of participation over the course of the campaign, and viewed themselves as its rightful owners. Beginning with their first contact with Local 1500, which UFCW organizers later described as an "interview" with the union, the workers continuously expressed their opinions, recommendations, and criticisms to the union staffers. The most outspoken worker, Sophia, a night-shift logistics worker and a leader of the workers' committee, never hesitated to articulate any frustration she felt or to demand the floor during a committee meeting. When an organizer called her on short notice to be photographed in the *New York Times*, she responded sharply, "This is not the way you do things" and insisted that she be given more time to gather more team members for the shot. During the recess of a NLRB hearing, Sophia criticized a UFCW lawyer who she believed was trying to keep her out of a strategy session. Such experiences, far from causing friction, endeared the workers to the organizers. They knew from experience that the alternative—a less passionate, less involved committee—was far worse.[14]

Yet the workers' committee did have some serious weaknesses in connecting to the workforce as a whole, especially because it disproportionately drew from the overnight shift (which comprised less than one-third of the store's overall workforce). As a result, even when the whole worker committee was assembled, they could not recognize the names of one-third of the store's workers.[15] Experienced union organizers emphasize the necessity of having a committee spread across all departments and shifts. Without a strong voice in each department countering the company's campaign, identifying influential workers, and reaching out to the rest, large numbers of workers can be expected to vote "no." The union's data suggests that overnight "logistics" and backroom workers were evaluated as "yes" votes by nearly a 3–1 margin (with only a small number identified as uncontacted).[16] These workers tended to be older, had more structured shifts than the rest of the workers (typically from 10 or 11 p.m. to 6 or 7 a.m.), and particular grievances that did not affect workers on other shifts, such as the prohibition on personal music and being locked in the store overnight.[17]

The one day-shift department with an identifiable prounion majority, by a 2–1 ratio, was "soft-lines"—Target's lingo for clothing. The key difference between this department and others on the day shift was that Tashawna Green, one of the store's most outspoken prounion workers, worked there. By contrast, in the cashiers' department, where the tide was 2–1 against the union, not a single worker was a member of the committee. Even more lopsided was the sales floor, which has a higher supervisor-to-worker ratio than other departments and in which workers are more dispersed. There, nine of eleven evaluated workers were expected to vote against the union.[18]

Another problem was that the group of worker-activists was disproportionately older than the rest of the store's workforce. Almost all of the activists were over thirty and some were in their forties and fifties. Three-quarters of the committee members were women, although the causes and consequences of this gender imbalance are unclear.[19] Almost all committee members were also parents who relied on their jobs at Target as their primary source of income. By contrast, the campaign did not successfully connect with the large number of young part-timers in the store. Of the dozen or so young workers who did sign cards for union representation during house visits, many had older prounion family members standing nearby.[20] On other house visits, some young workers stated that they saw their Target job as merely transitional, to help get through college. Whereas the older workers were supporting families, many of the young part-time workers appeared to be living with their parents and not necessarily paying rent. Whereas having a steady number of hours is of critical importance to workers with family responsibilities, college students and other young workers may react more positively to a "flexible" scheduling regime. Issues such as health insurance and seniority-based promotions are also less likely to be of immediate concern to them. Even the issue of respect may play out differently with young workers. Some of the Target workers stated that they had so little previous work experience that they had nothing with which to compare their treatment at Target. For all these reasons, as Stuart Tannock (2001) found, unions often find it difficult to effectively organize and communicate with young retail workers who view their employment—accurately or not—as temporary or as a "stopgap."

Adding to the intergenerational tension was the fact that the store's "team leads"—the equivalent of low-level supervisors—tended to be relatively young themselves. Indeed, some of them were connected to other young workers in the store through external social networks, and this appears to have facilitated their hiring in some cases. On several occasions, older prounion workers complained that these young supervisors showed favoritism toward their generational peers; they chafed at the disrespect they perceived from supervisors young enough to be their children.[21]

Generational Dynamics within the West Indian Immigrant Population

As Mary Waters's (2001) study of West Indian immigrants documents, the experience of first-generation immigrants' contrasts in several respects with that of their 1.5-generation and second-generation children. (The "1.5 generation" includes immigrants who arrived in the United States before adolescence.) West Indian immigrants do not conform to the traditional narrative whereby the second-generation immigrant's assimilation leads to upwards social mobility; instead, "becoming American" in U.S. racial categories specifically means "becoming black," a process that often leads to *downward* social mobility. Because of the special forms of oppression and discrimination facing African Americans, Waters argues, West Indians tend to resist such assimilation, retain their ethnic distinctiveness, and construct their own economic niches.

With regard to work, Waters found that second-generation West Indian youth were far less likely to accept the low-paying jobs that their parents had, and that those who did so tended to attach less value to such jobs. Doubtful that society will reward hard work with upward social mobility, the children of working-class West Indian immigrants tend instead to embrace the "oppositional identity" of their African American peers, who live in the same neighborhoods and attend the same schools. By contrast, the children of middle-class West Indian immigrants, who have more access to economic and educational opportunities, are more likely to prioritize their West Indian identities and differentiate themselves from African Americans.

Waters also argues that white employers tend to perceive West Indian immigrants as more willing to take orders and to accept jobs with long hours and low pay. Yet she also finds that West Indian immigrants are typically quite militant about confronting episodes of racism and outspoken about other indignities on the job. Although there are clear risks in making such broad generalizations, the immigrant workers' actions at the Valley Stream Target store largely confirm Waters's observations. A disproportionate number of the long-time workers in the store were middle-aged and foreign-born West Indians. Several of the key figures in the union campaign were employees who had been in the store since it opened over a decade earlier—a testament to their consistency and record of positive evaluations. Whereas management viewed these West Indian immigrants generally as "good workers," they were by no means passive. In fact, committee members repeatedly identified their West Indian immigrant background as one reason they were taking their prounion stand.

Waters's analysis also offers insight into the generational aspect of the Target case. According to several committee members, most of the store's young workers—1.5-generation and second-generation West Indians—had grown up in the United States, attended its schools, and adopted its cultural values. In interviews, the older workers often disparaged their younger counterparts for their uncritical adoption of American values, for failing to think long-term and see the dignity in their work. Moreover, several committee members considered the "brainwashed" young people to be the most decisive obstacle to their campaign. Similarly, Amy Foerster's (2006) study of first- and second-generation West Indian immigrants in a New York City social service union found that union consciousness was limited among the younger members. Although that union's Jamaican-themed cultural activities helped boost attendance from young second-generation members, it rarely translated into consistent union activism.

Some of the Jamaican immigrants active in the Target campaign credited their prounion beliefs to their home country's education system. Daniel, a committee member in his thirties, explained: "The young people here aren't thinking long-term. We come from a place where you pay for high school . . . and it's a better education because you have to show your work and use your head, not just fill in multiple choice." Aaron expressed his views of the younger workers even more bluntly, stating: "They go to college, but they're dumb. They don't know about their basic rights." He too suggested that Jamaican schools better informed young people about how their rights had been won through collective struggle.[22] Immigrant workers often suggested they had a different work ethic compared to their counterparts who grew up in the United States. "The type of people that say 'Immigrants are taking our jobs' are usually talking about jobs like this [at Target]," Sophia, the matriarch of the workers' committee who had been a teacher in Jamaica, declared. "But do you think if I was born here, I'd be working at Target?"[23]

Alongside the generational differences and those between the foreign and U.S.-born workers, there were economic differences among Target workers as well, which may also have contributed to the election outcome. Here the evidence is fragmentary, but it is striking that workers living in the more affluent town of Valley Stream, Long Island (where the Target store is located) were considerably less likely to vote for the union than those residing in Queens, as table 1.1 shows.

Although the workers at Target all received essentially the same wages, their relationship to their work varied across economic strata. Teenagers or college students living in a Long Island home with multiple incomes, for example, might be less likely to see the need for a union, and indeed might even consider it beneath them in class terms.[24] At the other end of the spectrum, in the poor and working-class neighborhoods of Queens where many Target workers lived, there was a much stronger prounion tendency as table 1.1 shows. In St. Albans, the workers were prounion by nearly a 2–1 margin, far higher than any other

TABLE 1.1 **Predicted union support among Target workers, by location and selected characteristics, 2011**

LOCATION	NUMBER OF ASSESSMENTS	MEDIAN HOUSEHOLD INCOME	UNEMPLOYMENT RATE	PERCENT PROUNION
Valley Stream, Long Island	20	$66,970	3%	30
Rosedale, Queens (Zip code 11422)	23	$82,525	7%	48
Springfield Gardens, Queens (Zip code 11413)	27	$77,352	8%	48
St. Albans, Queens (Zip code 11412)	28	$69,796	13%	64
Jamaica, Queens (Zip code 11434)	25	$57,027	13%	54
Jamaica, Queens (Zip code 11433)	12	$41,274	14%	33

Source: U.S. Census Bureau, 2007–2011 American Community Survey: Selected Economic Characteristics. Accessed online at http://factfinder2.census.gov/.

Note: The union evaluation data displayed are slightly distorted in favor of the union because in each location shown some workers were never contacted and thus not evaluated. Given that the union won most of the votes it was counting on, it is likely that such uncontacted, unevaluated workers voted against the union. The data shown, then, overstate support for the union, but do so for all locations shown. They are nevertheless useful for comparing prounion sentiment across neighborhoods.

area. At the poorest end of the economic range, in the Jamaica neighborhood of Queens (zip code 11433), workers voted *against* the union by a 2–1 margin. The company's repeated threats of job loss and store closure presumably weighed even more heavily there than for workers in other areas; the 11433 zip code has a 25 percent poverty rate and 14 percent unemployment rate, some of the highest rates in the state.[25]

Obstacles to Outreach

To win a union organizing campaign in the twenty-first century, when employers routinely deploy a vast arsenal of antiunion tactics, requires a great deal of effort (see Bronfenbrenner and Hickey 2004). Union staff must spend significant amounts of times studying the shop, uncovering its social networks, identifying leaders, learning about workers' grievances, and identifying pressure points within the company, while steadily building up a committee of core workers. The Target Valley Stream campaign was launched before these tasks had been completed, forcing organizers to scramble to gather information at the same time they were attempting to contact daytime workers to which the largely night-shift committee had few ties.

The union assigned twelve organizers to the campaign.[26] They devoted most of their time to "house calls." On average, a worker's house would be visited around ten times, with some requiring as many as seventeen visits, before the union finally made contact.[27] This arduous process not only drained staff resources but strengthened management's antiunion campaign: every day that passed without contact was a day that the company continued to control the conversation and convey its often intimidating antiunion message to undecided workers. The union also risked being perceived as a nuisance to family members and neighbors as it repeatedly showed up at the front door.[28] A week before the election, a narrow majority of the evaluated workers were listed as "yes" votes—but another ninety workers had not been reached or evaluated at all. In the final week, the union managed to contact around fifty-five of them, and all but a handful were identified as "no" votes. In the end, the union lost by fifty-two votes, 137–85. Thirty-six eligible workers, or 14 percent, did not vote at all.

The difficulty of making contact with workers is a common feature of most union organizing, and hardly exceptional in this campaign. House calls are of proven value (see Bronfenbrenner and Hickey 2004), but considering the difficulties they involve, one might ask if there were anything else the union could have done to reach workers. Attempting to make contact directly outside the stores of big box retailers such as Target, with their staggered and inconsistent shifts, is impractical. Organizers were reluctant to wait for workers in the mall parking lot. When they did so, it attracted immediate attention and confrontation from managers, who repeatedly told organizers, accompanied by security officers, that there would be no "soliciting" on company property, even if workers were off the clock. They refused to give a precise definition of "soliciting," but used the term to forbid any conversations about the union. Customers who sympathized with the union and prounion Target employees who attempted to approach coworkers during breaks or after work in the parking lot were subjected to similar treatment. The NLRB later ruled that such behavior from the company was illegal.[29]

The location of the Target store in Valley Stream's Green Acres Mall was also an impediment. Because there is little to no pedestrian traffic, and the parking lots are privately owned by the mall, there is no public area in which organizers can approach workers free of company harassment. Store executives also lied about the parameters of Target's parking lot, pushing organizers further away from the store. But even if Target owned none of the outside parking lot, it undoubtedly would have called on the Green Acres Mall management to police it.[30]

Local 1500's lead organizer was ordered to leave company property for "soliciting" one week before the election. A store manager told her, "You can't talk to my team members." When she replied, "They're not yours," the manager replied, "Target is a corporation, we can do whatever we want." Indeed, the supervisors' frequent refrain that "you are free to talk to team members about the union off company property," which was meant to sound like a concession instead implied ownership over employees—as if Target could decide what employees were free to do in their nonwork time.[31]

Some workers did take the bus to work, but organizers were reluctant to clandestinely wait at the nearby bus stop and approach workers. Moreover, because "team leads"—the first-level supervisors who were outside the prospective bargaining unit—wear the same uniform as the workers, it would be impossible to distinguish one from another. The union staff only approached workers at the bus stop when prounion employees accompanied them. Having a coworker present made the initial encounter less awkward, but the workers still tended to appear tight-lipped in such close proximity to their job. Moreover, the store is so large that many workers only recognized, but did not know, each other. Union organizers and supporters twice organized cookouts in a park in Springfield Gardens, a part of Queens where many Target workers reside. They hoped to attract team members that they had not been able to reach at home, while further identifying the union as approachable and "normal," not an outside force. The cookouts, however, did not result in any new contacts.[32]

Target, Walmart, and Big-Box Retail: The Shaping of Union Priorities

Local 1500—which knew before the election that it was likely to be a defeat—could have withdrawn from the process entirely. This is a common practice among some unions that prefer not to be on record with a defeat, which can create negative momentum. Nor is it unusual for a union to file for an NLRB election primarily to obtain the list with all the workers' contact information; the union then withdraws from the election before it is held and uses the list to plan a longer, sustained organizing campaign.[33] So why did Local 1500 go forward? The lead organizer presented the decision as one rooted in the union's obligation to the workers who had committed so much time to the drive. "It was a respectable loss," she explained, "and workers need to see the process" in order to understand the next round of the campaign.[34]

As noted above, the store was not quite a hot shop to begin with. The relatively low number of cards with which the union filed, and the decision to proceed despite the predictable loss, implies that winning was never the main point. Ultimately the Target campaign, in which technically labor was on the offensive, might be better understood as part of a defensive effort. Local 1500 was aiming to put Target "on notice," to create enough pressure, headaches, additional expenses, and bad press that the expanding company would conform to the standards defined by the many unionized stores in the area.

Target's reputation and public image is as a "friendlier" version of Walmart, the industry leader that is notorious for ruthless antiunion campaigning, low wages, and pervasive gender discrimination. Identified as an enemy by labor unions and small businesses alike, Walmart has been the subject of numerous boycotts, as well as critical documentaries and books. Target has received entirely different treatment. Unlike the direct "always low prices" messaging of Walmart, Target nourished a hip image with low-priced versions of designer clothing and earned the French-inflected nickname "Tar-zhay." A national survey conducted during the Valley Stream union campaign found that Target ranked highest among all discount retailers in "consumer perception" (Wilson 2011). Target is also identified as more cosmopolitan and sophisticated, in part because of its well-publicized philanthropy for cultural institutions.[35] Journalists have referred to "Target shoppers" as a distinct "swing vote" demographic, while portraying Walmart shoppers as poor, conservative "rednecks."[36] *Saturday Night Live* once defined the poverty line as "the invisible line that separates Target from Walmart."[37] The differences in image—whether or not they have any basis in reality—have real political consequences. Manhattan Borough president Scott Stringer, for instance, who lined up with labor unions to oppose

Walmart's entry into New York, attended the ribbon-cutting ceremony for the local Target.[38]

Walmart was the central reference point for journalists covering the campaign and for the union itself. Were Target's labor practices any better? Would it be any less hostile to union activity? Would the company lose its relatively clean image and be obstructed—a la Walmart—from further expansion into the area? Could an organizing success at Target reignite union drives at Walmart? This was the constant subtext of the struggle at the Valley Stream Target, and explains the national news attention it received, including a story on the first page of the *New York Times* Business section (Greenhouse 2011). Whereas unionization efforts at Walmart had been blocked at every turn, the Target campaign raised the possibility, however remote, of a breakthrough in the big-box sector.[39] A victory at this Target, the union suggested, could pave the way for organizing the twenty-six other Targets in the region and potentially elsewhere. The field director of UFCW Local 1500, once a union representative for stores in the same mall, recalled the arrival of Target stores in the 1990s, along with Lowe's and Home Depot, which began displacing unionized discounters such as Caldor's, Bradlees, Rickles, and Pergament Home Centers. During contract negotiations, these stores would wring concessions from the union by pointing to their non-unionized competitors. From her perspective, the Valley Stream Target campaign was an attempt to recover those lost union jobs.[40]

Under closer scrutiny, however, it is clear that the union's main strategic objective is not organizing victories but to raise the floor on wages, benefits, and conditions in the retail and grocery industry as a whole. Knowing that they might not win union recognition inside the "big box" retailers in the short term, they hope that public pressure on these companies might lead them to raise their labor standards to a level roughly equivalent to unionized stores. In the New York City area, about 60 percent of grocery stores are unionized, but potential undercutting by nonunion stores like Target presents a serious threat.[41]

Target stores initially carried few grocery products, but that began to change in 2009. Within a year, the company had stocked nearly a fifth of its stores with fresh produce and a large selection of other food products, and planned to do the same in additional stores. As at Walmart, this "one-stop shopping" format competes head-to-head with unionized chain grocery stores. The Valley Stream Target workers approached UFCW with an interest in organizing just when this competitive threat was emerging, and the union immediately recognized that this offered a valuable opportunity to confront the threat.

Thus, notwithstanding the tireless work of the field organizers, the timing of the election filing, and the decision not to withdraw prior to defeat suggest that the union's chief aim was to put Target "on notice."[42] The election was part of a larger strategy to embarrass, expose, and pressure the company, even if the organizing campaign inside the store failed. This strategy also may have been linked to the union's ongoing effort to keep Walmart out of New York City. Walmart has repeatedly charged that the union and its political backers have a double standard, which gives its competitors, including Target, a free pass. Putting the union on record against Target helped inoculate both the union and its anti-Walmart allies on the New York City Council from such charges.

Target's Antiunion Campaign

Target's response to the union drive did not revolve principally around one-on-one meetings between supervisors and workers, although some took place informally. Nor did an antiunion workers' committee emerge. Instead, the company focused on bombarding workers with antiunion arguments. Everyone was required to attend frequent, sometimes daily, "captive audience" meetings—where they listened to antiunion presentations and arguments by management and watched antiunion videos. Workers were inundated with letters and flyers attacking the union as well. Indeed, management's most powerful weapon was, as history has shown for other union organizing campaigns, its "monopoly control of both media and campaigning within the workplace" (see Lafer 2005).

Target's messaging came from the standard antiunion campaign playbook. The company portrayed the union drive as an attack on individual rights and invasion of privacy. In a letter explaining the NLRB requirement that the company turn over the name and address of employees to the union, the store manager wrote, "I hope they don't use *your* personal information in this negative campaign." The company warned employees of expensive legal battles between the union and its members. One letter warned of "37 pages of rules" that if violated would put a union member "on TRIAL before the union bosses."[43] Management suggested that a union contract would be very difficult to achieve. "Nothing changes unless Target agrees to make the change," a flyer warned. "You could end up with lower wages or less benefits because it is all subject to negotiations and everything is 'up for grabs.'" Even though organizers had been careful to explain to workers that no changes could be promised in advance, Target highlighted the fact that union shops had failed to resist the "labor flexibility" regime, posing the question: "80 percent of the union's members are not full-time . . . how can they promise you full-time?" According to the union, this figure was actually around 65 percent, and they emphasized that their part-time members have far more stability than nonunion part-time workers.[44]

Most egregiously, the company repeatedly suggested that workers could lose their jobs if the union won. One of the first antiunion flyers distributed was titled, "Will the Store Close if the Union Gets In?" to which it answered: "There is *no guarantee*." Other flyers stated that the "union has a terrible record of store closings," noting that the unionized A&P/Pathmark chain had closed twenty-five stores in 2010. The same point was made in Target literature stating that "we all owe our jobs to the closing of the unionized Caldor store that was in our building."

Another management flyer alleged that the union "took $868,288.00 out of their pension plan for 'expenses.'" But these expenses, ominously placed in quotation marks on the flyer, turned out to be regularly scheduled distributions to retired members. Another flyer stated in all capital letters: "THE UNION COLLECTED OVER $44 MILLION IN MEMBERS' MONEY AND SPENT ZERO . . . NOTHING . . . 'ON BEHALF OF INDIVIDUAL MEMBERS!'" This was a reference to federal LM-2 forms that include a reporting line "On behalf of individual members" for cash disbursements to individuals. Presumably, very few unions pay out cash in such a way to their membership.

Target's campaign included many other standard antiunion arguments, including company responses to alleged "questions" or "rumors" that had come up. One letter began, "This is a really important question that has been asked . . . 'I signed a union card. Now they told me I will be fired if I do not vote for the union. Is that true?'" Another flyer began, "Dues are at least $309 up to $455 a year . . . not $2.00/week!" The union had never suggested dues would be so low, and in fact clarified early on to workers that dues would be in the range of $6/week. Similarly, in captive audience meetings, supervisors falsely warned employees that union membership came with two sets of dues—to the local and the international union.

In those same meetings, the company screened several antiunion videos, one of which was leaked to the press (Nolan 2011).[45] The thirteen-minute video "Think Hard Before You Sign" repeatedly referred to unions as failing and outdated "businesses," whose only hope of saving their bottom line was to dupe new groups of workers into joining. The video attacked the seniority system, presenting the victim as the talented, hard-working, and ambitious new employee. The video's key audience was the younger workforce, but workers like Sophia, who had been at the store for a decade but had their wages capped at $12 per hour, could hardly have been swayed by its message.

The video also suggested that a union contract might prohibit team members from assisting customers outside their department, implying that employees would suddenly be forced to be rude and unhelpful to guests as a result of overly rigid union work rules. The video also reminded team members that the company encouraged workers to become trained across departments so they could access more work hours. Although these claims were of dubious credibility, they made an impression on young workers, who often repeated them to union organizers during house calls. "When it comes to the videos, the twenty-somethings' minds are like sponges," an organizer explained.[46]

Many workers were put off by management's constant indoctrination attempts, throwing away the flyers without reading them, not opening the envelopes mailed to them, and tuning out during the "captive audience" meetings and video showings. But that sense of fatigue did not necessarily translate into "yes" votes. Although a few workers told committee members they became more interested in the union after seeing their supervisors so frenzied—indicating that the union genuinely scared the company—for most such workers it probably had a different effect: Tired of the constant barrage of literature and dreary meetings, many would vote "no" just to return to normalcy.

The Battle for the Break Room

In some of the captive audience meetings, prounion employees directly challenged supervisors. Aaron took the floor during one question-and-answer period to bluntly ask, "Is a union a good thing or a bad thing?" When the supervisor hedged—stammering that unions used to play an important role, but are now outdated—Aaron responded sharply, "Is it not true that Dr. King died fighting for workers trying to form a union?" And when the supervisor asserted that the establishment of government labor standards made unions obsolete, Aaron fired back, "So you're saying Martin Luther King died for nothing?" When the company explained to workers how unions take money "out of their pockets," a prounion worker replied, "If you're so worried about keeping money in our pocket, how about a raise?" April, a committee member, confronted Lisa, the store manager, about Target's extensive charitable contributions, proudly enumerated on a banner inside the store. "They're giving United Way our money!" April declared. Lisa replied, "I'm not going to sit here and go back and forth with you, because I already know how you're going to vote."[47]

According to prounion employees, the managers running the meetings seemed poorly prepared to deal with these confrontations. Even the smallest challenges embarrassed and confounded them. Lisa, the store manager who signed all the antiunion propaganda, once admitted in a meeting that she didn't "know much about unions." On other occasions, team leads and other supervisors admitted their family members were in unions, with which they were quite happy.[48] But the break-room confrontations faded away as the campaign progressed, and its effectiveness was hard to gauge. Soon the most outspoken union supporters were no longer invited to the captive audience meetings, and several committee members shied from such public challenges for fear of retribution.

A union-initiated petition demanding that the company allow union representatives to enter the store and address workers' questions and concerns also proved unpopular. Target repeatedly bragged of its "Open Door" policy to employees, and the petition simply asked the company to extend this policy to an open conversation about the merits of the union. But the union abandoned this effort when it became clear that the number of signatures was small; even some committee members were afraid to sign.[49] The union continued to struggle to reach workers at home, and organizers were forbidden from soliciting for such petitions on company property. Few employees were willing to sign anything at work. No other demonstrations of worker rebelliousness materialized inside the store.

Carrots and Sticks: " 'A Scared, Confused Worker Votes No' "

As the election date neared, the store environment became palpably tense—an odd mixture of extreme hostility and artificial friendliness. Team leads quickly surrounded any customers, journalists, and observers who asked workers about the upcoming vote—this writer included—aggressively asking "Can we help you find anything today?" Target imported an additional group of supervisors from its Employee Relations department, who continuously policed the store. Increased numbers of security guards—"more than Black Friday" (the day after Thanksgiving and the largest shopping day of the year), in the words of one organizer—were assigned to the entrance and parking lot to prevent potential "soliciting."[50] Heading the whole operation was Jim Rowader, the company's vice president of employee and labor relations and the "star" of the leaked anti-union video, who had traveled from corporate headquarters in Minneapolis in the lead-up to the vote. The day before the election, when union organizers assembled in the parking lot and began to march into the store in a final show of defiance, management quickly herded the workers on shift into the meeting room at the back of the store. When the organizers entered, the only people present were supervisors.[51]

Likewise, management worked hard to isolate and intimidate known prounion employees, making it almost impossible for them to approach their coworkers, even off-the-clock, on company property. Sophia, after twelve years of spotless reviews, was written up for allegedly making an antigay joke in the break room; she disputed the charge, saying that she and her coworkers had only been singing along to a song.[52] Tashawna Green, a committee leader, reported being following around at work by snickering team leads, as well as store security, even when she visited the bathroom. When she broke down under this pressure, she was told to go home for the day. The NLRB later ruled that Green had been "unlawfully threatened" during the campaign. She was fired a month after the election due to allegedly "hostile behavior."[53]

Various rumors also spread through the store, the origins of which are impossible to identify. Some seemed intended to discredit prounion employees and their motives. Others induced fear; on a home visit, one employee said she had heard that the break room was bugged with a recording device.[54] Another rumor was spread that Target had already summarily dismissed prounion employees. The NLRB later ruled that the company broke the law by threatening store closures, creating the impression that union activities were under surveillance, and telling workers they could not solicit on behalf of the union in nonworking areas (Massey 2011g).[55]

Alongside the sticks came the carrots. The overnight shift received unprecedented invitations to a free breakfast. At one point, free pizza was ordered on the workers' behalf, leaving the break room filled with boxes of uneaten pizzas.[56] Supervisors added an unusually chipper "You are doing a great job today!" to the ritual "Target Time" message broadcast via walkie-talkie to all employees. A few days before the election, a supervisor passed around cupcakes. More significantly, the union charged that the company illegally promised raises and promotions to antiunion employees. One antiunion worker allegedly admitted as much during a house call. Another vocal antiunion worker, Brianna—who was the first to sign a union card but later switched sides—received a highly unusual $1.00 per hour raise during the campaign. She soon became the company's go-to worker whenever journalists asked for an employee to interview.

The election was held in the same room where workers had been required to sit through antiunion captive audience meetings. Although the process generally followed NLRB protocol, with only one union representative and one company representative in the room, a gauntlet of supervisors idled outside the store's employee entrance. Given the forces arrayed against the union, the eighty-five "yes" votes exceeded some of the organizers' expectations. And when the final vote was announced, store manager Lisa reportedly broke down and cried—almost as if Target had lost.[57]

Conclusion

A comprehensive academic study of NLRB elections concluded that the "quality and intensity" of the union campaigns, judged by their use of "comprehensive organizing strategies," are "a better predictor of differences in election outcomes" than "employer opposition, bargaining unit demographics, or company or industry characteristics" (Bronfenbrenner and Hickey 2004). More specifically, Bronfenbrenner and Hickey identified ten elements of a successful union campaign: (1) adequate staff and financial resources; (2) strategic targeting (research about the company); (3) an active and representative working committee; (4) active participation of member volunteers; (5) person-to-person contact inside and outside the store; (6) benchmarks and assessments; (7) issues that resonate in the workplace and community; (8) creative and escalating internal pressure tactics; (9) creative and escalating external pressure tactics; and (10) building for the contract during the organizing campaign. Three of these elements—adequate resources, an active committee, and frequent assessments—stood out as the most important. These tactics alone were hardly enough to spell victory; rather, the win rates dramatically improved only when unions utilized clusters or five or more of these tactics (and increased with each additional tactic used).

How did the UFCW campaign at Target measure up against these criteria? Organizers made frequent assessments of the campaign. They also emphasized person-to-person contact, although their efforts in this respect confronted many obstacles inside and outside the store. The union devoted considerable resources to the campaign—twelve full-time organizers.[58]

On the other hand, organizers noted that the composition of the organizing staff—mostly Latino, with a few white organizers—did not reflect the store's mostly African American and West Indian workforce. No significant marketing or advertising campaign was deployed. There was an active, but not fully representative committee. The union made limited use of members from other worksites in reaching out to Target workers. While union organizers had laid plans to escalate internal pressure tactics and to encourage worker defiance in the face of company intimidation, these plans were later set aside.[59] Ultimately, the campaign incorporated three or four of the ten elements that Bronfenbrenner and Hickey identified. The NLRB ruling for a new election creates an opportunity for organizers to craft a more comprehensive approach the second time around.

The tactical questions do not in and of themselves solve the major strategic questions facing retail and grocery unions. After all, how would a victory at a single Target store slow the steady encroachments of the big-box giants? Considering the losses suffered in organizing campaigns over the years, shouldn't the union be looking for other ways to raise the floor on wages and work standards? This context largely explains why union leaders have prioritized a defensive strategy of public and political pressure over new organizing victories or the finer points of comprehensive organizing.

It is too early to evaluate whether the union's strategy will help save the unionized grocery stores or if the negative publicity generated around Target will lead to any change in its behavior or its wages. Undoubtedly, Local 1500 spokesperson Pat Purcell is correct that the national attention given to the campaign, and the later NLRB verdict, helped to unmask and "crush the image" of Target as a high-road, moral employer.[60] This negative perception may assist future political and public relations efforts against the company, as it does with campaigns against Walmart. But ultimately, again as with Walmart, it is difficult to expect significant breakthroughs against big-box retail without direct union victories inside the stores. Even a single victory at a big-box store such as the Valley Stream Target could potentially have a major effect on retail workers elsewhere and would puncture these megacorporations' aura of invincibility. This, after all, was the impact of the Flint 1937 sit-down strike victory over the "unorganizable" auto giants.

UFCW may not have envisioned the Valley Stream Target drive as the beginning of such an initiative, but the campaign offers important lessons, both positive and negative, about the formidable challenges of organizing in the retail sector. First, it reaffirms the fact that immigrant workers are far from unorganizable; their unique experiences from their homelands, tight social bonds, and long-term investment in their jobs can in certain circumstances make them more disposed to fight over their conditions of employment than their U.S.-born counterparts. Second, the Valley Stream Target example puts in sharp relief the structural challenges of organizing the industry, which not only relies disproportionately on part-time work but also presents itself as transitional employment and is widely understood as such. This reinforces the notion that the pay, benefits, and full-time employment structure that are standard in many other industries are unrealistic in retail. The structure and image of the industry also helps recruit employees from disparate class strata, combining upwardly aspirational high school and college students from a variety of backgrounds with a core of typically older employees who understand the job as more permanent. Given the fact that labor unions do not presently have the power to fight for a dramatic restructuring of the industry as a whole, how can they make themselves relevant and attractive to young part-time retail workers? Although it is tempting to propose slicker and smarter advertising, and an adjustment of the union message, it is doubtful that this alone will be sufficient. It will likely require long-term, focused organizing campaigns—as expensive as they are necessary—in which employees both exercise collective power and directly experience its benefits. Since it resulted in one of the few NLRB elections to take place in the big-box retail sector, the Valley Stream Target organizing campaign also highlights the structural difficulties of using the current legal process to challenge employer power. Clearly, unions and their supporters must continue to demand reforms to this process, and devise strategies to work around it.

2

ORGANIZING IMMIGRANT SUPERMARKET WORKERS IN BROOKLYN

A Union-Community Partnership

Ben Shapiro

"Our goal for the Workers' Committee is not only to get information to the twenty or thirty workers in the group," Miguel, a Mexican immigrant supermarket worker and an active member of the New York Communities for Change (NYCC) Workers' Committee, explained.[1] "We want the group to be two hundred or a thousand people that extends into one hundred or two hundred stores. And not just for the sake of making it grow. We want to change the fearful mentality of the Latino worker, so that we as a group can change this exploitative system."[2] Miguel got involved in the Workers' Committee during a union organizing campaign at the small supermarket where he worked in the Flatbush section of Brooklyn. That store and half a dozen others in the neighborhood were the focus of a joint organizing initiative by NYCC, a community-based organization (CBO) that inherited staff and other resources from the former New York City chapter of the Association of Community Organizations for Reform Now (ACORN), and Local 338, affiliated with both the Retail, Wholesale and Department Store Union (RWDSU) and the United Food and Commercial Workers (UFCW). Like Miguel, most of the workers involved in this effort were Latino immigrants from Central America or Mexico, a majority of whom were undocumented.[3]

Collaborations between CBOs such as NYCC and labor unions remain rare, and effective ones rarer still (see Fine 2006, 147). But those joint campaigns that do exist offer insight into the potential of such partnerships as well as the obstacles to their success. The NYCC-Local 338 Brooklyn supermarket campaign began as what Carola Frege and her colleagues (2004) call a "vanguard coalition," in which the union partner dominates and essentially dictates the strategy. In this case the initial focus was on a series of union representation elections under the auspices of the National Labor Relations Board (NLRB). After those elections yielded disappointing results, however, the union began to grant NYCC organizers more autonomy. That led them to focus on building the neighborhood-wide Workers' Committee that Miguel joined, with the longer-term goal of waging an industry-wide organizing campaign in Brooklyn.

In this chapter I recount the history of this effort and of the NYCC-338 relationship, against the background of the recent restructuring of New York City's retail grocery industry. After a series of flawed campaigns focused on NLRB elections, I show how the NYCC organizers developed a more effective approach to organizing undocumented immigrants in small, independent grocery stores in Flatbush, using a more *organic*, neighborhood-based strategy. That approach, in which the Workers' Committee was central, involved rank-and-file leadership development, workers' rights training, and popular education, a form of what Janice Fine (2006) calls "pre-union organizing."

Another key feature of the neighborhood-based strategy was its ability to draw on immigrant social networks to help spread the campaign to new stores. Drawing on Immanuel Ness's research into a similar campaign involving New York City greengroceries in the 1990s (Ness 2005), I make the case for industry-wide organizing within a given neighborhood. In the case Ness documented, victory depended on securing the formation of a neighborhood store owners' association with whom the union could bargain on an industry-wide basis within the local area, avoiding the danger that raising wages and labor standards in only a few stores would make them uncompetitive and drive them out of business. I argue that a union-CBO partnership like that between NYCC and Local 338 can be highly effective in achieving this, but only if sufficient resources are available and if the power balance between the partners allows the distinctive strengths of each organization to be fully utilized.

This organizing drive targeted some of the most exploited workers in New York City: Latino immigrants, many of them undocumented, employed in independent grocery stores in poor neighborhoods in the city's "outer boroughs." Most of these stores are small (often under thirty workers). Typically both the owners and the overwhelming majority of the workers—predominantly Latinos—are immigrants. Workers at these stores are often victims of wage theft and other violations of bedrock employment laws, in many cases paid less than the legal minimum wage, and working more than sixty hours per week for as little as $250 to $400 (Bernhardt, McGrath, and DeFelippis 2007). Like other recent immigrants from Latin America, they came to the United States because of limited economic opportunities at home. Many send remittances to support their families and aspire to return home with some capital. As Francisco explained, "Most everyone's plan when you come here is to save up enough to build a house [back home], to make a little money, and then go back." However, as previous research shows, most never return home and instead remain in the United States (Gordon 2005; Ness 2005, 172).

Structural Changes in New York's Grocery Industry

Two significant trends have transformed the New York City grocery industry in recent decades. First, union density has sharply declined. The expansion of larger nonunion supermarkets such as Trader Joe's and Whole Foods, smaller specialty food stores, and the sale of food in drugstores has meant increasing competition for the traditional supermarket chains that have been the bulwark of retail grocery unionism for decades (Bernhardt, McGrath, and DeFelippis 2007).[4] The share of the industry represented by RWDSU/UFCW Local 338 and UFCW Local 1500—by far the two largest union locals representing New York City grocery store workers—has plummeted, with a density in 2011–12 at only 15 percent in a sector that three decades earlier was highly unionized (Milkman and Braslow 2012).[5] With few exceptions, unions have been unable or unwilling to organize the new stores; as a result they have also been forced to make wage and benefit concessions at the union chains (Morris 2011), leading to a "race to the bottom" in the industry (Bernhardt, McGrath, and DeFelippis 2007).

A second trend is the proliferation of small independent or franchised grocery stores in poor and working-class neighborhoods, particularly in the outer boroughs (Ness 2005: 59–60). In these stores, which often rely on "informal" employment arrangements, wage and hour violations are more likely than in larger or chain stores (Bernhardt, McGrath, and DeFelippis 2007). Undocumented immigrants are especially vulnerable, because they have limited knowledge of their rights, limited options for employment, and often can be intimidated by threats of deportation (Ness 2005, 65–66). The lack of a union's watchful eye and the weakness of wage and hour law enforcement, combined with razor-thin profit margins, heightened competition, and a vast supply of undocumented immigrants, have all contributed to the problem. Some store owners have even asserted that "they cannot pay the minimum wage and still stay in business" (Bernhardt, McGrath, and DeFelippis 2007).

A New Partnership: RWSDU Local 338 and NYCC

By the end of the twentieth century, Local 338 had become "a conservative, bu-reaucratic service union" (Ness 2005, 128).[6] As one of its own staff members admitted, "338 for many years was half asleep."[7] Despite a steady decline in membership, the local had a healthy treasury, but had become highly dependent on its contract with one supermarket chain, A&P, whose workers represented almost 70 percent of Local 338's membership by 1999.[8] That year members elected a new progressive slate, with John Durso taking the helm as the local's president. He hired veteran labor radical Kevin Lynch as organizing director and began to invest resources in new workplace and political organizing.[9] The local's membership rose from eleven thousand to eighteen thousand through mergers with other union locals and growth in the drug store sector, and the share made up of A&P workers fell to about 40 percent.[10] The new leadership also reactivated the local's shop steward network, improved member servicing, and began to le-verage its political influence to advance the interests of supermarket workers.[11]

Local 338's new leaders were also eager to take on the challenge of organizing the new Latino workforce in the independent grocery store sector, although they had little experience with such efforts. The one exception was a 2009 campaign in which the union won recognition at two "hot shops" (a term union organizers use to describe workplaces where workers are angry at their employer and espe-cially eager to unionize). Both of them were Hasidic supermarkets in Williams-burg that employed about fifty immigrant workers in total. One of the shops was unionized through an NLRB election and the other by using wage and hour charges to pressure the owner into recognizing the union. Both stores are now under contract. Although these campaigns were modest in scale, they did signal 338's openness to organizing smaller stores employing immigrant workers.[12]

Soon after these successes, Local 338 entered into a partnership with NYCC to organize other independent grocery stores in Brooklyn. NYCC was born out of the New York City chapter of ACORN, which had deep roots in New York's poor and working class communities, having spent over three decades waging campaigns for affordable housing, quality education, living wages, and other progressive goals. Although it was best known for community organizing, ACORN's New York leadership had long recognized the importance of workplace organiz-ing in the low-wage economy. As NYCC executive director Jon Kest (and former director of New York ACORN) explained in an interview: "[The] low-wage worker stuff that we do, it's pretty simple: poor people are getting fucked. We cannot just focus on education, housing, and health. What is often a source of their problems? Lack of a living wage."[13] Several ACORN chapters around the country had been involved in union organizing in the 1970s and 1980s, partnering with willing unions or forming new ones (Atlas 2010, 53–57). In New York, ACORN had allied with the United Federation of Teachers (UFT) to organize twenty-eight thousand state-funded, home-based childcare providers, after winning a change in state law to allow the workers to bargain collectively. The UFT won recognition in 2007 and signed a contract in 2009 in one of the largest newly organized bargaining units in New York City in decades (Allen 2007; "UFT Reaches" 2009).

In 2009, ACORN was attacked by a coordinated group of right-wing activists, politicians, and media figures, as a result of which it lost most of its external funding and eventually collapsed. However, several local chapters started new organizations with many of the same staff, strategies, and goals. One of these was NYCC, which formed in the summer of 2010 and picked up where New York's ACORN had left off, although with a greatly reduced membership (falling from forty thousand to five thousand). NYCC's board includes experienced labor and community leaders along with NYCC members.[14]

Shortly before ACORN's demise, its New York leadership had begun to lay the groundwork for a low-wage worker organizing campaign, sending canvassers out to map wage and hour violations in the retail sector. The results suggested that violations were particularly concentrated in grocery stores.[15] In searching for a union partner, ACORN found that Local 338 was receptive, and conversations began between Kest and Lynch.

Both organizations recognized the benefits of working together. ACORN needed both funding and a union partner that was willing to experiment with new approaches, and 338 fit the bill. Over the preceding years, the RWDSU International had shown a willingness to try nontraditional organizing methods. In 2006, it had collaborated with another CBO, Make the Road New York (McAlevey, this volume), in a successful union drive at a chain of shoe stores in the Bushwick neighborhood of Brooklyn. Using the threat of a community boycott and lawsuits over violations of wage and hour laws, that campaign eventually won union recognition and a contract (Greenhouse 2006a).[16] ACORN (and later, NYCC) envisaged a campaign along similar lines focused on neighborhood grocery stores, with the notion that this could be the springboard for a citywide Workers' Committee that would support future organizing drives as well as fight for improved labor legislation.[17]

Although some of Local 338's leaders were open to this kind of approach, most of the union's staff had a more traditional organizing philosophy, focused on NLRB election campaigns. Within the local, Lynch was the main proponent of partnering with ACORN. As he recalled in an interview, "[The leadership of Local 338] was ambivalent about [organizing small shops]. They'd like to have it, but it was hugely problematic. For one thing, you cannot have the same contract provisions covering a large profitable supermarket with several hundred workers and a major corporation behind [it], and a small independent supermarket with twenty-five workers and nobody behind it." Lynch recognized the challenges it involved, but he thought this kind of effort could be successful with the aid of a community partner: "If the union tried on its own to organize these small stores, without the community supporting the effort, the guys who were working there would be so vulnerable to the employer that chances are you would not succeed in an election. And if you did succeed in an election, you would find it hard to get a contract, because these are very vulnerable workers, they need help."[18]

The campaign was interrupted by ACORN's collapse, but it picked up again in mid-2010, when NYCC hired two young bilingual organizers to work on it full time. One was Manhattan-born Kate Barut, who had spent two years in Mexico organizing and learning about popular social movements there, and identified as an anarchist and feminist. The other new organizer was Lucas Sánchez, who had emigrated from Colombia as a child, had experience as a community organizer in his New Jersey hometown, and described himself as a "student of socialism." Neither had much union experience, although Barut had spent a year as an organizer for the Teamsters Union, but both were motivated enough to work long, irregular hours for less pay than a typical union organizer.[19] Local 338 funded their salaries and other campaign expenses with the understanding that they and the rest of NYCC would take on primary responsibility for organizing the workers—an arrangement that was to be reviewed every three months. Local 338 also made available two of its organizers and Lynch to support the effort as needed.

The organizing strategy was influenced by Make the Road New York's earlier campaign in the Bushwick shoe stores, but it was also a "learn as we go" effort.[20] NYCC organizers made the initial contacts with workers in the stores, asking them to sign a petition that was part of a separate NYCC education campaign. At first, managers did not find this threatening, but after initially engaging workers about education issues, the NYCC organizers gradually shifted the conversation to working conditions and legal rights. If wage and hour violations surfaced, they offered to provide a lawyer to file suits. Besides obtaining back pay that workers were rightfully owed, such lawsuits could engage workers in helping "to pressure the owners into giving a [union] contract to the workers . . . so they can be represented and protected."[21] Essentially, the lawsuits provided leverage against the employers, as they could be withdrawn or settled on generous terms with those who agreed to maintain neutrality with regard to the union drive or to negotiate in good faith.

The initial target was Associated Supermarkets. Although Associated stores often are franchised to independent owners, it was a good target because the brand name was recognizable, and also because NYCC's research suggested that its stores had widespread wage and hour violations.[22] Moreover, Associated stores employed large numbers of Latino immigrant workers in neighborhoods where NYCC had a strong membership base.[23]

By the end of 2010, five months after Barut and Sánchez had been hired, Local 338 began to express frustration with the campaign's limited progress. Not a single worker had signed a union card, only one wage and hour case had been filed, and no union elections had been held.[24] There were at least two serious challenges at this stage. First, publicity about wage and hour lawsuits and New York State Department of Labor action against some of its stores (unrelated to the NYCC campaign) had led many Associated franchisees to bring their stores into compliance with the law, so that violations were not nearly as prevalent as was expected. Second, as the organizers themselves readily admitted, they had limited prior experience in labor organizing.[25] However, Local 338 made it clear that if tangible results were not immediately forthcoming, they would no longer provide funding for the campaign.

The Master Food Campaign and NLRB Elections

Facing this pressure, NYCC introduced a new tactic—offering free English as a Second Language (ESL) classes for the supermarket workers.[26] The ESL intake form included questions about the students' work situation, offering a means of pinpointing wage and hour violations.[27] Around this time NYCC received a phone call from Teresa, a Salvadoran woman who had recently been fired from Master Food, a grocery store on Church Avenue in Flatbush. Upon hearing Teresa's story, which involved generally poor treatment and allegations of sexual harassment, Barut decided on her own to help her confront her ex-boss by serving as a translator. After meeting Teresa and some of her coworkers, most of whom were undocumented Salvadoran, Honduran, and Mexican immigrants, Barut realized that wage and hour violations were rampant in the store as well. It also was obvious to her that Master Food was a "hot shop" where workers were angry and felt deeply disrespected. One worker told the organizers that the manager had punched him for speaking up. Another worker reported being locked in the basement overnight and directed to dispose of large quantities of broken recycled glass dust without proper safety equipment. Other workers complained that the Korean store owners treated and paid the Latino workers worse than the few Koreans who worked there. Barut also learned that these workers had relatives and friends who worked in nearby supermarkets, many of whom were also facing wage and hour violations and egregious working conditions.

While the Associated campaign languished, the NYCC organizers saw Master Food as a promising opportunity and convinced Local 338 to grant them two months to try to organize there. Although they had only a handful of contacts, NYCC wanted to display their mobilizing power at Master Food, drawing on their active community-based membership. With approval from their Master Food contacts, they planned a rally outside the store, and NYCC turned out its members for a "Backpay for the Holidays Bus Tour." They loaded a bus and held rallies in front of three stores, including Master Food and another nearby store, Nebraska Land, owned by the same employer, known as Mr. Cha.

At the Master Food rally, a Telemundo news reporter asked a worker, Jesus Najera, who had not previously been involved in the campaign, what his pay was, and he told the truth on camera: since 2004 he had worked seventy-two hours a week for $300 to $400, or about $4 per hour, well below the legal minimum wage ($5.15 in 2004 and $7.25 in 2009) and also without time-and-a half for overtime. The next day, workers received new swipe cards to keep official track of their hours, and suddenly began receiving the minimum wage and overtime premiums. Although Mr. Cha immediately reduced their hours to about sixty per week, their weekly pay rose by about $100. This was obviously a result of the bus tour and rally. As Azael, a Master Food worker, recalled, before the protest "many of the workers were scared and they took management's side because they just wanted to keep their job . . . but after the protests outside the store and [the owner's response], this gave us more confidence and we talked about it and decided to move forward." Similarly, Barut recalled later that these events "really bolstered the workers. . . . After [Jesus] went on camera, it was a done deal."

Within weeks, NYCC was holding Master Food organizing meetings of fifteen to twenty workers at a nearby church, and had filed a class-action lawsuit against Mr. Cha for wage and hour violations in the $2.5–$3 million range.[28] Workers were now signing union authorization cards, while taking care to keep the union drive hidden from management until at least 70 percent of them signed up. After a month of house visits and meetings, Local 338 filed for an NLRB election at Master Food, taking Mr. Cha completely by surprise. On March 7, 2011, the election was held and the union won by a vote of 14–11. This was a smaller margin of victory than the organizers expected, perhaps due to last-minute employer pressure—but it was a victory nonetheless.[29]

Winning one union shop of thirty workers in a sea of nonunion grocery stores was at best a first step. Unless the campaign expanded to other stores, winning significant gains in wages and benefits would damage Master Food's competitiveness. The organizers placed their hopes in the understanding that Latino workers in Flatbush exemplified what Immanuel Ness calls "identity enclaves"— immigrants of similar origin who work and live in the same neighborhood and find employment through ethnic social networks. Ness asserts that activating these networks can make a campaign spread "like wildfire" (Ness 2005, 32).

Indeed, Master Food workers' networks were the most effective method for recruiting workers at other stores into the campaign. After the bus tour, new organizing opportunities began to develop organically, as Master Food workers reached out to housemates, friends, and family who worked in other local supermarkets. As a result, by the time of the NLRB election at Master Food, workers at five other stores in the neighborhood had signed union cards, and NYCC had filed lawsuits or Department of Labor charges at four of the five, although the alleged violations were smaller in monetary value than those at Master Food.[30] The bus tour and lawsuits had already frightened some other local supermarket owners into raising their pay to the legal minimum, which in most cases meant a $100 per week raise.

Although the campaign was spreading, and new contacts and relationships were also being developed through the ESL classes, at this point the focus was almost exclusively on winning NLRB elections. The NYCC organizers had tried to start the NYCC Workers' Committee, but only four workers attended the first meeting and by the third meeting only one worker showed up. They blamed the time-consuming demands of the NLRB election process for this failure, since it left them insufficient time to devote to building the Committee, but they also had not yet fully won the workers' trust at this stage.

Moreover, as the various union drives surfaced at the Brooklyn stores, employers did not sit idly by. "I smell a consultant," muttered Lynch as he left a Master Food committee meeting where he learned that notices for an NLRB election with International Brotherhood of Trade Unions (IBTU) Local 713, an independent union, had been posted in two of Mr. Cha's other stores, Nebraska Land and Pioneer. By the time Lynch learned about these elections, they were only two days away. Meanwhile Master Food workers reported various other standard union-busting tactics, reinforcing Lynch's hunch that Mr. Cha had hired an antiunion consultant.

IBTU Local 713 was not the only other union the employers were courting in their effort to undercut the NYCC-338 campaign. At a nearby Key Foods, a sticker for Local 1964 of the International Longshoreman's Association (ILA) had suddenly appeared in the window, and the store owner claimed that the ILA now represented their workers. The NLRB ruled that Local 1964 had no legitimate presence in the store after workers testified that they had not authorized it to represent them, but at Nebraska Land and Pioneer NLRB elections for the IBTU went ahead. Workers at these stores had told NYCC organizers that managers had made them sign some forms, but having little experience in union campaigns, Barut and Sánchez thought little of it, and were blindsided when the election posters went up. IBTU Local 713 won these elections by 10–0 and 7–0, and although some workers were upset and claimed only a few of them—and some managers—had voted, none of them was willing to testify before the NLRB to that effect, so the elections were never challenged.[31]

Organizers faced another dilemma at three other stores in the neighborhood where some workers (but not a majority) had signed union cards and where employers had launched aggressive antiunion campaigns. At Fine Fare, after a wage and hour lawsuit was filed, workers were told they could not talk to each other and their hours were severely cut. Two prounion workers were fired and three others left because the work environment had deteriorated so severely.[32] At Key Foods, a worker was fired as well. At Golden Farm, the owner took a different approach, meeting with each worker and giving them $100–$150 more per week raises, depending on seniority. (These "raises" actually involved the owner bringing pay up to the legal minimum wage, plus $50 per week more for the most senior employees.) When workers informed NYCC organizers that Key Foods managers were asking them to sign ILA authorization cards, Local 338 quickly filed for an NLRB election with 338 on the ballot. "Not filing would have meant conceding the shop to ILA 1964, and although we had only 35 or 40 percent [who had signed union authorization cards], we had no choice."[33] At Fine Fare and Golden Farm, the organizers also filed for elections at the urging of 338 staff, on the grounds that they might win the vote and that filing also offered the workers some legal protections.[34]

NYCC organizers spent the month leading up to these elections doing house visits and staging a series of actions, culminating in a group of chanting NYCC members marching through Key Foods. But in June 2011 the union lost by votes of 18–3 at Key Foods and 6–6 at Fine Fare. At Golden Farm, the union withdrew from the election after support for the effort dwindled as a result of the "raise" workers received. In the wake of this crushing series of defeats, the organizers retreated to reevaluate their campaign strategy.

Although Local 338 had lost all but one of the NLRB election campaigns at these markets, the threat of lawsuits, along with a wave of negative publicity, did yield some positive results. Workers in several grocery stores throughout the neighborhood received substantial raises as owners began to comply with wage and hour laws.[35] Many workers won significant back wages, in some cases in the tens of thousands of dollars. Master Food workers had gained union representation and a union contract.[36]

The Master Food campaign succeeded for a number of reasons. First, organizers utilized a wide array of organizing tactics.[37] They also had the leverage of a $3 million lawsuit. And Master Food was a hot shop from the outset, where the manager was universally hated by virtually all the workers, fostering a strong spirit of solidarity well before the campaign itself began. The lack of an aggressive antiunion campaign—due to the fact that this campaign took the owner by surprise—was yet another advantage. The workforce was also relatively homogenous, made up mostly of Mexicans and Hondurans. Finally, as Lynch suggested, "[at Master Food] we had the good fortune of having a group of people that were very wise and very much able to stand together."

Conditions were not so favorable for the larger neighborhood campaign, however. And adding to the other challenges it faced was the negative effect of the lopsided balance of decision-making power between the union and NYCC. Both parties agreed on the goals of winning union contracts and building an immigrant Workers Committee. But while NYCC valued both goals, Local 338 seemed to place much more value on the first. According to NYCC organizing director Jonathan Westin, "[We] had always wanted to develop a Workers Committee . . . but [strategy] was probably too dictated by the union in terms of how they did their organizing. The union wanted them to collect cards, they wanted them to do elections . . . which certainly made sense from their vantage point." That Local 338 was paying the salaries of the NYCC organizers gave it the final say on campaign decisions—and it was clear to NYCC organizers from the outset that if there were no union election victories, funding would be pulled. By December 2010, Sánchez later recalled, "The pressure from 338 was, 'We're funding you guys, but no one has signed a card, we haven't filed for a new election, and nothing is moving.' And they were like, 'If you guys don't make something happen, we will pull the funding.'" Although NYCC wanted to concentrate on building the Workers' Committee and developing relationships in the community, the need to produce tangible results in the short-term forced them to narrow their focus to winning NLRB elections.

Another problem was the division of labor between union staff and NYCC organizers. Barut and Sánchez did the bulk of the labor-intensive work of getting cards signed and communicating with the workers, while 338 organizers only assisted occasionally—usually at meetings or public actions. And when union staff did talk to workers, they tended to push them to sign union cards, which at times threatened to undercut the trust and relationship development NYCC had so painstakingly tried to build. The division of labor also contributed to the failures at Nebraska Land and Pioneer, where organizers with more experience in NLRB election campaigns might have detected the employer's antiunion tactics in time to counterattack.

In contrast to Master Food, at the other stores where elections were held the organizing tactics fell short.[38] And whereas at Master Food Mr. Cha had been unaware of the union drive prior to the NLRB election notice, at all of the other stores the employers had ample time to mount a countercampaign.[39] Moreover, the wage and hour lawsuits were more limited in scale at the other stores; only at Master Food was the financial threat substantial enough to significantly alter the owner's actions.

Local 338 understood the need for an industry-wide approach to reverse the downward trajectory of wages and conditions in the grocery sector, yet it provided limited resources to this experimental campaign. Such community-based organizing is vital because, as many commentators have noted, the NLRB election process has become highly dysfunctional in recent decades, with long delays and routinized employer antiunion tactics—both legal and illegal—that have proven highly effective in dissuading workers from voting for a union. Even when employers are sanctioned for violating NLRB rules, the penalties are typically too modest and too late to act as an effective deterrent (see Mehta and Theodore 2005; Getman 2010).

The power of employers is amplified in settings where the workers are predominantly undocumented immigrants, because although most organizing drives engender worker fear, undocumented workers have special concerns.[40] As Miguel put it:

> The biggest obstacle for any campaign to succeed has to be the fear that workers feel. It's a real big obstacle because we as immigrants can't depend on any of the benefits that the government gives people, so if we lose our job, we're losing our means of paying rent, paying for food. The fear is not having a means to be able to survive. That is the biggest obstacle that there is.[41]

The aggressive antiunion responses of the employers (except Master Food) in the Flatbush grocery store campaign are consistent with the perspective that unions are at a structural disadvantage vis-à-vis employers. However, Bronfenbrenner and Hickey (2004, 54) argue that structural constraints can be overcome:

> It is too easy to simply blame employer opposition and the organizing environment. American unions themselves must shoulder a good portion of the responsibility for their organizing failures. Although our results demonstrate that even in the most difficult contexts, unions can dramatically increase their organizing success when they run more multifaceted strategic campaigns, the majority of unions organizing

today still run weak, ineffectual campaigns that fail to build strength for the long haul.

Indeed, the failure of these campaigns also reflects Local 338's limited efforts to adapt to the changing structure of the industry. Although for more than a decade before these organizing efforts were launched, Brooklyn's grocery workforce had been comprised predominantly of immigrants, including many undocumented immigrants, this was the first serious attempt to organize them. Local 338 had little or no familiarity with the strategies used elsewhere to effectively organize low-wage immigrants, such as those Jennifer Gordon (2005) has enumerated: providing multiple "paths to participation," fostering ethnically based solidarity, organizing around nonworkplace issues, as well as educating workers about U.S. unions and labor laws. Another difficulty was that Local 338's tactical repertoire had been developed for larger chain supermarkets, and was poorly suited to small, independently owned stores. Holding an NLRB election at a hot shop such as Master Food can be effective to establish a foothold, provide an example of success, develop relationships, and utilize immigrant networks to get new contacts at other nearby stores. But focusing on winning elections at dozens of small stores in a neighborhood is another matter entirely, extremely difficult even with extensive resources and when organizing best practices are fully utilized—neither of which was the case in this campaign.

Shifting Gears: Organizing Organically

After the election losses in June 2011, NYCC and 338 staff met to evaluate the campaign and develop plans for the future. Wary of pursuing more NLRB election campaigns, NYCC organizers made the case for a focus on community organizing, leadership development, and building the Workers' Committee. Both parties were aware that the lawsuits had been fully successful only at Master Food. At this meeting, NYCC organizers were granted much more autonomy than before. Sánchez recalled, "What we got out of that meeting was basically, we are allowed to work, and contact [338] when we feel the need to contact them." The two groups carved out three scenarios for the next phase of the effort:

(1) If no wage and hour violations were present in a store, but workers were highly aggrieved (that is, in a hot shop situation) NYCC would arrange for them to work with union organizers.
(2) If wage and hour violations were present, but support for unionization was limited, NYCC would take the lead, focusing on lawsuits and other

pressure tactics to win gains for the workers. In this situation, negotiating a settlement with the employer might not involve efforts to win union recognition.

(3) If wage and hour violations were present, and workers were interested in forming a union, NYCC and 338 would work together to use a lawsuit and pressure tactics as leverage to win union recognition and a contract. NYCC organizers would take charge of organizing the workers and the wider community, while union organizers would focus their work on more technical and legal aspects of the effort.

The NYCC organizers were happy with this agreement: "This way we can split our time more effectively," Barut commented. "NYCC organizers are not so busy doing union organizing, but when union organizing needs to be done, 338 can come in and do it through already trusting relationships."

During the earlier campaign, NYCC organizers had developed their own ideas about strategies and tactics, and had decided that building the Workers' Committee was their top priority. As Sánchez put it:

> It's got to happen at the Workers' Committee level, where people are having conversations about: Why are we in this country? Why are working conditions the way they are? What are the forces that are proposing this? People start having conversations about capitalism.... So ultimately the way we should be measuring this project is not only getting people back their money, not only winning elections, but ultimately having a Workers' Committee that's part of a broader alliance for immigrant rights, and workers' rights.[42]

The NYCC Workers' Committee convened in late June 2011 for the first time in five months. Whereas no more than four workers had attended the earlier Workers' Committee meetings, now, having developed deeper relationships through the NLRB elections and more time to focus on organizing the Committee, twenty-four workers showed up. They went on to meet on a monthly basis after that, with a core group of ten to fifteen leaders meeting in between the Committee meetings. About 150 workers in the local area attended Workers' Committee meetings at some point during the year following the disastrous series of NLRB elections. The meetings included trainings on workers' rights and recruitment techniques, workshops on immigrant organizing, brainstorming about how to expand the campaign, planning actions and other events, and discussing the goals of the Committee.

At least as important as the actual content of the meetings is the worker-centered, participatory democratic organizing method—what NYCC organizers call "organizing organically." As Sánchez explained:

> Our job in organizing is not to try to convince people, but try to help people convince themselves. And helping people convince themselves means people taking it upon themselves to act, to change conditions in whatever space they might be. And learning from that process as to what power they hold as individuals and what power they hold as a group. It should be led not by organizers convincing people but by the work of the tenants, or the neighbors working to change whatever they feel needs change.[43]

NYCC organizers are gradually becoming more skilled facilitators—knowing when to step in and when to hold back, even if the discussion is not always as focused as they would like. To encourage workers to take ownership of the Committee, the staff encourages them to sign up as NYCC members, and there is talk of making the Committee an NYCC chapter. Organizers also encourage Committee members to volunteer for actions such as phone calling or petitioning new stores. As a result, although the Workers' Committee has only grown modestly in size (between thirty-five and seventy typically attend its monthly meetings), its active members have become more comfortable taking on leadership roles and responsibilities.

The neighborhood-based Workers' Committee approach has the potential to circumvent many of the limitations of a store-by-store NLRB election strategy. Its success thus far reflects a strategic emphasis on "organizing organically." Elements of this approach—participatory democracy, popular education, leadership development, and worker rights trainings—are typical of worker centers (as other chapters in this volume demonstrate), which often function as "pre-unions" for undocumented workers in hard-to-organize low-wage industries (Fine 2006, 247).

In a different context, Francesca Polletta (2002, 10) further specifies the benefits of participatory democracy:

> For those who have been systematically excluded from political participation, participatory decision-making provides skills in negotiating agendas and engaging with political authorities. It trains people to present arguments and to weigh the costs and benefits of different options. It develops their sense of political efficacy. . . . [To move to] making an

overt and organized challenge to authorities takes the kind of confidence that people inexperienced in the rules of engagement with the state may not have. Rotating leadership, establishing a norm of participation, and working to consensus trains people to *do* contentious politics.

Only about half of the active Workers' Committee leaders were recruited from the stores where the NLRB elections had been held—stores to which the organizers had previously devoted most of their time and energy. That led them to conclude that to organize undocumented immigrant workers in a dispersed group of stores would require a deliberate and long-term focus on leadership development and building worker agency (see Clawson 2003).

Another advantage of a neighborhood committee-based approach involves its potential for a local industry-wide impact. Among immigrant workers, this approach can both draw on and help deepen ethnically based social networks, while also helping to develop leadership and organizing skills, and thus reducing their reliance on staff.[44]

New Opportunities

The Committee approach gradually bore fruit, and led to new union victories as well. A Committee member from Master Food introduced NYCC organizers to his brother—who works at another supermarket in the neighborhood, Farm Country. Soon seventy workers at that store had signed on to a lawsuit for $1.3 million in unpaid wages, and Local 338 was preparing to file for an election. The Farm Country owner tried to claim that Local 1964 represented his employees, but he could not produce a contract or other evidence. Therefore the NLRB went ahead with a three-way election on April 13, 2012, in which thirty-seven workers voted for Local 338, ten for Local 1964, and one for no union. A neutrality agreement was negotiated for the owner's other two stores, and, by June 2012, contracts had been signed covering approximately 140 workers (at all three stores combined). Meanwhile, workers at Golden Farm, some of whom were actively involved in the Committee, initiated a second union drive. This time the workers were completely committed and Local 338 won the election, albeit in a close 13–12 vote. Finally, when workers from Key Foods heard that the owner was planning mass firings, they decided that they too wanted to have another election and they too succeeded the second time around by a vote of 17–12.[45] The Key Foods owner also negotiated a neutrality agreement with Local 338 covering his other three stores, two of which are now under union contract.

As of May 2013, according to Sánchez and Barut, four hundred workers at ten stores were represented by Local 338.[46]

What made the difference in this new round of NLRB elections, which unlike the earlier round was able to overcome aggressive antiunion campaigns by the owners?[47] Critical factors included the continuing work of the NYCC Workers' Committee and the relationships, leadership, and organizing skills it helped develop. According to Sánchez:

> One of the most important lessons I've learned in this campaign has been . . . that losing an election is not the end. [We must] stay with workers even after a defeat. . . . Even after we were defeated at Key Foods and Golden Farm, we continued to have very strong relationships with the workers involved. And when situations changed in the stores, workers reached out to us to give this election process a second shot.[48]

Another important development was the deployment of more varied tactics, especially the greater emphasis on mobilizing community support through large rallies, petitioning, distributing flyers, and a community boycott at Golden Farm.[49] This aggressive approach may have influenced the owner of Key Foods to quickly grant a neutrality agreement at his other two stores.[50] Moreover, these changes were facilitated by the greatly improved working relationship between Local 338 and NYCC organizers. Whereas in the first round of elections NYCC organizers did not have enough autonomy to develop or implement strategy, in the second round, as Sánchez recounts, "We have found a sort of working equilibrium . . . . Over time, I have learned to recognize the strength of 338, and 338 has learned to recognize the strength that Kate and I have as organizers, and I think that has made the relationship a lot better." Although the working relationship has improved and roles are better defined, differences between the two organizations' culture and ideology are still palpable. As Barut explained:

> There are still some basic differences between us that must be addressed in order to rebuild the labor movement. [Local] 338 is traditionally a servicing union, and so they have a certain way of doing things. And they don't necessarily see the value or understand the importance of really building worker ownership over the union. . . . It's still an ongoing struggle. We constantly have to do pushback—'the workers have to vote on this, this has to go through the workers first.' I see it as part of our job to push the union towards bottom-up organizing. I can see them changing, but it's limited.[51]

Language barriers were among the manifestations of this problem. The contract for Master Food was signed in November 2011, and although the majority of the workers are monolingual Spanish speakers, the contract had still not been translated into Spanish as of June 2012. Furthermore, the Local 338 union representative assigned to the store was a monolingual English speaker.[52]

Voss and Sherman (2000) argue that local union revitalization is more likely when three conditions are met: the local has an internal political crisis causing a change in leadership, the international union supports local revitalization, and there is an influx of staff with experience in other social movements. Although the first two conditions are present in the case of Local 338, the third is more tenuous, met only through the partnership with NYCC—which may or may not be sufficient to stimulate significant changes within the union.

Although NYCC and Local 338 have had some success winning NLRB elections, this approach still faces formidable structural limitations. One key hurdle is that, in the absence of a truly industry-wide campaign in a given neighborhood, store closings remain a real threat if nonunion stores are able to undercut them with lower prices. Moreover, union contracts at the stores have not significantly improved wages, which has disillusioned some workers who expected more from a union contract.[53]

It is interesting to compare the Flatbush campaign analyzed in this chapter to Ness's (2005) case study of the Mexican workers' greengrocery organizing in Brooklyn's Brighton Beach and Manhattan's Lower East Side a decade earlier. The Mexican workers formed an independent organization, the Asociación Mexicano Americano de Trabajadores and eventually gained the support of Local 169 of the Union of Needletrades, Industrial, and Textile Employees (UNITE). In Brighton Beach, organizers used a store-by-store NLRB strategy, and after 75 percent of the workers across twenty stores had signed union cards, elections were scheduled. However, as in Flatbush a decade later, the employers used aggressive antiunion tactics including firings and threats of deportation, and raised wages to the legal minimum. In the end, the union won only one of the elections. After this debacle, in the subsequent campaign on the Lower East Side, the organizers decided to forego NLRB elections, instead demanding union recognition when a majority of workers had signed cards. They also pressured the owners to form an association, so that they could "negotiate a neighborhood-wide agreement that would ensure the economic viability of the greengroceries while improving the conditions of workers" (Ness 2005, 75).

By mobilizing the community through marches, lawsuits, and boycotts, they were able to get some stores to come to the table, although they soon confronted an aggressive antiunion campaign from other employers.[54] But the organizing momentum was so great that the former NYC Central Labor Council mobilization director claimed at the time that "if the union had put twenty or fifty [more] organizers into the field, the industry would have been unionized fairly quickly" (quoted in Ness 2005, 88). Instead, the untimely death of UNITE Local 169's president and other developments led UFCW Local 1500 to win a jurisdictional claim and to take control of the campaign. The ensuing friction between the organizational cultures of the Asociación Mexicano Americano de Trabajadores and UFCW finally undermined the effort.[55]

There are striking similarities between the greengrocery campaign and the more recent Local 338-NYCC effort in Flatbush. Both involved collaborations between progressive union locals and CBOs; both targeted small, independent grocery owners; and both learned the hard way that the NLRB store-by-store approach is limited and then turned to alternative strategies. At the peak of the greengrocery campaign, twenty-five organizers were on the ground; however, even that did not yield an industry-wide impact.[56] In the Flatbush campaign, NYCC organizers lament that two or even five organizers will not be sufficient to organize all the stores in a neighborhood, let alone an entire industry. The greengrocery campaign also exemplified the mutually beneficial potential of collaboration between a union and CBO, as well as the danger that an unbalanced power relationship between the two can hinder the effectiveness of organizing.

Some commentators argue that union-community partnerships are a promising strategy for reversing organized labor's continuing decline (for example, Clawson 2003). Unions tend to have far superior financial resources and political capacity, are able to sustain organizing gains over time through enforceable contracts, and have vast expertise in traditional forms of organizing, labor law and employer antiunion tactics. On the other hand, they are also limited by a variety of legal restrictions on strikes and secondary boycotts, and by the increasingly dysfunctional NLRB system.

CBOs are more experienced in community organizing and leadership development, and are not subject to the same legal chokeholds as unions (Needleman 1998). However, their financial resources are typically limited and precarious, they have limited experience in workplace organizing, and they often find it difficult to win and sustain significant economic gains for workers. In this respect, Local 338's contribution to the Flatbush grocery store campaign was irreplaceable. As Kest explained:

> Without 338 stepping up, investing emotionally and legally in this strategy, we would have been running a campaign to get a few workers well deserved back pay awards but nothing in the way of job protections, guarantees and [wage and benefit improvements]. Many unions have abandoned these workers, and the workers know that. 338 did not

abandon these workers and without Kevin and others from the union assuring these workers that the union was behind them we wouldn't have gotten nearly as far.[57]

Yet, as Fine (2007) has documented, many factors inhibit successful collaboration between unions and worker centers or CBOs. Specifically, cultural and ideological tensions often pose serious obstacles. In the case of the Flatbush grocery campaign, the experimental culture and radical democratic ideology of the NYCC organizers did not mesh easily with the more traditional culture and ideology of Local 338. This was exacerbated further by differences in organizational structure and strategy, at times producing communication problems, mutual distrust, and improper assignments.

Moreover, at least initially, the relationship resembled a "vanguard coalition" in that the union had far more control over decisions than its community partner. According to Steve Kest, the former executive director of the national ACORN, this is not unusual in union-community collaborations: "Too often union partners are quick to request community support for an organizing drive or a contract campaign, but are unwilling to utilize their power to support a community organization's goals" (Kest 2003, 91).[58] Lynch agreed, stating "one of the weaknesses of the union movement is that they're too impatient, they're looking for a quick return on investment." To the credit of both Local 338 and NYCC, however, they learned from their mistakes, and eventually were able to adjust their strategy and take advantage of their respective strengths. After NYCC organizers convinced the union to allow them more space and time to develop a new approach, the campaign evolved positively, although not without ongoing tensions. Union pressure for NLRB elections lessened but did not disappear; resources are still inadequate for achieving an industry-wide impact, and a comprehensive long-term strategic alternative to the store-by-store election approach has not yet taken hold.

Conclusion

In this chapter, I make three key claims. First, for organizing a large group of independently owned neighborhood stores, an industry-wide strategy is essential. Second, "organizing organically" by such means as building a neighborhood-based workers' committee like the one NYCC created in this campaign is a far more effective approach to organizing undocumented immigrants than a singular focus on NLRB elections. Third, a CBO-union partnership is much less effective when it takes the form of a vanguard coalition than when both organizational partners share power. Collaboration can be difficult, but it has huge potential payoffs, helping to develop more effective organizing strategies, transforming local unions, and empowering the community.

Despite the obstacles encountered in the Flatbush grocery campaign, it ultimately proved highly promising, and generated important strategic discussions within the union movement about organizing outside of the NLRB election process. At this writing, the RWDSU International and other unions have provided NYCC with additional resources to organize in other sectors, such as car washes, where they have already enjoyed some successes (Greenhouse 2012a), and also launched a series of strikes in the fast food industry (Greenhouse 2012b).

The Flatbush grocery campaign exposes the problems and possibilities of organizing in the growing low-wage retail sector. Whereas much has been written about the challenges of organizing giant retailers such as Walmart, the many thousands of workers in smaller stores who face worse conditions have been all but ignored. Unions must identify effective strategies to organize workers across the retail sector. That can only happen when unions dedicate significant financial and human resources to experimental collaborations and strategies, as Local 338 did in this campaign.

3

FAITH, COMMUNITY, AND LABOR

Challenges and Opportunities in the
New York City Living Wage Campaign

Jeffrey D. Broxmeyer and Erin Michaels

On a cold snowy evening in early 2011, nearly two thousand people gathered in Harlem's Convent Avenue Baptist Church for a mass meeting in support of the Fair Wages for New Yorkers Act (FWNYA). As a church choir sang in the balcony, a video of Martin Luther King Jr. played, invoking the civil rights movement legacy of faith-based organizing. The energized crowd clapped to the beat of the music as the choir leader urged them to sing along; many did. Under a "Living Wage Now!" banner hanging over the pulpit, Convent Avenue's pastor, Jesse T. Williams Jr., delivered a sermon, followed by speeches from other clergy, elected officials, and union leaders. The evening also featured testimony from retail workers themselves, including Linda Archer, a middle-aged woman employed at a McDonald's in Times Square, who told the crowd that she was unable to afford to rent her own apartment on $7.25 per hour so she slept in her mother's living room.[1]

Like many large development projects in New York City, the redevelopment of Times Square had been accomplished with considerable public subsidies. "The irony is that this place represents in many ways the epitome of free-market capitalism," explained the president of the Times Square Alliance, a nonprofit organization. "But its transformation is due more to government intervention than just about any other development in the country" (Bagli 2010). Times Square is hardly alone in its heavy reliance on taxpayer money for reshaping the urban landscape, even if most members of the public are unaware of it.

Equally invisible to most New York City residents is the reality that the same real estate developers and their corporate retail tenants that receive such subsidies have generated large numbers of low-wage jobs like Linda Archer's, even though the subsidies are often justified in the name of job creation. The "Living Wage NYC" campaign that began in early 2010 was an effort to challenge the "any job is a job" development paradigm with an alternative approach that would require jobs linked to city-subsidized projects to pay at least $10 per hour, with health insurance coverage, or $11.50 per hour without health benefits. Over the course of the two-year campaign, sustained mobilization by union, clergy, and community groups culminated in the passage of a compromise measure, the product of negotiations between City Council Speaker Christine Quinn and the leadership of the Retail Wholesale and Department Store Union (RWDSU). Far narrower in scope and coverage than the original version of the bill, the city's living wage law passed in April 2012 nevertheless provided the union and its coalition partners a foundation to build on in future campaigns.[2]

Although in other cities living wage campaigns have often involved a wider coalition of unions, the RWDSU was the lead union partner in the Living Wage NYC campaign. The RWDSU had already built an alliance with the Northwest Bronx Community and Clergy Coalition in a struggle over the proposed redevelopment of the Kingsbridge Armory in the Bronx in 2005. In that campaign, the RWDSU aimed to prevent non-union stores in the mall that would have been part of the new development from undercutting nearby unionized groceries. Building on that effort, the RWDSU formed the Living Wage coalition to strengthen its ties to community and faith-based organizations, to reach new workers, and to extend its influence through public policy.

A Hybrid Campaign

From its inception, the Living Wage NYC campaign was a hybrid, partly a social movement-based coalition and partly a lobbying effort in the tradition of insider city politics. The union built a broad community-labor coalition and then harnessed the political capital generated by that process to publicly pressure the New York City Council into taking action. The final bill, however, illustrates the challenges for labor to win even modest labor reform in New York City, in the face of the enormous political clout of business interests generally and the commercial real estate industry in particular. Despite the strength of the living wage campaign's coalition, the union's access to effective lobbying channels, the modest, pragmatic demands, and widespread public support, this campaign sparked massive opposition from the business establishment and its political allies.

Within the living wage coalition itself, chronic tensions over information sharing and decision making added to the formidable challenges of extracting concessions from city power brokers. Disruptive protest repertoires advocated by some members of the coalition were rejected in favor of the insider politics and traditional lobbying tactics to which RWDSU and many other coalition partners were long accustomed. In the course of the campaign, however, RWDSU's community and clergy partners did demand and eventually win increased access to decision making, which may allow the community and clergy groups to push the union beyond its traditional tactics in the future.

As the Living Wage NYC campaign developed, RWDSU's coalition-building effort attracted a wide array of community partners, including many faith-based groups, and succeeded in winning extensive media attention to the city's role in subsidizing low-wage employers. The core strategy was to build enough political momentum behind the living wage demand to force future mayoral candidates and undecided city council members to take the issue into account as part of their electoral calculations.[3]

As the 2005 struggle over the terms of redevelopment for Kingsbridge Armory in the Bronx had made clear, Mayor Michael Bloomberg's administration would resist any living wage proposal linked to the city's role in subsidizing development projects. The Living Wage NYC campaign's goal was therefore to build the grassroots and lobbying pressure necessary to override the mayor's inevitable veto with a two-thirds supermajority in the city council. Living wage advocates won majority support from the Council early in the campaign, and subsequently focused their energies on pressuring Speaker Quinn to move the legislation forward. Taking advantage of the uncertainty surrounding the 2013 mayoral election cycle, for which Quinn and others were already positioning themselves as potential candidates, living wage advocates hoped that if they could generate sufficient momentum, the next mayor would have no alternative but to fully implement the living wage legislation.

Table 3.1 summarizes the campaign's timeline, from its launch when the RWDSU hired Ava Farkas of the Kingsbridge Armory campaign to organize for a citywide living wage, until the fall of 2013 when Christine Quinn lost the mayoral race in the Democratic primary. Other key moments in the timeline include May 2012, when the mayor vetoed the final version of the bill after it passed the city council by a vote of 44–5. When the city council overrode his veto, the mayor challenged the measure in court. However, the Living Wage law went into effect in September 2012 and the mayor's lawsuit was finally dismissed in July 2013.

In the face of strong political opposition, the original living wage proposal went through a series of changes, all of which narrowed its scope. The most

TABLE 3.1 **Living Wage NYC campaign timeline: December 2009–June 2012**

DECEMBER 2009	City council vote on the Kingsbridge Armory redevelopment
MAY 2010	Living wage bill introduced in city council
FALL 2010	Early mobilizing and coalition growth
JANUARY 2011	First large rally at Convent Avenue Baptist Church
JANUARY–APRIL 2011	Growing clergy and council support; Brooklyn and Bronx rallies; mayor's Economic Development Committee report
APRIL–MAY 2011	Lobbying efforts and growing coalition
MAY 2011	First city council hearing
JUNE–AUGUST 2011	First compromise version introduced; ongoing mobilization and coalition growth
NOVEMBER 2011	Riverside Church rally; second city council hearing on the bill
JANUARY 2012	Quinn and the RWDSU negotiate final compromise bill
APRIL 2012	City council passes the Quinn compromise bill
MAY 2012	Mayor Bloomberg vetoes the bill
JUNE 2012	City council overrides mayoral veto
JULY 2012	Mayor Bloomberg files lawsuit challenging the bill
SEPTEMBER 2012	Living wage law takes effect
JANUARY 2013	RWDSU endorses Quinn for mayor
JULY 2013	Mayoral lawsuit against the living wage law dismissed
SEPTEMBER 2013	Quinn loses mayoral race in Democratic primary

important modification from the first version to the second raised the subsidy level that would trigger the living wage requirement from $100,000 to $1 million, expanded the exemption for small businesses, and shortened the duration of the mandate from thirty to ten years (or the life of the subsidy). The first two versions of the bill covered corporate retail tenants in large-scale projects such as malls and big-box chains, but the third and final version, whose provisions are summarized in table 3.2, exempted retail tenants entirely, so that the only retail workers covered are those few employed in stand-alone stores that receive direct city subsidies. The final version of the bill added three new provisions intended to partially compensate for these concessions: an administrative policy preference[4] setting a goal to maximize living wage jobs; a commitment by the speaker to modify Local Law 48[5] to increase reporting about jobs created by city subsidized development; and an experimental Pilot Program providing new financial incentives to developers who require their tenants to pay a living wage.

The Living Wage NYC effort was part of a series of living wage campaigns across the United States that first emerged in the 1990s. Most are grassroots efforts led by unions and their community allies to raise the wages of nonunion workers through local government laws or ordinances. Living wage campaigns

TABLE 3.2 **The Fair Wages for New Yorkers Act**

WAGE LEVEL	$10 per hour with health insurance coverage or $11.50 per hour without benefits
COVERAGE	All direct employees of a subsidized project, including on-site contractors, subcontractors, and concessionaires
INDEXED TO INFLATION	Yes
SUBSIDY TRIGGER*	$1 million
EXEMPTIONS	Nonprofits, small businesses (with less than $5 million in annual revenue), affordable housing projects and their commercial tenants, manufacturing businesses, ICAP and other as-of-right subsidies†
	FRESH program and Zone-3 adjacent to Hudson Yards§
LENGTH OF MANDATE	10 years, or life of the subsidy*
ECONOMIC DEVELOPMENT CORPORATION POLICY PREFERENCE	Yes
LOCAL LAW 48	Speaker's commitment to increased transparency in jobs created

* "Subsidies" are cash payments, grants, bonds financing, tax abatements or exemptions, tax increment financing, filing fee waivers, energy cost reductions, environmental remediation costs, write-downs in market value of buildings, land, or leases.
† ICAP is the Industrial Commercial Incentive Program. This program is an "as-of-right" subsidy, which is "usually a tax break, to which a company is automatically entitled," and thus the opposite of a discretionary subsidy (Good Jobs New York 2013).
§ Negotiated as part of the final political compromise that led to the FWNYA's passage, but not included in the bill's language. FRESH is a city-subsidized program to bring grocery stores to underserved neighborhood "food deserts." Hudson Yards is a multibillion-dollar mixed-use redevelopment project under way in midtown Manhattan's far west side; Zone-3 adjacent developments includes three blocks between Tenth and Eleventh avenues.

aim to raise wage standards above federal and state minimum wage levels (currently $7.25 per hour in New York), which have failed to keep up with the cost of living in recent decades. More than 120 municipalities and counties across the United States now have living wage laws, although they vary considerably in their breadth of coverage, the level of wage standard they set, and the extent of enforcement (Luce 2004; National Employment Law Project 2011).[6]

Prior to the FWNYA campaign analyzed here, New York City had passed two limited living wage laws in 1996 and 2002, each targeting narrowly defined groups of workers. The 1996 law, passed over Mayor Rudolph Giuliani's veto, focused on the outsourcing of work previously performed by unionized city workers. It covered building, food, security, and other services, setting pay at the prevailing wage in those occupations, or, if none existed, a living wage of at least $9 per hour (Greenhouse 1996). In 2002, as the result of a joint campaign by 1199 SEIU, the United Federation of Teachers, and ACORN, a second living wage law was passed covering fifty thousand home health and child care providers. It set a wage of $8.10 per hour, later raised to $10 per hour. Mayor Bloomberg signed the 2002 bill into law. But the 1996 and 2002 bills had little direct impact on the private sector; indeed, 90 percent of the cost of the 2002 bill was covered through Medicaid reimbursements. The FWNYA was substantially different from these earlier living wage laws in that it targeted private-sector real estate developers and (in the original version of the bill) corporate retail chains.

The roots of the FWNYA were planted during the previously mentioned campaign over the proposal to redevelop the Kingsbridge Armory, which began in 2005. In this effort, the RWDSU partnered with the Northwest Bronx Community and Clergy Coalition to create the Kingsbridge Armory Redevelopment Alliance (KARA) which pressed for a community benefits agreement (CBA) with the developer, Related Companies. The proposed CBA included provisions for union neutrality, community space, and living wage jobs paying a minimum of $10 per hour. When Related, with support from the Bloomberg administration, attempted to move the development forward without the CBA, KARA persuaded Bronx council member Oliver Koppell and ultimately the New York City Council as a whole to vote against the project, which they did in a 45–1 vote. The Kingsbridge experience convinced Koppell of the need for a citywide living wage mandate to avoid similar protracted struggles over CBAs for individual development projects. In May 2010, the Living Wage NYC campaign coalesced around Koppell's bill, which became the basis of the FWNYA.

Building the Coalition

The campaign for FWNYA was led by RWDSU, one of the city's key retail unions. Although retail is one of the fastest-growing industries in New York City, most of the jobs it generates pay very poorly. In 2006, 44 percent of the city's retail workers earned less than $10 per hour, and nearly a quarter less than $8 per hour. Contrary to media stereotypes, the vast majority of retail workers are not teenagers working for extra spending money, but adults struggling to make ends meet; 78 percent are over the age of twenty-five. Also important, the demographic makeup of the retail workforce is overwhelmingly people of color: 28 percent Latino, 26 percent black, and 18 percent Asian (Parrott 2008; see also Luce and Fujita 2012).[7]

As union density in the New York City retail sector has declined, RWDSU has turned to a variety of new approaches to improving pay and working conditions in malls and among large nonunion corporate retailers. The Living Wage NYC campaign is an example of one alternative approach, namely a policy campaign through which the union publicized the plight of low-wage workers in an environment that allowed workers to express their grievances with minimal risk of employer retaliation. In a series of earlier organizing and advocacy campaigns—in 2006 at Brooklyn's Fulton Mall, at Kingsbridge Armory in the Bronx from 2005 to 2009, and more recently at the Queens Center Mall—the union has searched for new sources of leverage over employers. By focusing on the city's economic development process in the FWNYA campaign, RWDSU sought to place a floor under retail wages and thus put a brake on the infamous "race to the bottom" among retail employers. This was not a unionization campaign but rather what RWDSU staff called a "pre-organizing strategy."

In recent years, traditional union organizing efforts have faltered in the face of an increasingly dysfunctional system of labor law and intransigent employer resistance (see Bronfenbrenner 2009; Logan 2006). RWDSU is a private-sector labor union affiliated with the United Food and Commercial Workers but with a high degree of autonomy within the larger UFCW organizational structure. As other commentators have suggested (Voss and Sherman 2000; Milkman 2006), such autonomy often facilitates union revitalization efforts and new organizing initiatives, offering local union leaders room to maneuver and opportunities to experiment with new strategies that deviate from traditional approaches to collective bargaining. In such contexts, union leaders may be more willing to "risk failure" through militant tactics, although limited financial resources, commitments to existing membership, and an unfavorable legal and political environment may also make them wary of such risk-taking (Getman 2010, 307). Even losing campaigns can help lay the groundwork for future struggle, as Eve Weinbaum argues in her analysis of "successful failures," teaching activists the power of collective action and expanding the capacity of progressive actors and networks (2004, 261).

RWDSU's search for new organizing approaches has also involved borrowing from the burgeoning strategic and tactical repertoire of worker centers (Fine 2006), which have increasingly replaced traditional unions as advocates for low-wage workers. Worker centers have often succeeded in winning public support for their efforts by drawing media attention to wage and hour violations and pursuing litigation to win back pay and other remedies for the workers affected. In the context of Los Angeles, Milkman (2010) noted growing strategic convergence between labor unions and worker centers. In New York, RWDSU stands out as the one union that has successfully adopted worker-center-like tactics, for example in its ¡Despierta Bushwick! (Wake Up Bushwick!) and Yellow Rat Bastard organizing drives (Shapiro, this volume), both of which focused on wage and hour violations. RWDSU has also undertaken joint projects with the Retail Action Project, a retail industry worker center the union helped create (Ikeler, this volume).

Many worker centers also engage in public policy organizing (Fine 2006, 101). And in other parts of the country many unions have experimented with CBAs like the one KARA sought in connection with the proposed Kingsbridge Armory development project, mentioned previously. CBAs involve binding legal contracts between real estate developers, public agencies, and community stakeholders (Warren 2005). The final iteration of the FWNYA included a living wage requirement administered through the city's Economic Development Corporation, an arrangement that in some respects resembles a CBA.

The Living Wage NYC campaign also drew on another innovative approach to which unions increasingly have turned in recent years, namely labor-community coalitions (Nissen 2004; Krinsky and Reese 2006). Just as there are structural and cultural mismatches between worker centers and unions (Fine 2007), so too labor-community coalitions face challenges. Community and clergy groups are structurally different from labor unions in terms of their organizational capacities, decision-making processes, membership accountability, and resource levels. Mutual collaboration between groups can involve sharing resources and working toward common goals, but even when agendas converge, organizational structures can collide. Union capacity and financial resources may be a major coalition asset for a campaign and yet constrain the possibilities for community partners' participation, cooperation, and power sharing. There are also potential cultural mismatches between unions, on the one side, and community and clergy groups, on the other. Differences in guiding philosophies and the social characteristics of leaders can generate tensions over coalition goals, strategy, and expectations. An action that seems pragmatic and reasonable to a union may utterly bewilder coalition allies. Conversely, the actions or recommendations of coalition allies may appear unreasonable to a union leader with insider status in city politics. Community groups are frequently rooted in specific geographic locations and concerned about the long-term outlook of their neighborhoods, while union interest in development policies may come and go. Clergy in particular operate on a distinct cultural terrain tied to spiritual and even biblical points of reference. In addition, many clergy have tremendous capacity to turn out their congregants to coalition rallies and other events, and may be puzzled as to why other groups have less ability to do so; they may also wonder why passion, commitment, and moral vision alone may not always carry the day. Furthermore, clergy who command great respect in their religious institutions place a high premium on trust, which can break down during critical campaign junctures when some groups are privy to information and decision making while others are excluded.

As Snarr (2011, 66–101) shows, religious activists can serve as bridge-builders in living wage campaigns and help to mediate some of these structural and cultural tensions. Another relevant case study is the Los Angeles security guard campaign in which outreach to black clergy played a key role in building orga nizing momentum. As Bloom (2010) notes, while both the union and clergy had a vested interest in working together on the campaign, it was funded by union resources and initially controlled by union officials. However, when Clergy and Laity United for Economic Justice expressed discontent about the power imbalance internal to the campaign, the union responded in a fashion that eventually resulted in mutual trust and made it possible for the labor-clergy alliance to build a successful campaign in a way that neither could have done alone. In this case, Clergy and Laity United for Economic Justice activists advocated greater militancy and more aggressive campaign tactics, which were decisive factors in the campaign's success (Bloom 2010, 174).

Corporate political culture, and above all the power of the commercial real estate industry, was the single greatest obstacle that the FWNYA campaign had to confront. Since the 1970s fiscal crisis, New York City's postwar social-democratic legacy has been severely eroded and the city has become increasingly reliant on the interdependent growth engines of finance and real estate (Freeman 2000; Sassen 2001; Moody 2007a; Brash 2011). As analyst Bettina Damiani from Good Jobs New York put it, "Texas has oil, and New York has real estate."[8] Mayors from Edward Koch onward have built conservative progrowth governing coalitions around redeveloping Manhattan's central business district and attracting large-scale investment through a mix of financial incentives and subsidies channeled through city agencies (Mollenkopf 1992). Organizations such as the Real Estate Board of New York, the New York Metropolitan Retail Association, and the Food Industry Alliance represent industries that receive city subsidies and spend heavily in elections and lobbying, giving them vast political influence.

The most delicate challenge for the Living Wage NYC campaign was how to win over Councilwoman Christine Quinn. As city council Speaker, she held the legislative fate of the bill in her hands by determining if and when it would receive a hearing and come to a full vote. Moreover, Quinn was the mayor's closest ally on the council and had played a role in the defeat of other high-profile labor-backed bills, such as a proposed paid sick days ordinance that she had declined to bring up for a vote. However, the fact that Quinn was also interested in running to succeed Bloomberg as mayor led her to attempt to strike a balance between appearing sufficiently attentive to business concerns and avoiding alienating important electoral constituencies. Quinn therefore avoided taking an official position on the proposed living wage law for the first two years of the campaign, until ultimately unveiling her own version of the bill in January 2012.

Social Justice Framing and the Role of Clergy and Community Groups

The Living Wage NYC campaign's public discourse drew on the tradition of religiously inspired social justice movements, invoking for example Martin Luther King Jr.'s 1968 support for the organizing efforts of low-wage sanitation workers in Memphis, Tennessee. Living wage advocates emphasized that King's call for economic and racial justice remained unfulfilled in New York City, pointing out that racial minorities disproportionally suffer from low wages. Faith leaders thus framed the living wage as both an economic and a moral issue, with a narrative that "punctuated" the problem of poverty by highlighting low wages, and then attributed responsibility to those who had the power to shape government policies (Snarr 2011).

Living wage opponents did not directly challenge the campaign's discursive frame that defined the issue as a moral struggle between right and wrong, justice and injustice. Instead, the opposition created an alternative narrative couched in the language of business, suggesting that the living wage mandate would be a "job-killer" if enacted. The opposition's main example was the Kingsbridge Armory where redevelopment was stopped, in part, because the developer refused to pay living wages. When interest group lobbyists or officials from the Bloomberg administration spoke about the living wage proposal, they invoked a discourse of business competition—an especially resonant theme during a recession.[9] In his public rhetoric, the mayor invoked the specter of central planning (and even made comparisons to the Soviet Union), describing the proposed living wage law as an anti-free-market imposition (Rubinstein 2012). But the living wage campaign's alternative frame of religiously inspired social justice proved highly effective and for many audiences trumped the opponents' business-oriented arguments. Despite vocal criticism of the bill from the mayor, the Real Estate Board of New York, retailers, two building trades unions, and the *New York Post*, supermajorities of New Yorkers expressed support for the proposed legislation.[10] An April 2011 poll conducted by the Baruch College School of Public Affairs found that 78 percent of New Yorkers approved of the FWNYA (Cordero-Guzman 2011); similarly, in December 2011 a Quinnipiac poll found that 74 percent of New Yorkers approved of the bill (Quinnipiac 2011).

Coalition building was central to RWDSU's strategy. As Ava Farkas, the campaign's lead organizer, explained:

> I think that there is a sense in our union that these kinds of coalitions and relationships are a necessity to revive the labor movement in general, that we can't just work in our own silos. We probably need the

whole community to help us organize a single retail store, or a chain of stores.

This approach to mobilizing community forces had already been deployed in successful organizing drives in Bushwick and SoHo, and the union carried these prior experiences and relationships into the FWNYA campaign. Over time, the effort won support from more than 110 organizations, ranging from unions, community groups, houses of worship, and neighborhood associations to anti-hunger groups and political clubs. By early 2012 when the final deal with Quinn was reached, the coalition had gained impressive momentum.

Families United for Racial and Economic Equality, Good Old Lower East Side, and New York Communities for Change were among the many community-based organizations that joined the campaign. These three groups had preexisting relationships with the union, and the living wage issue was also a good fit with their antipoverty and racial justice agendas. The union also actively recruited churches whose members represented the workers they aimed to organize, namely low-wage African American and Latino retail workers. Here RWDSU relied strongly on its relationship with the Micah Institute of the New York Theological Seminary, hiring several of its social justice-minded theology students as part-time organizing fellows who focused on recruiting other New York-based faith leaders.

Thus the Living Wage NYC campaign built a coalition that was far broader than those formed in previous citywide labor mobilizations. As one clergy activist explained:

> This campaign has been largely propelled by faith groups. There's a union behind it, but in terms of the actual on-the-ground organizing and mobilizing, it's been by faith groups around the city. The prime movers have really been the African American and Latino churches, largely Baptist and evangelicals—it's not the usual white liberal Pentecostals or mainline Protestant suspects—and their members are these low-wage retail workers. So there is an obvious self-interest, but it's a communal self-interest.[11]

Indeed, one of the living wage campaign's greatest achievements was building new alliances between the labor movement and faith-based organizations in communities of color. African American and Latino congregants, especially Baptists and Latino evangelicals, comprised the majority of participants in living wage campaign rallies throughout 2011. Notably, most church members attended as concerned citizens, although a few were also retail workers themselves.[12]

The campaign's core strategic planning process took place during weekly meetings convened by RWDSU with the Micah Institute's clergy organizing team and Rabbi Michael Feinberg, executive director of the Greater New York Labor-Religion Coalition. Community-based organization staff regularly attended these meetings as well. Representatives from the most active groups also participated in advisory committee meetings, although no official process for decision making crystallized until after the agreement with Quinn was reached in January 2012. Coalition planning meetings also included monthly clergy lunches organized by RWDSU and the Micah Institute. Clergy meetings drew a largely Christian but interfaith crowd representing ten to fifty separate churches and synagogues during the run-up to the campaign's large rallies.

The union also solicited input and advice from clergy and community representatives through informal channels of communication. Sometimes this consultation process was a point of contention. Most coalition members believed the union had genuinely good intentions, but some community and clergy members remained adamant about not simply agreeing to a prefabricated RWDSU plan. One community-based organizer explained the predicament of groups that received financial support from labor unions and then participated in coalitions with them: "Often what they [the union] want from that funding is not exactly what our members want. How they want to be involved in things isn't exactly always the same [as what we want]." Even community groups that received no union funds deferred to RWDSU as the force with the resources and political connections to assemble and sustain the living wage campaign. But the union's domination of the decision-making process began to rankle. As one clergy member noted, there was often nothing wrong with the union proposals, but collective input sessions frequently occurred after a proposal had already been effectively adopted.

Compromise Tests the Coalition

Over time, as their contributions to the campaign mobilization efforts expanded, clergy and community groups began to demand greater influence on the direction and shape of the campaign. A critical juncture for the coalition's decision-making structure occurred in January 2012 during the meeting called in the aftermath of the compromise deal struck by RWDSU leadership with Speaker Quinn's office. Some of the key community-based organizations and churches objected strongly to both the content of the deal itself and the fact that they had not been consulted in advance about its terms or the campaign's subsequent deescalation. Many of the coalition members only learned about the deal when

RWDSU president Stuart Applebaum publicly announced it alongside Speaker Quinn at a press conference at city hall. One key concern was that the Quinn compromise bill effectively removed retail tenants from coverage under the legislation, the very category of workers that had from the outset been a major focus of the campaign. The compromise bill only covered direct subsidy recipients such as large freestanding stores, and exempted the retail stores that rented space in those buildings. Several faith leaders expressed surprise and concern at the union's willingness to agree to such terms. During a series of animated meetings following the revelation of the Quinn deal, one clergy leader expressed his discontent:

> This was a coalition decision, and we felt left out. We're a team, and we believe in the message of movement. We're here, and we would have been there if you'd asked us. We have hundreds of congregations to explain this to, and we could have done something stronger.

The narrowing of the legislation's coverage was particularly difficult for the clergy to accept because the foundation of the campaign's discourse was one of moral clarity; the Quinn compromise reduced the scope of the coverage so drastically that the faith organizers were unable to see the final bill as transformative anti-poverty work. A union staff leader responded to the criticism, acknowledging the validity of the clergy's and community groups' concerns but also urging them to maintain the united front that the campaign had created:

> This is the most powerful grassroots coalition in NYC in a generation. What we created is important, and how we move forward [is important]. We live for struggles. This coalition cannot afford to lose. Mistakes are made, we learn from them. [We must] hold this together or we won't win the next fight.

Over the course of subsequent coalition meetings and informal discussions, trust was painstakingly reconstructed through the creation of a Policy Team composed of respected faith and community leaders that from this point on would have a direct line of communication with RWDSU's political director. The nine-person Policy Team took the lead in directing subsequent meetings, presenting the specific details of the bill, and answering questions from the activists in attendance.

Despite these internal frictions, the coalition was impressive by any standard, allowing the Living Wage NYC campaign to mobilize thousands of supporters. Living wage coalition members visibly dominated attendance at four major public rallies and two lengthy city council hearings, and recruited dozens of workers, faith leaders, and citizens eager and ready to testify on behalf of the

FWNYA. Such grassroots mobilization is crucial for living wage campaigns that must overcome fierce resistance from entrenched business interests and reluctant public officials. As Luce (2004) explains, however, it can be difficult to balance the demands of lobbying, a quintessential "insider" activity, and grassroots activism, an "outside" game that relies on the energy of everyday citizens.

The Living Wage NYC campaign included massive efforts to mobilize dramatic displays of public support. One of the first major actions in November 2010 was the delivery of seven thousand postcards from church members addressed to members of the city council. Later, the campaign continued to collect postcards from supporters who attended rallies and also coordinated several waves of phone calls from constituents targeting undecided council members. Prominent endorsements from dozens of local neighborhood groups and Democratic and progressive political clubs were also part of the strategy to pressure undecided members. Local groups supporting the campaign secured the endorsement of six community boards across Manhattan, including Community Board 4, in Speaker Quinn's home district.[13] Retail workers, community activists, and clergy turned out in force to testify before the city council's Committee on Contracts at hearings on May 12 and November 22, 2011. On both occasions, the campaign mobilized far more supporters than were able to testify.

During the fall of 2011, after an initial compromise version of the bill was announced, living wage activists struggled with the question of how best to move the bill forward. A number of approaches were debated at meetings, including expanding the size of the coalition, holding more public rallies, and targeting elected officials more intensely. Union staff deflected discussion of civil disobedience, which was periodically suggested by certain faith leaders, for whom it was an integral part of the civil rights movement tradition. Some community groups active in the campaign also suggested targeting specific council members with street actions to embarrass them into coming to the negotiating table. Much later, after Mayor Bloomberg vetoed the bill, some coalition members proposed picketing or blocking traffic around his uptown Manhattan home to draw attention to the veto. Such disruptive actions directly targeting political figures were generally discouraged throughout the campaign, especially after what many perceived as an unsuccessful action in April 2011, when forty activists marched to the office of City Councilmember James Vacca (D-Bronx) to deliver living wage supporters' postcards. This action led to dissension in the coalition, as some high-level clergy argued that elected officials should be approached with the goal of achieving the political equivalent of a conversion experience, which would become impossible if they were antagonized through confrontational tactics like the march to Vacca's office.

Throughout the campaign, the coalition leadership attempted to maintain a balance between the insider strategy of negotiating with politicians and the outsider strategy of grassroots mobilization. The delicacy of this effort at balance is illustrated by the final deal brokered between the Living Wage NYC campaign and Speaker Quinn. Throughout the preceding two-year period, Quinn had been careful to avoid publicly acknowledging any negotiations with the campaign. In briefings to groups during coalition meetings, RWDSU's political director, Ademoloa Oyefeso, emphasized that Speaker Quinn should be viewed as a potential ally and that confrontational tactics directed at her should be off the table. This was a repeated point of disagreement with many of the community and clergy groups, however, who believed that Quinn was not friendly to either the coalition or the living wage.[14]

Shortly after the negotiations with the union leadership in January 2012, Quinn allowed the compromise bill to go to a city council vote that April, and it passed easily. However, the ongoing tension between Quinn and the advocates erupted into public view at the living wage coalition's press conference on April 30, 2012, celebrating the passage of the FWNYA. In coalition meetings held prior to the press conference, there had been prolonged debate about whether or not to ask Speaker Quinn to appear at a joint press conference. Despite ongoing reservations a consensus formed to invite her to do so. But as she was delivering her remarks to the media in front of fifty living wage supporters and other city officials, Quinn overheard one activist call the mayor "Pharaoh Bloomberg," at which point she proceeded to chastise the individual at length before storming off in anger. "You stand here talking about democracy and wanting people to listen," she exclaimed. "In a democracy, people have a right to have different views, and we do not have a right to then call them names."[15] Quinn's outburst dominated the news coverage of this event and exposed the campaign's limited influence over her and other elected officials who would be essential to the law's implementation.

A "Successful Failure"

The Living Wage NYC campaign can be understood as a "successful failure" (Weinbaum 2004) despite the tremendous vitality of the campaign and the commitment of its activists. Legislation was passed, but the victory was largely symbolic. The attempt to shift the power relationship between RWDSU and the larger coalition that led the campaign, on the one hand, and the city's powerful real estate and retail industry groups, on the other, made little headway. Pay and conditions for low-wage retail workers in New York City remain essentially unchanged.

Considering the energy and resources mobilized during the two-year campaign, the bill's final version was at best a limited victory in terms of the number of workers covered. Although before its passage the bill was estimated to impact only four hundred to nine hundred workers per year, the RWDSU released a report in July 2013 claiming the law covered 12,488 workers across 18 projects in its first nine months.[16] However, the report is overly optimistic in at least two respects. It includes projected job creation fifteen years into the future, five years beyond the term of the legal mandate. The report also fails to note that 88 percent of the covered jobs are from two projects subsidizing the airline industry, which already boasts higher wages and greater union density than the low-wage retail jobs that the law originally targeted.

The living wage campaign illustrates both the possibilities and limits of efforts to win local labor reform in the current political and economic climate. It did succeed in building a broad coalition and mobilizing popular support, as manifested in the effort to collect and deliver supporters' postcards by the thousands, and by holding large rallies and other high-profile public events that put pressure on elected officials. Activists enjoyed a great deal of success in mobilizing support and attracting positive media coverage, winning support for their effort from the vast majority of New Yorkers.

Yet the campaign was reluctant to "rock the boat," or use more confrontational approaches like direct action or public shaming of powerful political figures. Unions in particular tend to be highly risk-averse, often shying away from militancy in favor of protecting long-term relationships with influential elected officials. Those officials, in turn, were unwilling to put their own ties to business interests at risk.

To be sure, RWDSU has creatively and effectively deployed militant protest tactics in some of its recent workplace organizing drives, but the union's aggressive posture in organizing retail stores has no counterpart in its consensus-based approach to policy work. The union's community partners in the living wage campaign were receptive to the idea of adopting more aggressive tactics from the standard toolbox of community activists, but ultimately RWDSU's cautious approach carried the day.

Over the two-year span of the campaign, however, in response to internal pressure from other coalition members, RWSDU did begin to move out of its tactical comfort zone, especially after the final compromise with Speaker Quinn when the union agreed to create a Policy Team to increase accountability and share decision-making power with its coalition partners. But this occurred only after the political deal on the bill was already finalized. Prior to that point, allies did not exercise sufficient decision-making authority within the coalition to successfully convince the union to engage in the type of risk-taking that might have enabled it to win broader coverage and a stronger mandate.

After several revisions, each of which involved concessions to business opponents, the final living wage bill passed the city council in April 2012 by an overwhelming 44–5 vote. The bill did achieve some of the campaign's original objectives, such as a wage mandate and wage disclosure law through an amendment to Local Law 48. The deal also included newly added items, like the experimental Pilot Project. Perhaps most important, the final FWNYA set a precedent for regulating private-sector employment in one of the city's fastest-growing industries, potentially paving the way for future struggles over economic development and wage standards. The campaign also achieved a symbolic victory: as organizers frequently pointed out, it "changed the conversation" about city-sponsored development and the worth of retail workers in the city, offering popular policy alternatives to the hegemonic business discourse of tax cuts and "job creation." RWDSU also could now credibly claim to represent not only its own members but also the city's working poor by championing this effort to raise wages at the bottom of the labor market.

The campaign also succeeded in building RWDSU's institutional capacity, developing and sustaining relationships with community and clergy groups, and expanding its influence in relation to city power brokers as well. Other coalition members also gained greater political influence through their involvement in the campaign. For example, through RWDSU-funded fellowships, the Micah Institute acquired a citywide reputation as a leader in faith-rooted activism, attracting new students, and gaining access to community-clergy activist networks. Other living wage coalition members also benefited by learning new skills and in some cases developing a different political consciousness. As Weinbaum (2004) points out in her analysis of "successful failures," experiencing the power of collective action and learning new organizing skills, even in unsuccessful campaigns, can lay the groundwork for future efforts at social change. It is impossible to predict the impact of the FWNYA campaign on future struggles, but there are already hopeful signs. For instance, one first-time organizer from the living wage fight subsequently turned his energies to a statewide campaign to raise the minimum wage and also was involved in RWDSU's successful 2012 car-wash unionization campaign in Queens.

Despite a legislative victory, the future of the living wage remains uncertain. Mayor Bloomberg vowed to block the new law through legal action, but has been unsuccessful. On July 2, 2013, a federal judge from the Southern District of New York dismissed his lawsuit. Yet, one month later the State Supreme Court ruled that a separate prevailing wage bill won by SEIU 32BJ was preempted by the state's minimum wage law. This ruling blocked the law's coverage of building services tenants who indirectly receive city subsidies, which may bode ill for other city wage mandates. If this decision is not overturned on appeal, it could prevent the expansion of the living wage law to include tenants, which was the coalition's original goal.

Following the negotiations with Christine Quinn over the living wage law, the RWDSU endorsed her for mayor early in the 2013 Democratic primary contest, when she was leading in the polls. Quinn lost badly in the primary race, to William de Blasio, who has expressed his support for the living wage as well as a commitment to address the broader issue of growing inequality in the city's population. Given the uneven track record of implementation of other living wage laws around the country (Luce 2004), however, even a sympathetic mayor may not effectively enforce the law in the absence of ongoing grassroots pressure. The new mayor will inherit a city of extreme social inequality with a political system dominated by corporate interests, and implementing the new living wage law is among the many challenges that lie ahead.

4

UNITED NEW YORK

Fighting for a Fair Economy in
"The Year of the Protester"

Lynne Turner

The Service Employees International Union (SEIU) launched a national campaign it called Fight for a Fair Economy (FFE) in early 2011, which included a
New York City campaign called United New York (hereinafter United NY).[1] This
effort was launched a few years after the results of the 2008 election failed to deliver labor law reform that many hoped would lay the groundwork for a private-
sector union resurgence, or to stem the tide of continuing cuts in public services,
assaults on unions, and deterioration of workers' wages and working conditions.
SEIU had spent over $67 million on political activities and lobbying in 2008, and
had mounted an intensive grassroots mobilization for Barack Obama's presidential campaign.[2] Now, SEIU, like the U.S. labor movement as a whole, confronted the grim reality that despite Obama's electoral victory, corporate power
and populist right-wing movements remained intact. Stephen Lerner, long-time
labor strategist and architect of SEIU's Justice for Janitors campaign, has argued
in a much-quoted essay (Lerner 2011a) that labor unions, despite their substantial institutional resources and professed anticorporate agenda, "are just big
enough—and just connected enough to the political and economic power
structure—to be constrained from leading the kinds of activities that are
needed" to challenge that power structure. More specifically, he suggested that
"unions with hundreds of millions in assets and collective bargaining agreements covering millions of workers won't risk their treasuries and contracts
by engaging in large-scale sit-ins, occupations, and other forms of non-violent
civil disobedience that must inevitably overcome court injunctions and political pressures."

Continued concern about the relentless efforts of the Right, along with the continuing decline in union density (by 2010 down to 11.9% nationally and 6.9% in the private sector), led the 2.2 million member SEIU to attempt a break with standard union behavior and to launch the national FFE campaign in seventeen cities where the union had a strong footprint in an effort "to do something radically different."[3] The union that had made "organizing the unorganized" its mantra, and had done so with notable success, now recognized the limits to this approach, and attempted what one commentator (Meyerson 2011) dubbed a "Hail Mary pass."

To restore the labor movement's diminished clout, SEIU leaders now believed, "the environment needed to change in order to . . . create the space for workers to organize."[4] Internal discussions about a community-based initiative that might help alter the political landscape and create a drumbeat of protest across the country for jobs and other progressive policies began soon after Mary Kay Henry was elected SEIU president in May 2010, succeeding the often-controversial Andy Stern. After the Republican landslide in the 2010 midterm elections, the union unveiled its plans for FFE, first within the union, and soon after to the wider public. For the union, this involved a commitment to "reorganizing the International staff behind this campaign . . . freeing up a lot of resources to do a kind of organizing we had never done before, and it called for redirecting what had been traditionally straight-up worker organizing campaign resources into something broader without clarity about what the payoff would be."[5] By February 2011, as unprecedented attacks on public sector unions were unfolding in Wisconsin and other states, new hopes for a resurgence of labor and grassroots activism were kindled when students, union members, and allies staged an eighteen-day takeover of the Wisconsin State Capitol in response to Governor Scott Walker's move to end public sector collective bargaining rights.

This chapter examines United NY, FFE's New York City campaign, whose efforts fortuitously coincided with the emergence of Occupy Wall Street (OWS) in the second half of 2011. I argue that United NY's strategic decision to foster a grassroots protest movement within the city's existing landscape of community-labor coalitions and embrace what Dan Clawson (2003) calls "fusion" with other social movements enabled it to play a positive and synergistic role in OWS. In addition, while United NY was able to capitalize on prior SEIU efforts to build alliances with community-based organizations in the city, its explicit focus on collaborative work facilitated greater acceptance of "fusion" within local SEIU unions. That in turn enabled United NY to transcend bureaucratic constraints and embrace OWS's risk-taking and militancy, counterbalancing the gravitational pull of "insider politics."

United NY and its Partners

United NY functions as an "organization of organizations" and describes itself as a "coalition of neighbors, community groups, faith organizations and labor united in the fight for good jobs, corporate accountability and stronger communities."[6] As figure 4.1 shows, it brings together three key SEIU units with large memberships in New York City—SEIU Local 32BJ; 1199 SEIU; and Workers United, the laundry, distribution, food service, and apparel union, now affiliated with SEIU—as well as three of the most effective, deeply rooted community organizations in the city, Make the Road New York (MRNY; see McAlevey, this volume), New York Communities for Change (NYCC),[7] and the New York Civic Participation Project (see McFarland, this volume). United NY's goal was to stimulate a local mass movement, which leaders hoped would also generate national-level influence given New York's size and status as home to the financial goliaths of Wall Street.

SEIU Local 32BJ and 1199 SEIU, in contrast to Workers United and many other unions, have large memberships and have not experienced the broader crisis of declining density that has plagued organized labor in recent years. Nevertheless their leaders recognized the urgency of addressing the national free fall in union power and ongoing right-wing attacks on workers.

Local 32BJ, the largest local in SEIU's property services division, is a regional entity with 120,000 members in eight states and Washington, DC. But the majority of its members—seventy thousand commercial office cleaners, residential building service workers, window cleaners, and security officers—are located in New York City. In an earlier era, 32BJ epitomized "business unionism," especially during the tenure of former president Gus Bevona. Spared the membership losses that SEIU building services locals in other cities suffered in the 1970s and 1980s and maintaining relatively high standards for existing members, in those years 32BJ was not engaged in organizing the unorganized or internal organizing to increase membership participation. But a year after Bevona's resignation in 1999 and a subsequent trusteeship, reformer Mike Fishman was elected 32BJ president. Soon after that, the local embarked on large-scale and successful unionization drives targeting suburban janitors, residential building porters, food service workers, and, more recently, security officers.

Under Fishman, 32BJ also launched a membership engagement program and an effort to recruit and develop stewards for its fifteen thousand worksites, and initiated internal discussions of leadership and the union's guiding principles among its members.[8] Among other effects, these internal organizing efforts enhanced the local's contract mobilization for twenty-two thousand commercial office cleaners during the second half of 2011. For Local 32BJ, which was thriving

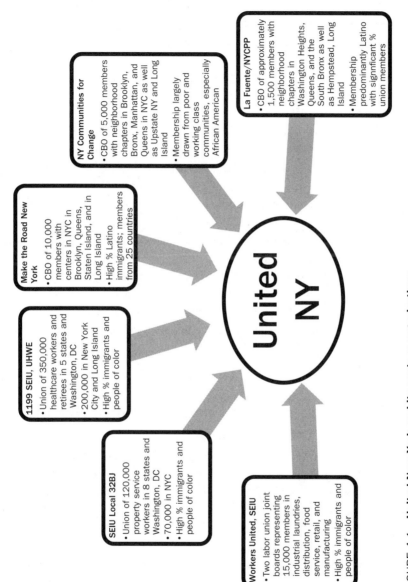

1199 SEIU, UHWE
• Union of 350,000 healthcare workers and retirees in 5 states and Washington, DC
• 200,000 in New York City and Long Island
• High % immigrants and people of color

Make the Road New York
• CBO of 10,000 members with centers in NYC in Brooklyn, Queens, Staten Island, and in Long Island
• High % Latino immigrants; members from 25 countries

NY Communities for Change
• CBO of 5,000 members with neighborhood chapters in Brooklyn, Bronx, Manhattan, and Queens in NYC as well as Upstate NY and Long Island
• Membership largely drawn from poor and working class communities, especially African American

SEIU Local 32BJ
• Union of 120,000 property service workers in 8 states and Washington, DC
• 70,000 in NYC
• High % immigrants and people of color

Workers United, SEIU
• Two labor union joint boards representing 15,000 members in industrial laundries, distribution, food service, retail, and manufacturing
• High % immigrants and people of color

La Fuente/NYCPP
• CBO of approximately 1,500 members with neighborhood chapters in Washington Heights, Queens, and the South Bronx as well as Hempstead, Long Island
• Membership predominantly Latino with signnificant % union members

United NY

FIGURE 4.1 **United New York and its partner organizations.**

as a local, FFE was about the survival of the broader labor movement. As Organizing Director Rob Hill put it, "Even if we have an aggressive organizing plan for our union, we're increasingly going to be an isolated island of unionization; we're still looking at the end of the labor movement." Counteracting this would require unions to "actually start a real offensive, engaging the private sector workers who are unorganized to start demanding more."[9]

The other large SEIU affiliate in United NY, 1199 SEIU—United Healthcare Workers East, represents over 280,000 active members in New York, New Jersey, Maryland, the District of Columbia, Florida, and Massachusetts[10]—including approximately 192,000 hospital, home care, nursing home, and other health care and human service workers in New York City and Long Island.[11] 1199 has a storied history as an independent health care workers union that spearheaded the unionization of hospital workers half a century ago through successful community-supported strikes, and went on to organize 85–90 percent of the city's health care workers and become a powerful force in New York politics (Fink and Greenberg 2009). Like 32BJ, it has defied the national crisis of unionism and has thrived in recent years. For Larry Bortoluzzi, 1199's coordinator of special projects and United NY board member, the purpose of FFE is movement building and changing the political environment: "We're trying to impact the debate: since New York is the media capital of the world, we think we can help influence the rest of the country."[12] Both 32BJ and 1199 saw FFE as an effort to shift the union's focus from organizing and representation so that it would, in Bortoluzzi's words, "go forward in a more broad way and stop being parochial."[13]

Insider/Outsider Politics and Coalition-Building

United NY, and FFE nationally, sought to prioritize "outsider politics" and grassroots mobilization over the "insider politics" and high-level political relationships long nurtured by labor unions—reflecting organized labor's frustration at the political impasse following Obama's election. With FFE, SEIU hoped to reignite the grassroots power of the labor movement, the civil rights movement, and other social movements. As Bortoluzzi put it:

> Historically, the only way that there's ever really been major change in this country is when people are in the streets, a popular movement. In the '30s, in the '40s, the New Deal only happened because people were out there. . . . What happened in the '50s and '60s with civil rights, it's because people were in the streets. The antiwar movement was all about keeping people in the streets and making noise. That's why we

were taken aback by the attacks from the Right, these Tea Partiers attacking people at town halls. We were just completely taken by surprise by it because *we* hadn't mobilized that kind of grassroots support for our agenda.[14]

To signal this new direction, the national SEIU leadership cancelled the political convention it had traditionally held every four years with all of the local unions "where all the presidential candidates parade through and make their pitch and kick off SEIU's participation in the presidential election," as 32BJ's Mary Anne Collins later recalled. Instead the union launched the FFE at a March 2011 meeting of fifteen hundred members in Los Angeles, "creating a core of activists in the union who were going to go back and commit themselves to this campaign for good jobs and organizing rights and organizing the communities. It was a real sign for the party politics people that we were going to do something different."[15]

According to Hector Figueroa, then 32BJ's secretary-treasurer, a crucial yardstick for FFE and United NY would be their effectiveness in challenging the market fundamentalist narrative:

> While politics is important, you need to do something in addition to politics. Martin Luther King used to say that civil disobedience is a way of bringing attention to the plight of the oppressed, and to those who are oppressing them. To have a narrative, you have to have a narrator, and the narrator cannot just be the president or Congress. It has to be ordinary working people, who can tell the story, tell what the priorities should be, and are ready and willing to take action both with their ballots but also in the streets and in demonstrations.[16]

With a Democratic president in office and the 2012 presidential election looming, SEIU had to consider the extent to which FFE's effort to forge an "outsider politics" would jeopardize their preexisting relationships with Democratic elected officials. This was hardly a new dilemma. As Mike Davis (1986) observed decades ago, labor's "seat at the table" within the Democratic Party was established during the New Deal era and fortified after World War II with the demobilization of rank and file militancy and the establishment of "a new legal labyrinth of time contracts, government mediation and legislative lobbying." Davis famously characterized labor's loyal support for the Democratic Party as a "barren marriage" that yielded meager rewards.

Other commentators dissent from this view. Taylor Dark (1999), for example, argues that unions maintained substantial political clout in the second half of the twentieth century, despite sharply declining membership and workplace power. Dark acknowledges the long-standing failure of Democrats to enact labor law, but maintains that labor's "insider" political power was crucial for winning passage of key progressive legislation, ranging from the Civil Rights Act, the Voting Rights Act, and Medicare during the Johnson administration to the Family and Medical Leave Act under Clinton. In addition, he points out, the AFL-CIO and many individual unions have been granted consistent access to Democratic administrations, have benefited from prolabor administrative appointments to the Department of Labor and the National Labor Relations Board, and have warded off many Republican legislative attacks on labor rights and labor standards such as prevailing wage protections.

Whether one applauds or condemns it, the record of U.S. unions' continuing support for Democratic electoral campaigns is beyond dispute, and labor's get out the vote (GOTV) efforts remain highly effective. During the 2008 presidential race, for example, union support translated into Democratic votes even among Republican-leaning demographic groups like gun owners and veterans (Francia 2010, 299; see also Francia 2006). It is equally indisputable that in recent years, organized labor has received comparatively little in return (Francia 2010, 294; Reed 2010). The Obama administration did make several union-friendly political appointments, particularly within the U.S. Department of Labor. But in the wake of the failure of labor law reform, and as the dividends of insider politics fell to a new low, key union leaders decided to move beyond "politics as usual" and intensify efforts to generate grassroots power from below. The national FFE campaign was born out of this sentiment.

In New York, a similar challenge faced powerful unions like 32BJ and 1199, both with relatively high union density and accustomed to wielding "insider" political clout (Hauptmeier and Turner 2007). Although they had some previous experience with community-based organizations and campaigns, United NY's effort to bring these giant SEIU locals into closer collaboration with leading community organizations to mobilize grassroots power was a major departure from routine. This created a series of dilemmas for United NY similar to those facing FFE at the national level. How could the SEIU remain loyal to the Democratic Party and yet hold Democratic politicians accountable? Would the FFE devolve into old-style GOTV mobilization as the 2012 election approached? In short, how could the FFE resist the pressure to retreat into "insider politics" while trying to build an aggressive "outsider politics" movement?

The FFE vision of workers' power relied on partnerships with community-based organizations. In this respect, SEIU was part of a broader tendency among unions, in the United States as well as other countries, to ally with community-based organizations to press for progressive change and to expand "the reach of union activity beyond job regulation, narrowly conceived, to pursue wider social and political change," as Carola Frege and her collaborators point out, adding that the diminishing returns of traditional "insider politics" have spurred many unions "to exert pressure on state agencies through industrial action or generating popular protest" (Frege, Heery, and Turner 2004, 138). In the case of United NY, as NYCC executive director Jon Kest explained, "The notion was that enhancing the capacity of the two main organizations in the city that were organizing poor people would have huge benefits for the issues that the unions care about."[17]

Born out of alarm over organized labor's weakness, FFE sought to build "coalitions of protest" through partnerships that could amplify the power of both unions and their community partners. As United NY steering committee member and MRNY co-executive director Ana Maria Archila put it:

> United NY is . . . bringing powerful institutions together to push a coordinated agenda on jobs and economic justice. In New York, most progressive institutions are advancing their own narrow issues. So convening a table where everyone that is working on economic justice has some shared strategy is a huge contribution.[18]

In this respect, FFE represents what Clawson (2003) terms "fusion" between labor's agenda and that of other progressive social movements. Clawson contends that both labor and social movements must do "far more to connect with each other and to take up each other's causes in ways that transform the movements." Unions can't succeed within the narrow confines of contracts and business unionism, he argues, but need to capture the "bottom up mobilization and vitality essential for movements" (Clawson 2003, 14).

SEIU's effort to move beyond traditional union strategies and work together with social movement allies to transform the nation's politics is not the only labor movement initiative with this goal. The AFL-CIO's Working America campaign, founded in 2003, which does grassroots canvassing and organization building among working-class voters in swing states, is the best-known such effort.[19] Another recent example is the National Nurses United's Main Street Campaign to Heal America/Tax Wall Street, which centers on the demand for a financial transactions tax.[20] These initiatives share many common elements, yet each takes a distinctive approach. Working America focuses largely on white, middle-class voters who—although adversely impacted by the wrenching economic changes of recent decades—may or may not share labor's political perspective. It prioritizes long-term relationship building and legislative efforts rather than disruptive protest tactics. In contrast, FFE explicitly targeted cities where SEIU already had a strong membership base. Building on that foundation the FFE local groups, working in coordination with community organizations, sought to reach out to low-income communities most impacted by the crisis and generate public protests to disrupt the status quo and shift the political landscape. The National Nurses United Main Street campaign focuses specifically on the financial transactions tax and—while like FFE engaging in disruptive tactics and working with community allies—emphasizes member mobilization more than coalition-building.

Launching United NY

FFE began in April 2011 with coordinated canvassing efforts in New York and several other cities. In New York the canvasses focused on neighborhoods with average household incomes of $35,000 to identify working people now "sitting on the sidelines" who might later be activated in campaigns for good jobs, for increased taxes on corporations and the wealthy, and against budget cuts affecting the middle class and poor. The purpose was to locate people who were angry and open to participating in such efforts. MRNY and NYCC conducted the canvassing for United NY in three Brooklyn neighborhoods (East New York, Brownsville, and Bushwick), five Queens neighborhoods (Jackson Heights, Elmhurst, Corona, Jamaica, and Southeast Queens), and in the South Bronx.[21] By the end of June, canvassers had completed 330,000 door knocks and had 122,000 face-to-face conversations with residents, more than half of whom signed cards expressing their support for United NY.[22]

MRNY's Archila recalled that while "it felt monstrous" to be doing a canvass of that scale, taking on the work offered organizational benefits for MRNY, helping to "expand our capacity, allowing us to train our members to become awesome canvassers, allowing us to engage more people in our work, and to learn how to set up an operation of that scale." The canvassing also helped MRNY identify people who "are perfect material for organizing, and who are connected in very deep ways with people in their neighborhood." Archila was especially struck by the extent of unemployment in the neighborhoods canvassed: "So many people who answered the doors were unemployed. So many! Even though we knew the numbers, really knocking on every door in some of these neighborhoods brought it home in a real way. People are not working. They can't find jobs. That was very powerful."[23]

The original plan had involved coordinating the New York effort with other canvasses run by FFE across the country. However, after the United NY canvass was completed, there was a delay as the coalition partners assessed the results and debated next steps. SEIU 1199 and 32BJ—both large and opinionated locals accustomed to forging their own organizational programs—were hesitant to move ahead with a national campaign without first determining how to link it with local fights in New York City in an effective manner. Should United NY have a separate organizational identity at the neighborhood level, or should it focus on building the membership and capacity of the community organizations? Should it focus on advancing legislative initiatives or on generating protest activities—or both? Which policy initiatives should be included—raising the minimum wage, promoting an extension of the New York State millionaires' tax, enacting sick day legislation, or others? Finally, given that New York was "saturated with community organizations"[24] and various coalitions advancing progressive programs, it seemed important not to "reinvent the wheel and to reach out to existing organizations, see what they are doing to see how we can fit into what's already going on."[25]

Follow-up on the canvass was delayed for months as United NY pondered these issues internally. The canvass itself had confirmed the urgency of addressing the issues of unemployment and economic disparities and persuaded the coalition of the urgent need to engage low-wage and nonunion workers "as community members, as students, as retirees, as people who are unemployed, people who are nonunion."[26] But in October 2011 United NY chose to broaden the campaign beyond those reached by the canvass, "to find folks that are willing to take action."[27] Now MRNY and NYCC were tasked with building on the canvasses to reach out beyond their existing base, through community meetings, phone calls, and other methods, to recruit new people into their organizations.[28]

Meanwhile, United NY was expanding its own capacity. It established itself as a 501(c)(4) organization with its own office and a small but growing staff, including an executive director and staff responsible for communications and politics. For a few months it also drew on 32BJ's thirty-eight member summer youth brigade for support. Later a field director, member engagement coordinator, outreach person, youth coordinator, and others were added, so that by fall 2011, United NY had eight staff people on its payroll.[29] At this point United NY also added another community partner, the NY Civic Participation Project. SEIU continued to provide funds, and representatives from 1199, 32BJ, and Workers United sat on the steering committee; community partners were consulted as well through the "partners' table."[30]

As Amanda Tattersall (2010) has pointed out, labor-community coalitions' success often depends on the leadership capacity of particular individuals who "act as bridge builders and broker relationships between organizations." United NY's executive director, Camille Rivera, exemplified this bridge-building role.[31] Born and raised in the Bronx, she became a single mother at the age of sixteen. Striving to complete her education while raising her child, she confronted many obstacles, including cuts to child care programs and welfare restrictions. She passed a New York Public Interest Research Group table one day after her classes at Bronx Community College and "was organized" to attend one of its meetings. NYPIRG soon hired her as an organizer. She helped coordinate their committee on homelessness, founded a chapter at her campus, and became its chairperson. She later joined the staff of Local 32BJ, eventually becoming a deputy political director. She was drawn to the directorship of United NY because it offered her a new opportunity to work with community groups building power in low-income neighborhoods like her own in the Bronx and others across New York, reengaging her "organizing brain" in a setting where she could "add to the dynamic and think of activities that would change the narrative and drive the work forward."[32]

During the summer of 2011 transition period, even as its priorities were being debated internally, United NY rolled out a series of public protest actions calling for jobs, an end to cuts in social programs, and for holding banks accountable for the economic crisis—actions that also provided opportunities for solidarity among United NY partner organizations as they joined together to support each other's efforts and press for larger economic demands.[33] United NY also demonstrated its willingness to confront politicians from both parties when, in the weeks following the August debt ceiling deal, it joined with allies to target Congressman Michael Grimm, a Republican representing Staten Island and Brooklyn (Staten Island Advance 2011), and Congressman Gregory Meeks, a Democrat from Queens (Costella 2011), for voting for the deal and "putting private interests in front of working people."[34]

United NY gradually became more visible as a labor-community alliance promoting good jobs and opposing service cuts. Its actions, designed to maintain a steady drumbeat of activity (rather than major large-scale mobilizations), began to generate media attention. It also provided opportunities for coalition partners to support each other while drawing public attention to larger economic issues. A union picket in support of soon to be laid-off food service distribution workers represented by Workers United in Sunset Park, Brooklyn, brought out about 150 supporters, including labor and community contingents from all of the United NY partner organizations. Even at this early stage, Rivera recalled, these actions suggested "what United NY could do as a coalition organization and show that once we're at full throttle we'll be in a really good place to begin a larger, more extensive program."[35]

However, United NY's member engagement efforts were slower to come to fruition. Union members from the three New York City-based SEIU affiliates had convened in the spring of 2011 to discuss ways that they could be involved in the FFE campaign and, over the summer, "train the trainer" sessions were held on issues such as wealth inequality, the tax shift, and immigration. United NY hired a member engagement coordinator from the 1199 staff, Florence Williams-Johnson, an African American activist from Southeast Queens who had been an 1199 member for twenty-four years and a staff member for eight years. She helped build a Member Leaders in Action Committee in United NY to engage union members in upcoming actions and to help develop members' leadership capacity both on the job and in the community. The committee supplemented the union's ongoing efforts to engage members around FFE, including "train the trainer" sessions and meetings on community and political issues in each borough of the city.[36]

At the outset, United NY spent several months shaping its organizational mission and structures, building collaborative relationships among its partner organizations, and gearing up its capacity to launch protest mobilizations. Conducting the large-scale canvass described above took place in the absence of a longer-range strategic vision for the new organization. Although that limited the potential for extensive follow-up, the canvass did bring some organizational benefits to the community organizations. Meanwhile, the ongoing process of crafting United NY's organizational mission ultimately resulted in two strategically crucial decisions. The first was to focus on building and utilizing the existing capacity of its community partners rather than creating new United NY neighborhood groups; the second, closely related decision was that United NY would work to build the capacity of, and position its campaigns within, the city's existing labor-community coalitions.

Expanding Collaboration and Building for Fall Actions

As the summer of 2011 drew to a close, FFE's national leaders decided to launch a campaign to spur legislative action on infrastructure spending and other job-creating bills. The plan was to time actions around congressional activity, including deliberations of the "super committee," the congressional panel that faced a November 23 deadline to propose budget cuts to reduce the federal deficit.[37] On September 22, United NY held an event in coordination with other FFE efforts across the country to support President Obama's jobs speech delivered on a crumbling Cincinnati bridge.[38] And FFE laid plans for a series of events around the country culminating in a national day of nonviolent direct actions highlighting structurally deficient bridges on November 17, timed in relation to the super committee's deadline. Such grassroots protests were meant to add "outsider" politics to the union's "insider" support for Obama's proworker initiatives, with the upcoming 2012 election in mind. As Rob Hill explained:

As long as we're only about electing certain people, we stay boxed in. This is a movement about demanding things. . . . It's about creating a narrative. The way you do that is you get people on the street demanding jobs. Not just the unions, the working people, going out there every day, saying we want you to focus on good jobs, we want the wealthy to pay their fair share, we want corporations to pay their fair share.[39]

United NY's fall 2011 activities also involved supporting the Strong Economy for All coalition focused on New York City and State budget issues. That coalition included 1199 SEIU, Local 32BJ, NYCC, and MRNY, as well as the New York City Central Labor Council, the New York State AFL-CIO, the New York State United Federation of Teachers, the local affiliate of the Communication Workers Union, and many other labor and community-based organizations. In addition, United NY supported the ad hoc Beyond May 12 coalition that had emerged in the aftermath of May 2011 anti–Wall Street protests that had called on "Mayor Bloomberg to save our jobs, human services, schools, pensions and communities."[40]

United NY hoped that supporting such coalition efforts, which bridged labor and community interests, would expand its capacity to affect the national debate and, more broadly, help spur organized labor to break out of its political isolation. At the national level as well, the SEIU, the AFL-CIO, MoveOn.org, and coalition efforts such as the New Bottom Line and Van Jones's Rebuild the Dream were developing plans for actions around jobs and corporate responsibility.

In September 2011, the Beyond May 12 coalition convened a meeting of one hundred organizations to plan a week of actions for the following month. The demands it focused on included renewing the state "millionaires' tax"; creating new jobs though investments in infrastructure, transit, and energy; restoring city and state budget cuts; and at the national level, congressional passage of the American Jobs Act and tax reform.[41] United NY, Strong Economy for All, and NYCC were key players in this broad effort, which also included plans aimed to attract media attention such as actions targeting Chase Bank and a bus tour of billionaires' homes on Park Avenue framed as "a visit to the richest of the rich who are getting a tax break while school budgets are slashed."[42]

Enter Occupy Wall Street

The political landscape suddenly changed on September 17, 2011, when approximately one thousand people responded to a call by the Canadian magazine

Adbusters to "flood into lower Manhattan, set up tents, kitchens, peaceful barricades and occupy Wall Street for a few months."[43] Invoking the spirit of earlier uprisings from Tahrir Square to Wisconsin to Madrid, the Occupy Wall Street protest that would spread to hundreds of other sites around the country and the globe was born when a few hundred occupiers settled in Zuccotti Park, a few blocks from the New York Stock Exchange. With the slogan "We are the 99 percent," OWS soon captured worldwide headlines and won widespread support from the public—gaining far more traction in calling attention to growing economic inequality than any previous efforts by unions or community groups like those comprising United NY.

United NY and the SEIU affiliates sponsoring it embraced OWS and began to actively support it soon after the encampment began. United NY began delivering pizzas, Local 32BJ brought blankets to the park, and 1199 president George Gresham offered an early endorsement, providing not only verbal support but also vowing to "feed the occupation for a week, to have 1199 nurses help train those staffing the first aid stations at the occupation, and to set up an 1199 task force charged with help in whatever ways possible."[44] After the widely publicized pepper-spraying of protesters and the hundreds of arrests of peaceful marchers on the Brooklyn Bridge, NYCC's Jon Kest and others pushed United NY to "do something big." Local 32BJ asked United NY to host a conference call with all its community partners to determine how to best support OWS. As Kest told a reporter from *Crain's New York*, "It's a responsibility for the progressive organizations in town to show their support and connect Occupy Wall Street to some of the struggles that are real in the city today. They're speaking about issues we're trying to speak about" (Massey 2011a).

The Beyond May 12 coalition developed plans for a Community/Labor March to Wall Street in support of OWS on October 5, for which they hoped to turn out a few thousand people. Transit Workers Union Local 100 and 1199 SEIU had already voiced their solidarity with the occupiers. At the 1199 executive council meeting, although some of those present expressed wariness about OWS, the fact that so many 1199 members, staff, and officers were already involved led to a unanimous endorsement.[45] The early TWU and 1199 support and the official call for a solidarity march helped spur a surge of endorsements from over sixty other New York organizations, including fifteen labor unions.[46]

Turnout for the march exceeded all expectations. As Kest recalled, "I still thought it would be 5,000 people there on October 5, just the day before, because I was looking at all the numbers and the counts."[47] An estimated twenty thousand people participated in the rally and march, including large contingents of union members. Linking OWS to earlier protest movements in Spain and elsewhere, 32BJ secretary-treasurer Hector Figueroa declared from the rally stage,

"We are the *indignados* [indignant ones] of New York, the *indignados* of the United States, the *indignados* of the world" (*Informador* 2011). United NY contributed its logistical expertise as well—lining up the permit, prepping speakers, and providing safety marshals, who wore red United NY T-shirts with the slogan "Fighting for a city that works for all." Although its efforts were largely invisible to the public, this was an important moment for United NY, itself only a few months old.

Rivera, who "as a person of color" admitted to some initial reservations about the mostly white OWS movement, soon came to recognize its emergence as a "defining moment." "We had been struggling to create a movement and a narrative in this country," she explained. "United NY was lucky enough to be able to work on this rally and help coordinate it. We became part of something big. It's humbling."[48]

The outpouring of support from established unions and community organizations in the October 5 march helped to legitimize OWS, even as the spectacular rise of OWS unleashed new energy inside those organizations. Buoyed by the success of the march, Beyond May 12 coalition organizers scaled up their plans for upcoming actions. The October 11 Park Avenue bus tour, originally planned for a hundred participants, became a much larger "March on the Billionaires" that attracted close to a thousand people—and throngs of media—to Park Avenue where protesters carried oversized checks representing the upcoming $5 billion gift billionaires would soon receive from New York taxpayers should the New York State tax surcharge on married couples earning over $300,000 and singles earning over $200,000 expire on December 31 as scheduled (Massey 2011a).

The next day featured a rally and picket at Chase Bank headquarters that began with about one hundred people, including members of MRNY and NYCC, and then swelled as hundreds more marched from Zuccotti Park to join them. The newfound mutualism between OWS and the traditional community-based organizations and unions spurred many other such street protests during the fall of 2011, which captured extensive media attention. While OWS shunned specific demands, United NY and others continued their campaigns for an extension of the millionaires' tax and various job creation programs. As Stephen Lerner (2011b) noted, both OWS and the already established movements benefitted from the new synergy as they worked to "challenge inequality and the power of big banks" with militant protests targeting "Wall Street, big banks and runaway corporate power" in New York and other cities around the nation.

United NY's role in these efforts helped to raise its profile within the larger coalition as well as with the media, and supporting OWS rapidly became one of United NY's highest priorities. It helped with everything from finding bathrooms to providing computers and various forms of financial support; staff members also participated in OWS working groups and other activities.

Before OWS emerged, FFE, along with United NY and the Beyond May 12 coalition, had laid plans for a November 17 National Day of Action to spotlight the need for job creation and infrastructure investment. The original expectation was that a few thousand union members and low-wage workers would engage in nonviolent civil disobedience on city bridges during rush hour. But OWS's success now made larger ambitions possible.

November 17, which marked the two-month anniversary of the Zuccotti Park occupation, was a very important date for OWS. In New York, OWS worked together with the Beyond May 12 coalition to develop a day-long schedule of activities, starting with an early morning OWS direct action meant to delay Wall Street from opening for that day's business, citywide university student walkouts, and a variety of other protest events around the city—including the outer boroughs—to engage community-based organization members. The day's events would culminate in a large, permitted, evening rally and march to the Brooklyn Bridge to maximize the participation of union and community members. In contrast to October 5, the plan for this rally did not include speeches from elected officials or union leaders; instead members of "the 99 percent" were invited to the stage to tell their stories. The slogans of the day—"Resist Austerity," "Reclaim Democracy," and "Rebuild the Economy"—replaced the jobs message FFE had initially envisioned, and explicit support of President Obama's job-creation legislation was off the table.

The plans changed again on November 15, two days before the planned day of actions, when the New York police raided Zuccotti Park in the middle of the night without warning, forcibly dismantling the encampment. The next day hundreds of organizations, including United NY, MoveOn.org, Rebuild the Dream, NYCC, and many others, issued a call to support the protests already planned for November 17, adding protests against the eviction to the day's agenda. The turnout for the protests that day far exceeded that of October 5 with reports of more than thirty thousand in attendance (RT 2011). Participants included students, activists, community members, and large, visible contingents of union members. Both 1199 and 32BJ mobilized strongly—with 1199 having over three thousand members signed up to participate prior to the rally.[49] Rob Hill noted that for 32BJ members who served as marshals, the November 17 events made the power of "the 99 percent" message palpable.[50] Over two hundred people were arrested for peaceful assembly and civil disobedience throughout the day, including SEIU International president Mary Kay Henry, 1199 president George Gresham, 32BJ executive vice-president Kevin Doyle, and other labor and community leaders, clergy, and city council members (Newman 2011).

United NY once again provided logistical coordination for the November 17 protests. Even as the mutually reinforcing efforts of OWS and the labor and community organizations magnified the energy and impact of the day's events, explicit tensions also surfaced. When the first line of marchers approached the Brooklyn Bridge, the United NY marshals, many of them members of 32BJ and 1199, positioned themselves between the protestors and the police. While their intention was to protect the protesters, many participants complained that United NY was doing the work of the police.

Labor Unions and Fusion with OWS

Labor was a follower, not a leader, of OWS, but many unions responded to the movement with enthusiastic support once it emerged. SEIU's 1199 and 32BJ were cases in point. 1199 began offering food and financial resources to the Zuccotti Park occupiers within days, was the second union to officially endorse the occupation, and provided meeting space for OWS meetings and events. 1199ers, from members and staff to the president of the union, participated in OWS activities and took various initiatives to fortify the movement's alliance with labor.[51] Similarly, 32BJ incorporated explicit support for OWS into its mid-October contract mobilization rally and relocated the event to Wall Street. At the rally, 32BJ executive vice-president Kevin Doyle called on union members to stand with OWS, and then led a march to Zuccotti Park. In mid-October, when the New York Police Department made its first unsuccessful attempt to evict the occupiers, 32BJ and 1199 SEIU members, staff, and leaders were highly visible among the thousands of supporters that rallied to defend Zuccotti Park in the middle of the night.

These two SEIU affiliates exemplified the broader support for OWS offered by a broad array of labor unions in New York and in other cities throughout the United States where occupations were sprouting up. AFL-CIO president Richard Trumka offered to "open our union halls and community centers as well as our arms and our hearts to those with the courage to stand up and demand a better America" and came to New York to have breakfast with the OWS protesters at Zuccotti Park.[52] The preexisting efforts to build community-labor alliances that many unions had already begun—not only FFE but also Working America and a range of local coalitions—helped to pave the way for this positive labor response. Lerner's vision of a movement that "taps into and builds on union resources—both financial and organizational—but denies unions' 'veto power' over campaign activities" had begun to emerge (Lerner 2011a).

United NY allowed its union partners to work through their own internal processes to determine their support for OWS, but as Camille Rivera observed:

> People know that this is the right thing to do. *They've been waiting for this moment.* . . . Obama got elected and we thought there was going to be dramatic change, and then we realized that elected officials cannot change the world by themselves—that *we* actually have to do that.[53]

United NY facilitated a process of constructive "fusion," expanding the earlier investments of 1199 and 32BJ in community work into a dynamic alliance with OWS. That United NY had already engaged these two giant SEIU affiliates in coalition work with community organizations laid the groundwork for them to actively support OWS.

Synergies and Fusion

OWS radically altered the national political conversation. By targeting Wall Street—New York's most important industry and a key actor in the financial meltdown associated with the Great Recession—the new movement succeeded in shifting the narrative from deficits and cuts to inequality and corporate corruption of democracy within months. This helped established labor and community organizations like those in United NY to attract greater media attention to their initiatives, enhanced their mobilization capacity, and infused them with new energy and imagination. OWS led unions in particular to reach beyond their usual incrementalist politics.

United NY and its constituent organizations—in conjunction with the Beyond May 12 coalition and Strong Economies for All—helped to sustain OWS through providing direct resources and logistical support, as I noted above. In addition, although OWS itself eschewed the idea of specific demands, some of the political energy it generated helped advance campaigns for the millionaires' tax, job-creation programs, and opposition to foreclosures. In addition, the unions and community organizations helped bring to the Occupy movement the diversity that it lacked in its initial stages. Although systematic data are few (see Milkman, Luce, and Lewis 2012 for an exception), OWS participants were by all accounts predominantly young, white, and middle class. Union and community organizations helped bring more immigrants, people of color, and working-class people into the movement.

Unions and community organizations were also able to sustain some of the energy of the movement after the eviction of Zuccotti Park, when OWS itself became more fragmented. 1199's Larry Bortoluzzi commented in late 2011: "We hope this will be a real movement for the long haul but we're only three months into it. There's going to be setbacks, things are not going to go totally smoothly . . . but the main idea is to keep people thinking that the way things are today can be changed; it doesn't have to be this way."[54]

In the aftermath of the eviction, in hope of helping to maintain movement momentum, 1199 SEIU's president George Gresham convened a series of meetings with other local union presidents to explore ways to sustain labor's solidarity and commitment to its work with OWS in spite of the lack of a physical space to house the movement. Meanwhile, 32BJ achieved a major contract victory when real estate developers reversed their demands for two-tier wages and other givebacks, averting a threatened New Year's strike of twenty-two thousand New York City commercial office cleaners (Massey 2011b; Beekman 2012). Prestrike member mobilizations—energized by the earlier investment in rebuilding steward capacity and magnified by OWS's "common unifying message"—were a major factor in the success of the negotiations.[55]

The end of 2011 brought a key policy victory as well when, on December 6, Governor Andrew Cuomo reversed his prior refusal to extend the millionaires' tax, which was due to expire at year's end, and worked out a deal with the legislature to reform the New York State tax code (Kaplan 2011). Although the deal didn't represent the systemic change that OWS called for, the governor's reversal vindicated the determination of the labor-community alliance that had targeted Cuomo as "Governor 1%." As Michael Kink of the Strong Economy for All coalition noted: "The fact that lawmakers came together to take action is a credit to the organizing and advocacy of the community, labor, student, and faith coalitions that have been working tirelessly on these issues for the past year, and to the courageous protesters of the Occupy movement."[56]

Both FFE and Occupy Wall Street emerged in response to growing economic inequality and the corrosive influence of money on American democracy—yet they also reflected distinct missions, analytic frameworks, and organizational cultures. FFE, the top-down creation of a large labor union, aimed to utilize "leverage politics" to reverse the growth of inequality and to recapture the New Deal-era power of labor unions and working people; as such it emphasized explicit public policy objectives. By contrast, OWS, a bottom-up upsurge fiercely committed to direct democracy, embraced an explicit critique of capitalism and a vision of societal transformation largely absent in twenty-first-century labor unions and community-based organizations; and it famously shunned pragmatic, compromise-prone political engagement. Yet it was not their differences, but the ability of OWS and the traditional unions and community organizations to find commonalities and synergies, that nurtured them both.

Post-Eviction and the 2012 Elections

United NY and OWS continued to move forward on parallel tracks with periodic intersections after the eviction of Zuccotti Park. Rivera understood the anger that many OWS activists felt toward the Democrats and their lack of interest in the 2012 elections. Although she felt it as well, she also worried that if young people engaged with Occupy opted to stay home rather than come to the polls, the result would be even greater consolidation of right-wing Republican political control. However, that didn't mean that United NY believed that the Democrats should be let off the hook. "Occupy Wall Street should go after the Democrats, they need to be held accountable," Rivera insisted.[57] Meanwhile United NY utilized grassroots mobilization and creative actions to target the Republicans during the 2012 election campaign while shining a spotlight on Republican candidate Mitt Romney's links to private equity firm Bain Capital and its contributions to tax evasion and job losses.[58] Alongside SEIU's GOTV efforts on behalf of Obama and other Democratic candidates, United NY continued its efforts to generate grassroots protests to advance proworker policies. As Rob Hill of Local 32BJ explained:

> How do we break out of the constraints of the two-party system? I don't know, but that's what we have in this country. But it's movements that make, historically, all the changes, big, broad movements like the civil rights movement. . . . Without that, just electing people doesn't seem to get us much power. You've got to elect people, but the bigger issue is you've got to have enough of a movement and power.[59]

During 2012, United NY began to expand its alliances and the scope of its campaigns, working with a variety of non-SEIU union locals in New York for legislation to raise the minimum wage and close tax loopholes.[60] By the summer, United NY had enough organizational capacity to help launch community-based campaigns among some of the city's most exploited workers in the fast food industry, airports, car washes, and supermarkets—an effort that harkened back to its original mission to spotlight and elevate the struggles of private sector, low-wage workers.

Working with its constituent organizations and allies, United NY coordinated a rally in Union Square in July 2012 that mobilized hundreds of low-wage workers across employment sectors and thousands of supporters to highlight the dire need for a hike in New York's minimum wage of $7.25 per hour. The goal was to shine a spotlight on their common struggles in a city where low-wage workers comprise 40 percent of the labor force, according to a report released jointly that month by United NY and ALIGN (2012).[61] This was part of a broader effort to foster new organizing efforts among low-wage workers in various industries. A week before the rally, United NY and its partners hosted an executive-boardroom-style planning meeting where "instead of chief executives and other top officials, the seats were occupied by low-wage workers" joined by clergy, community, and political allies (Edwards 2012). Throughout the summer and fall of 2012, United NY's constituent organizations launched a series of low-wage worker organizing campaigns—32BJ among airport security officers, NYCC among grocery and car wash workers, and MRNY among car wash workers. The car wash campaign, organized jointly with the Retail, Wholesale and Department Store Union, was the first to come to fruition, with a series of five unionization victories in the fall of 2012 (Semple 2012; Greenhouse 2012a; Pearson 2012).

Another low-wage worker campaign made headlines at the end of November, when hundreds of fast food workers from McDonald's, Burger King, Wendy's, and other chains in New York City staged an unprecedented one-day strike calling for a pay raise to $15 per hour, better working conditions, and rights to unionize. The organizing efforts were led by forty organizers fielded by NYCC, with sponsorship from United NY, the Black Institute, and SEIU as well. The New York Civic Participation Project and MRNY also actively supported the effort, and OWS activists and supporters were visible at the rally in support of the strike (Greenhouse 2012b; Jaffe 2012). Rather than relying on traditional unionization methods, this Fast Food Forward campaign instead drew on the strategic repertoire of the worker centers, with a longer-term vision of militant action and minority organization that could expand solidarity across employers. The fast food strikes, in conjunction with the Black Friday nationwide walkouts and rallies at Walmart stores the week before, focused attention on the plight of precarious workers in unstable, low-wage jobs.

Conclusion

United NY helped bring New York City's SEIU affiliates together—with each other and with key community partners—and engage them in larger coalitions such as Beyond May 12. This positioned United NY to rapidly embrace the unexpected rise of OWS in the "American Autumn" of 2011, which in turn helped to amplify United NY's own efforts. Ultimately it provided an avenue for the unions to become more engaged in coalition efforts and to break out of "insider politics" and to take greater risks. United NY's involvement in citywide coalition efforts and OWS helped it—and the SEIU affiliates that initiated it—expand their horizons in an example of the kind of "fusion" of unions and social movements Clawson (2003) suggested a decade ago.

As it continues to build and expand its work, United NY will inevitably face numerous challenges. Among these is to continue to fuel "outside power" without losing the "inside" political power that SEIU affiliates have long relied on to win new organizing campaigns, contract fights, and to maintain high wage and benefit standards for their New York City members. Another key challenge involves United NY's status as a creation of SEIU and reliant on the union for funding—making it vulnerable to losing that funding should the union shift its priorities. At this writing, following the successful reelection of Barack Obama in 2012, United NY anticipates that there will "be a need for a 'United NY' as long as corporations and the wealthy are allowed to get away with paying the minimum, while everyone else is forced to sacrifice."[62] That suggests the hopeful prospect that the union is keeping its "eyes on the prize" well beyond the shifting winds of the election cycle.

Part II

ORGANIZING THE PRECARIAT, OLD AND NEW

5

INFUSING CRAFT IDENTITY INTO A NONCRAFT INDUSTRY

The Retail Action Project

Peter Ikeler

On an overcast February afternoon I enter a nondescript office building in midtown Manhattan, head to the fifth floor and into a large room. The far wall has a plaque fixed to it with "RWDSU"[1] projecting out in silver letters. Below this stands Alicia Canary,[2] middle-aged, speaking animatedly to a crowd of about twenty-five. The Retail Action Project's two-day "customer service training" has just begun. The crowd seated around six tables is predominantly black and Latino, and most look to be less than thirty years old, though a few are older. Alicia explains the purpose of this ten-hour training session, spread out over two days: "We will be helping you develop interview skills, put together resumes, and provide you with a better understanding of customer service."[3] This is what the participants have signed up for: customer service training for retail sales personnel, complete with a certificate at the end.

But just as Alicia, who is a full-time organizer, speaks these words, she turns to introduce a young man, one of RAP's worker-members: "How's everybody doing out there? Good? Great. I'm here to tell you guys about the Retail Action Project, or RAP as we call it. RAP is a member-run, nonprofit organization with over eight hundred members.[4] At RAP we work to improve retail jobs through organizing, media and policy." After a short hesitation, he continues: "Even though retail is one of the most profitable industries in the city, we all know about the low wages they pay, the disrespect at the workplace and the crazy shifts we deal with." Some of the attendees look around at each other, surprised at the sudden change of tone. When the young man mentions wages and scheduling, though, a number of them nod and one or two laugh.

A young woman seated toward the front raises her hand. She says she always tries to be "straight" with her supervisor and doesn't let him give her crazy shifts. At this point David Jimenez, a full-time organizer, steps in from the side: "It is very important to address issues of worker abuse and to raise grievances against them. But it's even more important that we address these problems *as a group*, and not just individually, because then we have more *power*."

After this exchange the presenters shift to a discussion of RAP's various committees, the organizing campaigns it has been involved in, and its goal of providing a network for skill transfer and job mobility from low-end to high-end industry tiers, and even into wholesaling jobs (which typically pay more than retail). At the mention of skills, a middle-aged man at the center of the room raises his hand. "There is a lot of skill in what we do," he says. He talks about how people in his job are often referred to as "unskilled" but argues that, in fact, there's a lot of patience, "people skills," and knowledge of the product necessary to be an effective salesperson. His comments get approval from the rest of the room and even a few claps.

David steps in again: "We're going to do some group work now. Each group gets to talk about and answer one of these three questions. One: What challenges do you face with regard to economic and occupational advancement in retail? Two: What challenges are faced in the retail industry by workers? And three: How can we elevate our voices and advance workers' interests in the retail industry?" After ten minutes of small-group discussion, the class reconvenes to share their responses. Grievances are many: erratic scheduling, low-pay, "dirty politics by management," discriminatory hiring practices, and lack of benefits are among the most common.

One type of grievance, however, appears several times, and comes up repeatedly at two similar sessions in the following months: lack of on-the-job training, "no money for training," and the common practice by managers of "just dumping you into a job and expecting you to figure it out." A young woman describes starting at the Gap and being promised a one-week "apprenticeship" with her supervisor. The supervisor gave this up after two days and left her to "figure it out." An older man states that even though he has worked in retail for over twelve years, he can't advance because he "needs more training within the industry." And a younger man, clearly frustrated, tells of a manager's response to his question about a sales display: "he told me, 'stay in your place as a salesperson and don't ask questions'—and then he hired his stupid-ass nephew a week later."

The Dilemma of Retail Organizing

Training sessions such as these are a primary way for RAP to engage unorganized retail workers. Through online postings and targeted store outreach, the organization promotes its free events in pragmatic terms: as a means of improving one's resume and networking to find jobs. Once inside, however, attendees become subjects in a consciousness-raising effort—what might be called "*conscientização*," to use Paulo Freire's (1970, 67) term. The combination of service provision and consciousness-raising, in line with the organization's stated aim of "improving opportunities and workplace standards in the retail industry" places RAP squarely in the framework of worker centers that have proliferated in recent years (Fine 2006, 2).[5]

But several points distinguish RAP from the majority of worker centers. Of the 137 that existed in the United States in 2005—of which RAP was not yet one—the vast majority (122) were specifically oriented toward immigrant workers. Eighty-six percent originated from nonunion organizations (such as ethnic NGOs, legal service organizations, or faith-based organizations) and 85 percent maintained no or only occasional contact with traditional unions. And of the 56 percent that targeted specific industries, none of these went after retail (Fine 2006, 3, 15, 23, 121). RAP is thus among the small minority of union-seeded, non-ethnic-specific worker centers. As of 2012, it is one of only two such centers in the United States focused on retail.[6]

RAP arose in the context of declining union membership for U.S. retail workers, along with falling wages, weakening job security, and increasingly erratic scheduling. By 2011, just 4.9 percent of the nation's retail workers were union members, down from 8.6 percent in 1983 (Hirsch and Macpherson 2013). Between 1990 and 2008, mean hourly earnings for nonsupervisory retail workers grew just 1.9 percent, from $12.63 to $12.88 in inflation adjusted dollars—against the backdrop of an 80 percent increase in per-hour productivity (U.S. Bureau of Labor Statistics, Current Employment Statistics, Labor Productivity and Costs, 1990–2008). In popular media discourse, from Janeane Garofalo's Gap-worker character in *Reality Bites* to the depiction of Walmart work as the epitome of downward mobility in *Fun with Dick and Jane*, to Barbara Ehrenreich's (2001) first-hand account of the same, retail has become synonymous with low-wage, unstable, "stopgap" work (Tannock 2001). Yet the prospect of raising wages and workplace standards through renewed unionization or some other form of organizing is, at best, distant.

Myriad attempts to organize on a store-by-store basis through NLRB elections have failed, often due to intense employer opposition (see Becker, this volume). Where successful, as at Walmarts in Palestine, Texas, and Jonquière, Québec, employers have displayed their ability to "cauterize the wound" by closing down unionized departments or entire stores (Lichtenstein 2009, 137). Growing recognition of the challenges of the single-workplace model of NLRB-sanctioned organizing motivated the RWDSU's support of RAP's formation, in collaboration with the community-based organization Good Old Lower East Side (GOLES), as an independent worker center.

Calls for unions to break out of the workplace model and pursue alternative modes of organizing have become increasingly urgent since the 1980s, in response to organized labor's precipitous decline. Many proponents of new organizing *forms* (as distinct from new strategy or tactics) advocate renewed craft, occupational, or what some call "full-service unionism" (Lopez 2004, 6; see also Heckscher 2001). Most systematically explicated by Dorothy Sue Cobble (1991a), this type of unionism is analogous to that practiced by many building-trades unions, past and present. It has four basic components, as Cobble argues:

(1) occupational identity;
(2) control over the labor supply in the occupation;
(3) rights and benefits as a function of occupational membership rather than of worksite affiliation, and;
(4) peer control over occupational performance standards. (Cobble 1991a, 421)

RAP's vision of nonworkplace unionism is broadly similar. RAP founder and director Carrie Gleason envisions RAP as a "flexible form of worker representation for the unorganized in the retail economy,"[7] highlighting the potential of open membership structures (anyone may join, regardless of occupation, industry, or employment status) and referring explicitly to Cobble's proposals for "organizing the postindustrial workforce" (1991a). "RAP's portable membership," Gleason states, "is carried with workers as they move along industry tiers."[8] Operating as it does in archetypically "postindustrial" New York City, RAP's work to date offers an opportunity to assess the viability of the occupational union model for retail sales workers. This is one goal of this chapter. RAP, however, is not simply an occupational proto-union; indeed, the likelihood of immediate unionization on a significant scale is remote. "The underlying problem," according to Jeff Eichler, RWDSU's recently retired director for New York organizing, "is scale."[9]

Gleason describes the organization's goals in more general terms as "building a wide network of retail workers to try to change the industry through strategic organizing and policy campaigns."[10] In its first five years, RAP organized workplace-based campaigns for back wages, several of which resulted in unionization by the RWDSU, and launched its "career development" program—skills training, certification, and job placement—which has evolved into a nascent form of occupational unionism. Since 2010, having greatly expanded its activity, staff, and membership, RAP has become increasingly autonomous from its parent organizations (RWDSU and GOLES), and has turned to policy initiatives and media outreach to highlight and improve working conditions in New York's retail industry, in what I suggest involves a shift in focus from organizing to advocacy.

"The defining feature of the advocacy model," argues labor lawyer and worker advocate Steve Jenkins, "is the client's relative powerlessness to change his or her own circumstances." Instead, he suggests, "professionals such as lawyers and social workers *mobilize elite institutions* . . . to help clients achieve the changes they are seeking." Organizing, in contrast, aims to "creat[e] democratic organizations that are accountable to the specific needs of the people being organized." For Jenkins, successful organizing depends on the structurally determined "social power" of members "to *coerce* the decision-maker to make the changes they seek," rather than persuading them through legalistic means (Jenkins 2002, 57, 61–62; emphasis in original).[11] The key distinction is between challenging existing social relationships via the collective power of members ("organizing") or ameliorating inequality through appeal to elite institutions ("advocacy"). The second goal of this chapter is to use this distinction to assess RAP's efforts to date. I argue that while RAP maintains many aspects of the occupational union model, based on the social power of its members, it has increasingly shifted its focus to advocacy on behalf of retail workers.[12]

Background: Retail Unionism in New York City

Retail trade and retail unionism have a long and peculiar history in New York City. By the early twentieth century, the city was already a mecca of mass merchandising, home to many of the nation's most emblematic department stores, such as Macy's, Gimbels, Saks, and others (Strasser 2006). These stores catered to a middle and upper-class clientele, while early discounters and five-and-dimes were oriented to the burgeoning and mostly immigrant working class. In a city whose industrial base consisted largely of small-scale garment manufacturing, "department stores . . . housed some of the largest congregations of workers" (Freeman 2000, 19). Indeed, the upsurge of industrial unionism in the 1930s and '40s found vibrant expression among New York City retail workers, under the aegis of the United Retail Employees of America–CIO (forerunner of the RWDSU).

Formed as a breakaway from the AFL-affiliated Retail Clerks, it was the seventh largest union in the CIO by its mid-1940s peak. Some of the industrial locals it established through strikes and mass picketing, at stores such as Macy's, Saks, and Bloomingdale's, still exist today (Harrington 1962; Opler 2007).

By 1954, five different unions claimed a total of ninety thousand members among New York City's retail workforce, with the largest group, fifty-four thousand, in the RWDSU (Estey 1955, 562).[13] The city's retail workers numbered slightly more than three hundred thousand at that time (New York Chamber of Commerce 1951, 1966),[14] suggesting that union density was about 30 percent (although given the propensity of unions to inflate membership figures, 25 percent may be more realistic). This was the high point of New York City retail unionism. Department stores and other retailers were already branching out into the suburbs and union attempts to organize these stores largely failed (Ziskind 2003; Opler 2007). But in the city and beyond, RWDSU Local 1199 grew rapidly, first among drug store workers and later among nonretail health care workers. The eighty-thousand-member New York component of this local split from its parent union in 1986, later affiliating with the Service Employees in 1998 (see Fink and Greenberg 1989; Chaison 1996, 38–41). Unionism also flourished in the expanding grocery sector, primarily under the Retail Clerks and the Amalgamated Butcher Workmen, which merged in 1979 to become the United Food and Commercial Workers (UFCW) (see Harrington 1962; Brody 1964; Walsh 1993).

Since the early 1990s, New York City sales activity has resurged, thanks to the growing population of immigrants, on the one hand, and of high-income professionals—or "gentrifiers"—on the other (Sassen 2001 [1991]; Moody 2007a). In this period big-box chains such as Home Depot, Target, and Best Buy entered the city, alongside the proliferation of high-priced boutiques, mostly in Manhattan (see Angotti 2008; Zukin 2004). Virtually all of these stores operate on a nonunion basis, however. After the initially successful organizing in the 1930s and '40s, retail unionism stagnated. The RWDSU, New York City's largest retail union, suffered especially dramatic erosion. Following the disaffiliation of Local 1199, the rest of RWDSU merged with the UFCW (which by then included its former parent union, the Retail Clerks), in 1993. Overall, although it remains far higher than in the nation as a whole, union density in New York City's retail industry had declined to only about 9 percent by the early 2000s, with considerable variation across industry subsectors, as table 5.1 shows. Unionized workers earn slightly higher pay (averaging $15.12 per hour) than their nonunion counterparts ($13.21).

As table 5.2 shows, the composition of New York's retail workforce is diverse in terms of gender, race, ethnicity, nativity, age, and education. This is among

TABLE 5.1 **Workers, wages, and unionization rates in the New York City retail industry, by subsector, 2003–2011**

	NUMBER OF WORKERS	PERCENT OF ALL NYC RETAIL WORKERS	MEAN HOURLY WAGE	PERCENT UNIONIZED
Food and beverage stores	86,688	24.0	$10.43	13.2
Health and personal care	32,141	8.9	$15.45	7.5
Clothing and accessories	65,036	18.0	$14.67	4.9
General merchandisers	47,180	13.0	$11.94	15.5
Other sectors	130,613	36.1	$14.84	6.8
Total	361,658	100.0	$13.43	9.2

Source: U.S. Census Bureau, Current Population Survey, Outgoing Rotation Group, merged data for 2003–2011.

the many challenges that are involved in organizing the vast nonunion component of this burgeoning industry. On the other hand, the aggregated data shown obscure the fact that in some of its subsectors the workforce is far more homogeneous. For example, in nonunion supermarkets and greengrocery stores, the bulk of the workforce is comprised of Latino immigrants. Efforts to organize such stores provided the context that eventually gave rise to RAP.

Workplace Campaigns

RAP's formation in 2005 was partly inspired by two nontraditional unionization drives: an effort in the late 1990s and early 2000s to organize city greengrocers, and the RWDSU's 2005 ¡Despierta Bushwick! (Wake Up Bushwick!) campaign with immigrant rights organization Make the Road New York (see McAlevey, this volume). Local 169 of the Union of Needletrades, Industrial and Textile Employees (UNITE) launched the greengrocer campaign, with no initial involvement on the part of the UFCW or RWDSU.[15] Three things set it apart from traditional union drives: its reliance on coalition-building with vibrant immigrant workers' groups; its use of strikes, boycotts, and mass demonstrations; and its leveraging of wage-and-hour lawsuits, supported by the New York State Attorney General's office, to bargain for employer neutrality in union organizing. The campaign ultimately succeeded in gaining union recognition and contracts at several stores, raising wages to the legal minimum, and obtaining an enforceable Code of Conduct in 2002 (Ness 2005, 58–96).

Local 169's organizing director, Jeff Eichler, joined the RWDSU staff shortly after the greengrocer campaign ended. Convinced of "the need to find other sources of worker identity and solidarity" beyond the often precarious low-wage

TABLE 5.2 **Selected characteristics of New York City retail workforce, 2003–2011**

TOTAL EMPLOYEES	361,658
Percent female	42.9
Percent non-Hispanic White	26.2
Percent non-Hispanic Black	23.3
Percent Hispanic/Latino	30.3
Percent non-Hispanic Asian	16.7
Percent non-Hispanic Other	3.5
Percent foreign born	52.2
Percent age 16–24	22.6
Percent age 25–55	65.2
Percent over age 55	12.2
Percent with less than high school education	20.5
Percent with high school diploma	37.0
Percent with some college	23.3
Percent with bachelor's degree or more	19.2

Source: U.S. Census Bureau, Current Population Survey, Outgoing Rotation Group, merged data for 2003–2011.

workplace, Eichler helped initiate the ¡Despierta Bushwick! campaign in 2005 as a joint effort with Make the Road.[16] This was one of RWDSU's first community partnerships, targeting low-wage retailers on Knickerbocker Avenue in the Bushwick section of Brooklyn. Like the greengrocer campaign, it began with a wage-and-hour lawsuit, proceeded to consumer boycotts, public rallies, and eventually the threat of sanction by the state attorney general, all of which resulted in a union contract for workers at ten Footco stores across the city (Hetland 2009). As Eichler recalled, Footco's owner was "very confused by the multiple fronts of attack" and, in return for an end to the boycott, signed a "good business community agreement" providing for neutrality in union organizing.[17]

This successful campaign led RWDSU organizers to seek out other wage-and-hour violators as strategic targets. The union decided to target the lower Manhattan neighborhood of SoHo due to its growing density of branded retail outlets and flagship stores for national and international chains. Another plus was the nearby presence of GOLES, a tenants' rights organization that had roots in the neighborhood dating back to the 1970s. "At the time," director Damaris Reyes explains, GOLES was "working on some economic justice, small business issues, job readiness stuff, and we wanted to look more at some of the workers' rights issues." To GOLES organizers, "it seemed like a good fit" when the RWDSU approached them with the idea of a partnership, and it was Reyes, in fact, who coined the name "RAP."[18]

Once a framework for cooperation was agreed on, two RWDSU organizers began researching SoHo retail employers with wage and hour violations. One of them was Carrie Gleason, a Cornell University graduate and visual artist who had spent several years organizing hotel workers and would later head RAP. Gleason and co-organizer Sadatu Mamah-Trawill, who also came from the hotel workers' union, soon discovered wage and hour violations at the Yellow Rat Bastard (YRB) clothing chain. Workers were being paid as little as $5.25 per hour when the legal minimum was $6.00 (and even after it rose to $6.75 in 2006), with many West African immigrants relegated exclusively to stock work and suffering the most egregious violations. The organizers were amazed to learn that YRB workers received accurate pay stubs that documented their hours and the illegal rate of pay. Jennifer, a former sales associate who was eighteen when the campaign began, recalls:

> A lot of the time I was working for free,[19] it was off the books, six dollars, maybe a little less, and I was paid in cash. And not only that, they also had me working like a manager, they would have me do everything a manager would do: I trained employees, I would help hire, I also did visual displays, so I had the position of three, but I was getting paid nothing. But you know, I was young, I was happy, I was like 'oh my God, maybe they'll promote me!' Maybe, even though in that company they don't promote women—there's no such thing as that. Everyone in management was men, there was no women, we were like lower class.[20]

Her first conversation with Gleason was a turning point in her attitude toward the store, her job, and management:

> When Carrie came to me—she was the first person [from RAP] that ever spoke to me—and told me all of these things that were going on, I didn't even feel like it affected me that much, it was other workers there who were close to me, immigrants from Africa and it was really affecting them. And when I saw the difference—they were being treated literally like slaves, they were working eighteen hours sometimes straight, and they were always in the basement and it was like, really bad. So that was the turning point for me when I saw the big change for them.[21]

Along with Mamah-Trawill, who is of West African descent, Jennifer went on to play a key role in the campaign. The first challenge was to build trust for RAP's effort among the immigrant workers at the store. Though deeply dissatisfied, they were unfamiliar with the fledgling organization and wary of management retribution. Several LGBT workers, however, who had "faced intense homophobia by their managers" and thus felt "less allegiance to the company" (Gleason), became crucial to winning over others.[22] Eventually, a group of YRB workers agreed to be party to a back-wage lawsuit filed by the state attorney general's office. RAP organized weekly one-day boycotts and storefront rallies of workers and community members mobilized by GOLES. When the owner was arrested in late 2007 for violation of state labor law, he agreed to settle the back-wage suit for both frontline workers and first-line supervisors. "That was the [end] goal—we didn't go in to organize them to become union members," according to Mamah-Trawill.[23]

As the 2008 economic downturn ate into company revenues, the owner claimed he would be unable to make further payments. RAP managed to turn this crisis into an opportunity, persuading the employer to accept card-check union recognition. The final settlement included $1.4 million in back pay for over one thousand current and former YRB employees, as well as union recognition for RWDSU on behalf of workers at New York City's seven Yellow Rat Bastard stores. The workers won their first union contract with the RWDSU in 2009. This became the defining success story of RAP's initial phase.

Three further RAP campaigns grew out of the YRB struggle, all directed at local retail chains based in or near SoHo. Back-wage cases were launched at Shoemania, Scoop NYC, and Mystique Boutique (owned by the brother of YRB's owner), with one of these (Shoemania) leading to union recognition and a contract in 2012. All three cases exhibited similar dynamics to YRB: small, New York-based stores, flagrant wage-and-hour violations, and ethnically divided workforces (predominantly West African stock workers and native-born sales workers). The Scoop and Shoemania campaigns began in late 2008 with back-pay lawsuits, and in the Scoop case, charges of discrimination as well.[24] The Mystique drive followed in mid-2009. All three efforts utilized worker committees, public demonstrations, and regular customer service and workers' rights training sessions conducted by RAP organizers. At Scoop, divisions between backroom stock and front room sales workers proved insurmountable, with the latter declining to sign onto the lawsuit or join the campaign. According to RWDSU organizers, this prevented the negotiation of a neutrality agreement that could have aided unionization. At Shoemania, one organizer declared, attaining such an agreement was "the only thing that allowed the [union] win—we couldn't get people to sign cards until we got the employer to stop the terror [against union supporters]."[25] Even so, the card-check majority was twice disputed by the owner and only resolved through arbitration. In February 2010, these efforts culminated in a "March of Hearts" down Broadway that united workers from all three campaigns as well as the YRB drive. The Scoop back-wage case was settled in 2010 for an undisclosed amount, and the Mystique case in 2012 for $925,000.

Taken together, these four campaigns were the highlights of the first phase of RAP's development, when it was still an internal project of the RWDSU. The success at YRB in particular validated Gleason's perspective that organizing was possible among Manhattan-based, nonfood retailers, while raising the profile of the nascent organization in the local area and among immigrant workers. All four campaigns depended on significant rank-and-file worker activism to pursue the lawsuits, to turn people out for rallies, and, in the cases of YRB and Shoemania, to gather union cards. As one organizer put it, through RAP the "RWDSU has now developed a model to organize these specific [New York-based, non-corporate] employers on a store-by-store basis."[26] The model included back-pay lawsuits, "hot shops" with some degree of ethnic solidarity, community support (GOLES), and geographic continuity (SoHo and environs).

But the applicability of this model for the city's overall retail sector is questionable, since corporate retailers—the giants of the industry—are very different from the small retail operations targeted in these early campaigns. Eichler notes that "healthcare and pensions are often too expensive for such low-ball employers, at this end of the industry, to even negotiate on."[27] This brings us to the question posed by Jenkins as to "whether a given group of people, if organized, would have the power to force changes from the institutions they are confronting" (2002, 58). Workers at YRB, Shoemania, Scoop, and Mystique were able, with RAP's help, to win back wages owed them by legal mandate; in two cases they also obtained union contracts that provided regular wage increases (although not health or pension benefits), paid sick leave and formal grievance procedures. The primary source of leverage, however, was not workers' social power to "stop production," or in this case, distribution (Burns 2011). Instead, it was the combination of employers' noncompliance with existing wage and hour law, a proactive Attorney General's office, and the RAP organizers' ability to channel workers' grievances into a formal lawsuit. Furthermore, because of the thin profit margins of such firms, workers at YRB and Shoemania, although "organized," have little prospect of making more substantial gains.[28]

These campaigns, then, were organizing efforts with a strong advocacy component, unlikely to significantly alter power relations between retail employers and employees in New York City. RAP organizers are well aware of this. Indeed, the inherent limitations of store-by-store, back-wage-lawsuit campaigning motivated RAP's shift in late 2010 to an "open membership model" and what Gleason calls "the project of really building RAP as an organization."[29]

Career Development

One key interest that RAP identified among retail workers in this early phase of its development was skills training. The organization therefore began offering skill-building workshops like the one described at the beginning of this chapter. What RAP calls its "career development" program not only certifies members' skills but helps some of them gain greater employment security and upward mobility. It also attracts new members, expanding the organization's reach beyond individual workplaces and sometimes bringing hot shops to RAP's attention, which can become the focus of later campaigns. RAP's career development program contributes to the four components of occupational unionism defined by Cobble, as quoted above, each of which I briefly consider in the remainder of this section.

CONTROL OVER THE LABOR SUPPLY. At the heart of occupational unionism," states Cobble, "lay a reliance on union-run hiring halls and the closed shop" (1991b, 138). The key source of leverage for any occupation-based as opposed to workplace-based union is thus control over the labor supply in a given market, or what Wright terms "marketplace structural power" (2000, 962). Achieving this has two aspects: (1) organizing workers to seek work through the union instead of individually, and (2) organizing employers to hire only, or at least preferentially, through the union. The first entails making clear the benefits of membership and delivering on those benefits, which in turn depends on members' active participation in upholding standards for pay, conditions, and work rules. The second is more puzzling: Why should employers give hiring preference to union members? Some might argue that union workers are better trained and more reliable, providing a form of "value added." But in most cases "organizing" employers requires pressure tactics, such as "top-down" legal or corporate campaigns, or more "bottom-up" forms of direct action, such as boycotts, strikes, or slowdowns, or both (see Milkman 2006, 150–55).

RAP's main focus is on recruiting workers, although it has taken initial steps toward employers as well. Among the services offered to RAP members are help with job searches, resume preparation, interview training, and referral to open positions. RAP has set up an online job bank called CREW (Connecting Retailers with an Exceptional Workforce) through which it has placed members in various Manhattan stores. In the context of a weak economy and high unemployment since 2008, job search help has become an increasingly significant part of RAP's service provision and a primary means of outreach to new members. When asked why they have stayed with the organization, long-term members often cite hiring help. For example, Jennifer, who played a key role in the YRB campaign, recalls, "They helped me find other jobs; they helped me with resumes, workshops, all sorts of things."[30] Similarly, another active member, Angelo, explains that RAP has "enabled me to either find other gigs or to meet people who want to collaborate on different projects."[31]

RAP has also facilitated hiring for some members at RWDSU-organized stores such as Macy's; at YRB, the union obtained a preferential hiring clause in its contract. Obtaining more such agreements and enforcing them could be a key mechanism for RAP to gain control over the retail labor supply. Since RAP is not a union, however, it cannot be party to these agreements; it therefore can only accomplish this goal by collaborating with the RWDSU or other traditional unions.

Training and job placement also constitute attempts to control the labor supply by creating mobility paths within the retail trade. According to Gleason:

> Our professional development trainings provide the opportunity for workers to talk about what they've done, what their knowledge is. It's a revaluing of skills, and because people have worked in so many stores, it gives them industry analysis where they can compare from one store to the next and think about what their career might be and what their opportunities for advancement might be.[32]

Such "bridging" occurs not only through job referrals by members and RWDSU allies who work in higher-wage retail but also through RAP's workshops on customer service, visual merchandising (developing floor plans and attractive displays to boost sales), and "from retail to showroom" (about moving into higher-paying wholesale occupations). At one such workshop, an older RAP member with twenty years experience as a showroom saleswoman and fashion designer explained to participants how trade shows are organized, how one develops a client book, and how skills gained in retail—product knowledge, selling ability—can be transferred to wholesale work. In developing such paths of mobility, RAP is challenging employers' erosion of internal labor markets through deskilling and increased use of part-time, nonpermanent positions (Lambert 2008; Lichtenstein 2009; Braverman 1974, 248–60). At present, however, RAP's job search and placement services are precisely that—services. They help to expand and maintain membership through what Gleason terms the "services-to-organizing model"[33]—to access the full range of services, one must be a dues-paying RAP member and regularly attend membership meetings and other events. But, as RAP's leaders are aware, this alone is not likely to lead to truly "controlling the labor supply."

RAP has also compiled a list of friendly stores and chains through "employer outreach" by members and staff. However, these efforts remain at what Eichler calls "an embryonic stage."[34] To significantly impact employers' hiring practices and gain meaningful control over the retail labor supply in New York City—or even Manhattan—RAP would have to provide either such superior retail employees that companies would actively seek them out or collaborate with traditional unions to pressure employers into preferential hiring agreements.

PEER CONTROL OVER PERFORMANCE AND STANDARDS. In contrast to Fordist-era industrial unions, which "lost the will and ambition to wrest control of production from capitalist hands and turned ever more to bargaining over labor's share in the product" (Braverman 1974, 8), occupational unions provide mechanisms for skill maintenance and enforcement of work rules. As Cobble notes, this is achieved through training and apprenticeships (1991b, 141), an approach that RAP is actively developing. It offers a variety of course offerings, the most frequent and best attended of which—customer service training—provides participants with a certificate from a local community college upon completion. This process actively engages members, as an organizer explained:

> We do trainings and they are a way that we develop our members to become teachers. So we can see that they have skills, and some will come in and I'll do their resume and be working with them and realize that, 'you have so much experience, would you be interested in sharing this with the other members?' And so then they come, we sign them up to be a trainer with CWE [Consortium for Worker Education], and they come in a few times and work with me to develop, to kind of tease out all the information and develop a curriculum, and practice with them to develop a workshop.[35]

RAP's skills-training is aimed at developing workers' confidence, awareness of their tacit skills, and the ability to articulate and pass these on to peers. Another aspect is purely utilitarian: helping unemployed people find work or helping those in low-wage, dead-end jobs to move into more lucrative sectors of the trade. The consistent emphasis on member-led training sessions and the interaction of growing numbers of New York City sales workers with RAP's educational program has created a space for peer-based construction of occupational norms. As Cheryl, a five-year retail veteran who first attended a RAP customer service workshop in July 2011 and has since become an active member, explains: "Going through the training, that's when we started to get a more in-depth idea, feeling of what we've already been through [in retail], what we have yet to experience and being able to feel like we're prepared for the future as far as customer service and retail is concerned."

Asked what she thought of the workers' rights portion of the workshop, she adds:

> That was one of the key components that drew you in even more, be-
> cause it was like, "Wow, I didn't know that I am getting paid next to
> nothing and there are other people getting paid worse than me!" And to
> know that I have a voice, that I can speak up, that I can do something
> about it, make it change, as far as my living standards and arrange-
> ments is concerned. So it was good to know about the workers' rights.[36]

In its efforts to raise worker confidence and generate peer-based norms—and eventually control—of performance and standards, RAP's worker rights training plays a key role, as Cheryl attests. But as in the struggle to gain control over the labor supply, RAP is swimming against the tide of management-driven deskilling and the devaluing of emotional labor central to sales work (Hochschild 1983; Benson 1986; Leidner 1993). Talisa Erazo, a long-time member and current retail worker who serves as president of RAP's board of directors, notes:

> Management and people high up are realizing that by cutting hours and
> making turn-around a lot faster for workers—people who quit or firing
> people—they are saving money. They don't need to give raises, they
> don't need to give benefits, it's just ten hours a week and they'll proba-
> bly just quit in the end. Their idea is that we'll make as many profits as
> we can and we're going to figure out how to do that the fastest way pos-
> sible, the easiest way possible.[37]

OCCUPATIONAL RIGHTS AND PROTECTIONS. As Cobble notes, whereas industrial unions seek job security for their members in a given workplace, occupational unions instead aim to offer workers employment security, through hiring halls and other mechanisms. Because job shifts are frequent, occupational unions commonly provide members with portable health, pension, and other benefits that workplace-based industrial unions typically obtain from employers through collective bargaining. With this in mind, RAP is in the process of setting up group-sponsored benefit packages for health care, unemployment, professional development, and banking services. Other New York-based workers' organizations—the Taxi Workers' Alliance, Restaurant Opportunities Center, and the Freelancers' Union in particular—offer models of benefit provision that RAP's leaders hope to emulate (see Gaus, Brady, King, all in this volume). RAP is already able to offer its members consumer benefits, such as discount cards for dental work, basic health and mental health services, medication, and public transport. RAP staff also counsel members with pressing needs as to where they can access services.

Unlike the other components of occupational unionism, benefit provision seems feasible even at this early stage of RAP's development. But the more robust goal of providing employment security—through a hiring hall that can offer members regular work—is at best a distant prospect.

OCCUPATIONAL IDENTITY. If control over labor supply is the *structural* foundation of occupational unionism, occupational identity is the *subjective* basis for sustaining member involvement and collective self-management. RAP actively seeks to foster such a common identity among its members, with some results, as Joseph, a long-time RAP member who previously worked at Target and is now an organizer for a nonretail union, explains:

> I thought [organized] labor was like guys in overalls with jackhammers and hardhats, you know, spittin' tobacco and I was like, "Why retail? That's a joke—you know, retail sucks, this is for kids!" . . . I didn't realize how many people work in retail and for how many it's their main source of income, and I saw that through RAP all the time. . . . I was able to learn how important changing retail is. . . . Whether or not they want to stay there forever, but to think this job is important, it does produce value for society, it deserves dignity, it's worth fighting for, it is organizable—off the bat, that was the big lesson that I learned from RAP.[38]

Joseph alludes to a significant hurdle in RAP's attempt to build occupational identity: the social devaluation of retail sales and customer service work and the view that such jobs aren't "real jobs," which is widespread among many retail workers.

RAP organizers understand this well. As Gleason relates, "There's this idea among some workers that retail is something you're doing while working toward something else."[39] Training sessions are thus a conscious attempt at "infusing a craft identity" into a largely noncraft industry. To this end, the organization integrates long-term sales personnel into its activities whenever possible, since such workers tend to have stronger occupational identification than their younger counterparts. This is aided by RAP's organizational and physical proximity to the Macy's workers' union hall—RWDSU Local 1-S, one floor above: several 1-S members regularly participate in RAP planning meetings, workers' rights and skills-training workshops, and a former 1-S shop steward is now a full-time RAP organizer.

As with controlling the labor supply and achieving peer-based performance standards, RAP is fighting an uphill battle in its attempts to build occupational identity among an increasingly deskilled and socially heterogeneous workforce. Yet this may be RAP's most original contribution to retail organizing: rather than trying to win union representation elections in isolated workplaces, or organizing around nonwork identities such as race, ethnicity, or nativity, RAP is creating a community of workers organized around occupational identities.

Policy and Media

In the fall of 2011 RAP conducted a survey of retail workers in New York, interviewing 436 workers from 230 nonunion stores across all five boroughs. Earlier that year, the organization had acquired its own office, filed for 501(c)3 status, and added several new staff members. But the survey project signaled a new level of visibility and activity. Members were present in the office more often than before, working in teams of two or three, discussing protocol, heading into the city and returning hours later with completed questionnaires, debriefing about their experiences and preparing for the next day. RAP issued a report on its findings, *Discounted Jobs: How Retailers Sell Workers Short*, on a rainy Tuesday in January 2012 outside the annual conference of the National Retail Federation, the dominant employers' association in the industry. This garnered front-page coverage for both the study and RAP in the *New York Metro*, as well as an article in the *New York Times*.

A primary finding of *Discounted Jobs*, which reflected RAP members' own experience and confirmed the results of earlier research by Susan Lambert (2008), was the pervasiveness of unpredictable "'just-in-time'" scheduling practices and the havoc they wreak on employees' lives. As Dominique, a RAP member and long-time retail worker, explains, "Scheduling is a huge problem—they often make schedules in a way that you don't actually have a life, so that you will revolve around your job."[40] Similarly, Joseph, a former Target worker, recounted his experience:

> I explained to them [management] that I was in school and had to be there two days a week. So it was quite easy—don't schedule me then. They still would. If I told them they would take me off, but it was always grudgingly and it was like, oh I'd signed a contract that said I can't possibly do that. I found out after they had hired me [that although] I put on my application that I was part-time . . . it's not possible to work less than five days a week.[41]

RAP's study uncovered five aspects of retail scheduling that are especially oner-ous for workers: involuntary part-time status, "on-call" shifts where one is ex-pected to be available without guarantee of work or other compensation, being sent home early, frequent schedule changes, and hours being given by managers as "rewards" for high sales. As the report put it, "Workers are now competing with each other over sales, not for commission, but just to 'get on the schedule'" (Luce and Fujita 2012, 14).

In response to employers' scheduling tactics—what Naoki Fujita, RAP's pol-icy coordinator, argues is "part of an antiunion strategy"[42]—RAP has developed its Just Hours policy campaign designed to "win stronger state policies that give retail workers stable, predictable, and livable work hours."[43] This cam-paign was launched on October 17, 2012, with twin rallies in front of Aber-crombie & Fitch and Urban Outfitters stores on Fifth Avenue in Manhattan featuring workers from each store who had suffered low or unpredictable hours and had since joined RAP. This direct action component of Just Hours targets individual employers' scheduling practices. As Fujita explains, the goal is to "cre-ate a code of conduct and ask a good employer in New York to sign onto it,"[44] and then pressure other, "less good" employers to comply with the same stan-dard.

Another aspect of Just Hours is the proposed Predictable Scheduling Act, which RAP is promoting with support from the National Employment Law Project and the advocacy group "A Better Balance." This legislation, if passed by the New York City Council, "would apply to large retail employers operating in the New York City market. These companies would be required to provide weekly schedules with advance notice before the workweek begins, would re-quire workers' consent for scheduling changes and would give workers the right to make scheduling requests" (United NY and Center for Popular Democracy 2013, 21).

Closely connected to these policy initiatives are RAP's growing efforts to gain media attention. Since early 2011 the member-composed Art and Media Com-mittee has met on a monthly basis to develop creative ways to highlight the plight of retail workers and raise RAP's profile. One of the most visible results of the committee's work was its flash-mob "Interns' Night Out" in September 2011. Staged as a mock fashion show during fashion week's "Fashion Night Out," the action involved more than twenty RAP members who wore T-shirts, passed out flyers, and sang songs condemning the industry's widespread use of unpaid interns. The concept was developed entirely by RAP members, with staff assisting in the planning and execution, and sought to build links with under-paid (or unpaid) workers in the retail-related field of fashion, with which many members already had an affinity. Another committee project is a "RAP rap" about scheduling hassles set to the tune of Jay-Z's "Hard Knock Life."

RAP is also engaged in more conventional media outreach. In late 2011 the organization hired Yana Walton as a full-timer dedicated to communications and media work. "All these big retailers," she explains, "have massive PR teams and huge budgets to be able to make sure that everything is heard from their point of view. . . . [Getting] coverage for what it is like for people who actually *work* there—that's how I see my job." *Discounted Jobs* came to the attention of U.S. Senator Tom Harkin (D-Iowa), who then invited a leading RAP member to testify about her experiences with erratic retail scheduling before a hearing of the U.S. Senate Committee on Health, Education, Labor and Pensions in May 2012. "Media is the ultimate legitimizer of what we are saying," Walton said. "It's like a huge microphone and essential part of any legislative campaign."[45]

RAP's policy offensive counters the employer-dominated discourse and legal framework for retail employment relations, while also educating members about the systematic character of workplace injustice and developing their skills—such as public speaking and strategic thinking. This helps to set the stage for future workplace or occupational organizing. At the same time, however, an aspect of RAP's messaging has the potential to divert members' focus away from power-based organizing. A central component of RAP's policy narrative is that it is in employers' interest to institute "high-road" employment practice. As Erazo explains:

> [Employers] are not realizing that their profits can go up if they keep the same workers, keep them happy and make sure they're not getting sick and making other workers sick. So those profits that they are seeing in making those quick turnarounds and hiring a lot of different people, they could be making the same ones if they kept the workers and treated them well, but nobody's bringing this realization to management or the people at the NRF [National Retail Federation].[46]

But RAP's own successes at YRB and Shoemania provide evidence counter to this: even though workers gained union contracts with the RWDSU at both chains, they have been unable to obtain health care and pension plans or even middle-class wages from their employers, due to thin profit margins. And large national chains, such as Walmart, Target, or JCPenney that *do* have large surpluses but invest millions in internal union prevention and antiunion lobbying, are deeply committed to the low-road path. RAP's appeal to employers' self-interest as a pathway to improving conditions in the industry not only seems quixotic in the face of the dominant approach of employers in this sector, but may also deflect members' energies away from building workplace or market-place social power. Although RAP has not abandoned workplace organizing or the development of member power, its increasing focus on policy and media—combined with employer-friendly rhetoric—highlights this risk.

Results and Prospects

Originating in 2005 as a campaign-oriented coalition between the RWDSU and GOLES, RAP has evolved into an autonomous, member-based worker center with an active career development program, budding policy initiatives, and an expanding public presence. Its most original contribution to the field of retail organizing is its avoidance of the traditional workplace-based, electoral path to worker representation and its embrace of an open-membership, activist-based model. Occupational organizing, as outlined by Cobble, is one avenue down which RAP may continue to travel, but in doing so it must confront significant challenges.

The biggest challenge involves scale: less than one in ten retail workers in New York City are union members, or about thirty thousand workers. But just over two thousand workers are part of RAP's network. Without significantly greater organization, RAP cannot hope to exercise meaningful influence over retail employers. Another critical challenge is deskilling, which has been pervasive in retail in recent years. Little to no specific training is required for a majority of entry-level positions, which translates into fewer opportunities for RAP to act as an intermediary between retail employers and job-seekers. In implicit recognition of these formidable obstacles to occupational unionism, RAP's leaders are pursuing a multipronged strategy that includes a policy and media component, career development programs, as well as workplace campaigns.

Advancing on the policy front—winning improved enforcement of existing laws, new legislation, or instituting a voluntary code of conduct with key employers—can open the door to further occupational organizing, further workplace organizing, or it can be limited to advocacy, in Jenkins's terms. The career development program, birthed during RAP's campaign phase, helps to recruit new members while providing job-help services for existing members and engendering a mechanism for possible labor-supply control and worker self-management in the future. In the short run, however, it primarily involves service provision rather than organizing, and is unlikely to contribute much to RAP's stated goal of "improv[ing] retail jobs." RAP's multipronged strategy, in which policy initiatives, service provision, and legal advocacy serve as means to the broader end of transforming the industry and opening up new possibilities for member-based organizing, reflects the limitations on what is possible in any one field (workplace, occupational, or policy).

In the short run, however, RAP functions primarily as an advocacy-based incubator of workplace-based campaigns and a mobilizing force for policy initiatives. It continues to embrace several aspects of the occupational union model, but it has recognized the many challenges that involves and will likely not pursue this as a long-term goal. Meanwhile, RAP is providing much-needed support to retail workers in New York City while familiarizing a new generation of workers with the ideas of economic justice and collective organization, a task that may help spark a resurgence of a broad-based postindustrial labor movement.

6

STREET VENDORS IN AND AGAINST THE GLOBAL CITY

VAMOS Unidos

Kathleen Dunn

Virginia grew up in the Bronx, where both her Mexican-born parents have worked as street vendors for as long as she can remember.[1] As a child, she regularly accompanied them to work in the street. Vending was the only way they could find to earn a living. As Virginia puts it, "Ask my father. He says he's been looking for a job for twenty-two years."[2] Virginia herself began vending as a teenager, selling a range of products depending on the season, from flavored ices in the summer to hot dogs in the winter. Frustrated by numerous tickets and harassment from the police, Virginia and her family joined Esperanza del Barrio, a Harlem-based Latina/o street vendor group. Esperanza would eventually dissolve in 2009, but in 2007 several of its members, including Virginia and her family, decided to found a new Latina/o organization of vendors working in the Bronx, Brooklyn, and Queens.

This was Vendedoras Ambulantes Movilizando y Organizando en Solidaridad: VAMOS Unidos (which means "let's go together" in Spanish), in which Virginia is now an active leader. She volunteers in the office, working on legal case management, including translation for vendors appealing violations; she conducts outreach alongside other vendor leaders and volunteers; she helps facilitate monthly meetings, where members participate in strategic planning; and she organizes VAMOS marches and protests.

Like Virginia, many VAMOS members live and work in the same outer-borough neighborhoods, as familial obligations often make trekking their wares to the more lucrative streets of Manhattan difficult. Nearly 70 percent of VAMOS members are women, about half of them single mothers. Working close to home enables them to both care for their children and vend within ethnic enclaves where they can communicate easily with customers.

The street vending industry in New York City has long been comprised of first-generation immigrants like Virginia's parents. But commercial property owners and city officials alike have long been opposed to the ways in which these recent immigrants use public space, and consider street vending to be a source of urban disorder. In their view, vendors create congestion and obstruct pedestrian flows, and "unfairly" compete with brick-and-mortar restaurants and retail stores. Moreover, their goods are suspect as low-quality "street meat" served from "roach coaches." These perceptions are interlaced with contempt for the working poor and with racialized views of "Old World" practices that tarnish the "modern" urban order.

Efforts to restrict street vending are ubiquitous in cities around the world (Swanson 2007; Hunt 2009; Crossa 2009; Cross 1998; Kothari 2008; Martinez-Novo 2003). In New York, the surveillance and criminalization of street vendors is deeply institutionalized and bureaucratically complex. Depending on the kind of goods sold and their physical location, New York City street vendors are governed by a combination of federal, state, or city laws, as well as regulations promulgated by no less than seven municipal agencies.[3] This vast regulatory matrix actually intensifies the informality it aims to stamp out (see Devlin 2010). The zealous enforcement of regulations is often (and not unreasonably) experienced as injustice, which in turn spurs vendors to form or join vending organizations.

Street Labor in the Global City

Although VAMOS is a locally based organization, its members' working conditions are profoundly shaped by national and global dynamics. Because they work in city streets, vendors confront these dynamics within the ever-contested politics of public space. Struggles over public space, which capital and neoliberal regimes seek to control (Davis 1992; Low and Smith 2006; Mitchell 2003; Sorkin 1992; Zukin 1995), have fueled street vendor activism across the globe. Yet curiously, few scholars have explored the growing movement of labor and community-based organizations in support of street vendors' rights. This case study documents how VAMOS Unidos strives to improve the working conditions of the Latina/o immigrants that comprise its membership, and analyzes a vital if underrecognized immigrant workplace in the global city: the street itself.

Immigrant street vendor organizations like VAMOS Unidos are part of a *street labor movement*. Street labor consists of informal microeconomic activity located in public space, typically involving economically marginal groups, often immigrant or indigenous, and disproportionately performed by women (Chant and Pedwell 2008; Gallin 2001; Chen 2001). Street labor's global expansion since the 1970s is one aspect of the larger macroeconomic trend of informalization (Slavnic 2009; International Labor Office 2002a; 2002b; Sassen 1991). According to a 2009 OECD policy brief, nearly two-thirds of the world's workers now operate within the informal sector.[4] The proportion is far lower in wealthy countries than in the Global South, where street labor organizing has flourished (Celik 2011; Devenish and Skinner 2004; Gallin 2001; Chen 2001). As Gallin (2001) has documented, informal workers' organizations typically take the form of either trade unions, such as India's one-million-strong Self Employed Women's Association (Agarwala 2013), or of nonprofit community-based organizations like VAMOS Unidos.

Although celebrated by some commentators as entrepreneurial (Cross and Morales 2007), street labor, like other types of informal self-employment, is embedded in structured relationships of dependency (DeFilippis et al. 2009). Street vendors' primary dependence is on access to public space, which is precisely what makes them subject to intensive state regulation.

The regulation of public space has been increasingly privatized, especially within the global city (Zukin 1995). In New York City, "public-private partnerships" called Business Improvement Districts (BIDs) have been central actors in regulating public space since the 1975 fiscal crisis.[5] That crisis sparked a highly racialized "moral panic" over the growing visibility of the poor in the city streets. As Miriam Greenberg (2008) argues, the "branding" of New York in this period reasserted its business- and tourist-friendly status as a global city. Alongside graffiti artists, street vendors were considered "quality of life criminals" (Street Vendor Project 2006) whose activities disrupted the brand security of global New York. Solving the vendor "problem" thus became a central strategy for "reclaiming" public space in order to attract more elite business investments to the city.

In recent decades, BIDs have gained increasing influence over the New York City Council, which in turn has implemented dozens of laws restricting street labor, and street vendors in particular. The BIDs' expanded role in the governance of public space makes them formidable adversaries for those whose livelihoods involve working in city streets. Street labor organizing in New York is thus largely a defensive endeavor. Yet by claiming public space as a legitimate workplace, and uniting to improve their conditions, street vendors illustrate how labor organizing can and does shape the ever-shifting economic geography of capitalism, as Herod (1997) has argued. The struggle of street laborers to restructure public space, indeed, is an emerging component of the twenty-first-century global labor movement.

Public Space as Workplace

Because it occurs within public space and not private property, street labor embodies a series of class contradictions. In the case of vendors, multilayered legal restrictions dictate where, when, and what one may sell in the street. The allure of being one's own boss is continually disrupted by inspections and ticketing by police and other state enforcement agents. Though many vendors entered the industry as a preferable alternative to untenable low-wage work, the high cost of fines for vending violations can significantly disrupt vendors' income stability. Otherwise pleasant interactions with customers can be tempered by turf wars with fellow vendors.

Vendors occupy a liminal class position: they are both small-business people and yet also part of the city's rapidly growing precarious workforce. VAMOS members themselves overwhelmingly identify as workers, even though by objective criteria most are self-employed. The majority of VAMOS members turned to street labor either because they could not access the formal labor market or because they could not withstand its degraded conditions. As Virginia explains, "If they're not giving you a job, you can't get money, you can't pay your bills, you have nowhere to go. So you have to make your own work."[6] Although VAMOS members typically describe vending as an occupation of last resort, almost all of them did have some prior experience with waged work, most commonly in factories, restaurants, cleaning services, and domestic work.

Compared to low-wage jobs like those, street labor offers autonomy and flexibility that, for many, offsets the challenges inherent in working in public space. All but one of the VAMOS members I interviewed preferred vending to other occupations they had tried. As Juana put it:

> I go out every day. Even if it's raining, I'm going to sell. To pay the rent, pay for electricity, send a little to Mexico. Because right now with a [waged] job, they give you nothing. I used to work cleaning and that paid $350 a week, six days of work, sleeping there. Sunrise to sunset, 7 a.m. to 9 p.m. And what's more, I have kids. Now my daughter is still working there cleaning, she says it's just a pittance they give her . . . She would be better off selling *elotes* [corn on the cob]. You could make $40 or $50, but you wouldn't have to spend your whole day doing it.[7]

Control over one's schedule, being free of supervision by a boss, and independence come up again and again in VAMOS members' accounts of why they became vendors and why they prefer vending to waged work. For them, vending constitutes a form of resistance to the unacceptable conditions of the formal employment available to them (see Itzigsohn 1994).

However, even as they free themselves from employers' exploitation, vendors encounter state surveillance and criminalization, which threatens their economic self-sufficiency and undermines the control they might otherwise have over their working conditions. Street labor organizing efforts therefore target the state, especially at the municipal level, not only in New York City but in cities across the globe (Celik 2011; Skinner 2010; Cross 1998; Lund and Skinner 2004).

Solidarities and Stratification

New York is currently home to three nonprofit organizations working to expand street vendors' rights. These groups reflect a hierarchy among vendors that is structured by class, race, ethnicity, and gender. The two largest groups, the Street Vendor Project (SVP) and VAMOS Unidos, closely resemble worker centers, community-based organizations that advocate on behalf of, organize, and provide services for precarious immigrant workers (Fine 2006; Gordon 2005; Jayaramen and Ness 2005; Milkman, Bloom, and Narro 2010). In contrast, the third and most recently established vendor group, the New York City Food Truck Association is a trade association that represents a more affluent constituency of predominantly native-born "gourmet" food truck owners.

Many Food Truck Association members are brick-and-mortar restaurant owners who use food trucks to build their brand. Some run multiple trucks and employ staffs of up to thirty people. They enter street vending not as an occupation of last resort but as a less capital-intensive and lower-risk alternative to conventional restaurants. The Food Truck Association only admits branded food truck companies into its organization, and charges monthly dues of $200. It has engaged a high-profile lobbying firm to represent the organization at the city council on issues pertinent to business ownership, such as reducing the time it takes to obtain street food handler's licenses for their employees. While gourmet food trucks garner a disproportionate share of media attention, they represent a small—although growing—minority of the city's estimated twenty thousand street vendors.

Unlike the Food Truck Association, SVP and VAMOS focus their efforts on expanding vendors' social and economic rights, including immigrant rights. Any street vendor can join SVP, which currently represents over thirteen hundred food, merchandise, and art vendors, most of them Asian, African, or Latino immigrant men working in the Financial District or Midtown Manhattan, with smaller numbers in major shopping districts in Harlem, Brooklyn, and Queens. A small number of military veterans, mostly African American men, are another

SVP constituency. While some employ other vendors, most SVP members are self-employed or work as informal subcontractors on permitted food carts. Many self-identify as workers, although some do see themselves as small-business owners, especially military veterans and artists.

SVP members pay yearly dues of $100, which guarantees them free legal services; there are no other membership requirements. SVP staff provide legal assistance and educate vendors about their rights and how best to navigate municipal regulations. Along with the staff, a small but highly engaged core of vendor-leaders advocate and carry out campaigns targeting the city council's vending regulations. The group regularly issues press releases and reports highlighting the injustices that vendors face. SVP also holds an annual food vendor award ceremony, the Vendy Awards, which has been replicated in Philadelphia, Los Angeles, New Orleans, and Chicago. Their public relations efforts help to keep street vendors in the news, and often succeed in winning public support; for example, the *New Yorker* magazine recently expressed its editorial disapproval of vendor criminalization in an article detailing the latest Vendy Awards event (Frazier 2011).

VAMOS differs from both the Food Truck Association and SVP in that it is primarily focused on base-building and membership engagement. Its nearly five hundred members are all Latina/o, and mostly women. The vast majority are self-employed food vendors who work without full municipal authorization in the outer boroughs and Upper Manhattan. Like SVP, VAMOS provides legal assistance to members; but its efforts more often extend beyond vendors' rights to immigrant rights, in collaboration with other immigrant advocacy groups and coalitions. Membership requirements are more robust than in SVP, including mandatory participation in monthly meetings and street actions. Yearly dues are only $30, reflecting the lower earnings of VAMOS members, and their location in less affluent areas of the city. Some VAMOS members earn as little as $2.00 per hour and can work up to fourteen-hour shifts. Like most street vendors, their daily income fluctuates dramatically; on a lucky day a VAMOS member can earn up to $100, but some days she may earn as little as $10, due to bad weather or police fines.

VAMOS's advocacy efforts are also largely defensive, but they are more actively engaged than SVP with the police and the various city regulatory agencies. For example, VAMOS regularly carries out negotiations on behalf of its members at local police precincts, and staff visit the Department of Consumer Affairs on a weekly basis to help members obtain or renew needed municipal authorizations. Directly challenging the powerful BIDs that so strongly influence vending oversight, and which often seek to evict vendors from the street entirely, is far more difficult.

In other arenas, VAMOS explicitly links workers' rights and immigrant rights. This reflects the organizing background and vision of the group's staff, but also the members' experiences as self-employed immigrants. VAMOS simultaneously seeks to strengthen members' economic self-sufficiency and to forge solidarity among them as co-ethnics operating on the margins of the formal economy.

In the rest of this chapter, I document VAMOS's work in the context of the wider panorama of street vendor activism in New York City. I analyze the group's achievements as well as the internal tensions and challenges it faces as part of a street labor movement that struggles against the *revanchist* dispossession of public space.[8]

Regulation and Resistance among NYC Street Vendors

A comprehensive count of the city's street vendors has never been conducted. Census data is of little help, as street vendors are only enumerated as part of a larger aggregation that also includes door-to-door and newspaper salespeople. No license or permit is required for vendors selling artwork or printed materials, who are protected by the First Amendment (Duneier 1999); there is therefore no effective way of estimating their numbers. In addition, no data exist on the number of merchandise and food vendors who operate without official authorization.

Municipal data does capture the number of vendors who possess licenses and permits needed for street vending (see table 6.1).[9] For general merchandise vendors, only a license is required. Food vendors, however, must have both a permit for their cart or other mobile food vending unit, and a street food handler's license; in addition they are required to store their mobile food vending units in one of approximately ninety city-licensed commissaries.

With the exception of military veterans, who can still obtain general merchandise licenses, merchandise licenses and food vending permits have been capped for over thirty years. Holders of food vending licenses may participate in a biannual lottery for a food vending permit, but since 2007 less than three hundred permits have been distributed through the lottery. Thus food vendors seeking legal ownership rights often turn to the underground economy, where permits are currently sold for $15,000 or more for a two-year term. An article in the *Wall Street Journal* (Reddy 2011b) detailed that some vendors are encountering dramatic increases in the price of their permit rentals, which in all likelihood derives from an increased demand for food vending permits since the recession—precisely when the gourmet food truck trend emerged.

TABLE 6.1   **New York City street vending licenses and permits, 2009–2011**

- General merchandise vending licenses (capped): 853
- General merchandise licenses issued to military veterans (2009): 1,900
- Food vending permits (capped):
  - 2,800 year-round permits
  - 100 citywide permits for disabled and nondisabled veterans and disabled persons
  - 200 borough-specific permits (outside Manhattan)
  - 1,000 seasonal citywide permits (valid April to October)
  - 1,000 GreenCarts permits (unprocessed fruits and vegetables only)
- Street food handlers' licenses: 18,968 (2011)

Sources: Independent Budget Office, New York City 2010; personal correspondence, Department of Health and Mental Hygiene executive 2011; Street Vending Fact Sheet, http://www.ci.nyc.ny.us/html/sbs/nycbiz/downloads /pdf/educational/sector_guides/street_vending.pdf.

Whereas most merchandise vendors are self-employed, the nineteen thousand licensed food vendors typically work as employees or informal subcontractors of permit holders from whom they rent a cart in exchange for a percentage (usually around 30%) of the daily sales revenue. The legality of this practice is dubious at best, as permits are officially nontransferable; thus even food permit holders operate with some measure of informality. In addition, many food vendors possess a food handling license yet lack a permit for their carts or trucks, as is the case for most VAMOS street vendors. Informal employment relations between merchandise vendors and unlicensed "helpers" are also common.[10]

The arcane web of state regulations wreaks havoc for vendors on a daily basis and is often poorly understood even by those charged with its enforcement. Vendors who obtain a license or permit from the city receive a fifty-six page packet of vending regulations from the Department of Consumer Affairs, thirty-five pages of which consist of a list of streets on which vending is prohibited or restricted throughout the five boroughs. Most major corridors in Midtown and the Financial District, along with key sites in Queens, the Bronx, and Brooklyn, are closed to vendors entirely. There are also myriad individual regulations regarding how far vendors must be from curbs, crosswalks, and storefront doors, as well as regulations on the size of vendors' tables and where merchandise may be stored.

Vendors are thus regularly fined for a wide array of missteps. Yet the vast majority of violations go unpaid; of nearly $16 million in fines issued in 2009, only $1.4 million was collected (Independent Budget Office 2010). This is due to a variety of factors, including improper citations on the tickets issued or the effective contestation of tickets by vendors individually or through the legal services of SVP and VAMOS. Moreover, unauthorized vendors have no incentive to pay such fines, as they are excluded from the license and permit system. Ultimately the city does not profit from its efforts to regulate vendors, spending approximately $5 million a year on vending enforcement, far more than it collects in fines.[11]

Regulations and their enforcement are the major focus of street vendor organizing. Since spatial restrictions and the caps on vending permits and licenses were introduced in the late 1970s and early 1980s—just as BIDs began to take hold in New York—street vendor associations have actively contested vending oversight, principally with regard to vending caps and street closures, and more recently with regard to the violation fine structure.

Litigation by food vendor trade associations effectively delayed the enforcement of some street restrictions, although only for short spells. Three large-scale vendor strikes, one in 1987 and two in 1998, generated extensive public support that forced reversals of proposed street closures. These strikes were organized by a now-defunct vendor trade association, Big Apple Food Vendors, and by a group called Artists' Response to Illegal State Tactics (ARTIST). Several vendor groups have folded, such as the 125th Street Vendors Association in Harlem, which unsuccessfully sought to block a massive street vendor eviction effort in 1994 under Mayor Rudy Giuliani (Stoller 2002; Foner 2001). ARTIST launched two successful litigations that won First Amendment vendors the right to operate without licenses, and it survives to this day, although only as a network with no paid staff or funding.

VAMOS Unidos: Structure and Campaigns

VAMOS Unidos is a community-based social justice organization that seeks to win greater economic security for low-income Latina/o street vendors. The organization holds frequent meetings and mobilizations, and has a strong political education program aimed at leadership development. Although most of their activities are local, VAMOS has a multiscalar strategy. At the neighborhood level, the organization works on issues of police accountability; at the municipal level, it helps vendors comply with regulations and campaigns to expand access to vending authorizations; at the national and international levels, it works in solidarity with immigrant rights groups and street vendors networks to advance social and economic rights.

VAMOS has two full-time employees: Rafael Samanez, the executive director, and Jennifer Arieta, the development manager and head organizer. The group also has two volunteer vendor-leaders (one full-time and one part-time), as well as a larger group of active members who contribute to strategic planning, fundraising, and development efforts, as well as political education and service provision. Samanez was a cofounder of the group, along with several members of the disbanded Esperanza del Barrio. He recruited Arieta, whom he met when they were both involved in a group called Immigrant Communities in Action. The staff and core volunteers are all Latina/os under the age of thirty-five, most of them women.

Ninety percent of VAMOS's funding comes from foundation grants, mostly obtained on the basis of the organization's commitment to supporting women in the informal sector, a current focus of NGO funding around the world. The group's annual operating budget is just under $300,000, which limits the size of its staff as well as its capacity to expand.

Although they do not systematically track members' national origins or immigration status, VAMOS staff estimate that over half of the organization's members are Mexican immigrants, with the rest from various Latin American countries. Half the membership is based in the Bronx, and the rest are divided between Upper Manhattan, Queens, and Brooklyn. Though women comprise the majority of the members, vending for many of them is a family business that also employs husbands, brothers, and sons.

Members are largely drawn into the organization through word of mouth; part of each member's responsibility is to actively recruit new members. Many are attracted to the group by the legal and financial services it offers. Some members have had prior experience in labor or community organizations in their home countries, including unions and community councils, as well as farmworkers' and squatters' movements. As Samanez points out, "People have come from places where, since they were born, they were fighting and struggling."[12] For some members, the challenges of single motherhood or experiences with domestic violence are among the reasons they joined VAMOS.

VAMOS takes pride in the fact that it has been a member-led organization from its inception. Meeting attendance is mandatory, a policy instituted by members to bolster participation. If a vendor misses four meetings in a row, her membership is suspended and thereafter a modest fee is imposed for any services provided. Meeting attendance is monitored by staff, as is participation in mandatory marches and protests, such as the annual May Day immigrant rights march in Manhattan's Union Square. Even those who volunteer to bring food to meetings are held accountable; those who fail to bring their promised food are asked for a donation.

VAMOS's monthly meetings, or *juntas*, usually last three hours. They focus on discussion of current issues facing members and strategic planning to address both long- and short-term problems. Leadership development is also a regular feature of the meetings, which strongly emphasize rank-and-file participation. "We try to have it be very participatory, so we focus a lot on capacity building within our meetings," Arieta explained. "All of our campaign decisions, and even things like deciding the difference between active and inactive membership, all those organizational decisions are made in our *juntas*, our general membership meetings."[13] Members such as Elena, a founding VAMOS vendor, view active participation as vital to being in the organization. "The most important thing is to attend the meetings and the marches," she declared. "If we don't join together there is no power. . . . Because with one or two or three, who can do anything?"[14]

Though its main office is located in the Bronx, where most membership meetings are held, in 2008 the group began convening additional monthly meetings in Queens and Brooklyn for members who live in those boroughs. In addition to the meetings at each site, monthly orientations for new members are offered in each borough. Members from one borough occasionally attend the meetings in other boroughs to keep the three groups informed about one another's initiatives and activities.

Street mobilizations also bring together vendors from the various boroughs. VAMOS organizes between five and ten street actions every year, most of which members are required to attend. In July 2010, for example, after a pregnant member was pushed to the ground in Brooklyn during a confrontation with a city Parks Department employee, members from all the boroughs mounted a protest in front of the Parks Department's office in Prospect Park. "It wasn't just the members from Brooklyn who were going to go to the protest," Arieta recalled. "We asked people from Queens and the Bronx to show their solidarity and support."[15]

Education is another defining feature of VAMOS's organizational culture; many members describe the organization as being like a school. Staff and member leaders organize educational programs for the monthly meetings, as well as separate workshops. Topics include Latin American history, civic participation, globalization, and migration. VAMOS has also partnered with Project Enterprise, which provides financial literacy classes as well as microloans to members, and with Teachers Unite to offer English as a Second Language classes.

VAMOS's educational programs are part of its commitment to leadership development. Members' own life experiences often provide the starting point for this work. At a political education class I attended in Brooklyn, for example, members spoke at length about the political and economic factors that had spurred their own migration trajectories, and then analyzed their personal situations in relation to the history of Mexico-U.S. relations. According to staff, members' working class and *campesino* backgrounds provide invaluable material for the leadership development process. As Samanez commented, "To make

$10,000 a year and be able to take care of a family of three or more takes a lot of good leadership skills."[16]

Vendor leaders who get involved in organizing are often self-selected. For example, Teresa, a middle-aged single mother, began by helping to facilitate monthly meetings and assisting with office administration, her eight-year-old daughter often by her side. After taking part in the political education classes, Teresa gradually became more involved in the day-to-day work of the organization, helping to recruit new members and organizing street actions. She enrolled in a course on Latin American history at a nearby college along with another VAMOS volunteer, and eventually she began to lead political education classes herself.

For many VAMOS members street vending is a family affair. For example, Teresa's mother, Rocio, is also a street vendor and is active in VAMOS's outreach and organizing efforts. The group also runs a youth program for members' children, educating them about community organizing both as a community-building practice and also as a viable career option for the future. In addition, because of the large number of single mothers and families among their membership, VAMOS provides free child care at required monthly member meetings.

VAMOS devotes much of its energy to assisting its members in negotiating the thicket of vending laws and codes. Lacking full municipal authorization, VAMOS members regularly accrue tickets that can easily total $2,000 in a single day of vending; indeed, the lack of a permit or a license alone can trigger a $1,000 fine.[17] Such fines are often devastating, given vendors' minimal income levels. VAMOS advises members to negotiate with police and ask for criminal instead of administrative summonses for vending violations; in an ironic but telling twist, criminal fines are far less expensive than administrative ones.

VAMOS provides legal representation for its members through a partnership developed in conjunction with Common Law, a nonprofit legal services organization. VAMOS staff and Common Law attorneys often accompany vendors to appeal tickets at Environmental Control Board hearings, where they conduct translation, and help vendors prepare evidence and documentation, taking photographs and obtaining testimony from bystanders or vendors' friends or family members.[18]

As a volunteer at VAMOS's main office, I helped staff log and manage hundreds of tickets for vending violations. The most common tickets VAMOS members receive are for display-related infractions (such as protruding boxes or goods that exceed legal cart dimensions), rather than for violations that endanger public health or safety. Operating without a permit or a license is the next most common—and far more expensive—violation. Through its legal representation program, VAMOS and Common Law have contested around three hundred tickets since 2008, with almost half being dismissed as a result. This saved VAMOS members about $50,000 and enabled forty-five members to renew their licenses.

Most members cannot afford to sublease a permitted cart or to buy a permit in the underground economy. But with VAMOS's guidance, the vast majority of them have obtained food handlers' licenses, on which there is no cap. This greatly reduces the fines vendors are likely to incur. Members attest that help in obtaining this license, along with assistance with quarterly and annual sales tax filings, are the most vital services that VAMOS provides.

Having a food handlers' license not only increases vendors' income security but also reduces the likelihood of arrests. Guillermina, a middle-aged mother, was detained for three days before VAMOS helped her to secure her food license; many other members recounted similar experiences. Having a license also provides vendors with a form of municipal identification that in itself often deters police from arresting them, further increasing their physical security and limiting the confiscation of their goods.

VAMOS staff also have helped members access the city's GreenCarts program, which provides permits for fruit and vegetable vending the neighborhoods in which most VAMOS members live and work. In a recent two-year period, while only eight VAMOS members had secured permits through the food permit lottery, approximately thirty were able to secure a GreenCarts permit.

Marcellino and Claudia operate a GreenCart just off Fordham Road near the VAMOS office. The couple had been vending without authorization when they first joined the organization. VAMOS was instrumental in securing their Green-Cart permit, and also in providing a space for them to learn from other vendors. As Claudia recalled:

> We realize this talking with other members, that there's no respect for anyone working in the street. Between the other vendors we talk a lot about immigration too; we learn from each other how to protect ourselves from the police, from the Department of Health—just how to defend ourselves. I don't think I could do it without the other members; on the contrary, it's really thanks to them that I am here.[19]

VAMOS staff not only help members negotiate municipal bureaucracies, as Claudia's account suggests, but members also view one another as a source of mutual aid.

At this writing, the organization has four key areas of work: an Economic Justice Campaign; struggles for police accountability; immigrant rights work; and global justice and solidarity efforts. VAMOS's Economic Justice Campaign seeks to increase the number of food cart permits available to city vendors, an effort that involves introducing bills and advocating with city council members to lift the existing caps. Although staff coordinate this campaign, members actively participate as well, a process facilitated by the simultaneous translation that VAMOS provides at council meetings, an example of what Jennifer Gordon (2005) calls "non-citizen citizenship." The immediate goal is to increase the caps on permits in the outer boroughs and upper Manhattan, working with city council members who are supportive of this idea.

At the heart of the campaign is the goal of economic self-sufficiency for vendors. As Samanez explains, "If they don't work as street vendors, there is no other income. A lot of them don't qualify for public assistance. They're under immense pressure to make enough of an income to support their families here and sometimes their families back in their home countries."[20] The campaign also helps to promote vendors' business efficiency. For example, VAMOS is developing a system to buy food in bulk for the vendors, which would create revenue for the organization while also reducing costs for members. Other business education efforts include arranging for experienced vendors to share their expertise on issues such as cart presentation and customer relations. And for those few members who have employees, VAMOS has established a $12 hourly wage floor (although enforcement of this policy is difficult).

Police accountability is another key area of VAMOS's work. Staff schedule regular meetings with local police precincts around the city to discuss various aspects of vendor ticketing and harassment. This work is labor-intensive, involving street-by-street, day-to-day interventions and negotiations with police officers responsible for the enforcement of vending policy. For example, as Arieta recounted in an interview, "We met with the inspector of the precinct, because children of vendors were being arrested while they were protecting their parents' carts or waiting for their parents to go to the bathroom. Children or family members were being arrested, or fined, just for being there and not having a permit. So that was an issue we were able to address."[21] To date VAMOS has worked with seven police precincts in Brooklyn, Queens, and the Bronx; as members often attest, these negotiations have greatly reduced harassment and ticketing. Vendor leaders can spearhead meetings with police, with staff involvement limited to providing simultaneous translation and negotiating in English when needed. This is an example of leadership development, with the staff seeking to lessen its advocacy role.

Immigrant rights advocacy and organizing is a third focus of VAMOS's work, inextricably connected to vendors' economic security. In 2010, VAMOS took the lead in organizing a protest against Arizona's SB1070, in which over two thousand people participated. Their march across the Brooklyn Bridge united several human rights organizations across New York and won support from politicians, churches, and other immigrant rights advocates. In this effort, VAMOS leveraged its ties to local and national immigrant rights networks, reflecting both the importance of the organization's multiscalar agenda and the close connections it makes between labor rights and immigrant rights.

VAMOS has a limited history of collaboration with SVP, reflecting differences in the two organizations' structures, cultures, and politics. But they did cooperate in an effort to block a 2008 initiative by City Councilmember Daniel Squadron to fingerprint vendors who incurred fines for vending violations. As a result of their joint advocacy and education on the issue, Squadron changed his position and subsequently became more supportive of vendor rights. More recently, VAMOS offered its support to SVP's successful Reduce the Fines campaign, introducing two city council bills with Council Member Stephen Levin that rolled back fines for vending violations to the pre-2006 fee schedule (from a maximum fine of $1,000 to $500). This was the first time that the city council ever reduced violation costs for street vendors.

National and international organizations and networks are another key focus for VAMOS. These include the National Network for Immigrant and Refugee Rights and Immigrant Communities in Action. Although it is not a formal member of StreetNet International, a network of street vendor organizations in over thirty countries that share strategies and carry out global campaigns, VAMOS is in regular contact with StreetNet leaders. The network provides research and education materials to all its affiliates. Partly as a result of its dialogue with StreetNet, VAMOS is exploring the idea of developing a national network of U.S. street vendor organizations.

In and against the Global City

A street labor movement in a global city such as New York at first appears to be a highly improbable proposition. Compared to cities in the developing world, New York's street vendors are relatively few in number, scattered across the city, and highly diverse not only in terms of national origin but increasingly in terms of socioeconomic status as well. The collusion of state and private-sector forces aligned against street vendors in New York is both formidable and politically opaque.

VAMOS has responded to these splintering conditions by building a base unified by ethnicity, class, and gender. Members' bonds are deepened through the organization's participatory approach to leadership development, which bolsters the group's strong capacity for mobilization. VAMOS prides itself on its high level of membership participation. According to Arieta:

> A lot of people participate. I've worked in other organizations where it was very difficult to get a high percentage of participation. And that's something our members have really been able to do well. You know, when I was first volunteering, I thought it was crazy. You can't do two meetings a month [in the Bronx]. People are not gonna come to these. But they do![22]

Member engagement is further reinforced by the group's political education efforts, which effectively link members' individual struggles to municipal, national, and transnational justice movements.

VAMOS's social justice framework, unlike a more narrow workers' rights agenda, allows the organization to engage both aspects of street labor's liminal class position: providing services that help to secure vendors' position as micro-business owners, and developing political education that builds both working class and immigrant solidarities. This dual approach illustrates that, in New York, street labor organizing is simultaneously an immigrant rights struggle. On this basis, VAMOS has been able to empower and unite a spatially dispersed group of precarious workers, while acting as a bridge between the traditional labor movement and the more recent immigrant rights movement.[23] Street-level organizing among informal-sector workers is a vital contribution to the rapidly shifting economic landscape that both these movements now confront.

The street labor movement is also part of the ongoing political struggle over the "right to the city" (Lefebvre 1968). Despite intensive surveillance and criminalization, and the new force of gentrification that the gourmet food truck trend portends, New York's public spaces remain a vital resource to tens of thousands of precariously employed recent immigrants. Their willingness and ability to organize a collective claim to the city streets suggests that recent proclamations about "the end of public space" under neoliberalism (e.g., Sorkin 1992) may well turn out to have been premature.

7

PROTECTING AND REPRESENTING WORKERS IN THE NEW GIG ECONOMY

The Case of the Freelancers Union

Martha W. King

Riding the New York City subway, one is likely to see advertisements for the Freelancers Union like this one. Many of its members, indeed, first learned of the organization's existence in this way. The Freelancers Union (or the union hereafter) issues six different ads each year and places them in six thousand spots in subways and commuter trains. Noteworthy for their provocative calls to action, the ads have sleek abstract designs, created by a freelance design team.

Sara Horowitz founded the Freelancers Union in 1995; as of 2013 it has grown to include 223,203 members nationwide, with the majority residing in New York State. The organization's mission is "to promote the interests of independent workers through advocacy, education, and service."[1] Combining organizational features typical of labor unions, professional associations, and worker centers, the union offers health insurance to its members; provides professional development and networking opportunities; and advocates and organizes for legislation and policy change, while supporting "freelancer-friendly" politicians. Like many unions, it provides benefits—health, dental, disability, life and liability insurance, retirement plans, and discounts—that can be accessed solely through membership, and it has built a sustainable organizational infrastructure, as well as the ability to influence electoral politics. Like a professional association, it strengthens the networks and resources of its members, many of whom work alone in their homes, by bringing them together. And finally, like a worker center it has low barriers to entry, aims to engage its members in mutual aid, or in Freelancers Union's language "new mutualism," and advocates for policy changes in labor and employment laws to meet the needs of independent contractors and other "contingent" workers.

The union's membership is made up of independent workers in a variety of predominately professional fields, such as arts, education, graphic design, health care, and information technology. About 66 percent of them are independent contractors; the rest are full- or part-time employees or temporary, contract or on-call workers. Although the union's members' occupations and incomes vary widely, they all face exclusion from many of the nation's basic employment and labor laws and maintain employment that is highly precarious. The union is a bold experiment that seeks to address the vulnerability and insecurity of this significant segment of the U.S. workforce that is mobile, including a growing middle-strata "precariat" (Standing 2011) that was underorganized until the union emerged.

The union has three defining characteristics. The first is a strong organizational infrastructure, rooted in the insurance company it established, which provides a steady stream of funding to support the group's organizing and advocacy efforts. Unlike many worker centers and community-based organizations, the union is not dependent on foundation support, philanthropy, or dues; instead it is sustained by the revenue of its social enterprise, which also meets a salient need of its members. The union's second defining characteristic involves branding, which both reflects and reinforces the aspirations of its constituency. If the union were a person, one might describe her as creative, brazen, and thinking outside the box. The union's brand is welcoming to independent workers, confirming what they think about themselves as individuals and professionals while also linking them, through a broader identity and shared interests, to freelancers who work in other industries and occupations. Third, the union is defined by its "new mutualism" philosophy. In lieu of a focus on collective bargaining, to which independent workers have no rights under U.S. labor law, the union embraces the tension between collectivism and individualism, supporting members' individual aspirations but at the same time promoting collective solidarity.

In this chapter, I first briefly describe the massive changes in the labor market that have generated the expansion of precarious employment in recent decades. Then I offer an analysis of the development of the Freelancers Union and its organizing and advocacy activities, as well as the demographics and other characteristics of its membership. Against that background, I document in more detail the three key characteristics outlined above which, taken together, distinguish the union from other worker organizations: infrastructure, branding, and mutualism. I conclude with a discussion of the ways in which, despite the fact that its diverse membership includes many middle-class professional workers, the union's structure and strategies are relevant for the larger precarious workforce.

The New Precariat

As many commentators have noted, various forms of precarious employment have proliferated in the United States, and in many other industrial societies as well, since the mid-1970s (Standing 2011). Sometimes called nonstandard or contingent work, precarious work is "uncertain, unpredictable and risky from the point of view of the worker" (Kalleberg 2009, 2). Although risk, uncertainty, and employment insecurity are hardly new features of market economies, they were moderated during much of the twentieth century. In the case of the United States, New Deal social reforms and labor legislation, along with the growth of organized labor, led to a system of labor market regulation that provided far more security to workers than had existed before the 1930s. However, that system has been severely eroded since the 1970s, by deindustrialization and outsourcing, new technologies, deregulation, and union decline. As a result, precarious forms of employment have sprung up across the labor market, affecting not only low-wage workers but also those in relatively skilled and well-paid professions. Employers have become increasingly adept at transferring market risks, once borne by firms, to workers themselves. As early as 1996 a representative survey of U.S. businesses found that three-quarters were using some type of labor "flexibility" strategy, such as hiring temporary workers directly or through agencies or subcontractors (Kalleberg 2011, 74). At some well-known firms, such as Microsoft, temporary workers comprise over 20 percent of the workforce (Greenhouse 2008b, 133). In some cases, individuals who had previously been regular employees have been laid off and then rehired as temps or contractors (Greenhouse 2008b, 118). In the twenty years after 1972, the temporary agency industry grew at over 11 percent annually (Kalleberg 2009, 8).

What is often labeled "contingent" work includes a variety of work situations: part-time work; temporary work; seasonal or short-term jobs; and the proliferating ranks of "independent contractors." The U.S. Bureau of Labor Statistics (2005, 2) defines contingent workers as "those who do not have an implicit or explicit contract for ongoing employment." Many of these workers are not considered "employees" under the law, and thus are not covered by government-provided unemployment insurance and workers compensation, or by the Family and Medical Leave Act; many also are excluded from such employer-provided benefits as health insurance, paid sick days, and paid vacations. Temporary workers and independent contractors have been dubbed

"America's new migrant laborers, moving from job to job without security and without benefits" (Osterman 1999, 54).

The most recent effort to enumerate contingent workers is an analysis of data from 2005 by the U.S. Government Accountability Office, depicted in table 7.1. Defining contingent workers as those who "do not have standard full-time employment, that is, are not wage and salary workers working at least 35 hours a week in permanent jobs," it counted 42.6 million contingent workers, or about one in three U.S. workers (U.S. Government Accountability Office 2006, 1). Although the absolute number of contingent workers grew from 1995 to 2005, the proportion of the total workforce they made up did not change significantly over that ten-year period. The GAO enumeration included agency temporary workers, directly hired temporary workers, on-call workers and day laborers, contract company workers, independent contractors, self-employed workers, and standard part-time workers.

Part-time workers (those employed for less than thirty-five hours per week) make up the largest category of "contingent workers," and are distinct from the other categories, in that many of them *are* covered by basic labor and employment laws, such as the Fair Labor Standards Act and the Occupational Safety and Health Act. They generally earn less than full-time workers, however, even when controlling for education, experience, and other factors (Kalleberg 2000, 345). A growing portion of part-time work is involuntary, that is, the workers so employed would prefer to work full-time. But as Tilly (1992) pointed out years ago, some part-time jobs offer high pay, stability, and high skill levels, while others pay poorly, offer little job security, and have minimal skill requirements. "Part time jobs are good or bad for the same reasons that full-time jobs are," Tilly

TABLE 7.1 **Contingent workers as a proportion of the U.S. labor force, by type of employment, 2005**

TYPE OF EMPLOYMENT	PERCENT
Full-time employee	69.4
Standard part-time	13.2
Independent contractor	7.4
Self-employed	4.4
Direct hire temp	2.1
On-call and day labor	2.0
Agency temporary	0.9
Contract company	0.6

Source: U.S. Government Accountability Office 2006.

concludes. "There is nothing inherent in part-time jobs that dictates that they must have low productivity and compensation" (Tilly 1992, 339). This point applies to other forms of contingent work as well.

Unlike other contingent workers, independent contractors often operate their own businesses, find their own clients, set their own hours, are paid for services performed or goods provided, and have no "boss" other than themselves (Kalleberg 2006, 564). Independent contractors are disproportionately male, white, over twenty-five years old, and college-educated, and have higher earnings than other contingent workers (and higher than many standard employees as well). Unlike other contingent workers, about three-fourths of independent contractors have health insurance, though they typically pay for it themselves or obtain it through a spouse. Eighty-four percent of them, moreover, prefer independent contracting to standard employment (Cohany 1998, 6). Independent contractors generally have high levels of education, professional occupations, and relatively good work conditions, but nevertheless they are facing what Horowitz and others have identified as "middle class poverty" (Horowitz 2011b; Bazelon 2009).

The Rise of the Freelancers Union

The Union is a multioccupational professional association that has successfully attracted members from more than fifty industries. Sara Horowitz, the charismatic founder and leader of the union, started Working Today in 1995, the predecessor to the union and now its research arm. Horowitz's conception of the union is predicated explicitly on the legacy of the U.S. labor movement, to which she has personal ties. Her grandfather was a vice president of the International Ladies Garment Workers Union and her father was a union lawyer. After graduating from Cornell University's School of Industrial and Labor Relations, Horowitz organized health care workers, practiced criminal defense, and went on to become a labor lawyer. She often mentions her two role models, New Deal leaders Sidney Hillman, who headed the Amalgamated Clothing Workers of America, and Eleanor Roosevelt, first lady and civil rights advocate.

Horowitz founded the union in response to the rise of what she calls the "gig economy," a profound shift in the way work is organized in the United States. "No longer do we work at the same company for 25 years, waiting for the gold watch, expecting the benefits and security that come with full-time employment," she points out. "Today, careers consist of piecing together various types of work, juggling multiple clients, learning to be marketing and accounting experts, and creating offices in bedrooms/coffee shops/co-working spaces"

(Horowitz 2011a). Horowitz was also inspired by Charles Hecksher's (1996) conception of "an open professional association with a willingness to pressure employers," or what he called "associational unionism."

Although some accounts of the union's history highlight the fact that Horowitz was misclassified as an independent contractor while she was a labor attorney, her lifelong commitment to worker organizing is probably more fundamental to the inspiration for the union.[2] She developed the idea for an organization called Working Today when she was studying at Harvard's Kennedy School of Government. Noting that labor laws and the industrial union model that presumed a stable workplace and a single employer did not match the needs of freelancers and other independent workers in the late twentieth century, she began to explore new strategies to help them protect themselves. She secured support from the Rockefeller and Ford foundations, as well as resources dedicated to social enterprises and entrepreneurs (Dart 2004). In 1999, she was awarded the prestigious MacArthur Foundation Fellowship, widely known as the "genius" award, and has since received many other honors and awards.

By the late 1990s, lack of access to affordable health insurance had emerged as a signature issue for freelancers. Working Today explored a series of approaches to addressing this need, and in 2001 it collaborated with twenty-three other organizations representing independent workers to form the Portable Benefits Network. This was a breakthrough because it organized freelancers into a group, enabling them to obtain cheaper group rates for health insurance. The Network also offered life and disability insurance. To make this model feasible, Horowitz had to convince the New York State Insurance Commissioner that a freelancers "association" like Working Today was as legitimate as a group of employees at a corporation for purposes of group insurance.[3]

Two years later, Horowitz and her Board of Directors launched the Freelancers Union as a 501(c)4 organization. The name change reflected a broader vision for providing benefits, resources, and a voice for independent workers, while also invoking the labor tradition to which Horowitz subscribed. With loans and grants from philanthropists totaling $17 million, the union went on to establish its own Freelancers Insurance Company (FIC) in 2008. This helped ensure access for its membership to lower-cost, quality insurance and also provided a secure economic foundation for the union's ongoing work. In 2011, twenty-two thousand independent workers in New York State purchased health insurance from FIC.[4] In 2012, monthly premiums for individual coverage ranged from $225 to $604 (depending on the deductible), well below the level of premiums available to self-insured New Yorkers on the open market. The union earned $75 million in gross revenue from the FIC in 2010 and has been able to cover operating costs with this revenue since 2008. In 2012, the federal government awarded the union $340 million in low-interest loans to launch and manage health insurance cooperatives in New York, New Jersey, and Oregon (Greenhouse 2013). Building on the initial success of FIC, the union launched a retirement plan in 2009. Its retirement fund is set up with the freelancer lifestyle in mind: there is no minimum investment and contributions can be adjusted to accommodate the irregular incomes of freelancers. The current monthly fee is $11 but will go down as more members join (Wilkinson 2009).

But the union does far more than offer insurance to its members. It also seeks to engage members in advocacy campaigns and to develop their leadership skills. At new member orientations, gaining "a political voice" is regularly cited as a benefit of membership. The organization uses four mechanisms to develop freelancers' political voice: member organizing and leadership development; a 501(c)4 tax designation (which unlike 501(c)3 status, permits lobbying and other political activities); federal and state Political Action Committees (PACs); and promoting legislation that benefits freelancers.

At the time of this writing, the union has over sixty full-time staff, the majority of whom work for the insurance company or on information technology projects intended to link members digitally.[5] The organization has a six-member Board of Directors, which includes Horowitz; one member representative; a psychotherapist and former director of policy for the union; a vice president in the urban investment group at Goldman Sachs; a union-side labor and employee benefits lawyer; and the union's former chief technology officer.

Members already vote in large numbers, but before the union existed relatively few participated actively in advocacy or in political campaigns directed at professional advancement and protections for independent workers—indeed, few if any such efforts existed at that time.[6] One goal of the organization is to change that. Since late 2010, the union has held monthly membership meetings in New York City, as well as regular working group meetings. These offer members a regular forum, or an "inside track," as union staff call it, to plan political campaigns, develop practical solutions to the problems their own businesses face, share ideas with union staff, and network. Members, who often work alone and at home, also attend meetings as a social activity and to find community connections. The union sees these meetings as the foundation for building and developing member-leaders and broadening "new mutualist" activities. Approximately thirty members come to a typical meeting, and usually about one-third of attendees are first-timers. Members in attendance are diverse in age and typically one-third or more are nonwhite.[7] Members mingle, eat pizza, move through a detailed business agenda, and then network at a nearby bar. Meetings that I observed have focused on the Get Paid Not Played campaign (discussed below), constituent meetings with elected officials, and PAC fund-raising.

Working groups have between five and ten members and meet weekly, often reporting back and asking for additional support and input at membership meetings. Working groups have addressed strategies for PAC fund-raising, creating a sample contract that members can adopt for self-protection, and plans for meetings with state legislators. The other formal outlet for member leadership development is the member representative position on the union's Board of Directors. Thirty-three members applied for this position in 2011; they were vetted by an endorsement committee appointed by the Board of Directors, which selected three members to compete in an election by the membership.[8]

Over the course of 2011, the union aimed to swing away from staff-intensive organizing and activities that "push" ideas out and toward a better balance with a membership-based model that "pulls" in rank-and-file contributions. By the end of that year, monthly meetings were regularly planned by a member facilitation group, and then led by members. That has shifted the focus away from politics somewhat, since the topics that members are most eager to address during meetings involve strengthening their skills and businesses. Members recommended using meeting time for workshops on accounting, marketing, business planning, résumé writing, cold calling, public speaking, and hiring techniques. Other suggestions involved developing programs to help members learn how to start and grow their own businesses, a guest panel to critique member sales pitches or other promotional materials, and related training sessions. These member-generated ideas highlight the professional services, advice, and networking members seek from the Union and one another; many of these have also been provided in fee-based workshops for members in the past.[9] Providing the solutions and resources to meet these and other member-generated needs and ideas is at the root of new mutualism as well.

At the same time, member meetings and working groups provide an operational foundation for the Union's policy agenda and campaigns, which are articulated in a 2011 seven-point proposal for a "new" New Deal. The seven recommendations are:

(1) Create an alternate unemployment protection program for freelancers;

(2) Increase independent workers' access to affordable, portable benefits;

(3) Combat nonpayment;

(4) End misclassification of all workers as incorrectly full-time or independent;[10]

(5) End discrimination of all workers by extending protections to independent contractors;

(6) Document the scale of the independent workforce; and,

(7) Encourage entrepreneurship by means of a tax credit for sole proprietors in their first years of starting a business.

The union's first legislative victory was reforming New York City's Unincorporated Business Tax, which had imposed a double tax on freelancers' business and personal incomes. The tax was eliminated for those earning less than $100,000, and the city also introduced a tax credit for freelancers earning up to $150,000, which affects virtually all of the union's New York City members. The union's membership is spread across fifty states but about 63 percent of the total membership is in New York State. The union was also successful in convincing the GAO to conduct its 2006 study on contingent workers and also in persuading the U.S. Bureau of Labor Statistics to request money to reinstate the Contingent Worker supplement of the Current Population Survey.[11] Other items on the union's policy agenda include payment protection and unemployment coverage.

The union's annual surveys of freelancers have found nonpayment for work performed to be a widespread concern; the 2007 survey, for example, found that over 75 percent of respondents had faced nonpayment or very late payment at some point in their careers. A study by Rutgers University economist William Rodgers (2010, 2) showed that 42 percent of New York State's nine hundred thousand independent workers had trouble collecting payment for their work in 2009. He found that the average payment past due was almost $12,000 and that nearly 14 percent of independent workers were not paid at all, losing $8,000 on average (Massey 2010).

Since many freelancers are not consistently employed, late payment or outright nonpayment can mean the loss of months of living expenses, depletion of savings, and even bankruptcy. Since they are not employees, independent contractors do not benefit from the protections of the 2010 New York State Wage Theft Protection Act or from other employment laws that offer legal recourse to collect late or unpaid wages.[12] The only recourse for a freelancer is to document his or her case and take a client to small claims court (if owed less than $5,000) or to hire a lawyer, which can be quite costly.

The union created a multilayered campaign to address this problem. It proposed legislation that sets a two-month window for independent workers to get paid upon completion of a project and gives the New York State Department of Labor jurisdiction over businesses that violate work agreements with freelancers or fail to pay them within a reasonable amount of time.[13] The union estimates that the recovery and payment of unpaid wages to independent workers could generate up to $323 million annually in state tax revenue. In addition to this legislative proposal, the union's Unpaid Wages Campaign includes efforts to educate the public about the nonpayment problem; find solutions based on the "new mutualism" model—such as a Web-based roster of clients launched in 2011 that highlights "good" clients or those who pay late or not at all; engage members actively in the campaign, and build a coalition of support for the issue. The campaign has generated extensive media coverage and many members have actively lobbied for the bill.

The union also is exploring plans to promote employment security for independent workers. In order to avoid overburdening the existing unemployment insurance system, it is promoting "a parallel program allowing freelancers to set aside savings in a tax-advantaged account. . . . Freelancers could access these funds to pay for basic expenses such as health care, utilities, child care, or tuition during times of long-term unemployment" (Horowitz, Erickson, and Wuolo 2010, 10).[14]

Narratives about Freelancing

There are two competing narratives about the growth of white-collar freelancing. One blames corporate greed and restructuring while the other celebrates the independence of workers eager to escape the rigid constraints of corporate life. Whereas the latter narrative is prominent in the union's advertisements, when members talk about their own experiences they often invoke the former as well. One member told me: "I started freelancing full-time seven years ago when I was laid off. I wanted to take a break and detox from what was a very toxic situation. Insurance was my biggest concern then. I came across the Freelancers Union and started immediately as a member accessing their discounts. [Afterward] I didn't want to go back on staff unless it was for a job that is impossible: making a lot more money and leaving me alone to work where and how I wanted."[15]

It is common to hear members talk about being laid off from full-time jobs in the context of downsizing or restructuring. But many of these same workers embraced freelancing, citing more control over their careers, more flexibility, and greater choice and range of assignments (van Jaarsveld 2006, 356). "I became an independent worker after I was laid off from a full-time job. I had been freelancing on the side, and was then having to crash on a friend's couch while looking for an apartment with my new position," a member recalled, adding, "I love that freelancing gives me flexibility, and the chance to be creative. I know people who don't like what they do, but I have never felt that way."[16] Although many long to return to the security of full-time work and benefits, 81 percent of respondents to a 2011 union survey say they prefer freelancing because of the lifestyle.[17] The top five reasons freelancers say they prefer freelancing are flexibility of schedule, diversity of projects, freedom from office politics, creative control, and the potential to earn more money (Horowitz, Erickson, and Wuolo 2010). Some freelancers note that with nonstandard arrangements, they are not subject to unpaid overtime; instead their hourly rates better approximate their investments.[18] Others favorably compare the benefits of their lifestyle, with stories of insecurity in full-time positions, unbearable office politics, and unreasonable employer expectations. As contract workers, freelancers can create a "dispassionate distance" between themselves and the negative aspects of office life, a distance based on their short-term commitment (Osnowitz 2010, 109).

Whether their work arrangements are freely chosen or not, freelancers face constant uncertainty and often refer to cycles of "feast and famine." Their level of insecurity varies by sector and occupation, as well as by the extent and viability of the networks through which they find work. There are also wide disparities in freelancer wage levels, even within a given occupation. For instance, one study found that writers and editors reported fees as low as $15 per hour and as high as $95 per hour, and wage differentials among computer programmers and engineers of as much as $150 per hour (Osnowitz 2010, 39).

The union collects limited data on its membership. For instance, race and educational attainment data are not available. As mentioned earlier, 66 percent of the membership work as independent contractors or consultants. The next largest work category for members is full-time work (14%). The rest of the union's membership is part-time (7%), temporary (6%), contract (4%), and on-call (3%). The union's data reveal a roughly equal gender breakdown in membership (53% men and 48% women). Thirty-six percent of union members are in their thirties, 23 percent in their forties, and 23 percent in their fifties. The data also indicate that approximately 58 percent of its membership earns $49,999 or less annually, as figure 7.1 shows. Members are employed in a wide variety of fields, as table 7.2 in the appendix to this chapter documents.

When staffers talk about members, they are often hesitant to generalize and prefer to describe them simply as diverse. Members' self-described industries spread widely. One staffer described them this way: "Diverse. We have lots of twentysomething graphic designers and lots of very savvy freelancers in their fifties and sixties. What they all have in common is that they feel like they've been going at it alone. They are independent and outspoken advocates for themselves. They like to maintain their independent identities."[19] The staff celebrates diversity as beneficial to the union, but it also makes building solidarity and a freelancer identity more difficult. "Our membership overall is so diverse," one staffer noted. "Beyond these differences, we are all looking at the same challenges and this makes the vision powerful."[20]

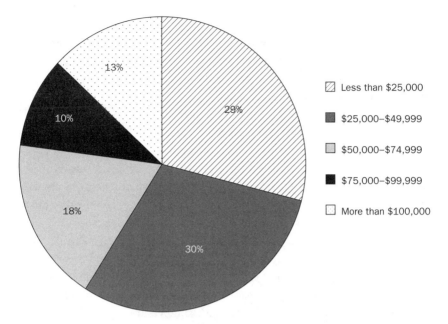

FIGURE 7.1   **Freelancers Union membership by annual income, 2012.**

Data from Freelancers Union internal surveys, 2012.

Barriers to Organizing Freelancers

Although many freelancers are precariously employed and hold concerns that could be addressed by collective action, research has found that for many independent professionals and creative class workers traditional labor unions are anathema. In addition, some argue that nonstandard work arrangements undermine the opportunity for workers to act collectively (Kalleberg 2011, 76). Previous research has found that freelancers generally have high levels of mobility, satisfactory working conditions, and a strong culture of individualism, all of which tend to make union mobilization unlikely (van Jaarsveld 2004, 364, 366). Compounding these factors, independent workers often work alone or at home, so that they have few opportunities to build rapport and community with colleagues; and their working conditions are not subject to public scrutiny.

Freelancers' clients are often seen as customers, and many view customer service as fundamental to their success. They therefore tend to avoid overt conflict or any expression of anger or frustration. "Conflict avoidance," Debra Osnowitz (2010, 181) writes in her ethnographic analysis of freelancers' work, "is one component of a contractor's expertise." This contrasts sharply with the adversarial tradition associated with unions and other traditional workers' organizations; indeed, Osnowitz's informants were wary of all forms of collective governance. Some conceded that a professional organization might enhance the legitimacy of freelancing, but they did not want to lose their autonomy and control over their work decisions.

Laurie Milton's study of the attitudes of high-tech contract workers toward labor unions, similarly, reveals barriers to collective organizing. Her informants felt that they already had a voice at work and reported a high sense of individual self-efficacy in negotiating their employment conditions. They viewed labor unions as unduly adversarial and a potential threat to their autonomy and creativity, and feared unionization would undermine their ability to be recognized for their individual merits (Milton 2003).

More generally, the basic characteristics of the "creative class" (Florida 2002) present challenges for organizations like the union. Accustomed to strict self-discipline and long hours, freelance professionals, especially those in the creative industries, are deeply devoted to their work and take great pride in their expertise (Gill and Pratt 2008, 14). Most value flexibility and the lifestyle associated with independent contracting, which they experience as empowering rather than oppressive. Successful freelancers can pick and choose the jobs they take, and often can command high fees for their skills (Pofeldt 2011); in this context, the appeal of collective action and organizing is limited at best.

Despite all this, the union has managed to attract many freelancers (including highly educated creative professionals) who reject the view that unionism is incompatible with freelancing. Before Working Today launched the union, it conducted focus groups and market tests of the words "union," "association," and "guild," and found that having "union" in the organization's title was very popular among participants.[21] Further evidence of members' receptivity to collective organizing is that nearly half (49%) of the union's members also belong to other professional or union organizations that represent specific occupational groups, such as the Authors' Guild, the Editorial Freelancers Association, the Graphic Artists Guild, the International Alliance of Theatrical Stage Employees, and the National Writers Union.

Members at monthly meetings—to be sure, a highly self-selected group—are especially enthusiastic about collective action. "I'm into union solidarity," one member declared. "The more of us that participate, the more power we will all have." Another said, "I first came to Freelancers Union for health insurance and to try to reform the status quo. We need to band together; otherwise the status quo continues."[22] Another member recounted his journey toward active involvement in the organization:

> Early on I went to a seminar on contracts and networking. I got more involved when I started working more from home. I would listen to WNYC and they had ads for the Freelancers Union, and I heard a news story three or four years ago on the UBT [Unincorporated Business Tax]. The Freelancers Union had successfully lobbied to get that repealed. I heard the story and thought that is really powerful and that was the beginning of my getting more involved. I felt the need to give back and contribute since I had decided to stay freelance for life.[23]

Many members embrace the slogan "1099 for Life," feeling a strong affinity for freelancing and finding it difficult to imagine returning to a full-time job.[24] "I'm just not cut out to be working in an office or, especially, a cubicle," a member who is a journalist and editor, explained, adding:

> I know some people who are the opposite: They can't take the haphazard pay and nonworking hours of a freelancer and need structure. I tell people the best thing about working at home is that I can work whenever I want. The worst thing? I can work whenever I want. But it would have to be an incredible job in a very stable publication (do they exist anymore?) to tempt me out of my apartment."[25]

Defining Characteristics of the Freelancers Union's Approach

Since under current U.S. labor law, independent contractors and self-employed individuals are not eligible for conventional forms of unionization and collective bargaining, the union has turned to alternative forms of organizing to improve the situation of freelancers. Its primary appeal has been making affordable health insurance and other benefits, which salaried professionals traditionally received from their employers, available through membership. Far from challenging the affinity of members for flexibility, this approach helps make it possible for them to thrive as independent workers.

As noted above, the union has three defining characteristics: (1) a self-sustaining business model, predicated on the revenue stream its health insurance company generates, that ensures its own organizational survival; (2) a "brand" that appeals to freelancers' identities and values; and (3) "new mutualism," which constructs a nonadversarial form of solidarity among members. I discuss each of these in more detail below.

Sustainability, Self-reliance, and Market Power

The union devoted its first ten years to creating a basis for organizational survival outside of traditional models of dues or foundation funding. Although it still raises some funds from philanthropies, the FIC earns enough revenue ($75 million gross in 2009) to fund most union staff and projects. This sets the union apart from most worker centers that are constantly struggling to raise funds (see Heckscher and Carre 2006; Fine 2006). Indeed, Horowitz states that her biggest accomplishment to date has been "figuring out how to pay for it,"[26] and she remains committed to figuring out the business model for the next form of unionism. Among the data the union considers in evaluating potential new strategies or organizing campaigns is whether they will generate a revenue stream.[27]

Staff often talk about the union as a social enterprise, stating "We are not a charity"; "We focus on the triple bottom line";[28] and "We need revenue to build power and sustainability." For Horowitz, social enterprise is rooted in a long-standing labor tradition of institution-building. She likens her focus to the work of American Federation of Labor leader Samuel Gompers a century ago, when he pioneered the development of strike funds and was criticized for it. "Today's labor movement should focus on its past successes in entrepreneurship and sustainability," Horowitz said. "When labor was building its own institutions, it had more power." Horowitz believes tapping into sustainable revenue is key to the long-term sustainability of the labor movement. "In 1994, the AFL-CIO raised $100 million from a credit card," she notes. "Their credit card is what allows them to operate in the black. These are things we have to look at. . . . The labor movement needs a new sustainability model."[29]

The Freelancer Union Brand and Identity

The union claimed 175,000 members in 2012. Critics and supporters alike agree that this high number reflects the low barriers to membership. Anyone who enters their contact information on the union's website and clicks on an e-mail to affirm membership is a member; there are no eligibility requirements or dues, and the organization is open to those who belong to a conventional union for collective bargaining purposes or health insurance (as is often the case for members in the film, television, and entertainment industries). Apart from its accessibility, the large number of members it has attracted is a testament to the union's success in building a brand that resonates with many freelancer workers' sense of self-identity. It "confirms" the identity of its members as creative, entrepreneurial, independent, outside the box, and solution driven (see Milton 2003).

This identity is reflected in the ways in which Freelancers Union staff describe their membership, often citing fierce independence as a defining characteristic of freelancers. "They are the architects of the next safety net. They have to put together things to protect themselves," Horowitz observes. "They have to get out there and hustle . . . they are super savvy people."[30] The union's branding builds on its recognition of freelancers' core identity, and is regularly represented in its subway ads, online presence, and member materials. For example:

- A federation of the unaffiliated;
- Doing it without dues. (Not your grandpa's union.);
- Revolutionizing the rules of the game;
- Over 100,000 rebels with 1 cause;
- Help your country by helping yourself, be part of the new model of portable benefits;
- A constituency of free spirits large enough to count;
- Cynics may shake their heads, but cynics don't really do much anyway;
- There is an I in union. Be a squeaky wheel.[31]

The union's advertisements are overwhelmingly positive and reflect a love of one's work, upholding freelancing as a source of pride. Their most recent tote bags, distributed to PAC donors giving more than $50, read, "Meet someone who loves their boss." Many of their advertisements blend these characteristics. Some of the following reflect the Union's identity as savvy, intellectual, unique, and proud:

- Who knew something as practical as buying health insurance could help do something as noble as shaping the future of health care;
- Become a practical revolutionary;
- Working for the radical notion of fairness;
- All that we want is a fair shake. If that makes us idealists, well, we've been called worse;
- Working together turns individual kvetching into collective problem solving; and,
- Listening, improving and other gerunds.

A young staff, many of whom freelanced at some point in time, and an organizational culture that borrows heavily from the high-tech sector, further contribute to the brand. Staff speak about the entrepreneurial nature of the organization and strive to avoid becoming rigid or bureaucratic. The union's brand thus challenges the conventional wisdom that workers join unions purely to improve the terms and conditions of their employment. Instead, it embraces its members' values and identities, in part by integrating members themselves into the organization's leadership.

The "New Mutualism"

Charles Heckscher, former union board member and sociologist, sees the organization as pioneering what he calls "associational unionism." He comments, "Craft unions built communities of occupation; industrial unions built communities, albeit much weaker ones, around the companies and industries they represented. An 'associational union' which encourages flexibility and mobility, and which involves a very diverse set of organizations, can't rely on either of those" (Heckscher 2001, 18–19). Instead, the union's associational unionism is predicated on what Horowitz calls "new mutualism." As the union's literature articulates it:

> Underpinning the philosophy of new mutualism is the belief that political and economic life flourishes in social networks, and that social change requires individuals to shift their thinking from "I" to "We." At the core of this new movement is a culture of interdependence, mutual support, and affinity, with building sustainability, rather than maximizing short-term profit, as a goal.[32]

This approach, unlike craft or industrial unionism, is nonadversarial in relation to both employers and government. Paradoxically, it combines working together in social networks or communities and an ethos of self-reliance. The FIC is a good example: A group of freelancers have come together to buy their own affordable health insurance plan. More generally, new mutualism involves building sustainable, market-oriented models that offer collective solutions to people's problems, effectively meeting their needs and desires. In this regard, Horowitz and other staff see their organization as similar to other groups that are dedicated to collaborative consumption or production, from collective online projects like Wikipedia or online marketplaces like Craigslist and Etsy; groups building financial resources like Kickstarter and microfinance; companies offering shared office space like LooseCubes or cars like ZipCar; to food and workplace cooperatives. In their view, new mutualism is developing organically in the context of a transformed society in which neither employers nor government adequately provide security or basic social protections.

The union has identified six core elements of new mutualism:

Sustainability. New mutualist strategies ideally have a self-sustaining revenue model and "all resources generated by the community must be invested in or returned to the community [in the short or long-term]."

Independence. Organizations must be independent of state and market institutions and instead driven by the needs of membership.

Leadership. The leadership of new mutualist strategies is membership-driven, accountable to the short- and long-term needs of the community, and able to build trust, affinity, and solidarity.

Associational power. New mutualism means using the collective strength of supporters to advocate for the group, influence political change, and provide benefits and services to the group.

Mutual exchange. Another key element is that strategies must be "structured to encourage cooperation and exchange among their members, with the aim of producing collective benefits that far outweigh returns for rational exchange." New mutualism cannot occur without social networks and community, but exchanges also reinforce social ties and promote community building.

Affinity. Finally, members must feel a group affinity, which could be based on risk sharing, solidarity, collective identity, or mutual interdependence. Individuals' affinity for the group allows people to connect self-interest to a common group interest.[33]

Future Challenges

In conclusion, I will briefly highlight the directions in which the organization is moving and the future challenges it must confront. The union's recent efforts have increasingly focused on member organizing and leadership development, both in face-to-face interactions and by means of a new online platform for new mutualist member activities. One challenge this raises is developing member-based, democratic decision-making processes in what began as a staff-driven organization. The union is also exploring why members join and developing strategies to engage them more actively. In 2001, Heckscher warned of the risk that the organization might become purely a deliverer of services. "Working Today provides no special value in this arena [health insurance] unless it also brings a reputation for concern about the interests of its members as employees," he wrote. "It has to create more than an economically self-interested bond; members have to see themselves as part of a larger community with a sense of shared values and interests" (Heckscher 2001, 17). The union's branding of a proud, positive freelancer identity has done much to bring freelancers together; indeed, the majority (89%) of respondents to a 2011 union survey see themselves as freelancers. To what extent this identity will contribute to collective action remains to be seen, however.

Another challenge is the tension between the union's open membership and its more sharply defined freelancer identity. The union's vision for membership is that nearly all workers might become members at some time in their lives; but the brand it has developed seems to appeal primarily to highly educated, better-paid, creative and professional workers. The majority of the forty-two million contingent workers in the United States do not fit this profile, and the union hopes to recruit more of them as its membership grows.

The union is also seeking more influence and impact in regions outside of New York. It plans to start health insurance plans in other states as well as an online platform that will facilitate "new mutualist" member-to-member organizing on a national basis and in other individual states. If these expansion efforts succeed, the union will likely face internal challenges associated with orienting an expanding staff to its mission and strategies and capturing the active investments of a wider swath of members.

I have argued that three key features define the union: financial self-reliance, an organizational brand that matches its membership's identity, and the new mutualist philosophy that encourages solidarity among members. All three would appear to be replicable and all three hold promise for other types of organizing efforts among the growing precariat. Indeed, the union's success offers valuable lessons for other groups interested in meeting the needs of twenty-first-century workers struggling to thrive in a deregulated, high-risk economy. At the very least, the union's history demonstrates the importance of organizational sustainability and of strengthening and reflecting the culture, aspirations, and identity of members. New mutualism, perhaps the most intriguing feature of the union's work, is still at an early stage of development, but it nevertheless suggests potential routes, borrowed from traditional unionism's origins in mutual aid, to sharing resources and building power among the rapidly growing ranks of precarious workers.

Appendix: Freelancers Union membership by industry, 2012

TABLE 7.2

INDUSTRY	PERCENTAGE OF TOTAL MEMBERSHIP
Film/television	10
Advertising	5
Graphic design	4
Health care/hospitals	4
Information technology/computer	4
Journalism/writing	4
Education/training	4
Fashion	4
Financial services	3
Visual arts	3
Nonprofit	3
Internet	3
Performing arts	3
Photography	3
Publishing/information services	2
Music/radio	2
Marketing	2
Technology	2
Communications	2
Fitness/wellness/alternative health care	2
Legal	2
Print media	2
Architecture	2
Construction/building	1
Theater	1
Restaurants/food service	1
Accounting	1
New media	1
Retail	1
Real estate	1
Decorative arts	1
Engineering	1
Electronic media	1
Administrative/clerical	1
Sales	1
Manufacturing	1

(continued)

TABLE 7.2   (continued)

INDUSTRY	PERCENTAGE OF TOTAL MEMBERSHIP
Government	1
Banking	1
Apparel/textiles	1
Social service	1
Domestic worker	1
Insurance	1
Pharmaceutical/biotechnology	1
Travel/hospitality/leisure	1
Telecommunications	<1
Human resources	<1
Environmental services	<1
Transportation	<1
Automotive	<1
Sports	<1
Market research	<1
Photojournalism	<1
Staffing/outsourcing	<1
Utilities/energy	<1
Textile	<1

Source: Freelancers Union internal surveys, 2012.

Part III

IMMIGRANT STRUGGLES FOR JUSTICE IN AND BEYOND THE WORKPLACE

8

THE HIGH-TOUCH MODEL

Make the Road New York's Participatory
Approach to Immigrant Organizing

Jane McAlevey

The room went uncharacteristically silent after the two leaders in the front of the room, Amador Rivas and Augusto Fernandez, posed the question, "What do you think it means?" The leaders seemed at ease with the nervous looks and fidgeting that often accompanies silence in a large group. Then, from the back of the room, a commanding voice boomed out, "I think it means us. We are the ones who are an army of the good. Every day we fight to hold politicians and bosses accountable for the wrongs they inflict on our community." A round of applause and head-bobbing followed, signaling that the woman in the back of the room was speaking for everyone.

The scene was a Trabajadores en Accion (Workers in Action) meeting at the Bushwick office of Make the Road New York (MRNY).[1] Over fifty people were present for this gathering, a weekly event where MRNY members and prospective members meet to analyze the previous week's activities and plan future actions. The prompt that led first to silence and then to reflection asked those at the meeting to interpret the meaning of a quotation from former Dominican Republic president Juan Bosch, "No hay arma más potente que la verdad en los manos de los buenos" (There is no weapon more powerful than the truth in the hands of the good).[2] Such prompts are a regular feature of MRNY's public meetings, which are conducted in Spanish. First, everyone present introduces themselves, stating whether they are first-time visitors or members (and if so, how long they have been part of MRNY). Then the leaders open the discussion with a prompt designed to spark discussion that everyone can participate in—longstanding members and newcomers, old and young, men and women. The prompt is also intended to ensure that the meeting agenda includes a "big picture" question along with minutia like who will sign up for leafleting (a key form of outreach for MRNY) in the coming week, evaluating what did and didn't work at the last big public event or direct action, or who will volunteer to cook for the next meeting.

MRNY is the largest nonunion membership organization of immigrants in New York City, with over fourteen thousand dues-paying members, about one hundred full-time staff, and an annual budget of over $10 million.[3] Membership requirements include a one-time dues payment of $100 for those members over twenty-one years of age.[4] Members who have paid their dues can participate in meetings. To become a voting member and to take advantage of MRNY's legal services and English-as-a-Second-Language classes—which also include political education and leadership skills—requires a higher threshold, namely attendance at two meetings a month. In addition, all voting members must participate in a series of workshops during their first year in the organization. Workshop topics include "Understanding Sexism," "LGBTQ Tolerance," education on each issue area in the organization, and a session on effective recruitment. (This last workshop is crucially important, since MRNY members do most of the recruitment of new members.)

MRNY was formed in 2007 when two organizations—Make the Road by Walking and the Latin American Integration Center—agreed on a merger. Make the Road by Walking had been founded in 1998 by Andrew Friedman and Oona Chatterjee to advocate for immigrant welfare recipients in Brooklyn. Friedman and Chatterjee met as law students at New York University, and both were frustrated by the idea of legal work that involved defending poor people one at a time. "We thought if poor people had power, they would need fewer lawyers," Friedman recalled.[5] At the time of the merger, Make the Road by Walking had a $2.5 million dollar budget, forty-three full-time staff, and one office in Bushwick, Brooklyn.[6]

The Latin American Integration Center (LAIC) had been formed in 1992 by a group of Colombian immigrants in Jackson Heights, Queens, New York City's "La Pequeña Colombia," to promote mutual aid and citizenship assistance for Colombian and other Latin American immigrants. LAIC's founding director, Saramaria Archila, was a Colombian human rights attorney in Colombia who had fled her country in response to threats on her life by right-wing paramilitary forces. Upon arrival in New York, speaking no English and with professional credentials that were not recognized in the United States, she found herself cleaning houses like many Latina immigrants until she helped found and then became a paid staff member of LAIC.

In 2001, LAIC hired Saramaria's niece, Ana Maria Archila, to open a new office in Port Richmond, Staten Island. Archila had emigrated from Colombia in 1997 at age seventeen and joined the LAIC staff after she graduated from college. In Port Richmond, she organized citizenship and adult literacy classes; later she succeeded her aunt as LAIC's director when Saramaria died from cancer. In 2006, the year before the merger, LAIC had a $702,295 budget and a dozen full-time staff.[7]

MRNY has won a series of significant victories involving immigrants, poor people, and low-wage workers during a time when many other organizations were experiencing setbacks and defeats. In this chapter I document MRNY's work and explore the factors contributing to its growth and success.[8] One such factor is the favorable political environment of New York City, which has higher union density than any other major U.S. city (Milkman and Braslow 2011), an enduring social-democratic tradition rooted in its labor history (Freeman 2000), and a relatively immigrant-friendly political culture. These conditions make New York fertile ground for the kind of immigrant rights and worker rights organizing to which MRNY is dedicated. But these same conditions are also present for all the other organizations and campaigns documented in this volume, yet none can claim as strong a record of accomplishment as MRNY, which has amassed a larger staff and budget than any comparable organization in the city.

I identify three specific factors that have contributed to MRNY's extraordinary record of success. The first is an aspect of what Marshall Ganz (2000, 2009) calls strategic capacity. Among other things, Ganz emphasizes the importance of diverse leadership teams composed of highly motivated individuals, with access to salient information and relevant life experience and knowledge, for enabling social movement organizations to be successful in both quantitative and qualitative terms. MRNY has adopted a highly collaborative organizational model that reflects exactly this kind of approach, with "leaders who take part in regular, open and authoritative deliberation and are motivated by commitment to choices they participated in making and on which they have the autonomy to act" (Ganz 2000, 1017).

The second factor is MRNY's highly deliberative and participatory organizational style—referred to internally as a "high touch" process. Here I draw on Francesca Polletta's (2002) analysis of participatory democracy and prefigurative politics. Polletta particularly emphasizes the importance of *process* for strengthening internal solidarity and enhancing the political impact of social movements. As I document below, MRNY operates along lines very similar to the participatory democratic model she outlines. Moreover, efforts to win and enforce progressive change, whether through the courts, the ballot box, negotiated contracts, or legislative bodies, can only succeed in the long term when large numbers of ordinary people are participating at levels high enough to enable them to hold institutions accountable.

The third factor is the organization's multi-issue character. MRNY's strengths have enabled it to operate effectively on a range of issues, including but not limited to workplace justice. As MRNY deputy director Deborah Axt, an attorney and former union organizer, and MRNY founder Andrew Friedman have noted, "Make the Road differed from many worker centers in the breadth of issues it addressed that were not directly related to worker or workplace organizing, and in its broader use of in-house legal, education, and other services" (Axt and Friedman 2010, 577). A broad issue spread with open and democratic organizational structures helps increase motivation among leaders and members alike because different individuals will feel passionately about different issues.

I argue that MRNY is not an advocacy group but an "organizing organization." Advocacy groups (such as the Center for Constitutional Rights, the American Civil Liberties Union, or Greenpeace) campaign *on behalf of* some broad societal goal or *on behalf of* a constituency or constituencies, or both. By contrast, organizing organizations' members are central players in campaigns and have decision-making power in such key areas as hiring and firing staff, approving budgets, and deciding on the direction and priorities of the organization. Not only are members the central actors but they also understand that mass collective action is their *primary* source of leverage. And, crucially, the goal of an organizing organization is not simply to win specific legislation or material benefits, but to make long-term, structural changes in the power structure of the wider society, shifting the balance of power toward the organization's base constituency and away from the forces that oppress them.

My argument that MRNY is an organizing and not an advocacy organization takes issue with a widely cited analysis by former staff member Steve Jenkins (2002). Jenkins cited MRNY's early worker rights campaigns as examples of the difficulties that face advocacy organizations, and suggested that unions had greater ability to build effective worker leverage against employers and were therefore a superior organizational form. However, Jenkins ignored the fact that many unions engage in an equally leverage-less form of activity often called "hot shop organizing," which means organizing isolated workplaces in response to immediate worker discontent (rather than as part of a broader industry-wide or regional organizing strategy).

Jenkins's focus on the forms and sources of power that different types of organizations can deploy is very important, but I take issue with his claims about the superiority of traditional unions. I argue that what matters most is not whether a group is a formal labor union but instead whether the group's members are directly defining the changes they seek and whether their own exercise of collective action is the basis of their leverage. Union or nonunion organizations that fail to meticulously and accurately assess the power structure of their opposition will wind up losing. Jenkins does not acknowledge that most U.S. unions have long ceased to deploy their members in militant, collective action. As a result, on the ground many unions behave similarly to the advocacy organizations Jenkins criticizes.

MRNY tightly blends top-down strategic savvy and bottom-up mobilizing in its public campaigns. In addition, it continually strives to expand its membership base while encouraging high participation among existing members by providing vital survival services that are contingent on participation.[9] These efforts operate in synergy with MRNY's multi-issue spread, yielding results that often exceed the sum of the parts.

Among MRNY's many policy achievements are two outstanding examples that help to illustrate my argument. The first is the passage of the New York State Wage Theft Prevention Act in December 2010; the second is a successful multi-year campaign, ending in 2011, to pressure New York City and New York State to withdraw from the Secure Communities program promulgated by the federal Immigration and Customs Enforcement (ICE) to involve local and state law enforcement officials in deportations of unauthorized immigrants.

WAGE THEFT. MRNY has been active throughout its history in campaigns to rectify minimum wage and other workplace violations, winning over $25 million in settlements for back pay and wrongfully denied government benefits between 2007 and 2010 alone.[10] Frustrated by the slow pace of the legal process and the persistence of wage theft in the low-wage labor market despite the many highly publicized efforts to combat it, in early 2010 MRNY members decided, in committee meetings and eventually in a board meeting, to launch a campaign to strengthen the existing state law.[11] This gave rise to a successful coalition effort to pass the New York State Wage Theft Protection Act, which was signed into law in December 2010 and took effect on April 9, 2011.

The new law increases both criminal and civil penalties for minimum wage and overtime violations. Awards range from 25 percent to up to 100 percent of back wages, with additional penalties of up to $10,000 for employers who retaliate or threaten to retaliate against workers for complaining about wage theft. The new law also strengthens employer payroll record-keeping requirements and requires more detailed written notice to employees regarding pay rates and deductions than before, including a new provision that these notices must be in the employee's primary language. Although the latter provision may seem like a modest victory, its thrust is important for an organizing organization because it directly enhances the ability of ordinary workers to understand their employers' actions and also provides access to enforcement mechanisms similar to those in union contracts. By forcing employers to document pay rates and deductions in each paycheck in the native language of the employee, the law enables workers themselves—with assistance from MRNY staff in some cases—to fight back if the employer has cheated them out of the pay to which they are entitled. Thus the law "makes the hammer of reach and enforcement much bigger," as Axt put it in an interview. "Our members are really proud of this victory and are now involved in outreach and education to all sorts of organizations across the city who we are teaching how to use the new tools afforded by the law."

THE CAMPAIGN AGAINST THE "SECURE COMMUNITIES" PROGRAM
On November 22, 2011, Mayor Bloomberg—flanked by members of Make the Road—signed a city council measure ending the city's cooperation with federal ICE authorities. Unlike the Wage Theft Protection Act, which was developed and passed in less than a year, this campaign took years of careful work. "When we first decided to launch this campaign, everyone said, 'You are fucking crazy,'" recalled campaign leader and MRNY deputy director Javier Valdes, a longtime immigrant rights advocate formerly on the staff of the New York Immigration Coalition, New York City's main pro-immigrant coalition, formed in 1987 with over 200 member groups.

In early 2009, Peter Markowitz, director of the Immigrant Justice Center at Cardozo Law School and a trusted collaborator of MRNY, approached the group with a plan to challenge New York City's cooperation with ICE. Because this campaign idea did not originate directly from the base, MRNY staff conducted a membership survey to see whether the issue mattered enough to members to warrant a shift in organizational priorities.

In response, members described cases of family and friends being deported after arrests for minor infractions, and in some instances even when they were found innocent. At the time, Rikers Island prison officials were holding immigrants suspected of being undocumented for up to forty-eight hours after their scheduled release and turning them over to ICE officials to be "interviewed." This was during the heyday of the city's "Stop and Frisk" program, in which thousands of mostly black and Latino young men were stopped by the police. Between 2004 and 2008, over thirteen thousand undocumented immigrants had been shipped from Rikers to detention facilities outside of New York (Bernstein 2009). According to Valdes, Rikers officials were deceiving immigrants into thinking they were going to meet with an attorney about their case, rather than with an ICE official.[12] The interviews would begin with innocuous questions that were intentionally misleading, to encourage detainees to reveal how they had gotten to the United States. As the survey documented, MRNY members saw this as an urgent issue and this soon led to board approval for the campaign.

Along with the New Sanctuary Coalition and the Northern Manhattan Coalition for Immigrant Rights, MRNY demanded that Rikers Island officials be required to explain to immigrant detainees in very explicit terms that these "interviews" were *not* with friendly attorneys. In June 2009 the campaign scored its first victory when officials from the city's Department of Corrections agreed to provide a written form in multiple languages to every detainee at Rikers *before* the interviews, explaining that the interviewers would be ICE officials, and detailing what could result. Rikers officials were also required to get signed consent forms from any detainee before any such "interviews" could occur.

By February 2010, thirteen more groups had signed on to the campaign.[13] MRNY then successfully drove what had become a large coalition effort that eventually persuaded newly elected Governor Andrew Cuomo to announce in June 2011 that Secure Communities would not be implemented in New York State (Reddy 2011a). Six months later, on November 22, 2011, in a move that gave new meaning to Thanksgiving for many New York City immigrants, Mayor Bloomberg signed City Council Bill 656, which prohibits the Department of Corrections from using city funds to detain immigrants, effectively ending the city's collaboration with ICE.

Concurrent with the three-year-long Secure Communities campaign, MRNY also led several other successful efforts that had a significant impact on public policy. Among the results were the 2009 Language Access in Pharmacies Act requiring that three thousand chain pharmacies in New York City provide translation and interpretation services; the 2010 Multiple Dwellings Registration Act that strengthened enforcement of tenants' rights; Governor Cuomo's Executive Order #26, signed in fall 2011, extending to all of New York State an earlier MRNY victory requiring New York City agencies to provide interpretation and translation services; and the 2011 Student Safety Act, making the relationship between police actions involving students and in-house school discipline more transparent.

MRNY was active on many other fronts in this period as well. In 2010 the organization negotiated a settlement with the retail chain American Eagle over discrimination against transgender employees. That same year MRNY's Youth Empowerment Project successfully blocked a city plan to cut funding for subsidized student Metro Cards. And MRNY filled forty-two buses with protestors for the May 1, 2010, immigrant rights march in Washington, DC—the largest turnout of any single group in the nation.[14]

This list illustrates the wide range of issues in which MRNY directly engages. The organization's multi-issue agenda contributes to its strength and dynamism. Since leaders often develop new skills in the heat of battle, having multiple campaigns that address the interests of all the members not only generates multiple victories but also helps to expand the bench of leaders in the organization.

Strategic Capacity

How does Make the Road get so much accomplished? A large part of the answer hinges on what Ganz (2000) calls strategic capacity. As he argues, "A group is more likely to achieve positive outcomes if it develops effective strategy, and it is more likely to develop effective strategy if its leaders can access diverse sources of salient information, employ heuristic processes, and demonstrate deep motivation—their strategic capacity." He adds that strategic capacity varies with "leaders' life experience, networks, and repertoires, and organizations' deliberative process, resource flows, and accountability structures."

MRNY's five-member Strategic Leadership Team (SLT) includes three women (two are people of color, one of whom, Ana Maria Archila, is also an immigrant) and one male of color, Javier Valdes. Valdes was born in the United States but when he was three months old his parents' visas expired and the family, originally Argentinian, moved to Venezuela. Valdes returned to the United States at age eleven when his father, a civil engineer, was hired at Texas A&M—a job that allowed him to obtain permanent resident status. Archila and Valdes both went to college in the United States and both took jobs in progressive organizations soon after graduating. SLT member Oona Chatterjee was born in the United States to Indian immigrant parents. She was influenced by family stories about the fight for Indian independence; similarly Archila and Valdes were shaped by their parents' experience of fleeing repression in Latin America (in Colombia and Argentina, respectively). The other two SLT members, Andrew Friedman and Deborah Axt, are white and U.S. born; Friedman had politically progressive parents.[15]

All five SLT leaders are passionately devoted to their work, exemplifying another aspect of strategic capacity, namely motivation. Ganz (2000, 1014) argues "motivation is critical to creative output because of its effect on the focus the actors bring to their work, their ability to concentrate for extended periods of time, their persistence, their willingness to take risks, and their ability to sustain high energy," The following excerpts from interviews with SLT members illustrate their level of motivation:

> Friedman: "We lose before we even start if we remain risk-averse. We constantly take risks here!" (March 17, 2011)

> Archila: "I fell in love with the folks I was teaching and knew I was hooked." (February 18, 2011)

> Chatterjee: "We want to build power. We want to be consequential in everything we do and move the ball forward." (March 17, 2011)

> Axt: "We are not so good at slow, methodical approaches. This is both a strength and a weakness—we tend to go head-long into an effort." (April 7, 2011)

> Valdes: "It's a magical space here. The level of commitment to the cause, I have never experienced it anywhere as much as here—it's not just the leadership, it's everybody. Every member and all the staff know this institution matters." (November 28, 2011)

The relationships among and between just about everyone I observed start and end with respect for each other, both within the leadership team and between the leaders and MRNY members and staff. For Ganz, this combination is key to the success of organizations fighting for social and economic justice. The frequent use of the word love (Chatterjee, "We love each other here"; Valdes, "We are rooted in love and community here") reflects the deep commitment of the SLT to a highly participatory and equally diverse membership.

The full-time MRNY staff as a whole is also highly motivated, with a group of talented, accomplished organizers who work around the clock with extraordinary dedication. As table 8.1 (prepared as part of a grant proposal submitted

TABLE 8.1 **Make the Road New York staff, by gender, race, and ethnicity, 2011**

	Underrepresented racial and ethnic minorities		Total number of staff members	
	FEMALE	MALE	FEMALE	MALE
Board of directors/trustees	9	7	10	11
Professional staff	48	17	61	22
Support staff	8	3	8	3

Source: MRNY Proposal to the Ford Foundation, January 15, 2011 (copy in author's possession).

to the Ford Foundation) shows, the staff is also extremely diverse in terms of gender, race, and ethnicity.[16]

Participatory Democracy and Make the Road's "High Touch" Model

Polletta (2002) argues that participatory democracy strengthens social movements and their organizations. Among "people with little experience of routine politics, making decisions by consensus and rotating leadership has helped create a pool of activists capable of enforcing the gains made by this movement and launching new rounds of activism. Participatory democracy's potential benefits . . . cannot be reduced to 'personal' or 'cultural' changes. They go to the heart of political impact," she argues, adding: "Participatory democracy . . . can advance efforts to secure institutional political change . . . [and] can be strategic" (Polletta 2002, 2–3, 7).

MRNY has adopted a detailed and transparent decision-making process. Most SLT decisions are made by consensus. Outside of the SLT, rotating leadership is standard practice at meetings, and each MRNY committee defines for itself whether a super majority or simple majority vote is required. The MRNY "Decision-Making Authority" document (available to members in both Spanish and English) specifies in detail how people are chosen for every role and every sub-body in the organization, and specifies the authority embodied in each role and sub-body.[17]

MRNY has committees focused on key programmatic areas, including core issues that have long defined the organization's agenda such as immigrant rights, civil rights, affordable housing, workplace justice, and environmental justice, and more ad-hoc committees devoted to campaigns like those described above on Wage Theft and Secure Communities. Each MRNY member is involved in one or more of these programmatic committees, all of which hold weekly meetings concurrently at MRNY's four offices in Port Richmond, Staten Island; Bushwick, Brooklyn; Jackson Heights, Queens; and Brentwood, Long Island. As Javier Valdes explained, "The weekly meetings serve the same purpose as church, it's a ritual. . . . It's the same time, the same day, every week, in the same office." He added, "Having access to the membership so frequently provides a constant opportunity for growth and political education. The members all run the meetings and . . . spend time every week thinking about the agenda and about how to run an effective meeting."

Members actively participate in the process of hiring new staff, and are included on hiring committees and interview teams. After multiple and sometimes grueling interview rounds, finalists are asked to demonstrate their skills in front of members by either facilitating a meeting or running a workshop. As Sabrina Harewood, a twenty-year-old Afro-Caribbean member of the LGBT working group, explained, "We want to see the potential staff facilitate a meeting . . . we want to see how they respond to members' questions, if they can teach us anything new, and how they get along with people."

MRNY's "high touch" decision-making process is also illustrated by the Trabajadores en Accion meeting described at the beginning of this chapter. In 2009, as part of a comprehensive strategic planning process, MRNY adopted a new set of leadership-development protocols for both volunteer members and staff. Members who want to become leaders meet one-on-one with the organizers responsible for each programmatic area, and carry out a series of assignments (in this case, learning to run a large meeting). This is one of several prerequisites for running for election to the MRNY board of directors—a very active and hands-on board of directors, the majority of whose members are elected from the membership.

About two hours after the meeting began, Augusto, who was cochairing the meeting as part of such a leadership development assignment, asked for "*silencio*" and then approached each person in the room to ask them, "Que le gusta sobre este reunion and que no le gusta?" (What do you like about this meeting and what do you not like?) When he got to the third person, the front doors to the room opened and a few members began to carry in enormous pots of rice and beans.

The fragrant smell wafting through the room was a challenge for Augusto at this point—almost two hours after the meeting began—but he pressed on with his questions undeterred. The answers he got were all variations on a theme: People liked being able to participate in the discussion and having a clear agenda; what they didn't like was "that this meeting is going on too long, look—see— our dinner is here and we should be eating it." This exposed the time-intensive aspect of MRNY's "high touch," participatory decision-making process.

MRNY's self-understanding is predicated on the idea that its success depends on its ability to recruit, develop, mobilize, and retain members. In many respects, then, it exemplifies Polletta's model of participatory democracy. But the deep commitment to democratic practice and leadership development is also a source of tension and what Andrew Friedman refers to as "democracy fatigue," describing the more than thirteen regular weekly meetings—all of which require tremendous energy and attention. There is, according to Friedman, a dull but persistent discussion of the endless search for fewer and shorter meetings. But Javier Valdes (who would later replace Andrew as a co-executive director) and others involved in building MRNY's member participation program insist that any compromise in the highly participatory nature of the organization would weaken the organization's effectiveness.

Future Challenges

MRNY has its critics, as became apparent at a December 2011 press conference about the proposed New York State DREAM Act, where one youth group—the New York State Youth Leadership Council—accused Make the Road of insider politics and deal cutting.[18] MRNY leaders and some other groups in the coalition countered that the issue in contention (whether to support the New York State bill's limited expansion of state-based financial aid to undocumented youth) had already been resolved in previous meetings. When asked about such tensions in coalition politics, MRNY staff and leaders defend themselves with the claim that they put considerably more into coalitions than they get out of them.

Earlier in 2011, MRNY officially withdrew from the New York Immigration Coalition, a move that led some coalition members to accuse MRNY of arrogance and of being unwilling to share power with others. Yet at the December DREAM Act press conference, the New York Immigration Coalition defended MRNY against the youth group's accusations. MRNY's success does open it to the danger of becoming arrogant and isolated, as is the case for any group that quickly pulls ahead of its peers. Indeed, a similar dynamic emerged nationally when the rapid growth of the Service Employees International Union in recent decades outpaced that of many other unions.

The special burden of the most successful organizations across all sectors is to maintain their own momentum while exercising a kind of solidarity that lifts the floor of success across the entire progressive social movement spectrum.

Aside from such external accusations of insider dealings—accusations that typically arise when one organization gains considerably more power and therefore access to the power brokers than its counterparts— Jenkins's (2002) critique of MRNY as an advocacy organization that is limited in its ability to build worker power remains influential. One of his key claims is that reliance on foundation funding—which is characteristic of MRNY as well as other worker centers and community-based organizations for which dues income is limited— creates dependency on philanthropic elites that set strategic and tactical limits on the types of activities the organization can undertake. Jenkins contrasts this to the case of labor unions, which are funded almost exclusively by members' dues and thus enjoy more autonomy.

However, he all but ignores the fact that unions' strategic and tactical repertoires are also highly constrained by such mechanisms as the no-strike clauses in collective bargaining agreements, to which dues "checkoff"—the source of almost all union revenue—is tightly linked. In addition, unions have deep institutional ties to political and economic power-holders that limit their effectiveness. The SEIU, where Jenkins now works, has at times limited the options available to its members by signing organizing rights accords with employers, some of which mandate that the union must stand down on legislation, organizing, bargaining, and other forms of activism in the name of targeted base expansion (McAlevey and Ostertag 2012). In addition, many union leaders restrain their own rank-and-file members and leaders from engaging in direct action, based on strategic decisions that involve cooperation with key employers. This parallels the constraints faced by groups dependent on foundation support that Jenkins highlights. Risk aversion and a lack of faith in the intelligence of ordinary people are the key issues here, for unions and other types of worker organizations alike.

Jenkins's argument that unions are the superior organizational form becomes even more problematic in the context of the contingent labor force and the informal economy, which includes a rapidly growing number of workers who are excluded from the laws governing collective bargaining and for whom developing alternatives to traditional unionism is urgent. As MRNY's Deborah Axt states, "We are trying to fill in the holes of what a collective bargaining agreement can get workers, for the workers who don't have a collective bargaining agreement. For the many workers in the informal economy, we are trying to put as many pieces together as we can to offer protections as if they had a contract." Moreover, MRNY is doing something that many unions that are parties to collective agreements fail to do, namely keeping their membership base active and engaged and therefore *able to enforce the agreement*.

Hard-won union contracts are enormously important, but they are only effective if the membership is sufficiently organized to enforce them through mobilization and legal action. That can also occur in nonunion organizations, as exemplified by the rule making in the Wage Theft Prevention Act described above. Like union contracts, such legislation demands enforcement by a base of actively engaged people, informed by an accurate power structure analysis. Workers' leverage is not a function of the type of organization they form, but rather of the skill of the leaders and the extent of the active participation of the members.

The high participation nature of MRNY's "high touch" model separates it from most unions and from the many advocacy groups in which "membership" is nothing more than subscribership. MRNY's ability to engage its members in active civic participation is palpable at legislative hearings, on street corners and marches, in the forty-two buses they sent to Washington, DC to demand immigration reform, and at its many press conferences. In these and other set-tings, the words and actions of organic members of the community not only move foundations to write checks but also inspire the mainstream media to write stories highlighting key issues and sometimes even win concessions from employers and the state.

Ten years after Jenkins published his critique, he clarified his views in an interview:

> I was writing for a world where unions are either ignored or reviled and where the most basic market analysis that a first-year union researcher would undertake was ignored in favor of proclamations about the power of oppressed workers. And if I criticized MRNY, it was simply because I worked there and thought that was the most honest and effec-tive way to make the point I was making. In actuality, they would have been at the bottom of the list of organizations to go after, as they under-stand these dynamics and struggle with them every day.[19]

It is true that MRNY has not had to confront the kind of opposition that *or-ganizing* unions routinely face. However, such unions are themselves a rare phe-nomenon within the twenty-first-century labor movement, which includes many "do-nothing" unions (Lopez 2004) that at best engage in defensive strug-gles. Relatively few unions are actively organizing the unorganized. Those that attempt to do so often face fierce resistance from employers, who routinely threaten workers with loss of their livelihood, divide them along racial and ethnic lines, and more. But such opposition is by no means limited to unions. Any organizing organization that is seriously contending for power faces formi-dable threats. Immigrants (including many MRNY members) regularly con-front livelihood-threatening measures, such as the threat of deportation. People of color routinely encounter police brutality, disenfranchisement, and mass in-carceration.

Like most successful organizations, MRNY's pace is so frenetic that its leaders barely have time to ponder the urgent questions embedded in Jenkins's critique: Ultimately, what forms of power can the organization exercise, why, and how? Andrew Friedman poses a key question: "We are having some successes, but is it enough? Can we be doing things better? Are we doing well compared to other groups or compared to what needs to get done?" MRNY has yet to successfully engage in electoral politics, limiting its ability to influence city and state policy-making. But its large and highly participatory base, strategic savvy, multi-issue spread, and impressive track record position the organization well to take on this challenge and to escalate to still higher levels of effectiveness.

9

BRIDGING CITY TRENCHES

The New York Civic Participation Project

Stephen McFarland

On a brisk and bright Saturday morning in early fall 2011, members of the Washington Heights Neighborhood Committee of the New York Civic Participation Project (NYCPP) set up for their annual Back-to-School Education Fair. A block is closed to traffic just east of Broadway alongside an elementary school in this mostly Dominican neighborhood, with bright balloons moored to the police sawhorses. The event has been a central focus of the group's monthly committee meetings all summer, and it is finally coming together. NYCPP's staff organizer for the neighborhood resigned just a few weeks before and has not yet been replaced, but the committee members are not at a loss as to how to conduct the event. They erect canopies and tables with leaflets in Spanish and English with information on topics such as education; diabetes, obesity, and asthma; voter registration and redistricting; upcoming meetings and rallies; and NYCPP itself. A woman opens a large cardboard box and starts handing out oversized T-shirts in NYCPP's trademark orange, marking the occasion with the date and their slogan "¡Sí se puede!" emblazoned on the front. She calls out the names of those who are slow to gather round. The orange-clad members gather for a photo, then fan out to greet passersby on either end of the block, and set up tables for free school supplies, health insurance information, and after-school tutoring. The DJ sets up his sound system, and soon bachata and merengue rhythms fill the air. Children line up for facepainting, and tigers, clowns, and spidermen trickle out of the tent, rejoining parents who now grip flyers and pamphlets. An elderly woman shuffling down the street with her younger relatives comes alive as she draws near to the DJ, swaying and bouncing to the music with a grave smile, one hand on her cane and the other pointed to the sky. She draws the merry attention of the crowd and not a few dance partners. Word goes round in Spanish—"She's 95!" By lunchtime, news has spread of the Mangu Festival put on by the tenants' organization Mirabal Sisters Cultural and Community Center in a schoolyard a few blocks away, and some NYCPP members walked over there for the Dominican specialty of mashed green plantains, passing a health fair put together by Columbia Presbyterian Hospital. It is a busy day for community organizations in Washington Heights.

The New York Civic Participation Project is an initiative created by a partner-ship of New York City labor unions and community-based organizations (CBOs) in 2002 to engage union members in local community organizing. It was incor-porated in 2004 as a project of the newly created nonprofit La Fuente (which means The Source in Spanish). Since then, NYCPP itself often has been referred to as La Fuente; the two names are used interchangeably here. Since its founding, NYCPP has developed neighborhood committees composed primarily of Latino members in Washington Heights, Queens, and the South Bronx, and created the Long Island Civic Participation Project in Hempstead, Long Island. NYCPP has engaged in organizing and advocacy at the neighborhood, city, state, and national levels around issues such as immigrants' rights, language access to public institutions, education reform, public health, and green space. It also aims to address historically low levels of political participation by Latinos and other recent immigrants in the United States (see Jones-Correa 1998; Wong 2006).

In addition to promoting civic participation and leadership development among its members, La Fuente is committed to building labor-community con-nections. In this regard, it constitutes an effort to bridge the long-standing split—famously analyzed by Ira Katznelson in his 1981 book *City Trenches*—in American workers' consciousness: the divide between workplace politics and community/ethnic politics. In what follows, I explore the work of La Fuente in Washington Heights—the same Manhattan neighborhood that Katznelson ana-lyzed in the 1970s—to assess the extent to which the organization has succeeded in bridging those "trenches," in the context of the many changes that have taken place in New York City since the 1970s, and the growth of the immigrant popu-lation in particular. Although I find that the division that Katznelson identified is still present forty years after he conducted his study, it has been signifi-cantly weakened both by the work of La Fuente and by the survival strategies of working-class Latino immigrants who now make up the dominant group in Washington Heights.

Trenches and Bridges

Katznelson aimed to explain why the U.S. working class has been "uniquely militant as labor and virtually non-existent as a collectivity outside the workplace," and why U.S. urban politics developed not on the basis of class issues but instead as "essentially a system of ethnic bargaining and accommodation" (Katznelson 1981, 71). Building on the spatial separation of the workplace and the home that is a feature of all industrial societies, he argued that in the case of the United States, that separation assumed a unique form,

> governed by boundaries and rules that stress ethnicity, race, and territoriality, rather than class, and that emphasize the distribution of goods and services, while excluding questions of production or workplace relations. *The centerpiece of these rules has been the radical separation in people's consciousness, speech, and activity of the politics of work from the politics of community.*" (Katznelson 1981, 7, emphasis in original)

The "city trenches" that Katznelson highlights are the divisions between labor unions, the political party system, and government services provided at the community level (1981, 55). Historically, he points out, each of these emerged as a distinct arena of working-class politics in the United States: early unions disdained political participation while political parties operated at the neighborhood or ward level, and that historical legacy remains important. Unions, he argues, still focus mainly on workplace issues while both political participation and modern social services are organized at the neighborhood level, often on the basis of ethnic and racial affiliations. In the conclusion to his book Katznelson insists that "community-based strategies for social change in the United States cannot succeed unless they pay attention to . . . the split in the practical consciousness of American workers between the language and practice of a politics of work and those of a politics of community" (1981, 194).

He developed this analysis through a case study of Washington Heights, which when he conducted his research in the 1970s was home to a diverse multiracial population in which the Dominican immigrants that have made up a majority of the neighborhood's population since at least 1990 (Bergad 2008) were a relatively small presence. There were already about thirty thousand Dominicans in the area at the time Katznelson studied it in the early 1970s, the vast majority of whom were recent arrivals; at that time they made up only about 15 percent of the population of the Heights, which was also home to African Americans, Cubans and Puerto Ricans, as well as whites, who were mostly Jewish and Irish (see Katznelson 1981, 98–102, 242). Today Latino immigrants make up the bulk of the population of Washington Heights, and Dominicans are by far the largest nationality group, even with the recent gentrification of the neighborhood. The U.S. Census Bureau's American Community Survey estimated that 99,670 Dominicans, nearly half the total population (205,338), lived in the area of Washington Heights and Inwood in 2008.[1]

The neighborhood's population is not the only thing that has changed since the 1970s; the political economy of New York City and that of the nation have undergone enormous shifts in the intervening decades, of which immigration is but one notable feature. But for the purposes of this chapter, the key question is whether the system of "city trenches" Katznelson documented during the 1970s is still intact, given the sweeping changes that have affected Washington Heights since that time. More specifically, to what extent have the divisions between community and workplace organizing remained intact, and to what extent have they been bridged?

There are at least two reasons to think that the trenches in Washington Heights might be less salient today than they were when Katznelson studied the area. One involves immigration itself. Not only are there many noncitizens in the immigrant community, who are therefore largely excluded from electoral politics, but the fact that Latino working-class immigrants tend to have strong neighborhood-centered social networks and often find jobs for one another in the same workplaces may tend to break down the neighborhood-community divide. The second reason that one might expect the neighborhood to have changed in this respect is La Fuente, which emerged as a labor movement initiative and retains a strong connection to trade unions in the city, but focuses its organizing on immigrant civic participation and community organizing, including accessing government-provided social services. Indeed, La Fuente's mission is precisely to bridge the "city trenches" Katznelson wrote about, and Washington Heights is among the neighborhoods in which it is most active.

NYCPP's Origins and Development

NYCPP was conceived in 1999 with the goal of "developing a way for pro-immigrant unions in the city to work together and with key community allies to support pro-immigrant/pro worker policies which would help set the groundwork for future union organizing efforts in immigrant communities in the city" (Sadhwani and Fine 2007). Three years later, the organization was formally launched as a partnership between three influential New York City unions and two of its most vibrant community organizations. The unions were Local 32BJ of the Service Employees International Union (SEIU), District Council 37 of the American Federation of State, County and Municipal Employees (AFSCME), and Local 100 of what was then HERE (now part of the merged union UNITE HERE). Local 32BJ of SEIU has been the dominant union presence in NYCPP, however. The other NYCPP affiliates were the National Employment Law Project, and Make the Road by Walking, a community organization based in Bushwick, Brooklyn (now called Make the Road New York, see McAlevey, this volume). Initial funding came from a grant from an AFL-CIO fund for post-9/11 recovery.

NYCPP was premised on a critique of previous efforts to build union-community partnerships in New York City. According to Gouri Sadhwani, NYCPP's founding director, some unions had largely ignored the growing constituency of immigrant workers, and where partnerships with community groups existed, they tended to be top-down, with cooperation between the leadership of union and community groups, but with little direct engagement and collaboration at the base. They also tended to be transactional, with each organization participating based on calculation of gains to its own organization, rather than out of any broader vision of building power among immigrant workers. As Amy Sugimori, La Fuente's executive director from 2007 to 2011, and a founding advisory committee member, recalled:

> There were some examples of some positive interaction, but there were a lot more examples of mistrust, hostility, questioning on both sides, labor being dismissive of immigrant worker organizing, or immigrant community organizing, and immigrant community organizing being extremely mistrustful of labor to the point of seeming antiunion at times.[2]

NYCPP's founders drew inspiration from work that had been done in Los Angeles and elsewhere in the 1990s by worker centers and in service sector union organizing drives. Ann Bastian, an officer at the New World Foundation (a progressive organization that makes grants in the areas of education, the environment, civic participation, and labor organizing) played a vital role in envisioning NYCPP. She recalls the inception of the project:

> When we looked at how issues like the living wage were unfolding here, we asked "Why can't New York do better than this?" with all the density of labor unions and membership. What we saw was the decline and even absence of energetic connections between the unions and broader working class communities. . . . There were letterhead coalitions, but not deeper relationships or deeper commitments to each

other's issues. . . . We wanted to renew the labor-community-immigrant nexus in the City, to discuss new approaches, and draw from some of the national experience that was so much in advance of what was happening in New York. Early on, we identified the vast pool of the newest immigrant communities—3 million strong—that was virtually untapped in terms of labor organizing, in terms of progressive politics, certainly in terms of labor-community alliances. It was a really important task, in this period, for progressives in the labor movement to be forging genuine ties with these new communities.[3]

NYCPP was initially controversial among existing immigrant organizing and advocacy groups. Sadhwani recalls that several of the city's worker centers, including Domestic Workers United and the Committee Against Anti-Asian Violence, sent a letter to the founding partner organizations urging them not to go forward with plans for the project. The letter voiced concerns that NYCPP might undercut ongoing work by existing organizations; in Sadhwani's view this was motivated by a history of negative interactions with unions engaged in community organizing.[4]

NYCPP moved forward nevertheless, initially focusing its efforts on two working-class immigrant neighborhoods, Washington Heights and Bushwick, both of which were home to many members of the three union partners involved in NYCPP. Sugimori recalls:

We did some mapping, and the goal was high levels of union density, high immigrant population, working class population, and a place where there isn't already a lot of other [organizing] going on. [Washington Heights] was picked [because] it had an extremely high level of immigrant density, people of color, [and] language density.[5]

Bushwick was chosen as the other initial neighborhood largely due to the presence there of NYCPP partner Make the Road.

NYCPP organizers began their work by reaching out to residents on union partners' membership lists. A year later, a third neighborhood committee was formed in the South Bronx at the request of SEIU Local 32BJ members who lived there. Unlike the other neighborhood committees, the Bronx committee was not selected based on research, but proposed by Bronx residents who were familiar with NYCPP's work in Washington Heights, some of whom had been displaced from Upper Manhattan by rising rents. "The Bronx picked us. We did not pick the Bronx," Sadhwani recalls. "I will never forget the day they came into my office, and there were many of them, and they were as sweet as could be, but they were like, "Why aren't you doing this in the Bronx?"[6]

In 2005, NYCPP formed yet another committee in northwest Queens (including Jackson Heights, Woodside, Elmhurst, and Corona), another immigrant-dominated area. (Sadhwani 2007, 6). Sugimori recalls:

> The Queens committee was built up around a broader sort of nation-wide, citywide immigrants rights movement lens . . . It was also a more diverse committee in terms of national origin. It's still predominately Spanish-speaking. But there are some who are South Asian, and from other backgrounds, because the issues weren't so much about identity per se as about immigration status. And so that committee . . . had a different makeup: a smaller percentage of union members, a bigger percentage of people who identified more as immigrant community members, more mixed in terms of immigration status and more diverse in terms of national origin.[7]

Around the time the Queens committee formed, the one in Bushwick was disbanded because it seemed redundant given community partner Make the Road's presence in the neighborhood.[8]

In 2004, NYCPP incorporated as a 501(c)3 nonprofit organization under the name La Fuente: A Tri-State Worker & Community Fund, Inc. With this change, NYCPP became a project of La Fuente. La Fuente's staff as of 2011 consists of seven people: La Fuente's director, a director of organizing support, the NYCPP project director, three organizers (one for Queens, one for Washington Heights and the South Bronx together, and one for the Long Island Civic Participation Project), and an administrative assistant. The organization's budget as of 2009 was roughly $625,000, of which over half went to NYCPP (the Long Island Civic Participation Project is the other main recipient of these funds). Revenues come from a combination of sources, with one-third coming from foundations, one-third from unions, and one-third from an annual fund-raising event called Bridge Builders, in which unions and their contacts give donations. Support from 32BJ amounts to roughly 10 percent of the budget, and in addition 32BJ provides in-kind support such as office space at below market rent.

At the end of 2011, 835 people were NYCPP members, with 320 in Queens, 290 in Washington Heights, and 369 in the South Bronx. Among these were some two hundred "active members" as well as seventy-five "somewhat active members."[9] Union membership among NYCPP activists in 2007 ranged from 60 percent in Washington Heights to 80 percent in Queens to 90 percent in the South Bronx. Sussie Lozada, NYCPP director, estimates that 50 percent of NYCPP members are 32BJ members or their relatives;[10] the second largest union group is composed of members of the Locals 78 and 79 of the Laborers, which became La Fuente partners in 2009 and 2006, respectively.[11]

The neighborhood committees have engaged in a variety of campaigns over the years, including community-level campaigns for translation services in neighborhood institutions such as community boards and, in the case of the Washington Heights committee, Columbia-Presbyterian Hospital. Access to parks and green space has been another focus, along with struggles to keep local public library branches open, as well as local school reform campaigns.

NYCPP is also active in citywide coalitions such as the Coalition for Educational Justice and the Coalition for Muslim School Holidays (which advocates for the inclusion of Muslim holidays in the NYC public school calendar). Statewide, a key milestone for NYCPP was the campaign for immigrant driver's licenses, which, though ultimately thwarted, signaled a new level of political influence. "The driver's license campaign was what NYCPP really became known for," Evangeline Echeverria, La Fuente's director of organizing support, recalled. "We were able to . . . build a very broad coalition, were able to build some real political power. It was a huge, meaningful accomplishment for the community."[12]

At the national level, NYCPP has mobilized for comprehensive immigration reform, lobbying in Congress and participating in mass rallies and demonstrations such as the spring 2006 mass demonstrations for immigrant rights (Sadhwani and Fine 2007, 11). "We played a crucial role because we were able to connect with and speak to both worlds: the labor world and the community folks," Sadhwani recalls. "In New York, the immigrant rights groups didn't have the money that was needed to be able to have this kind of demonstration. So unions paid for it, and we helped facilitate that."[13]

The neighborhood committees typically meet monthly for two hours, with smaller meetings of committee leaders, subcommittees, and organizers occurring in the interim as needed. Neighborhood committee meetings I attended had between twenty and forty people. Meetings are social, with meals of stewed chicken, rice and peas, salad, and soda usually laid out thirty minutes before the meeting starts. Printed agendas are distributed in Spanish and in English, for the benefit of the small minority of one to three non-Spanish speakers that often attend. These participants usually sit close to a hired or volunteer simultaneous translator, who interprets the meeting into English in hushed tones. Headsets are also made available for this purpose, particularly at larger gatherings, but are often discarded due to static.

The agenda lists the items for discussion, alongside the names of the members who will be facilitating each item. Staff organizers take a hands-off approach to the meetings, encouraging members to present material and shepherd discussion. A welcome, introductions, and an icebreaker are usually the first orders of business. Attendees state their names as well as their affiliations with unions, churches, and other community groups. This ritual audibly manifests the links NYCPP seeks to make between unions and community groups. 32BJ is the most common affiliation claimed, and when enough 32BJ members are gathered the union's signature call and response "32? BJ!" chant will often resound.

The monthly meetings serve to update members on campaign developments and recent events and demonstrations, and give notice of upcoming events. They are an entry point for new members, who have the chance to meet existing members, find out about ongoing campaigns, and get a feel for the organization.

Major decisions about the strategic direction of the neighborhood committees are made in the Leadership Advisory Council, a group of three elected members from each neighborhood committee that meets with NYCCP staffers in the downtown office every few months. More specific decisions about local campaigns are made by subcommittees working with the neighborhood organizers.

The initial outreach that built the organization involved mailings and phone calls to union members in targeted neighborhoods. But most outreach is done by members, who organize social events, staff tables at local street fairs, and recruit friends, neighbors, and coworkers. Recruitment trainings during committee meetings give members the chance to role-play and reflect collectively on techniques and challenges involved in bringing new members into the organization. This is part of NYCPP's broader leadership development work, training members in the skills and building the confidence necessary to do things such as run a meeting, speak publicly, recruit new members and mobilize existing members, develop strategies, analyze the political and economic landscape, and make effective contact with politicians, officials, and journalists.

NYCPP's internal elections are another part of leadership development. Three members from each neighborhood committee are elected to serve on the Leadership Advisory Council on a rotating, staggered basis. In addition, one representative from each committee is elected to the Advisory Committee, a body that includes representatives from partner unions and community groups and gives broad guidance and suggestions to the organization. These member elections are seen as another way to build leadership, as candidates for the Leadership Advisory Council go through formal processes of nomination and make public statements of their aims and qualifications for the positions. In addition, NYCPP has convened an annual Leadership Development Institute since 2004. In 2011, 142 members of NYCPP and its partner organizations participated in the two daylong Institute training sessions, which follow a popular education model. Individual members gave presentations about successful NYCPP campaigns, and discussed tactics such as grassroots lobbying, mobilizing voters, community organizing, influencing mass media coverage, and pursuing legal remedies in small groups. Participants also analyzed capsule histories of previous movement struggles, drawing parallels and lessons for the present.

NYCPP's leadership development work, according to Amy Sugimori, is especially valued by its union partners, and particularly 32BJ, since it directly enhances the work these members do within their unions:

> For 32BJ, they have a real interest in increasing member engagement and in member leadership development. . . . If somebody was a bus captain for us [NYCPP], going to an immigration rally in DC, well, then they would probably be able to be a bus captain for the union in the future. [Those are] some very transferable skills. Or if somebody builds their confidence, becoming a public speaker, becomes really good at working with the press, great, then they can become a spokesperson.[14]

At the same time, the unions' political clout adds to the impact of NYCPP's community organizing. Sadhwani recalls:

> We began to tap into the institutional political power that the unions held and the relationship that they held with elected officials, and getting those relationships and using those relationships to work on issues that were beyond just the traditional issues that the unions would normally go to these people for. There's nothing funnier than watching [a] city councilperson's face when you go in there with a group of union members and they're actually not there to talk about their contract, or not there to talk about their workplace issues, but they're actually there to talk about their library, or about a hospital, or about language access, and they're all there with their union shirts, saying "as a union member, I know my union gives you money, I know my union helps elect you, and this is important to us."[15]

The 2008 economic crisis brought funding challenges for La Fuente, as it did for other groups in the nonprofit sector. Alongside this challenge, the immigrant rights movement that had burst into public view in 2006 had lost some of its momentum, and two of La Fuente's union partners, UNITE HERE Local 100 and AFSCME DC 37 had reduced their involvement in NYCPP. These developments prompted the organization to engage in a strategic planning process starting in 2010. Participants considered how large a network of union partners to include in the group's future work, and explored the possibility of narrowing their focus to concentrate entirely on work with 32BJ members. In the course of this planning process, Amy Sugimori left La Fuente for a job on the staff of 32BJ, and was replaced by Lucia Gomez as executive director. Ultimately the "visioning" document that resulted from this process did not change the previous union partnerships, but emphasized rebranding, an intense voter registration and get-out-the-vote endeavor, and renewed efforts to build youth leadership in neighborhoods where NYCPP was already active. Other goals highlighted in the document included enhanced recruiting efforts to expand membership, fund-raising, and bringing active members onto the board of directors.[16]

Washington Heights Then and Now

Since Ira Katznelson conducted his research in the 1970s, Washington Heights has been transformed in a variety of ways. Economic shifts in the city, a massive influx of Dominican and other Latino immigrants into the neighborhood, the emergence of Dominican political leadership at the city and state levels, the growth of nonprofit service organizations, and gentrification have all made their mark on the neighborhood. Do the observations and arguments Katznelson made about the Washington Heights of the 1970s hold for the neighborhood in the twenty-first century? Has the system of "city trenches" persisted despite the sweeping changes within the neighborhood? Has the division between neighborhood and workplace organizing that Katznelson highlighted broken down or has it been reproduced over the decades?

THE IMMIGRANT INFLUX. The single most striking change in Washington Heights in recent decades has been the influx of Latino immigrants and in particular the growth of the Dominican population. When Katznelson studied it, the Heights was a multiethnic neighborhood with significant numbers of African American, Jewish, and Irish residents. In 1970, East Washington Heights was already heavily Latino, with a growing population of Dominicans along with Puerto Ricans and Cubans (Katznelson 1981, 100). By 1990, thanks to a massive influx of immigrants—the bulk of them from the Dominican Republic—two of every three residents in the Washington Heights–Inwood neighborhood were Latino, and two-thirds of the Latinos were Dominican. By the turn of the century there were 116,000 Dominicans in the area, roughly four times the level in 1970. By 2005, Dominicans had become not only the dominant nationality among Latinos in the neighborhood (73%), but an absolute majority (53%) of all Washington Heights residents (Bergad 2008). A substantial second-generation Dominican population is now present, which has helped spur gains in income and educational attainment, as well as higher rates of English proficiency and citizenship (Bergad 2008; Hernandez and Rivera-Batiz 2003; Caro-Lopez and Limovic 2010).

The Dominican influx coincided with the erosion of New York City's manufacturing sector, so that the unskilled factory jobs that had employed so many earlier generations of immigrants were seldom available to Dominicans. As garment manufacturing and other light industry moved out of the city, Dominicans and other Latino immigrants moved into low-wage service jobs. A 1994 survey of Washington Heights found only 17.3 percent of Dominican respondents employed in manufacturing, with 48.6 percent classified as service workers (Duany 2008 [1994], 43). By 2006, 37.2 percent of Dominicans citywide were employed in the service sector, with 19 percent in production, transportation, and material moving, and others in white-collar fields (Limonic 2008). Many were also self-employed: a 1991 study found that Dominicans owned more than twenty thousand businesses in New York City, including bodegas, gypsy cabs, travel agencies, and restaurants (Duany 2008, 30; see also Jordan 1997).

As they moved into the service sector, Dominicans entered industries with strong unions, including 32BJ in building services but also 1199 in health care, which fought successfully in 1976–77 to unionize Columbia-Presbyterian Hospital, at the time the largest employer in Washington Heights. By the first decade of the twenty-first century, 28.4 percent of all Dominican-born workers in New York City were union members—slightly higher than the 25.1 percent average for all workers (Milkman and Braslow 2011, tables 3 and 4).

CITY TRENCHES TODAY. To what extent should Katznelson's observations about the city trenches dividing the politics of the workplace from the politics of the neighborhood be revised in light of the social and demographic changes that have taken place in Washington Heights since the 1970s? Two salient changes stand out. First, there is evidence that immigrant social networks and referral hiring among immigrants have generated increasing overlap in the social ties among neighbors and coworkers. Hernandez and Ortega's (2010) survey of Dominican residents of Manhattan and the Bronx in 2009 found that 63.5 percent of Manhattan respondents had Dominican coworkers. And as a union official explained, in the building services industry, referral hiring is pervasive: when a job opens, employers frequently ask workers if they know of anyone who would be suitable for the job.[17] The result is growing overlap between networks of coethnics in the workplace and in the neighborhood. Although no longitudinal data allows a systematic comparison of those networks today and in the period of Katznelson's study, it seems likely that the "trenches" have been at least partially bridged. Indeed, NYCPP's mission is precisely to fortify them by nurturing social ties that span the home and the workplace.

Second, the growing presence of undocumented and noncitizen workers who lack the right to vote complicates Katznelson's argument about the early achievement of white male suffrage as a feature of "American exceptionalism" and the weakness of labor and radical movements relative to western Europe, where the working class had to fight for the right to vote. Katznelson saw workers' incorporation into mainstream machine politics as an integral feature of the city trenches, undermining the potential for independent labor and political organizing around economic issues. This view is supported to a degree by the 2009 survey of Dominican residents of Manhattan and the Bronx referred to previously, in which 7.5 percent of respondents in both boroughs reported working for a political candidate as a volunteer or for pay, 8.2 percent reported contributing financially to a political campaign, and 14.3 percent indicated that they had contacted an elected official. A larger proportion of respondents, however, 20.6 percent, reported they had participated in a public debate, march, or political demonstration in their community (Hernandez and Ortega 2010, 16). The higher level of participation in marches and demonstrations as compared to more conventional forms of political participation suggests that today's immigrants are less likely to be drawn into the "trenches" of party politics than their predecessors. Even more suggestive, 88 percent of Dominican respondents to the 2009 survey agreed with the statement "Labor unions are important to protect workers" (Hernandez and Ortega 2010, 13).

Dominicans' robust social networks also are reflected in their high levels of civic participation. The number of Dominican organizations in Washington Heights grew from twelve in 1971 to over ninety by 1984 (Reynoso 2003), although this in large part reflected the growth of Dominican immigration over that time period. However, in apparent contradiction to the thesis of Robert Putnam (2000) that social capital and civic and political participation are declining in the United States, a recent survey (Reynoso 2003) of Dominicans in Washington Heights, the South Bronx, and Harlem found that 85 percent of respondents belonged to a formal organization or group. These included "educational" and "socio-cultural" groups as well as religious, sports, and professional organizations. Could it be that levels of civic participation are, contra Putnam's thesis, actually *on the rise* for Dominicans and other recent immigrants? Perhaps working-class immigrants, who depend heavily on social capital to find jobs, housing, child care, and financial support, are different from the U.S.-born population that Putnam focused on in his study. Immigrant social networks are much in evidence in Washington Heights, where Dominicans are not only putting down roots but also actively shaping the community and political life of their neighborhoods.

THE RISE OF NONPROFIT CBOS. When Katznelson conducted his research in the 1970s, city bureaucracies distributed a variety of services to neighborhood residents, but those residents had little input into how those bureaucracies operated. After the New York City fiscal crisis of 1975 and the deep social service cuts that followed (see Freeman 2000; Harvey 2007), nonprofit organizations entered the picture as contractors that administered city-funded social services on a contract basis, and foundation-supported community-based organizations also began to play a similar role (Marwell 2004; Kasinitz, Mollenkopf, and Waters 2004, 192). In Washington Heights, Alianza Dominicana/Dominican Alliance emerged as the "800 pound gorilla" of CBOs;[18] its $12 million annual budget and staff of 350 make it the largest social service nonprofit in the local area. Others include the Northern Manhattan Improvement Corporation, the Community Association of Progressive Dominicans, the Community League of the Heights, the Broadway Housing Communities, and the Dominican Women's Development Center.

Such service-based CBOs are the dominant players, but there are also groups that focus on community organizing and base building. Among the issues these groups address are education and housing. Struggles over schooling in the neighborhood include efforts in the early 1980s to establish bilingual education in the local schools (although later some of these were replaced by ESL programs), as well as new school construction and the hiring of Dominican teachers and administrators. Dominicans also won representation on the local school board, which would later pave the way to more influential political positions (see Reynoso 2003, 68; Jordan 1997). Tenants' rights organizations have been active in the neighborhood since the 1970s when Katznelson conducted his research; issues such as overcrowding, vermin, disrepair, and utility outages have continued to be the focus of housing activism ever since.[19] In the late 1990s and early 2000s, signs of gentrification began to emerge as well.[20] A quantitative study based on 2005 census data, however, found little evidence of displacement of Dominican residents (Bergad 2008). American Community Survey data show that the area's overall population declined between 2000 and 2010, which one would expect with gentrification. The Dominican population of Washington Heights/Inwood declined only modestly, however, from 52 percent of the total in 2000 to 48 percent in 2010 (Bergad 2008; U.S. Census Bureau 2012).

POLITICAL REPRESENTATION. The growth of the second-generation Dominican population, along with increasing naturalization among first-generation immigrants, laid the groundwork for growing immigrant political participation starting in the 1980s. Although many immigrants were noncitizens and thus unable to vote, this was somewhat counterbalanced by a strong cultural tradition of political engagement among Dominicans. As the saying goes, the Dominican Republic has two national pastimes: baseball and politics.[21] In regard to the latter, immigrants often remain deeply involved in homeland politics (Dominican-born U.S. citizens are permitted to vote in elections in the Dominican Republic). A 2009 survey suggests that the political interests of Dominican New Yorkers are nearly evenly split between the two countries, with 60.7 percent of respondents in Manhattan and the Bronx reporting an interest in the politics of the Dominican Republic, and 65.2 percent an interest in U.S. politics (Hernandez and Ortega 2010, 15). In recent years Dominicans in New York have become increasingly active in local and city politics. Noncitizens were authorized to vote in local school board elections from 1970 to 2003, and many Dominican immigrants in Washington Heights did so. More recently, in 2012, four city councilmembers engaged in a pilot project in participatory budgeting in which voting was permitted regardless of citizenship.

Those Dominicans (and other Latinos) who are eligible to vote in state and national elections in the United States have lower turnout rates than U.S.-born whites and African Americans, but their participation has grown over time. In November 2008, an estimated sixty-four thousand Dominicans (both immigrants and U.S.-born) voted in New York City, which was 41.3 percent of voting-age Dominican citizens. The city's Latino immigrants overall had a slightly higher (47.9%) turnout rate in this election, compared to 64.2 percent for U.S.-born whites (Mollenkopf 2011, table 2). As the literature on immigrant political participation suggests, this may reflect the fact that in New York, where voters are overwhelmingly Democratic, there are relatively few incentives to actively mobilize immigrant voters to turn out at the polls (Wong 2006; Jones-Correa 1998).

However, immigrants had more reason to become active in local elections in Washington Heights starting in the 1980s, when Dominican candidates began to run for positions in the neighborhood's Area Policy Board of the city's Community Development Agency, the local school board, and the Community Planning Board. As early as 1983, six Dominican candidates were elected to positions on Area Policy Board No. 12. By 1990, two Dominicans sat on Community School Board No. 6, and four on the neighborhood's Community Planning Board. Dominican political leaders also began to influence the local Democratic Party apparatus, beginning with the election of Julio Hernandez in 1985 as the city's first Dominican district leader, representing the 71st Assembly District within the Democratic Party structure.[22] In 1991, redistricting based on the 1990 census led to the creation of a Dominican-majority city council district, setting the stage for

Guillermo Linares's 1991 election as the first Dominican city council member. Five years later, Adriano Espaillat became the first Dominican member of the state Assembly (Jordan 1997). As of 2011, there are four Dominicans on the city council, and Guillermo Linares holds a seat in the state Senate.

NYCPP and "Urban Trenches" Reconsidered

The transformations in Washington Heights in recent decades, then, have been far-reaching and in some respects challenge Katznelson's "urban trenches" thesis positing a *"radical separation in people's consciousness, speech, and activity of the politics of work from the politics of community"* (1981, 7, emphasis in original). What difference has the work of NYCPP made here? The organization's stated mission is precisely to bring proimmigrant unions into collaboration with CBOs. The current NYCPP's mission statement reads in full:

> Our explicit theory of change is that base building, combined with leadership development of working-class community members and deep work in collaboration with partners, results in transformation. We contribute to social change by building bases of organized people in low-wage communities of color; helping members to develop their analysis and skills as leaders; collaborating deeply with other community-based organizations; *and bringing the power of unions into the communities where their members live.*
>
> Because low-wage communities of color are often pitted against each other, *we choose campaigns that help build a broader movement that unifies communities of color and builds a sense of solidarity across racial and ethnic barriers.* We see our work as part of a national and global struggle for justice; through educational programs and through campaign work we make connections between our campaigns and the civil rights and human rights movements in the US and at the global level. (emphasis added)

Some might argue that by creating a separate organization for their community work, the unions that founded NYCPP have reproduced rather than broken down the split between workplace and community consciousness that Katznelson highlighted.[23] However, NYCPP's intention is to bridge that divide, as board president and Local 32BJ SEIU secretary-treasurer Hector Figueroa explains:

> A lot of [our broader] social agenda, we try to develop it with partners, through NYCPP, or the Working Families Party, or Jobs with Justice—

these are the things we think we should be fighting for primarily with partners. And then we have [our own] distinctive political legislation or agenda—that is, to protect our contracts, our standards, our jobs—we try to [pursue] a lot of that through our union. . . . It's not a hard distinction. What [issues] give us an opportunity to go beyond ourselves, to look at the general interests of working people, as opposed to our distinct industrial interests? Our industrial interests we drive heavily through the [union's] political program and the more general interests we try to see if other people are interested and we work more in a coalition.[24]

By engaging members as union members and as community residents at the same time, NYCPP endeavors to bridge the divide between community life and work that Katznelson highlighted. Figueroa explains:

When you're working in this way, the members start to develop a different identity. They see themselves as being part of the union, but also part of an organization that fights for everybody in the neighborhood. And that's actually appropriate. The members are not seeing that they can only be union members. They are union members and they're activists and they're members of NYCPP, and some of them may belong to the Democratic Party or the Working Families Party or some other venue. They have to see themselves as leaders in the outside world, and not just exercising leadership through the union.[25]

The bridge metaphor is explicit in NYCPP's self-conception: the organization's annual fund-raising event is called "Bridge Builders"; presentations of NYCPP's work to new audiences often prominently feature a diagram of a bridge with "state and national networks" as towers and a span of "labor rights, civil rights, human rights, immigrant rights, and community access to resources" connecting the two anchors of "labor" and "community." The majority of NYCPP members are union members or their relatives, mostly from SEIU Local 32BJ. And the work of the neighborhood committees is a self-conscious effort to transcend the division between community and workplace.

NYCPP's mission statement also explicitly addresses another division highlighted in Katznelson's analysis, namely "the segmentation . . . dividing workers from each other along ethnic lines." On the other hand, NYCPP's decision to concentrate organizing among Latino communities, to conduct all meetings in Spanish, and to adopt the name La Fuente for its parent nonprofit, appears to reinforce rather than bridge ethnic divisions. But in fact NYCPP tries to simultaneously promote both what Putnam (2000) calls *bonding* social capital, or ties to the in-group, and *bridging* social capital, or ties connecting a given group to other groups or institutions. NYCPP's work aims to build bonding social capital based on local neighborhood networks and Latino identities, while also organizing across ethnic lines to build bridging social capital. An example is NYCPP's involvement in the Muslim School Holidays campaign. As Sugimori explains:

> We've been able to bring together our more established Latino grassroots leaderships with folks from different Muslim communities where we work, to start spreading that excitement about civic participation [. . . I]t's been really exciting to see this interest and willingness to work across language and culture, to see how much receptivity there has been. We've been mostly connecting with mosques, but instead of working just say with the Imam and saying "Hey, we're doing this as a policy campaign, you're leading, we're leading, let's get together," they've been willing to open up their membership so that members are getting involved in our committees, are getting involved in the mobilizations and the activities that we do in the workshops.[26]

NYCPP also participates in the Coalition for Educational Justice, a citywide coalition dedicated to progressive educational policy. These efforts suggest that, as O'Brien (2008) argues, ethnic and class identities need not be mutually exclusive, and that ethnically based organizing can reinforce broader solidarities.

Promoting civic participation is another key goal of NYCPP, as the organization's name suggests. From its founding NYCPP aimed to remedy the fact that "despite the significant immigrant population in the city, the direct voice of new immigrants remained very much silent in the public policy debates that were shaping the city's character" (Sadhwani 2007). Sugimori describes NYCPP's approach to promoting immigrant civic participation as follows:

> There are so many factors that create barriers or disincentives to participation, and we try to address a lot of them. . . . High up there is not seeing why it would be the best use of somebody's time. So for example, you're working two jobs and you have a family and you're super busy, and you don't have a lot of free time or money. Why would you get involved with an election, why would you even register to vote, let alone register others to vote or mobilize people to vote or care? Some of it is about cynicism. "It's a done deal, politicians are all corrupt, why should this have anything to do with me?" Some of it has to do with distrust of government: "They're just trying to deport us, they're just coming after us, I want to keep my head down. I don't want to get involved." Some of it is, "What do I have to offer? I have nothing to offer. I'm not a

leader. I'm just a person and I'm shy." Some of it is, "I don't speak English, so I just feel sort of disconnected from the process." Or some of it is, "I'm not a citizen, so I can't vote." So we start [by asking] "What do people care about? What might motivate somebody to want to get involved or get active?" . . . People start with the thing that "it's worth taking time out of my busy schedule to come to a meeting, because I really care about this." . . . [And then they] start to feel empowered, not like, "Oh, there's somebody who knows the answers, is gonna fix it for me," [but instead] "We've got to get together and figure out what the solutions are." We start meeting with elected officials, we realize the elected officials aren't brilliant geniuses compared to us, they're just people. You start . . . building confidence, and saying, "Hey, at least I can be a spokesperson." And also realizing there's a lot of spaces in which you can do it in your native language. . . . So it's thinking about how we can root things locally enough that people don't feel so disempowered, that it doesn't feel too difficult to get somewhere, that people don't feel like, "Oh, this is just a trap, and I'm going to get myself deported." . . . They start there, but we build out, and then it builds towards political power.[27]

In this manner, starting with local, winnable campaigns that members care about, NYCPP aims to create a culture of participation and overcome barriers to broader political engagement.

The language barrier illustrates NYCPP's approach. The organization has always conducted its meetings in Spanish, with simultaneous English translation, enabling monolingual Spanish immigrants to be fully engaged in the proceedings. In addition, NYCPP has led campaigns around language access to public institutions, with notable success in the 2005 translation campaign at Columbia-Presbyterian Hospital in Washington Heights. At that hospital, an estimated 70 percent of patients were not proficient in English, yet translation services were often "inadequate and sometimes nonexistent" (Sadhwani 2007). Along with other neighborhood groups, NYCPP's Washington Heights neighborhood committee conducted surveys and outreach on the issue, and brought public attention to it through demonstrations and other efforts to attract media coverage. NYCPP's union connections served well in this case, as SEIU 1199, which represented the workers at Columbia University Medical Center, provided crucial support for the campaign. More recently, NYCPP campaigned to insititute Spanish-language interpretation at community board meetings in the neighborhoods where it has committees. This effort succeeded in getting City Councilmember Ydanis Rodriguez to provide funding for interpretation in Community Board 12 in Washington

Heights on a trial basis, and in Queens Community Board 3, Councilmember Daniel Drumm has provided funding for NYCPP partner New Immigrant Community Empowerment to implement a pilot interpretation project at CB3 meetings. NYCPP director Sussie Lozada explains the origin of the campaign:

> We found out that people don't know what the Community Board [did], and others who knew didn't participate because of the language. We started the campaign because we found that the community board is the only [arm of city government] that people that are undocumented can be part of. In a few months we realized that this was an issue not only affecting the community board of [one] District but it was a general issue, a citywide issue.[28]

NYCPP's leadership development and skill-building work also contributes to overcoming barriers to civic participation. Among NYCPP members who responded to a 2009 Immigrant Civic Participation Survey, 73 percent had helped other immigrants become citizens in the previous year, compared to 31 percent of respondents nationwide (Scheie et al. 2009, 40). Respondents also reported personal growth in key areas of civic capacity, including "relationships with people from backgrounds different from mine, openness to feedback and self-improvement, [and] desire to listen to and understand people with different views from mine."

NYCPP also actively promotes voter registration through outreach in parks and at street fairs and in other public places. In 2011, NYCPP launched an ambitious get out the vote campaign. Also, in anticipation of redistricting on the basis of the 2010 census figures, NYCPP is actively organizing to keep community members informed about their stake in that process. But promoting voting is only a small part of NYCPP's civic participation work, which also involves lobbying, community organizing, and media efforts. Leading up to each May Day, in preparation for the immigrant rights rallies that have been held on that date annually since 2006, each NYCCP neighborhood committee hosts a breakfast with reporters for Spanish-language print, radio, and television media outlets, honoring them for their service to the community while also communicating the agenda of the marchers. Mobilizing members for street demonstrations in New York City, Albany, and Washington, DC is another key part of NYCPP's work, and in 2011 its members were also active in labor mobilizations in support of Occupy Wall Street.

NYCPP is a small organization with limited resources, and lacks the capacity to single-handedly demolish the system of "city trenches." Yet its decade-long effort to promote civic participation among working-class immigrant Latino communities—communities already richly endowed with social capital prior to

NYCPP's arrival on the scene—has done much to build bridges across the workplace-community divide, as well as across ethnic lines. The collaborative of worker centers and immigrants rights groups that La Fuente convened in 2011 has the potential to continue to make those bridges more robust, and to help immigrant workers find their voice and begin to build power in Washington Heights and other parts of New York City.

10

CREATING "OPEN SPACE" TO PROMOTE SOCIAL JUSTICE

The MinKwon Center for Community Action

Susan McQuade

In late December 2010, a group of workers and activists appeared with picket signs in front of Euodo Ishihama, a Korean restaurant located on 32nd Street in midtown Manhattan. The dispute involved four Korean workers, all of whom had been victims of wage and hour violations and were demanding back pay from the restaurant's owner. The picketing continued for three consecutive days during the busy winter holiday season, and the effort was highly successful: not a single diner entered the establishment during those three days, and the protest was widely reported in the local Korean newspapers. Fearing the loss of income, as well as upheaval among his present workforce, which was composed mostly of young immigrant students, the employer agreed to meet with the group to resolve the issue.

Each of these four workers had sought help from MinKwon, a Korean American community-based organization (CBO) in Queens, New York. Although they all worked for the same employer, they had each approached MinKwon independently, unaware that the others were seeking similar assistance in obtaining the back pay they were owed. All four had also reported the problem to the New York State Department of Labor (DOL), but they had received no response in more than six months. A MinKwon staff organizer convened a meeting, bringing the workers together to brainstorm about the problem they shared, to "fire them up," and to encourage them to decide among themselves on a course of action. One of the workers had previously led another campaign for back wages at a different restaurant, and the others soon agreed that putting economic pressure on the employer would be the most effective tactic. They decided to picket the restaurant and distribute leaflets to urge patrons to take their business elsewhere. MinKwon then facilitated a meeting with the state DOL, the protestors, and the employer, at which a settlement was reached, although further delays at the DOL made a final resolution elusive.

The MinKwon staff helped to build strong relationships among the workers and facilitate open communication among all concerned. For the organization, this case offered a potential template for future worker-run campaigns. They also planned to use it as a basis for expanded media outreach, and to seek support from non-Korean customers and tourists in the hope that such a broad effort would have a powerful impact and ultimately help to change working conditions. Korean restaurant owners are part of a tight-knit community, and MinKwon also hoped that the high-road owners among them would help pressure the bad actors to take heed.

The MinKwon Center for Community Action was founded in 1984 as the Young Korean Service and Education Center (YKASEC). At this writing, MinKwon occupies two floors of a small six-story building in the sprawling Main Street commercial center of Flushing, Queens, home to one of the largest Asian American communities in New York City.[1] The organization had started off in Jackson Heights, another section of Queens, where it functioned primarily as a social service and education agency for the growing Korean American community in the borough. In the early nineties, YKASEC moved to Flushing, where there was a large and growing Korean population, and where "the political landscape was changing rapidly," recalled Ju Bum Cha, the Center's education and communications director. The passage of Proposition 187 by voters in California in 1994 and broader attacks on immigrant rights led the organization to become more politically engaged, even as it continued to provide social and legal services to the Korean American community.[2]

Many of the original participants working in YKASEC were members of Young Koreans United (YKU), a student-led peace and social justice organization that traced it roots to the student movement in South Korea in the 1970s.[3] Although initially focused on the campaign for democracy in the homeland, after that goal was met in 1987, YKU activists shifted their efforts to improving the lives of Korean immigrants in the United States. In 1998, Yu Soung Mun, an activist who had immigrated to the United States in 1990 and had worked in Korean American CBOs in Los Angeles and Philadelphia, came to New York to become executive director of YKASEC, a position he would hold for the next decade. By the early 2000s, the Center had become increasingly involved in labor issues, especially in offering legal support for workers' rights in the face of growing labor law violations.

In 2009, after an extensive strategic planning process, YKASEC changed its name to MinKwon. The new name, which means "civil rights" in Korean, was chosen "because we wanted the image of the organization to broaden to include civic participation by our members in the local life of the community," Cha explained. "Saying that we do education and services was just too limiting, and didn't really reflect the work that we were doing, and what we wanted to do more of."

MinKwon's role in New York's Asian American community is larger than one might expect, especially given that Korean Americans comprise only about 1 percent of New York City's population (Asian American Federation of New York 2012). Building on the legacy of social movements in Korea, along with a strong national identity and a commitment to promoting and nurturing second- and third-generation immigrant leadership, MinKwon gained a highly visible and vital position within New York City's CBO landscape. It straddles many internal divisions within the Korean American community—including immigration status, class, and generation—while promoting a progressive agenda rooted in Korean traditions of social justice advocacy. MinKwon is actively engaged in pan-Asian coalition work as well.

The Center effectively serves as a cross-generational broker, uniting young and old around common concerns. It also takes on class issues and works to counter the myth of the "model minority" by fighting for the rights of those in the community who are economically marginalized and acting as an advocate for low-wage workers employed by their compatriots within the ethnic economy. This chapter focuses on MinKwon's workers' rights activity, although that is only one component of the organization's broad mission and activity. Indeed, its work on labor issues raises some eyebrows in a community that includes a large number of small business owners.

The "Model Minority" and Class Issues among Korean Americans

Asian Americans are often portrayed as a "model minority," programmed for economic success, with a strong work ethic and a relentless emphasis on education. Some view this designation in positive terms, while others see it as contributing to the chronic marginalization of Asian Americans. The "model minority" idea has also been criticized for pitting Asians against other U.S. minorities, weakening overall solidarity and power among people of color (Kibria 2002a).

Whatever stance one takes on these questions, the reality is that many Asian Americans do not fit the stereotype. In 2010, 17.5 percent of Korean Americans in New York City, almost 16 percent of the children, and more than 30 percent of

elderly Korean Americans lived below the poverty line. And while a disproportionate percentage of the Korean American population had some postsecondary
education—63 percent, compared to 43 percent of all city residents—a majority
(52%) of the city's working-age Korean Americans had limited English proficiency, restricting their job opportunities. Among elderly Korean Americans, a
much higher proportion (94%) had limited English proficiency, the highest
among all Asian groups. In addition, 10 percent of Korean American children in
the city do not have health insurance, twice the citywide average (Asian American Federation of New York 2012).

Debunking the "model minority" myth is central to MinKwon's mission. The
campaign to increase funding for Asian American social service agencies is one
example of this, drawing attention to the reality that many Korean Americans
are poor and in need of services, just like many other New Yorkers. MinKwon is
also active on the issue of political redistricting, seeking to ensure that Asian
Americans are treated equitably on the basis of their increasing population. In
alliance with non-Asian community-based groups, the Center participates in advocacy for immigrant rights and housing issues, as well as various efforts to increase Asian American influence in the city and the state.

As Sara Lee (2004) has argued, Koreans' reaction to the stereotype of the
model minority varies by social class. Noting that most research on Korean immigrants has focused on the middle class, Lee's study of New York City found
that many working-class Korean Americans feel disconnected from the larger
ethnic community. They often live in neighborhoods with non-Korean minorities, and their limited economic resources profoundly affect their life chances.
Lee shows that while most middle-class Korean Americans subscribe to the belief that hard work and sacrifice by their parents helped to bring them success in
their lives and careers, their working-class counterparts believe that the success
of the middle-class Korean Americans was the result of their preexisting economic advantages (Lee 2004).

Korean Immigration to New York City

Koreans have made New York their home for more than a century. The first immigration wave from 1900–1945 involved a relatively small number of Koreans
who came to the East Coast as political refugees or students; many returned to
their homeland once the Japanese occupation ended in 1945. After World War
II, a second wave arrived, made up of students, Korean women married to American servicemen, and adopted children, many of whose fathers were American
servicemen. In this period the number of Korean immigrants remained small,

and most were highly assimilated, with few visible markers of ethnic identity (Min 2011).

The third wave began after the 1965 Immigration Act, and soon dwarfed the earlier ones in scale. Between 1976 and 1990, more than thirty thousand Koreans emigrated to the United States annually. During this period Korea was the third largest source of immigrants to the United States (after Mexico and the Philippines). The low standard of living in South Korea, the hardships of the military dictatorship, and fear of escalated conflict with the Communist North were among the "push" factors that led to emigration (Min 2011). The flow ebbed in the 1990s, thanks largely to improved economic and political conditions in Korea following the fall of the military dictatorship. In 2000, however, the number of Korean immigrants rose once again as economic conditions at home deteriorated. Young Koreans continued to pursue educational opportunities in the United States, and many remained after completing their schooling. In addition, more than eight hundred thousand Koreans visited the United States annually in the first decade of the twenty-first century, many of them with some form of temporary legal status. (Min 2011)

As their numbers grew, Korean Americans gradually developed a stronger ethnic identity. Unlike some other Asian groups, they are culturally and linguistically homogeneous; many are affiliated with a Korean community church, and the ethnic media are also well developed. New York alone has three Korean newspapers as well as a Korean-language television station on which immigrants rely.

In 2010, 11 percent of New York City's Asian residents were of Korean descent, making them the city's third largest Asian group (after Chinese and Indians). Almost two-thirds of New York City's Koreans live in Queens, with approximately twenty thousand in the Flushing area alone. The number of Korean Americans living in the City grew by 14 percent over the first decade of the twenty-first century, to more than one hundred thousand. Roughly the same number live outside the city in the wider metropolitan area. Only Los Angeles has a larger Korean American population. Three-quarters of New York City's Korean Americans are foreign-born, and Korean immigrants naturalize at lower rates than all other Asian groups except the Japanese (Asian American Federation of New York 2012). An estimated one in eight, or twenty-five thousand, of all New York City area Korean residents are undocumented immigrants without legal status.[4]

Korean American Entrepreneurialism

MinKwon's regularly updated website reflects its efforts to be inclusive of both working-class Korean Americans and more affluent members of the ethnic community. In May 2011, the site featured a headline story about the mayor's effort to help publicize the New York City Small Business Survey. Directly underneath that posting was an item about MinKwon's involvement in the May Day immigrant rights rally, with a colorful photo of a contingent of Korean Americans, banner in hand, marching in the annual event that traditionally celebrated the rights of workers, but in recent decades has focused on the rights of immigrants. This juxtaposition illustrates the "big tent" approach MinKwon has adopted, dealing with issues that involve the Korean business community as well as the concerns of workers.

Much of the scholarship on Korean Americans focuses on entrepreneurialism (for example, Light and Bonacich 1988). In 2010, there were nearly five thousand Korean American business owners in New York City alone, comprising 7 percent of all foreign-owned businesses in the city, second only to Chinese and Dominican business owners. Moreover, entrepreneurs make up a larger proportion of the Korean American population than of either Dominicans or Chinese (Fiscal Policy Institute 2011).

Many college-educated Korean professionals who emigrated to the United States after 1965 became small-business owners, in large part because their limited English proficiency, along with licensing and credentialing requirements, curtailed their access to more prestigious and better-paying professional jobs (Min 2008). In addition, many came from middle-class backgrounds, had business skills and access to capital, along with strong ethnic networks, all of which facilitated their movement into business ownership (Min 2008).

Korean immigrants are highly concentrated in New York's ethnic economy, with 81 percent either owning or working in a Korean-owned business (39% are owners, the remainder work in the ethnic economy).[5] The majority (60%) of Korean businesses in the metropolitan area are in retail trade, including greengrocers, liquor, and fish stores, as well as stores selling products imported from Asia dry cleaning businesses, and nail salons. In the 1970s and '80s, many newly arrived Korean immigrants purchased small grocery stores, which required limited capital and could be cheaply staffed with family members or other Korean immigrants. They often bought these businesses from white ethnics, and many of the stores were located in minority neighborhoods (Min 2008).

The number of Koreans in retail has declined in recent years due to the growth of "big box" retail chains, boycotts of some Korean-owned greengrocers in some African American communities, as well as Mexican workers' struggles for better working conditions and the right to unionize that also led to boycotts in several neighborhoods (Min 2008, Ness 2005). By 2010, 30 percent of the city's Koreans worked in retail and wholesale trade, down from almost 60 percent in 1980 (U.S. Census Bureau 2012; Min 2008). The retail owners that remain are well organized in ethnic business associations, many of which provide financial support to Korean social service agencies and CBOs like Min-Kwon. The Korean American business community's involvement has made those organizations stronger and more visible.[6]

Low-Wage Korean Workers and the Ethnic Economy

The high concentration of immigrant workers in ethnic businesses may limit opportunities for them to compare experiences with workers from other ethnic groups, share grievances, or develop common values and standards, let alone engage in joint action to alleviate exploitation (Light and Bonacich 1988). However, the work of CBOs such as MinKwon is beginning to change that. MinKwon's legal clients are mostly Koreans, but it also provides services to some Chinese clients and some Spanish-speaking workers. Among those who come to the Center to seek assistance are grocery store workers, construction laborers, restaurant workers, nail salon employees, bus drivers with Korean tour companies, warehouse workers, and workers at small retail establishments. When a worker comes in for legal assistance, a staff organizer is asked to join the conversation, and after listening to the worker's particular circumstances, the organizer, lawyer, and sometimes other staff discuss the best path to resolve the problem. If there are several workers involved, or if a large employer is involved and staff believe that a significant campaign can be waged, then they explore that; other cases are typically forwarded to the state DOL.

Almost one-tenth of Korean workers in New York City are employed in restaurants; in 2005 there were 120 Korean restaurants in Queens, and 77 in the Korean business district in midtown Manhattan (Min 2008). As in the city's restaurant industry as a whole, cases of workers who are illegally paid below the minimum wage, or who do not receive legally required overtime pay, are commonplace.

Significant numbers of Korean immigrants also work as day laborers and other types of construction workers, typically organized in teams that travel together from job to job. Most are employed by Korean subcontractors on residential and small commercial construction projects. With the fall-off in construction since 2008, most of these businesses are doing poorly; often subcontractors tell the workers that the contractor is not paying them because they are owed money from the developer, and this chain reaction culminates in issues of unpaid wages. Worker compensation violations are also commonplace among these workers.

The Korean Nail Salon Association estimated that there were four thousand Korean-owned salons in the New York metropolitan area in 2006, providing employment for about twenty thousand Korean women. The number of salons has tripled since 1991, and in absolute terms this is the industry with the largest number of Korean business owners (Min 2008). Many Korean immigrant women, especially those shut out of white-collar jobs by language barriers and credentialing requirements, work in the salons, which they can easily access through ethnic networks; that training takes place on the job is another plus (Kang 2010). Although some do move on to start their own businesses, a typical salon worker earns about $500 per week as an employee. The work is demanding and strenuous, and the long hours create tension for many women between their roles as mothers and workers. Another issue is exposure to toxic chemicals in the nail polish fumes as well as known toxins in the polish removers and in the acrylics and glue used for tips and extensions. These chemicals include formaldehyde, toluene, benzene, and the banned but still widely used methyl methacrylates. Many salon workers leave after a few years because they develop allergies and other occupationally related illnesses (Kang 2010). These jobs are often stigmatized in relation to both traditional Korean values and many workers' premigration class identities (Park 2009, 123).

The size of the employer often drives MinKwon's decisions as to which cases merit more staff time. "We go after the cases where there are egregious violations where people haven't been paid, or have not been paid properly, sometimes for months," noted Grace Cho, a legal services attorney at the Center who assists workers with wage and hour claims and other employment issues. "It's often the same, with the worker telling me, 'They said they would pay me, but they haven't,'" Cho explained. Most of her clients are employed by Koreans, and don't speak English well. She also represents tenants in disputes with their landlords. A Californian who came east to attend law school, and with a background working on refugee and asylum issues for Korean immigrants, Cho interned at MinKwon before being hired full-time in 2009.

"Open Space" for the Community

MinKwon's mission statement notes that the organization "places a special emphasis on meeting the needs of our marginalized community members who have less access to resources, including the youth, the elderly, recent immigrants, low-income residents, and limited English proficient residents."[7] At the same time, MinKwon seeks to support the entire Korean American community, including business owners. The organization's resources are spread across five program areas: community organizing and advocacy, social services, civic participation, youth empowerment, and culture. Workers' rights issues are integral to both the social service and advocacy activities; not only does the legal clinic provide services to workers with wage and hour claims but increasingly MinKwon also organizes public protests such as the restaurant workers' picket described at the beginning of this chapter. To be sure, as Gordon (2005, 193) notes, workers often prefer litigation over organizing direct actions, and those who are willing to risk coming forward have often already quit their jobs or been fired, seeking back wages from their former rather than current employer.

MinKwon has undergone rapid expansion, with its budget tripling in the past few years. By 2012, it employed fifteen full-time staff members, as well as two full-time fellows from Americorps and VISTA and two full-time and five part-time interns. The staff members include first-, 1.5, and second-generation Korean Americans from both working and middle-class backgrounds. Three staff members are responsible for the Center's work on labor issues.

More than half of MinKwon's funding is from foundations; public funding also provides a significant share, and a small percentage comes from private donors. An annual fund-raising gala event that honors activists engaged in a wide range of social justice issues draws a large crowd. Decisions about the direction of the Center's activities are made at the monthly meetings of the steering committee, which includes both the Board of Directors and staff. The board, which meets twice a month, is composed mostly of long-time activists, many of whom were formerly members of YKU and have carried the principles of that group into their work with MinKwon. The board also includes members who are business owners. In addition, the staff holds weekly formal meetings, and every workday at 1:00 p.m. they eat lunch together, rotating responsibility for preparing the meal. All these meetings include strategic planning discussions, as well as dialogue on current events.

No dues are required to be a member of MinKwon; anyone can receive services on demand, but those who do so are also urged to become active in the organization. The concept of "*mah dang jip*," which means "house of open space," is a core principle of the Center that staff members emphasize when they describe MinKwon's mission and work. "Open space" guides their efforts to build relationships and understanding among all community members, and they aim to form highly inclusive alliances.

A committee of community members has been meeting for about two years as part of MinKwon's effort to promote grassroots activism. This committee seeks to operationalize the idea that the organization is an open space, a place to freely discuss the concerns of the Korean American community, to talk about struggles, and to celebrate achievements.

Ethnic identities and culture help to forge strong bonds at MinKwon, as the Center provides social services to immigrant children and families, building on and at the same time strengthening social networks in the Korean community. The Center also helps maintain connections to Korea for the Korean American community in Queens and throughout the city (Cordero-Guzman 2005).

Immigrant Rights Advocacy and Civic Participation Efforts

The Center's main focus is on advocacy on immigrant rights issues, especially support for the DREAM Act and comprehensive immigration reform. Indeed, MinKwon participated in large-scale rallies, meetings with elected officials, phone banking, and a National Day of Action as part of the campaign to oppose the federal government's Secure Communities policy, which was designed to engage local government agencies to help enforce federal immigration law. Working with the New York Immigration Coalition and other allies across New York State, this campaign had a major victory when Governor Cuomo announced in June 2011 that the state was suspending its participation in the program (see McAlevey, this volume). In another example, MinKwon took the lead in the 2011 "Stop Deportations" Pen Campaign, sending twelve hundred pens and signatures to the White House, 12 percent of those collected by the New York Immigration Coalition.[8] The Center regularly mobilizes its members to participate in state and city Immigrant Days of Action, and lobbies to fight budget cuts affecting programs serving immigrants, and for improved language access for those using government services. MinKwon's Youth Empowerment Program, a group of fifty teens, spent summer 2011 organizing for the DREAM Act; they followed up with a video project documenting their experience and reaching out to other youth. MinKwon's legal services include free consultations on immigration-related issues.

In addition to its strong connection with the New York Immigration Coalition—whose director, Chung Wha-Hung, is a former MinKwon staffer—the Center has built alliances with organizations such as the YWCA, the Korean Family Service Center, and the Chinese-American Planning Council. But most of MinKwon's coalition building involves Korean American community organizations and immigrant advocacy groups, including Latino and South Asian organizations in Queens. In regard to housing, a growing issue for the community during the current economic recession, the Center works with the Queens Housing Coalition and Woodside on the Move, as well as Catholic Charities, on rent regulation and repair issues. And on worker rights issues, the Center continues its strong relationship with the Asian American Legal Defense and Education Fund (AALDEF).

The deepening immigration debate has led to shifting political party alliances. Koreans tend to be socially conservative, but they have increasingly moved into the Democratic column due to Republicans' anti-immigrant rights positions. Recent data indicate that almost half (48%) of Korean Americans self-identify as Democrats; less than one-third (32%) identify as Republicans (Pew Research Center 2012).

Expanding civic participation by Korean Americans in local, state, and national politics is another major focus. MinKwon is a cofounder of the 13% and Growing Coalition, a group of Asian American organizations that is seeking greater equity within the New York City budget allocation process. The 2010 census numbers indicate that Asians represent 13 percent of the population of the city, a 32 percent increase over 2000; however, Asian American social service agencies receive less than 1 percent of all funding provided by the city to community organizations.[9] With rallies at city hall, briefings for the city council, and visits to legislators, the coalition was successful in increasing funds to the Asian communities by 38 percent in 2011.[10] The 2010 census also led to the formation of the Asian American Community Coalition on Redistricting and Democracy, a coalition of Asian organizations working to ensure that the recent growth in the Asian population will be accurately reflected in the New York State redistricting process. MinKwon plays a key leadership role in this initiative, which is coordinated by James Hong, director of the Center's Civic Participation Program.

Hong, who arrived in the United States when he was three, grew up in Miami and New Orleans, moved to New York and found out about MinKwon from a friend. "I didn't know an organization like this existed, one with Korean Americans working for social justice," he recalled. He began as a volunteer in 2009, and was hired soon afterward. He uses the organization's tax clinic, one of its most heavily utilized programs, as a point of contact with the community. "We try to get them involved, or at least thinking about civic participation, and how it matters in their lives here," Hong explains. He coordinates door knocking, mailings, and phone banking for each local election. The organization is also highly committed to voter registration, and takes credit for having registered more than fifty thousand new voters since 2004. With a database of twenty-eight thousand names, the organization's ability to educate and mobilize members on political issues is formidable. In 2009, it made more than seven thousand calls to get out the vote in the mayoral election. MinKwon does not endorse candidates, but it does hold forums, and urges community members to exercise their rights and take part in the process. It also informs members in detail about issues and candidates, with materials tailored to the Korean American community. At the candidate forums, there is simultaneous translation in Mandarin and Hindi as well. Along with AALDEF, MinKwon also conducts exit surveys at polling sites with large Korean constituencies to identify any instances of discrimination.

MinKwon and Worker Rights Issues: A Delicate Balance

The Center launched its Workers' Project in 2000 in response to the growing numbers of workers requesting legal assistance. "They had the double hardship of being workers and being immigrants," Mun recalled.[11] With assistance from AALDEF and a board member who was an attorney, the Center initially focused on impact litigation to bring to light the plight of those who had suffered the most egregious wage and hour violations.

Advocating for workers' rights came into sharper focus a few years later when Steven Choi came to work at the Center. Choi, a second-generation Korean American, grew up in a Westchester County suburb, where he had no real connection with the city's Korean community. During his college years in California, however, he studied the history of U.S.-Korean relations in the era of the Korean military dictatorship, travelled to Korea, and completed a master's degree in Korean Studies in Hawaii, where he also learned to speak the language. He spearheaded the founding of a Korean American students' association, and became an activist in and for the Korean American community. Returning east to attend law school, in 2000 Choi secured a position interning for YKASEC. The organization struck him as resource poor, but its core of committed and dedicated volunteers inspired him to make a deeper commitment. After completing law school, Choi received a Skadden Fellowship[12] to found the Korean Workers' Rights Project, a joint initiative of AALDEF and YKASEC. He worked with YKASEC members and staff to file numerous lawsuits, mostly involving wage theft. The project also launched outreach and education efforts directed at workers in the garment, restaurant, and construction industries, as well as those employed in delicatessens and nail salons.

Choi wanted to better integrate his legal work with organizing and advocacy efforts devised and led by community members themselves. In 2007, he was hired as a full-time MinKwon staff member, and was named executive director two years later. Paid staff increased almost threefold over the next two years, complemented by an active internship program; a worker-organizer was also hired as part of this expansion.

MinKwon is a leading member of the New York Unemployment Insurance Coalition, advocating for improved access for immigrants to unemployment benefits, as well as for a more generous unemployment insurance benefit rate to match the higher cost of living in New York. Another MinKwon-led campaign aims to increase language access for limited-English-proficiency workers, demanding improvements in translation and interpretation services, including Korean-language translation of key documents and guides to DOL services.

MinKwon's goal is to help Korean American workers become more self-reliant in addressing these problems, and thus decrease their dependence on lawyers. This meets with some resistance from Korean immigrants, many of whom express the idea that they are "in someone else's country," notes Liz Chong Eun Rhee, a staff organizer for worker issues since 2009. "So I tell them, 'This is your home, you have been working here, and you are a backbone of the American economy. You have rights and you are entitled to be paid for your work.' It's a challenge to get them to feel ownership in this way." Similarly, when she brings workers to meet with a labor attorney, "they will tell us that they have not been paid in a long time, and they often feel like the problem they are experiencing is their own fault," she recounts. "A big part of my job is to get them to have a better understanding of their right to be paid, and that's a big change in the mind-set of many. I tell them they don't need to be apologetic or scared, but it often takes a couple of meetings to make them feel comfortable about taking action."[13]

Rhee, who arrived in the United States when she was two years old, describes herself as a 1.75-generation Korean American. She remembers accompanying her father to YKU meetings as a five year old in the northern Virginia suburbs of Washington, DC. With a long-standing interest in Korean history, Rhee came to New York to attend college in 2000 and began to volunteer at MinKwon. She directs the Center's cultural program, and leads Binari, the drumming group (pungmul). Pungmul is a Korean art form that traces its roots to agrarian society, when farmers gathered at the end of the day to celebrate their toil. This folk music, later used in protest movements during times of political repression, is present on many American college campuses, serving as an alliance builder among first- and second-generation Koreans. More generally, Pungmul ritual is often seen as a unifying force.[14]

MinKwon staff members regularly do door knocking and street outreach to raise awareness about workers' rights issues, and convene open meetings for workers on the first Sunday of each month. The goal is for this group to become an active workers' committee. At one of the initial meetings, a half dozen restaurant and construction workers discussed a plan to build a network of workers to raise awareness of labor rights and the laws that protect them. MinKwon staff is grappling with how to expand this committee, and Rhee and others are looking at the work of other organizations that have similarly moved away from the legal services model to organize direct action on these issues. "They need to understand that their issue is much bigger than just their workplace; this is a community concern," she explained. "Some just want the lawyer, some do want to organize, but the cross-fertilization of ideas among workers is essential."[15] At a recent meeting of the workers' committee, two workers described their experiences:

> I worked in different restaurants and there are very bad conditions . . . employees are treated like servants. There's a lot of disrespect . . . sometimes I wonder why I came to the U.S. with conditions so bad. . . . The employer should feel bad about the conditions, but they act like it's normal. Korean employers think that even if your time is up, you should stay longer. . . . Employees sometimes give good ideas, but employers think we are taking away their power.
>
> I clean offices in New York and New Jersey, and have worked with the employer for eight years. We work in teams of eight, and we work twelve hours a day, six days a week. Sometimes there is less work, so we take less so no one gets laid off. Latinos are sometimes on the teams, but they don't want to be flexible on the wages, so we stick with Koreans. If it's busy, we get full wages, but if it's not, we share. I make between $1,600 and $2,800 a month, depending on how much work there is. . . . Yes, I understand the overtime law, but economic conditions are tough. It's tiring work, but it is better to have more work. Things have changed these last years . . . some places we clean, they used to contract for $3,000 . . . now it's $2,000. They always tell us they have a "different quote from another company" that is cheaper. So to keep us all working our wages go down, and if we say "Follow the law," businesses won't like it. Our employer is Korean, and we understand him because of the human connection. He is good to us, even though we sometimes are not paid accurately.

The Korean small-business community has strongly supported MinKwon over the years, and the staff and board are careful to avoid alienating them; indeed, the Center actively supports their efforts to thrive in the business community. Yet the organization's commitment to workers' rights does raise eyebrows among some in the Korean American community. "Worker's' rights issues are controversial," Choi acknowledges. "Many Koreans are small-business owners, or have a relative that owns a small business."

Recognizing that this could be a source of tension for some MinKwon members, Choi and the staff insist that the organization works for the entire Korean community, including those who have been marginalized or deprived of their legal rights. Although there is support for the small-business owners, MinKwon is not willing to ignore wage theft and other violations by Korean American employers. "We have a responsibility to be working for a more prosperous, whole community where labor rights are respected," Choi said. "We know it is sometimes a minefield, but it is a crucial part of our work. . . . It is a key part of what we do to build a stronger movement for social justice."[16] All staff interviewed noted that worker organizing is a challenge, but insisted that healthy discussion about this work needs to happen in the wider community.

"Some members need to listen to the workers' side . . . it's as if workers were not telling the truth about being robbed of wages. We need to fight the stigma on this," declared Choi.[17] The organization faces not only tension about labor issues because of the business owners' strong presence but also other internal divisions. Korean churches are a strong and often conservative force in the community; MinKwon meeting agendas often include announcements of events taking place at the various Christian churches in the area.[18]

Leadership and Bridge Builders

The fact that MinKwon's staff includes both first- and second-generation activists is an important resource in meeting this challenge. The small business path that enabled first-generation Korean Americans in the late twentieth century to regain their middle-class status has been rejected by many 1.5 and second-generation Korean Americans. Moreover, self-employed parents, many of whom are highly educated, and well aware of the hard work and difficulties entailed in running a small business, have been reluctant to encourage their children to follow their example. Many of those in the second-generation have left the ethnic economy for the professions; others work in nonprofit sectors that provide community services (Kim 2004). Yet Lee's (2004) findings on working-class Koreans reveal that some do not feel fully welcome in the community. MinKwon's youth program, which recruits teens to take part in the life of the Center, reflects the organization's desire to nurture ties across generations and across class lines. Most second-generation members are bilingual, and can seek employment in the ever-expanding ethnic/transnational economy. Others work in the mainstream economy, although some have noted that they are coming up against the glass ceiling there (Kibria 2002b).

In twenty-first century America, where cultural diversity is prized, transnational ties are acceptable and even celebrated, so that the second generation often feels pride in the connection to their parents' homeland (Foner 2002). In the

1960s, Asian American identities began to emerge, fostered by the movement against the Vietnam War. That generation of Asian American activists was mostly from middle-class backgrounds, and embraced the egalitarian and democratic politics of the New Left. Many, however, were more drawn to identity politics than leftist politics. They began to serve as cultural brokers between their isolated ethnic communities and mainstream society. Using their education and understanding of American bureaucracy, some learned how to obtain federal and private funds to improve the lives of their co-ethnics from working-class and immigrant backgrounds (Wei 2004).

In recent decades, another wave of Asian-American activism has taken shape among children of post-1965 immigrants, gaining visibility on college campuses, in social service organizations, and in a variety of social movements. This generation of Asian American students is more diverse in family socioeconomic background and political orientation, and has greater access to institutional resources than its 1960s counterparts (Wei 2004, 312). Lee (2004) found that Korean Americans with working-class backgrounds are especially involved in efforts to improve the lives of the oppressed and marginalized.

MinKwon staff plays the role of bridge builder across various generations in the community. Although immigration issues help to unite community members, on other issues there is often internal conflict. MinKwon's membership is diverse in terms of age and, partly for this reason, views on labor rights vary widely. At one recent membership meeting, about fifteen mostly middle-aged men and women were present, all wearing plastic-coated printed nametags. The agenda had been typed up and distributed to all. The meeting was led by Jae Sup Song, a first-generation immigrant and community organizer. He introduced the issue of workers' rights by describing the details of the restaurant workers' campaign for back pay. The idea was to educate those present about labor law, as well as to inform them of the actions MinKwon is taking to support workers who are being exploited by their employers, also Koreans. Members listened intently to Song's description of the situation. When he asked for their input, a few suggested that it is important "to listen to both sides, and to hear the owner's positions" on the matter. One noted, "Things like this happen in American society. . . . I see it sometimes. People carry signs that say, 'Pay the workers,' the reporters take pictures, then no one goes to those places. It's a big deal, and owners worry about it."

Another member related this incident to his own work life:

> I have seen this a lot, and it is bad thinking in our community. . . . Some owners are taking advantage of the workers. A long time ago, I didn't have a [green] card, and I had nothing to eat, so I went to a

church and worked for them but they didn't pay me. So I won't work for Korean people, but we need to educate the community about these issues. I am in favor of demonstrations, not in breaking the law, but in protecting ourselves. Sometimes the employers say that they can't pay, but they do have the money. It can be embarrassing for the community, but some situations are bad.

A longer discussion about "*chong*" ensued. "*Chong*" refers to a complex mixture of primordial relational qualities like love, affinity, empathy, obligation, entanglement, bondage, and blood (Abelman and Lie 1995). In this discussion, the key idea was that the back pay issue should be kept "within the community." Some of those present suggested that instead of staging public demonstrations, MinKwon should try to play a behind-the-scenes role in resolving the conflict. Others pointed out that these issues also arise in Korea, but that enforcement of the laws is much stronger there. Song told the group, "Sometimes we think it's more effective to demonstrate rather than dealing with the Labor Department," but then promised that the Center staff would take the discussion into account as they developed future plans for educating the community on workers' rights issues.

This meeting also included less controversial agenda items. Two young women, both recent arrivals from Korea, were introduced, and each member was asked to share ideas about where the newcomers should visit, shop, and dine in the city. Later, members of the MinKwon youth group described their visits to Washington legislators to advocate for the DREAM Act, and the importance of Asian American activism in promoting this legislation. They also reported on the video they are making on the DREAM Act and on a youth community relations project at Flushing High School to counter racial segregation. Questions arose about how the older generation can work with the young on these projects. The meeting ended with announcements on activities in the churches to campaign against the recent increase in deportations by the U.S. government. A member warned of impending budget cuts, and how Social Security, and the work of nonprofits such as MinKwon, needs to be protected.

Building Unity

Spanning other differences, immigrant rights is an issue that strongly unites the Korean American community,[19] especially in response to the recent increase in anti-immigrant sentiment throughout the country. Community members all recognize the importance of the issue not only for Korean Americans but for all immigrants. Long-time residents want to help more recent arrivals; they also see immigration reform as linked to the community's economic prosperity, especially if they own a small business. This issue is a top priority for MinKwon.

That equality and adherence to the law are core beliefs in the community is helpful to the Center's efforts to bridge the divided opinions around labor issues. MinKwon educates workers and the community at large on workers' legal rights, and on that basis works to rein in low-road employers who flout the law, and whose actions can stain the whole community. "We are all Koreans," as one staffer put it. The Center has won great respect for its commitment to empowering and assisting the marginalized members of the community. Yet it has done so in part by deliberately avoiding confrontation, unlike some otherwise similar organizations in other parts of the United States. For example, the Koreatown Immigrant Workers Alliance (KIWA) in Los Angeles, "from its inception . . . decided to be publicly aggressive, even at the risk of alienating the community's ethnic elites, and thereby cutting off potential sources of financial, political and co-ethnic support" (Kwon 2010).

Although both MinKwon and KIWA have historical ties to YKU, they have followed sharply different paths in this regard. KIWA sees itself as an instigator, an "insider" that uses its standing in the Korean American community to voice opposition, and an "outsider" that "challenges the entrepreneurial hegemony that sustains the interests of the ethnic elites" (Kwon 2010). As a result, however, KIWA has found it difficult to recruit Korean American workers, many of whom are ambivalent about its militancy. The organization also has an uncomfortable relationship with business owners, even if it has also won their respect (Kwon 2010).

MinKwon has taken a very different approach. It operates in a Korean community far smaller than that in Los Angeles, but also has adopted a less confrontational approach to improving the lives of Korean Americans. Widely respected both within and outside New York's Korean community, MinKwon is a key player in the pan-Asian progressive network and has won widespread respect for its work on voter registration, its provision of legal services on a host of issues, and the help it offers those with limited English proficiency. "The key is to have leadership, and we have been able to get the community trust by doing the right thing at the right moments," Mun, the former executive director and present-day secretary treasurer of MinKwon, noted, adding, "We are a small ethnic-based organization, and we work hard on issues like immigration reform, but we are small, only 1 percent of the population, so it can be difficult to move our agenda. We are always trying to work and build alliances to achieve our goals."[20]

On labor issues, the Center addresses the tensions between owners and workers by adopting the role of arbiter, providing a moral compass and community enforcer of the law when workers' rights are violated by low-road employers. "Our challenges are overcoming stereotypes, dealing with rumors, having workers clearly understand what their rights are," says Choi. "A cultural shift needs to take place in the community, and there is a need to develop an organization among Korean American workers. It's about building legitimacy for ourselves. What is the model that will emerge, that is distinct and represents Korean Americans' voices in this struggle?"[21]

Part IV

GOING NATIONAL: NEW YORK'S WORKER CENTERS EXPAND

11

AN APPETITE FOR JUSTICE

The Restaurant Opportunities Center of New York

Marnie Brady

The Restaurant Opportunities Center of New York (ROC-NY) has a strong record of strategic campaigns, helping make visible the low wages and working conditions of immigrants and other workers of color that would otherwise remain hidden behind the kitchen door or in the cellars below the city's fashionable eateries. ROC-NY's direct actions and legal cases have won significant improvements for restaurant workers and imposed large penalties on "low-road" employers who break the law, although this is just one component of the organization's work. ROC-NY has also developed alternative models of business "best practices," an approach that sets it apart from traditional labor unions and establishes a foundation for politically sustainable organizing despite decades of decline in restaurant unionization.

ROC-NY has developed a three-pronged strategy since it was founded in 2001. The first prong involves workplace organizing campaigns. The second focuses on active partnerships with high-road, responsible employers whose practices promote workers' career advancement. As part of this work, the organization engages in a variety of efforts to raise consumer awareness of such restaurant employment practices, and has established a worker-owned cooperative restaurant, COLORS. The third prong is ROC-NY's policy work, which includes extensive research and advocacy aiming to lift industry-wide labor standards (see Jayaraman et al. 2011; Bendick, Eanni-Rodriguez, and Jayaraman 2009; ROC-NY 2009a, 2009b, 2010; ROC-NY and New York Industry Coalition 2005). These three strategic foci are mutually reinforcing, bringing together diverse stakeholders in New York's powerful and growing restaurant industry.

New York City's restaurant industry generated an estimated $16 billion in sales in 2012 (National Restaurant Association 2013).[1] The industry also contributes greatly to the city's symbolic economy, creating social spaces that evoke cosmopolitanism and exclusivity. Indeed, for many restaurants profitability depends as much on ambiance and style as on the quality of cuisine and service. Through a strategy that exposes workplace violations among low-road restaurants and highlights the responsible practices of their high-road counterparts, ROC-NY leverages employers' dependency on a positive public image to promote dignity and fair pay, as well as race and gender justice for all workers. In a city where less than 1 percent of restaurants are unionized, ROC-NY's three-pronged strategy has been highly effective. ROC-NY has won all nine of its major campaigns to date, and in 2005 won a major policy victory that raised the New York State tipped hourly minimum wage from $3.30 to $4.60 (this is the legally required hourly wage, usually supplemented by customers' tips).

This case study explores ROC-NY's history against the background of the long-term decline of restaurant unionism in New York City.[2] Although ROC-NY organizers recognize that strong union contracts would be the ideal guarantee for the benefits, wages, and protections workers desire, the reality in the twenty-first century is that unionism remains a distant prospect for the vast majority of New York City's restaurant workers. In that context, ROC-NY's campaigns focus on racial and gender justice as well as the interests of the working class. As a 501c(3) nonprofit organization, ROC-NY has a unique strategic approach, differentiating it not only from past restaurant union organizing but also from many other independent worker centers dedicated to organizing immigrants and other low-wage workers (Jayaraman and Ness 2005; Ness 2005; Tait 2005; Fine 2006; Milkman, Bloom, and Narro 2010).

Origins

ROC-NY was founded through the active efforts of immigrant workers, whose example continues to inspire the organization. It arose in 2001 from one of the darkest moments in New York City's and the nation's history. Among the victims of the 9/11 attacks were seventy-three employees of Windows on the World, the unionized restaurant on the top floor of the World Trade Center's North Tower. Local 100 of what was then the Hotel Employees and Restaurant Employees union (HERE) represented Windows's largely immigrant workforce. (HERE merged with the garment and textile workers union UNITE in 2004, forming UNITE HERE.) With support from two other unions, Local 100 established the Immigrant Workers' Assistance Alliance (IWAA) immediately following the attacks to support the families of Windows victims as they navigated the complicated web of local and federal government assistance (Sen and Mamdouh 2008). IWAA also sought to help find new jobs for the 350 Windows workers who were not scheduled to work on the morning of 9/11.

Windows employees included immigrants from many different parts of the world, reflecting the owner's desire for a staff that could communicate with the restaurant's many international patrons in their first languages. In part because they had unionized in 1997, only a few years before 9/11, many Windows workers had a strong sense of solidarity and now turned to one another and to the union for assistance. Local 100 hired several former Windows workers, including headwaiter and shop steward Fekkak Mamdouh, to staff the IWAA. Shortly afterward the union recruited a Harvard- and Yale-trained lawyer, and former organizer from the Long Island Workplace Project, Saru Jayaraman, to join him.

Six months after 9/11, against the background of mass immigration enforcement sweeps, hate crimes, and the PATRIOT Act, Jayaraman, from a family of Indian immigrants, and Mamdouh, originally from Morocco, launched ROC-NY. It began with two staff members and a $500,000 budget, but grew rapidly, with eleven staff and a budget of $1.3 million by 2009. In those first eight years, the organization won $5 million in back pay for restaurant workers in legal settlements with employers that it had sued for wage and hour violations, as well as a variety of workplace and policy changes.

In 2006 ROC-NY opened COLORS as a cooperative owned by a group of former Windows workers (Sen and Mamdouh 2008). This project gave organizers and activists firsthand experience with the challenges of managing a successful fine dining business. In a tribute to the former and deceased Windows workers, COLORS adopted a global menu. As a high-road restaurant, it added a prefigurative dimension to ROC-NY's work as well. However, although Local 100 had hoped that the workers would be covered by a union contract, in the end the restaurant's staff was not represented by the union and instead adopted a traditional cooperative organizational structure. An operating restaurant at night, COLORS is also a job training center during the day, providing revenue through state-funded workforce training grants for ROC-NY helping lessen its dependence on foundation support.

In 2008, when Jayaraman and Mamdouh left ROC-NY to found the national organization Restaurant Opportunities Centers–United (ROC-United), Sekou Siby and Rekha Eanni-Rodriguez became codirectors of the New York organization. Siby, a former teacher and Windows' line cook, is from the Ivory Coast, where as a young man he had become politicized working for his brother's youth mobilizing campaigns. Mamdouh had recruited Siby to join ROC-NY as an organizer in 2003. As ROC-NY's codirector, Siby oversaw COLORS as well as the

CHOW (COLORS Hospitality and Opportunities for Workers) Institute, the organization's workforce development program (discussed in more detail below). Born in India, Eanni-Rodriguez is of Indian and Italian American origin, a former restaurant server and a graduate of Brooklyn Law School with experience in immigration asylum work. She first got involved with ROC-NY in 2005 when she was hired as a researcher. Her personal experience as a server also attuned her to the abuse women in the industry often face. Siby became ROC-NY's executive director when Eanni-Rodriguez moved to ROC-United in late 2011.

The Decline of Restaurant Unionism in New York City

Although Local 100's IWAA initiative laid the groundwork for the formation of ROC-NY, it was an independent organization from the outset. Against the background of decades of deunionization in the restaurant industry, this was a welcome development from the union's perspective. "We see [ROC-NY's] work as positive justice for hospitality workers," commented UNITE HERE deputy director of food services, Paul Schwalb, who serves on ROC-United's Board of Directors. "We don't think their power diminishes our power, we see it as additive. . . . There is a need for someone to bring justice to workers in these shops" (quoted in Elan 2007). Windows on the World, which had been the nation's highest-grossing restaurant (with $37 million in revenue the year before the attacks), represented approximately 10 percent of Local 100's independent restaurant worker members in 2001. In earlier years, more of the city's dining establishments had been unionized, but by then relatively few remained in Local 100.[3] Overall, about 35 percent of all New York City hotel workers are union members, compared to only 1 percent of restaurant workers (see Milkman and Braslow 2011).

As Dorothy Sue Cobble has shown, the history of restaurant unionization includes a complex mix of craft and industrial union models over the arc of the twentieth century, which both helped shape and was shaped by the racial, ethnic, and gender dynamics of the workforce. In the early twentieth century, restaurant unionism took a craft-like form, with hiring halls that provided access to jobs for workers and a reliable pool of skilled labor for employers. In that era, HERE was sex-segregated, with separate locals for waitresses, who were excluded from the male-dominated fine dining sector. Black workers worked in the kitchen and other "back of the house" restaurant jobs, while unionized servers were overwhelmingly white (Cobble 1991b; Bailey 1985).

Like most unions, HERE's membership grew in the 1930s, in part as a result of a surge in hotel organizing, which in New York led to the first citywide master contract in 1939. In this period the union transitioned from a craft union to an industrial union model with a multiracial membership, although craft union forms persisted in many nonhotel restaurants along with continuing gender and racial segregation. A 1955 change in federal labor law that prohibited closed shops for hotel and restaurant unions undermined the craft model further; it disappeared altogether after the 1964 Civil Rights Act made sex-segregated locals illegal (Cobble 1991b).

A variety of additional factors led to long-term decline in union density among restaurant workers, as the industry itself was transformed both in New York City and nationwide. HERE, the largest union representing restaurant and hospitality workers, experienced a 50 percent decline in the size of its membership, from a peak of 507,000 members in 1970 to 249,746 in 2011, even as the size of the industry's workforce grew. HERE was still trying to organize, but lost more and more union representation elections in the face of employer resistance; at the same time decertification elections eliminated unions in many previously organized restaurants (Murrmann and Murrmann 1990). The rapid rise of fast-food chains and immigrant-owned ethnic restaurants from the 1960s onward, virtually all of them nonunion, further eroded union power (Waldinger 1996; Bailey 1985).[4]

As the food service industry became increasingly nonunion, New York City's full-service restaurants began recruiting servers among the city's abundant supply of actors, models, artists, and students, while hiring immigrants in "back of the house" jobs that both U.S.-born whites and blacks had abandoned as wages and conditions deteriorated with the union's decline. In the same period, many black workers left the fine-dining segment of the industry due to discrimination (Waldinger 1996; Bailey 1985). Thus the city's restaurant workforce became increasingly female and foreign-born. The expansion of the fast-food and chain restaurants did provide employment opportunities, including a small number of management positions, for black workers in the growing nonunion sector of the industry. By the first decade of the twenty-first century, two-thirds of all New York City restaurant workers were foreign-born and nearly one-third (32.7%) were female. Whites were less than a fifth (17.3%) of the workforce, which was 39.7 percent Latino, 26.7 percent Asian, and 12.6 percent black.[5]

In 2006, shortly after the HERE merger with UNITE, the union decided to abandon freestanding restaurant worker organizing (that is, organizing small restaurants that are not part of hotels or other large entities with large enough numbers to justify the resources required by organizing campaigns). UNITE HERE nationally, and Local 100 locally, shifted their organizing focus to food service and cafeteria workers employed by large multinational firms. Against this background, ROC-NY entered the picture, seeking new strategies to organize the freestanding restaurant sector with its nonunion and largely foreign-born work-force. The goal was to create a space that brings immigrant and U.S.-born work-ers together across nationality, immigration status, race, ethnic, gender, and income levels, and to engage high-road employers and allies as well.

Immigrants of color today face a very different economic, social, and political context than European immigrants who began restaurant unionization in New York City in the early twentieth century. ROC-NY's founders focused their efforts on developing a strategy that could counter not only the absence of unions and the erosion of state regulation but also what De Genova (2007) refers to as immigrants' current state of "deportability." As Jayaraman (2006) has noted, today's undocumented immigrant workers' very presence in the United States and family unity is in question, a situation of great advantage to employers, and one that had no equivalent for white European immigrants a century ago.

Fine Dining: Workplace Justice and Industry-Wide Change

After a few years of experimentation, ROC-NY organizers concluded that they could not respond to every group of indignant restaurant workers in the city, however much they were underpaid, not paid at all, or discriminated against. Although the group welcomes workers from all segments of the industry as members of the organization and offers them training and support in regard to workplace rights, in order to maximize its impact on the industry as a whole ROC-NY's leaders chose to focus their campaign efforts on New York's fine din-ing restaurants, also known as "tablecloth restaurants," defined by an intake per patron of at least $40 excluding gratuities (ROC-NY 2009b, 11). Fine dining sets the standards for the industry as a whole, so that winning improvements there often benefits workers in the casual dining and fast-food segments as well.

Mamdouh and other ROC-NY worker-leaders had personal experience in fine dining, and many of the organization's members had extensive knowledge about this part of the industry, which enriched ROC-NY's "strategic capacity" (Ganz 2009). Among other things, organizers were aware of labor violations throughout the industry. Although fine dining is the segment with the highest wages, as ROC-NY's research (2009a, 2009b, 2010) documents, violations are present there as well as in the low-wage tiers of the industry. Moreover, in fine dining the racial and gender dynamics that permeate the industry are especially striking. Alongside the well-paid servers, bartenders, sommeliers, and floor cap-tains, who are disproportionately white and male, fine dining restaurants typically employ white women as hostesses (often in highly sexualized roles), and vast numbers of low-wage workers, especially in the "back of the house."

Executive and sous chefs are the "back of the house" exception that proves the rule; almost always men and as often white, they are handsomely paid and some have celebrity status. The porters, dishwashers, prep cooks, and other kitchen workers, who have little or no direct or social contact with restaurant guests, are typically immigrant Latino, Asian, and African men. "Front of the house" runners, barbacks (bartender assistants), bussers, and baristas are typically immigrant Latino men (ROC-NY 2009b). In their focus on fine dining workplaces, and specifically those in conglomerates, ROC-NY draws attention to "the culture of white, male dominance in the industry" (ROC-NY 2009b, 17), while also challenging employers' exploitation of immigrant labor and limited career advancement opportunities for workers of color and women.

Across the industry, ROC-NY has documented race- and gender-based earnings disparities. Controlling for education, experience, and English proficiency, women, immigrants, and people of color have far lower annual earnings than white men in New York City restaurants (ROC-NY 2009b, 2010). Sexual harassment is also widespread in the industry, as the Equal Employment Opportunity Commission has noted (see also Giuffre and Williams 1994).

A Worker-Centered Organizing Approach

Jayaraman and other ROC-NY staff emphasize that although they use legal tools in their workplace campaigns targeting low-road employers, the organization is committed to a worker-centered organizing approach, rejecting traditional legal interventions that reinforce workers' dependence on legal expertise. Instead, they adopt a community lawyering approach, directly involving workers in every phase of the work. ROC-NY members are required to attend a minimum of three public protests in the course of each campaign, and settlement negotiations include rank-and-file worker representatives (along with ROC-NY staff and the legal team). As staff member Daisy Chung stated, "Legal action is just one tool that can be used as part of a larger organizing strategy."[6]

The workers named as plaintiffs in the legal cases (usually cases involving violations of wage, hour, and antidiscrimination laws) stand to benefit directly and therefore have strong incentives to participate actively in direct action campaigns, regardless of whether they continue to work for the target employer. ROC-NY also asks workers who are plaintiffs in the lawsuits to agree to give back to the organization 6 percent of the final settlement award. The funds generated in this way are modest, and do little to defray the costs of campaigns, but they are important symbols of workers' commitment to the organization. In a few cases, workers have voluntarily shared their individual monetary awards directly with their coworkers.

ROC-NY tries to identify pro-bono attorneys and public interest law firms to litigate these cases, but more often standard legal fees come out of the award. Neither Eanni-Rodriguez nor Chung, the two staff members with law degrees, practice law on behalf of the organization. Along with the lawsuits themselves, ROC-NY campaigns bring to bear various forms of public pressure, including direct actions, to induce low-road restaurant employers to negotiate settlement agreements. Typically featuring sidewalk protests in front of the targeted restaurants or pickets at venues where owners are present, ROC-NY's direct action approach sets it part from traditional unions, whose right to picket and protest is constrained in any case under U.S. labor law.

In regard to the lawsuits, settlement negotiations typically begin in earnest early in the discovery process. Discovery not only involves owners and key managers in legal depositions, but also may require that companies open up their accounting and personnel records. This makes company practices transparent to a much greater degree than in a union organizing campaign, and may make employers vulnerable to additional lawsuits or government audits. Employers' willingness to enter settlement negotiations, however reluctantly, opens up opportunities for ROC-NY to obtain not only back pay and damages for existing violations but also changes in workplace policies and practices. These may include increased wages, paid sick and vacation days, the implementation of grievance procedures, and increased training opportunities and transparency in hiring to promote mobility for immigrant workers of color and women.

Settlement negotiations are often more advantageous than a court order for all concerned parties, reducing attorneys' fees and limiting the discovery process. Employers who opt for settlement can avoid potential court decisions providing for more extensive monetary compensation for violations; but on the other hand the types of settlement agreements ROC-NY negotiates may benefit workers unnamed in the original lawsuit, changing workplace practices in a lasting manner. Although employers tend to demand a confidentiality agreement as part of any settlement, ROC-NY generally seeks to ensure that key settlement terms are made public, a vital mechanism for empowering workers.

Enforcement of settlement agreements that result in workplace restructuring presents a major challenge, especially where worker plaintiffs are no longer employed at the restaurant involved. Although in some cases the New York State Attorney General's office, the U.S. Equal Employment Opportunity Commission (EEOC), or even ROC-NY itself are named directly as independent monitors, workers themselves must be vigilant to ensure that policy changes remain in place. Unlike union structures that might allow shop stewards or union staff representatives to monitor the implementation of a contract, ROC-NY does not retain ongoing access to the restaurants where settlements have been reached, so that workers themselves, albeit with ROC-NY's support, must defend or expand the settlement gains.

Organizing across Differences: The Fireman Campaign

ROC-NY's most substantive workplace victory to date was the result of a two-year campaign aimed at the high-end conglomerate Fireman's Hospitality Group, which operates several Manhattan restaurants. It illustrates the ways in which ROC-NY addresses issues of class, race, and gender, as well as its efforts to promote organizing across those boundaries. The campaign began in 2006, when two white servers, one woman and one man, contacted the organization about wage and hour violations at one of Fireman's fine dining restaurants, the Redeye Grill, located near Carnegie Hall. Both servers complained they were not being paid properly for their daily overtime hours.[7] ROC-NY organizers worked with them to recruit workers of color from the Redeye Grill staff into the campaign, and urged them to identify back-of-the-house worker-leaders. As a result, the campaign ultimately involved not only the unpaid overtime claims but also minimum wage violations and discrimination issues.

One of the Fireman worker-leaders recruited into this effort was Sekou Luke, who had held a host position before becoming one of two black servers at another Fireman restaurant, Café Fiorello, located across from Lincoln Center. Luke complained about blatant discrimination in hiring at Fiorello's, alleging that management explicitly favored Italian-looking men for front-of-the-house positions. He had been hired with help from a friend, the one other black server. Yet even after he got the job, what Luke called the "race component" persisted. "When the owner would come in, I always got sent downstairs to answer phones, and I never really got it at first, but then I was like, 'Oh, they don't want him to see me at the front.'" He concluded that the owner would not tolerate a person of color as the "face of the restaurant."[8] A highly skilled server, who also works as a professional photographer, Luke later became the cochair of the ROC-NY Board of Directors.

The Fireman campaign helped servers see how their grievances, such as overtime violations, were tied to abuses throughout the restaurant industry and the wider society. Servers in upscale restaurants, who often earn $60–$80,000 a year, are expected to emulate the social class of those whom they are serving through conversations, humor, and taste while also deferring to their customers. Many take pride in their interpersonal skills, which also help to maintain their privileged position in the restaurant workforce hierarchy. Servers are more likely than other restaurant workers to receive "emotional care" from managers and owners, as ROC-NY staffer Daisy Chung observed.[9] They potentially have much to lose by getting involved in workplace agitation. For example, their tip income will be threatened if patrons go elsewhere due to a campaign or if management retaliates against them by assigning them fewer or less desirable shifts. Furthermore, ROC-NY's goals emphasize mobility for underrepresented workers and an end to discrimination, a potential threat to white servers in fine dining. And servers with another career goal often do not see themselves as remaining in the industry over the long term. As Luke explained, "[servers say] 'I'm not really a working-class person. I'm just working in a restaurant. I'm doing this just to make a little money.' There's still this disconnect. . . . One of the big things we try to do at ROC is help to raise awareness of worker issues, workers' rights, helping workers identify what is wrong with the system. People identify more with the class that's above them than the class they truly are in."[10]

Indeed, servers at Fireman establishments were accustomed to "throwing other workers under the bus," Luke recalled. They often socialized together but had limited relationships with back-of-the-house workers. "The white workers thought the back of the house would drag them down," a white server who had helped initiate the Fireman campaign later reflected. "But when they started coming to meetings more than waiters, people got it" (quoted in Sen and Mamdouh 2008, 173–74). At first there was mutual suspicion, and Latino workers held their own committee meetings separate from the mostly white servers, who were also meeting to strategize on their own. According to Siby, it was the Latino workers who took the most convincing to link what were initially "two campaigns."[11] Luke himself was not fully committed to the Fireman campaign when he first got involved. "[In the beginning] I stood across the street from the protests," he recalled. "Slowly over the course of the campaign I got to the point where I would leave my shift and go right in front of the restaurant to be a part of the protest actions."[12]

Many of Fireman's back-of-the-house immigrant workers had even more reason to be wary. At one point, the Redeye Grill fired six immigrant campaign leaders for "documentation problems," an action later found to be illegal by the courts.[13] In light of the servers' privileged position, involving them in the campaign was initially controversial among ROC-NY staff members, although they ultimately decided that including the servers would help build the unity needed to win.

The racial divide remained an ongoing challenge as the campaign unfolded. For example, ROC-NY members had to press the legal team representing the Fireman workers to include a diverse group of plaintiffs in the wage and hour lawsuit. The "eloquent" white servers provided gripping testimony, and the lawyers continually favored them until ROC-NY members and organizers insisted that immigrants and people of color should play equally prominent roles in the legal action. Presuming that "the white face was the right face" before a judge only reinforced the racism they were fighting, members contended.

The Fireman settlement ultimately led to a $3.9 million dollar win, exceeding all ROC-NY's previous campaigns, and included as well an EEOC-brokered agreement to change racially discriminatory employment practices (Greenhouse 2008b). Luke stated that the campaign was transformative at his worksite: "The atmosphere has changed. The intimidation is gone."[14] However, there are no formal workers' committees present in the Fireman restaurants to ensure that the settlement terms are enforced, or to work for further workplace changes. Enforcement instead relies on the EEOC's and ROC-NY's continued monitoring, although individual workers regularly orient new hires, recounting the history of the struggle that took place.

Leadership Development

In its earlier efforts, ROC-NY had not always managed to bring together the front- and back-of-the-house, but the success of the Fireman campaign persuaded organizers of the viability of simultaneously confronting racial, ethnic, and gender boundaries. As Eanni-Rodriguez explained, "Now, when we have a group of workers [who come to us], we tell them to come back with a woman, or a person of color, or a cook from the back of the house." When one group of Latino workers was told to come back with women coworkers, they responded, "But the women are all white, what do they have to do with us?"[15] ROC-NY's organizers replied that just as the Latinos faced discrimination as immigrants, women most likely faced gender discrimination as well as sexual harassment.

To become members of ROC-NY, workers participate in individual conversations with organizers and must attend a general orientation meeting. Orientations for those seeking assistance with specific grievances or who wish to enroll in the organization's training programs take place twice each week. After that, potential members must attend three hour-long political education meetings on (1) workers' rights and organizing, (2) research and policy, and (3) "know your rights" health and safety training. Only then do they become full members who can propose campaigns or register for workforce development classes.

Members also contribute monthly dues of $5 (or $50 if they make a single annual payment).

By 2010 ROC-NY's membership had grown to about five thousand members, who were 42 percent Latino, 22 percent black, 21 percent Asian, 11 percent white, and 4 percent other (Chung 2012). Since that time more U.S.-born black members have joined, many of them recruited through the CHOW Institute, ROC-NY's workplace development program. About 30 percent of the members are women. The membership includes some servers earning as much as $80,000 a year, but the majority are bussers, dishwashers, and other low-wage workers who often earn less than the minimum wage.

Members with workplace grievances that could become the basis of potential campaigns must bring them to the general membership for discussion. Not all such cases can be pursued, even if there are legitimate grievances. Some restaurants fall outside of ROC-NY's fine dining focus. And if the organization is already involved in one resource-intensive campaign, the membership may decide against taking on another one at the same time. ROC-NY sometimes encourages workers to embark on "self-organized" campaigns instead, an aspect of its larger commitment to leadership development. As staff member Virgilio Arán explained: "As an organizer, you will train leaders, with the end goal that they become organizers, so they can run their own campaign, and that is their own struggle. They run their own campaign, and when they come out from that campaign they can go and train other people. If we just train people just to have a win . . . we will not have what we have now in the restaurant movement."[16]

Arán, who worked for HERE in Chicago, Toronto, and Vancouver, Canada, before joining ROC-NY, sees leadership development and the political consciousness it fosters as a vital element of the organization's work, outlasting the effects of specific campaigns. Individual grievances and needs may motivate individuals to contact the organization, but as Siby also stressed, workers' commitment is deepened by political education, leadership development, and collective action.

Advancing Opportunities for Workers

Another ROC-NY priority is expanding employment opportunities for women and for racial and ethnic groups that are underrepresented or excluded from jobs in the fine dining segment of the industry. One facet of the organization's political education and leadership development work focuses on what one staff person calls "seeing gender." Participants learn about sexual harassment in particular through peer-to-peer trainings modeled on domestic violence awareness education, and ROC-NY has an active women's committee. The organization is also committed to supporting black workers, who are conspicuously underrepresented in the fine dining segment of the industry. This work takes place primarily through ROC-NY's CHOW Institute, established in 2007 to help current restaurant workers gain entry into better-paying positions through skills training, as well as to help job-seekers with some restaurant experience for whom training can lead to new skills and job connections. CHOW students are offered college credit in partnership with Kingsborough Community College. Housed in the COLORS restaurant space, CHOW is funded through private foundations and New York State workforce development grants to offer training in both front- and back-of-the-house skills, free of charge. The state funding requires that participants in the program include ex-offenders, public benefits program participants, and people with little formal education (less than seventh grade).

Most of the job-seekers in this program are U.S.-born black men and women, who now comprise more than half of the members walking through ROC-NY's doors. CHOW trainees are also exposed to the organization's broader work and undergo political education as well as skills training. Yet the growing number of job-seekers recruited through CHOW presents a challenge for organizers eager to maintain ROC-NY's active base of currently employed restaurant workers. As Siby observed, bringing job-seekers and employed restaurant workers together across ethnic, nativity, and language differences is not easy. Some job-seekers freely admit that while they appreciate the organization's mission, their initial goal is to simply get a job, not to join a campaign.

Whether or not it succeeds in finding work for CHOW participants, ROC-NY seeks to engage them in its leadership development programs, which can be empowering in itself. Eric Brown, an African American worker who had two decades of on-and-off experience in the restaurant industry, was unemployed when he came to the training institute: "I remember thinking, free training for front-of-the-house, that's awesome. You can't get that anywhere."[17] He joined ROC-NY's health and safety committee after learning about it in the membership orientation; he had experienced injury and sickness in past restaurant jobs. Soon after that, he attended his first protest.

Brown later provided testimony for the organization's campaign for paid sick days at a city council hearing, and remembered a council member nodding throughout, and then making a statement acknowledging Brown's passionate testimony. "The ability to have my voice heard was so important," he recalled. "I can't describe how it felt to have someone in a position to do something tell me that they felt what I said."[18] Brown subsequently became highly active in the paid sick days campaign, attending rallies as well as ROC-NY policy committee meetings. In 2011 he became cochair of ROC-NY's Board of Directors.

CHOW promotes professionalism by upgrading workers' skill levels, and also has established an embryonic hiring hall, efforts reminiscent of the craft-based unionism of a century ago. In contrast to early twentieth-century craft unionism (see Cobble 1991a, 433), however, ROC-NY's training and job placement program is explicitly inclusive in regard to race, ethnicity, gender, and occupation. To date, however, ROC-NY's job placement program is far more limited than the union hiring hall model. While workers do receive training in fine dining skills, the program cannot ensure employment placement or set wage standards. However, staffer Kevin Scott, who works to place CHOW training graduates in restaurants, is gradually making connections with restaurant owners on behalf of CHOW graduates. "ROC-NY is a success when employers come to us seeking workers," Scott declared.[19] His goal is to build relationships with restaurants that respect established labor standards and that promote a healthy work environment. He identifies these restaurants through ROC-NY members, or through the New York City Restaurant Industry Roundtable, a high-road employer network that ROC-NY launched in 2005.

The Roundtable

The Roundtable, which brings together employers, advocates, workers, and government officials, helps ROC-NY in its research and policy work, and helps identify and convene owners who take "the high road to profitability."[20] High-road employers follow a code of conduct that includes compliance with all workplace laws, the publication of an employee manual, and support for such policy goals as expanding paid sick days and training opportunities for workers.[21] ROC-NY's first Exceptional Workplace Award was timed in conjunction with New York City Restaurant Week in 2009, when the organization issued a *NYC Diner's Guide to High Road Restaurants*. Since then about half of the twenty-five Roundtable participant employers have received Exceptional Workplace Awards. Awardees are urged to promote their high-road status to consumers on their menus and promotional materials. Most of these restaurants are casual to upscale dining, and several of them are owned by African Americans or immigrants of color. One prominent Roundtable participant is Colicchio & Sons, which is part of a national conglomerate.

As a ROC-NY staffer pointed out, even restaurant owners who comply with the law need support and information about best practices. In 2006 ROC-NY issued a comprehensive manual for employers through the Mayor's Office for Immigrant Affairs, which is provided to every restaurant that receives or renews a business license. The manual provides detailed examples of what employers must do to comply with workplace and immigration laws, as well as extensive information about penalties for discrimination or retaliatory firing in response to worker organizing. ROC-NY also offers monthly trainings on sexual harassment and health and safety to interested restaurant managers.

Roundtable members also contribute to ROC-NY's research and policy endeavors, such as the proposed city Paid Sick Days ordinance. (This legislation was blocked by the chair of the city council, who refused to bring it to a vote.) In another example, in February 2012 a member of the New York City Roundtable spoke at a congressional hearing on raising the federal minimum wage for tipped workers. Such efforts provide a crucial high-road employers' perspective, countering that of the National Restaurant Association and its New York affiliate.

Roundtable members are almost entirely nonunion, however, which makes it controversial among those who assert that the only high road is the union road. Indeed, in the view of some unionists, the "high road" as represented by the Roundtable lowers rather than raises the bar for acceptable labor standards. However, Eanni-Rodriguez defends the project, stating, "We take a fairness approach, we don't want to alienate industry. This could be a *good industry*." Advocacy groups such as the National Employment Law Project, along with ROC-NY's policy committee, focus on identifying policy levers to promote best practices throughout the industry. For example, they suggested that the recently established New York City restaurant health inspection scorecard could also serve as a means to evaluate and publicize labor code compliance, although they were unsuccessful in that effort.[22] ROC-NY also proposed rewarding restaurants that voluntarily include wage, benefits, promotion, and food source information in their applications for state liquor licenses from the State Liquor Authority.

Expanding Strategy and Building Up Scale

Whereas ROC-NY promotes a "high road" stamp for restaurant owners engaging in best labor practices, another much larger organization, Slow Food International, promotes restaurants with sustainable food sourcing practices. ROC-NY has begun to link the two concepts, in an effort to reframe food justice to include "fair food" that is both environmentally sustainable *and* free of labor exploitation at every node in the food worker chain. Thus COLORS restaurant sources from local organic farms, some of them immigrant-owned, and also promotes a model of just employment that includes a prevailing wage. ROC-NY is also a member of the Food Chain Workers Alliance, a coalition of unions and worker centers that promotes "a more sustainable food system that respects workers' rights, based on the principles of social, environmental and racial justice, in which everyone has access to healthy and affordable food."

In this way ROC-NY is actively connecting worker justice with the broader movements for sustainability and ethical consumption. The aim is to raise restaurant patrons' consciousness about the source and artisanship/preparation of their food, as well as the health and welfare of the human beings who pick, deliver, cook, and serve their meals. On its ten-year anniversary, ROC-NY highlighted the connection between worker justice, poverty, food access, and environmental sustainability by honoring Slow Food USA president Josh Viertel.

ROC-NY also links its organizing work to the movement for immigrant rights and the rights of precarious workers more generally. The organization participated in the 2011 Excluded Workers' Congress (later renamed the United Workers Congress), which includes several other independent worker centers throughout the country. Jayaraman and Mamdouh, ROC-NY's original cofounders, are now working with restaurant workers across the country through the national organization ROC-United, which by 2012 had launched new ROCs in eight U.S. cities outside of New York. All ROC local affiliates follow the three-pronged strategic model pioneered by ROC-NY, including workplace justice campaigns, promoting the high road to profitability, and conducting research and policy work to lift standards industry-wide.

In 2012, ROC-United created its own restaurant scorecard, the National Diners' Guide, which calls on consumers to take "action" by eating ethically, and lists both "low" and "high" road establishments throughout the country. ROC-United's policy efforts focus on developing a national high-road political platform that includes raising the federal minimum wage. Its quest for restaurant industry reforms is a potential harbinger of change in the service sector as a whole, since food service is one of the nation's largest job-creating industries (Jayaraman 2011). In the hope of spurring a national conversation about such reforms, Jayaraman (2013) documents restaurant industry conditions through the voices of both workers and owners in her book, *Behind the Kitchen Door* (2013). The book reflects the ROC strategy of reaching out to consumers as well as workers and employers, and argues for a sustainability movement that connects food justice to worker justice, without negatively affecting the industry's profitability.

Conclusion

Along with policy change, and winning concrete improvements in the lives of restaurant workers, ROC-NY is growing its membership, promoting best practices among restaurant employers, and partnering with workers, consumers, and high-road employers while actively promoting racial and gender equality. Through the grassroots involvement of workers, combined with the strategic use of lawsuits, ROC-NY has won significant workplace changes and raised public awareness of both abuses and of the "high road" potential of the industry.

Although the organization draws on union traditions by pursuing practices such as professionalization and job placement, as well as through negotiating legal settlements that raise labor standards well beyond the minimum level required by law, ROC-NY's workplace organizing leaves unionism to the unions. At a time when organized labor faces the ongoing challenge of creatively responding to changing conditions in the restaurant industry, ROC-NY has advanced change for restaurant workers. Rather than replacing traditional unionism, ROC-NY's three-pronged approach exposes by example that a resurgent labor effort for industry-wide change in the twenty-first century will necessarily include a movement orientation. Movement building extends beyond a narrow focus on traditional collective bargaining to instead create a broader alignment, in this case by addressing the sustainability of business models, environmentalism (food security), and the connection of workers' rights to racial, gender, and economic justice.

12

NOT WAITING FOR PERMISSION

The New York Taxi Workers Alliance and
Twenty-First-Century Bargaining

Mischa Gaus

For two days in September 2007 the considerable machinery of New York City's executive branch spun at full tilt, attempting to counter a strike among the city's yellow cab drivers. A special contingency plan divided the city into fare zones, attempting to entice some drivers to break the strike by increasing a driver's take on some fares. The mayor and press declared victory for the beleaguered commuter but had to quietly admit that thousands fewer cabs were trolling the city's streets—and five-minute airport lines had grown to half-hour waits (Lopez 2007). What fearsome labor organization had they crossed swords with? A group of immigrant workers who bring home about $100 for a twelve-hour shift, legally prevented from collective bargaining, who had sat at labor's table in the city for less than a year—and still were demonstrating their strike power for the second time in a decade.

Denied the right to organize under the National Labor Relations Act, New York's taxi drivers encounter the same fate as millions of other workers who are termed "independent contractors" in today's labor market: They have no collective bargaining rights, no job protection, low and variable pay, and little say over the essentials of the job. But they have turned that apparent powerlessness on its head. The New York Taxi Worker Alliance (NYTWA) is the oldest and largest of nineteen such organizations nationwide, claiming fifteen thousand on its membership rolls from among the fifty thousand licensed drivers in the city. Although the NYTWA was granted a union organizing charter by the AFL-CIO in 2011, it does not match present-day unions, because it lacks formalized collective bargaining and does not sign contracts with employers. Indeed, the alliance in many ways resembles a worker center, a type of nontraditional worker organization that sprang up in the 1990s among mostly immigrant workers excluded from the formal labor movement. But even without legal status as an exclusive bargaining agent or a contract with employers, the taxi alliance is exploring many avenues to escape the limitations on collective bargaining. The organization engages in virtually all forms of typical union bargaining, negotiating over income, grievances, benefits, and the conditions of the job. Why will the city and the cab-company owners bargain with the New York taxi alliance when the law provides no mechanism for the taxi drivers, as independent contractors, to do so?

In this chapter I suggest a number of reasons. Of first importance are the particularities of the taxi industry's structure that drive the city toward a stable relationship with the alliance. The city regulates the industry and governs workers' wages and working conditions by setting fare levels, enforcing myriad rules, and controlling the number of medallions—the legal permits needed to operate a cab in New York City. The structured relationships between the city, the owners, and the workforce give the NYTWA points of leverage that other low-wage contingent workers lack. The success of the alliance is also due to its construction of rank-and-file driver power that makes collective action possible in a key transportation node. New York's political leaders care deeply about the image- and commerce-crippling potential of logjams in the streets of the global city, and the NYTWA's ability to mobilize workers makes it a threat they take seriously. The long and slow work of member-to-member outreach and advocacy built the alliance's reputation as a trusted representative for the drivers. Finally, a leadership corps led by executive director Bhairavi Desai has mastered the language of policy and the art of politics, effectively inserting the alliance into negotiations that shape the working lives of drivers. Industry expertise and organizational longevity have helped to propel the alliance into quasi-bargaining relationships with city leaders and taxi bosses.

Structural (Dis)Advantages

New York's taxi industry is divided into three groups: yellow cabs that customers hail on the street, mostly clustered in Manhattan; livery cars which are dispatched to an address after a customer calls in, mainly outside Manhattan; and prearranged black cars and limos for VIP pickup in Manhattan. Yellow cabs are further fragmented by neoliberal financial innovation.[1] When a passenger steps into a cab—something that happens 485,000 times every day in New York City—she enters one of three different ownership scenarios: both vehicle and medallion are owned by a garage and leased to the driver, the driver owns the vehicle but a broker owns the medallion ("driver-owned vehicle"), or the vehicle and medallion are owned by the person sitting behind the wheel. The industry was split 60/40 between cabs owned by fleets and owner-operated cabs through the 1970s.

In the twenty-first century, however, there is a three-way split: 25 percent of the cabs are owned by fleets, 25 percent by owner-operators, and 50 percent by brokers. This reflects a shift in the industry's power structure that has increasingly reduced the number of owner-operators and made brokers the dominant force. Taxi ownership is spread across four tightly networked interest groups representing brokers, garages, hybrid gas–electric vehicle owners, and medallion financiers. The brokers are middlemen who exploited the gaps in the regulatory system to capture control of medallions that older drivers sold to generate retirement income, in the process morphing a state-issued permit into a financial instrument that gains value with every medallion auction.[2] The splintered nature of the industry feeds into drivers' disbelief in their potential power and their conflicted identity as independent workers.

The city's regulation of taxis gives the workers in the industry a key point of leverage, however. The Taxi and Limousine Commission (TLC) controls entry to the market through its power to auction new medallions and approve the qualifications of each potential new medallion purchaser (Schaller Consulting 2003). It also has the ability to shape wages and working conditions by setting fare levels and drafting and enforcing a variety of rules that drivers and owners must obey. As a result of a deal the NYTWA brokered in 2011, for instance, the TLC began dispatching undercover enforcement agents to garages used by brokers and fleets. In the first months of enforcement, NYTWA's complaints led to one broker receiving an $80,000 summons, and a garage owner receiving a $150,000 summons, for overcharges (NYTWA 2011f).

But the TLC is rarely a sympathetic forum for workers. Its nine members are appointed by the mayor, with the advice and consent of the city council, which is responsible for recommending five members, one from each borough. Composed of political appointees without industry experience, the panel has never had a member who drove a taxi, a tradition the current commissioner, former city councilmember David Yassky, defends as necessary to avoid potential "conflicts of interest."[3] The commercial and social ties that bind other commission members to networks of political and financial patronage apparently do not evoke such concern.

New York's taxi industry, like the nation's airline and trucking sectors, underwent radical restructuring in the neoliberal period that began in the 1970s (Hamilton 2008; Tilly 1996). In contrast to those industries, the city's taxi industry was not deregulated; indeed, the continuing oversight of the TLC would help enable the worker organizing that followed. But the restructuring that did take place led to a dramatic deterioration in wages and work conditions. Drivers episodically organized through the 1980s to resist the downward slide. The first substantial effort came from South Asian drivers who coalesced in 1992 into an ethnically based advocacy group known as the Lease Drivers Coalition. Desai was hired in 1996, and in disagreements over whether the group should answer to a board of nondrivers or to worker-representatives, the drivers' coalition split with its initial sponsor, the Committee Against Anti-Asian Violence, in 1998 and became the New York Taxi Workers Alliance, open to all yellow cab drivers.

From its inception, NYTWA called itself a union.[4] But the union it created is by no means the first in the industry. Taxi workers were part of the Transport Workers Union as early as 1937, although industry resistance and "company unions" that signed sweetheart contracts undermined their efforts (Mathew 2008). Although the taxi unions never could lift pay and work conditions to as high a level as their counterparts in basic industries in the post–World War II era, drivers had steady jobs with benefits and guaranteed paychecks in this period.

The advent of independent contracting spelled the death of the stable taxi job. In the old commission-based system, drivers earned a steady daily rate and enjoyed fringe benefits, whether they had a lucky day or not. When the TLC authorized the transition to "independent contractor" drivers leasing their cabs in 1979, they held out the promise of higher earnings without fully disclosing the risks drivers would face. The drivers themselves rebelled against becoming contractors with one garage launching a short-lived wildcat strike. The last taxi driver union, Service Employees International Union (SEIU) Local 3036, helped usher in the new era of precarity. Driver opposition to contracting was muted by a Lease Drivers Benefit Fund—and a vigorous campaign from union officers, who acted to protect their perquisites (Zeiger 1998). Bill Lindauer, a NYTWA leader who began driving in the 1970s, said union officials led retirees to believe that the fund would protect their pension benefits and mobilized them to vote for it (along with the leasing system); the resulting votes outweighted the opposition of active drivers. But the fund served a rather smaller class of beneficiaries. "The union officers were ready to retire and they wanted a cushy existence," Lindauer recalled.[5]

According to drivers, the SEIU local began to disintegrate in the 1980s as native-born workers retired or abandoned the increasingly degraded jobs under the lease system. Javaid Tariq, a NYTWA leader who started driving in 1990, said drivers scornfully called SEIU the "$3 union," because they had to drop that amount into a machine each shift to take the cab out of the garage, with the money going to the union. He has no memory of ever seeing a union rep or tapping any benefits from the dues he coughed up every day.[6]

Once the system of independent contracting was firmly in place, immigrant drivers were recruited to fill the new contracted positions. Diditi Mitra (2005) argues that the immigrants, overwhelmingly male, came to dominate the field in New York due in part to the declining numbers of low-skilled native-born residents in the city and the entry of newcomers who arrived following the 1965 liberalization of U.S. immigration law. With limited language skills and little access to public sector employment, they were willing to accept work that native minorities would not. Douglas Massey and his colleagues (2002), similarly, suggest that immigrants' acceptance of low-wage work is grounded in expectations rooted in their home-country experiences.

The rise of independent contracting was accompanied by an explosion in medallion prices, as brokers took advantage of owner-operators seeking to generate retirement income as they fled the industry. Since the supply of medallions is limited and the ability to generate healthy returns is all but assured for the owner,[7] investors flocked to the new opportunity and prices soared. In 1971, medallions were valued around $30,000 but by 2011 they sold for about $1 million (Grynbaum 2011b; NYTWA 2011d).

Medallion prices historically had been modest. The initial price was $5 when the medallion was first created in 1937 to regulate the supply of cabs (Mathew 2008). But unlike most other cities, in New York medallions were transferable, so that over time a private market developed in which they were bought and sold. Because the city limits their number, but not their circulation, medallion prices have skyrocketed. As valuations soared well above the reach of most individuals, the proportion of drivers who owned and operated their own vehicle plummeted. Instead of earning a percentage of the meter, most drivers now leased their cabs, typically paying more than $100 a day, and had to buy their own fuel (see table 12.1). "It doesn't take too long to figure out the deck is stacked against you," said Zubin Soleimany, who has been driving cabs for two years, trying to patch the holes in his budget as other work became slimmer.[8] Some observers compare the leasing setup to sharecropping. "Their day is spent trying to dig themselves out of a hole" (Surowiecki 2002). The TWA says yearly takehome earnings average just $27,000. Data from the U.S. Census Bureau's 2010 American Community Survey (ACS) pegs average hourly pay for taxi drivers in New York City at $12.50.[9]

Taxi drivers in New York are stereotyped as predominantly South Asian, but NYTWA's data indicates a much more variegated ethnic composition among drivers. The largest groups in the independent contractor era are indeed South Asian: Bangladeshis, Pakistanis, and Indians, in order of predominance, but these groups make up only 55 percent of the total. The 2010 ACS data also reveal

TABLE 12.1 **Typical shift expenses and net pay, New York City taxi drivers, 2011**

Typical gross bookings	$286	
COST BREAKDOWN	AMOUNT	% OF BOOKINGS SPENT ON INDUSTRY COST
Lease	$113	40
Fuel	$51	18
Credit card surcharges	$6	2
Subtotal	$170	60
Expenses not cited by city		
Shift incidentals (parking, tolls, and extras to garage), maintenance costs	$20	6
Typical total expenses	$190	66
		% OF BOOKINGS FOR DRIVER EARNING
Driver take-home pay (after 12 hour shift)	$96	34
Compared to minimum wage	−5%	
Compared to living wage ($10/hr)	−40%	

Source: Unpublished data from NYTWA.

a greater degree of racial and ethnic diversity (see table 12.2). Although those data indicate that 38 percent of drivers were foreign-born in 2010, very few if any undocumented immigrants are among the ranks of yellow cab drivers, because of strict licensing requirements.

Leverage in a Key Transportation Node

NYTWA consciously deploys the language of the global city, referring to drivers as the "city's ambassadors" and reinforcing the idea that the provision of their service is tied into the smooth functioning of the financial sector that dominates Manhattan's economy. Such a discourse lays bare the enormous economic, spatial, and social changes wrought by New York's transformation, and the disparities at their root. The old Fordist economy's promise of stability through wage-driven mass consumption has long since been replaced by a polarized social structure, with a caste of low-paid, contingent, racialized workers providing a variety of personal services to the increasingly affluent class of professionals concentrated in the financial sector (Sassen 2001; Castells and Mollenkopf 1991).

TABLE 12.2 **New York City taxi workers by national origin, race, and ethnicity, 2010**

National origin	
South Asian	55%
Haitian	15%
African	10%
Arab	10%
Latino	5%
Eastern European	5%

Race/ethnicity	
White	16%
Black	24%
Latino	27%
Asian	27%
Other	5%

Sources: For national origin data, unpublished data from NYTWA; for race/ethnicity data, 2010 American Community Survey.

Note: In the race/ethnicity section, figures for whites, blacks, Asians, and others do not include Latinos.

The NYTWA's capacity to mount effective strikes made it a formidable presence from the outset, and one result was that the TLC and others in the city's political elite viewed it as a potentially powerful organization. The alliance lost no time in demonstrating its willingness to act, launching a twenty-four-hour strike within months of its 1998 founding. That early action came in response to the attempt by the administration of Mayor Rudy Giuliani to triple fines for drivers and its casual attitude toward police harassment of drivers. From a base of only five hundred active members, the alliance used traditional organizing tactics—distributing flyers and talking with drivers in the airport lots—to mobilize enough of the city's taxi drivers to stop work and gain credibility (Moody 2008). Giuliani deployed riot police in armored vehicles and denounced the workers as "taxi terrorists," underscoring the threat he saw in their emerging power and the racism undergirding his administration's treatment of drivers (Mathew 2008).

This first strike showed the power of a collective approach in a key transportation node. Taxi alliance leaders immediately understood that the city would respond to their mobilizations, fueling their organizing efforts. In 2002, the alliance coordinated the participation of four thousand drivers in an advocacy campaign that allowed thousands to access federal emergency aid to repay debts incurred after 9/11 decimated business in Manhattan. A two-year bid to raise fares culminated in threats of another job action in 2004, which led city regulators to grant a rise in fares with 70 percent of the increase going to the drivers—more than they had seen in decades (Mathew 2008). "So many times we fight for raising the meter and they'd just raise the lease," said Mohammad Jamil Hussain, who began driving a New York cab in 1988. "They squeezed us every which way."[10] The alliance once again won the lion's share of a 17 percent fare increase in 2012, beating back intense pressure from the taxi lobby to boost lease rates at the same time.

These campaigns were marked by professionalized advocacy efforts, including a media strategy that netted sympathetic coverage and a report on drivers' stagnating wages from a third-party research partner (Waheed and Romero-Alston 2003). The alliance also deployed lobbying techniques to win its gains, including worker testimony, rallies, and other direct pressure tactics on decision makers.

For veteran taxi drivers, the wave of activism initiated by the alliance among the "hacks" who drive cabs is the most exciting development in a generation, stretching beyond the boundaries of a fragmented workforce to create a cultural and political unity unseen for decades (Hodges 2007). But while it describes itself as a union, the NYTWA shares many of the characteristics of the worker centers that Janice Fine (2006) analyzed, such as provision of legal and health services, outspoken advocacy on immigrant rights, and careful nurturing of member-leaders. At the same time, by normalizing dues paying as part of membership requirements, attempting to set labor standards across an industry and not employer by employer, and not shying away from mass collective action, the Taxi Worker Alliance has functioned more like a union than a worker center. Widely acknowledged as the largest and most powerful organized group of drivers in the country, NYTWA also offers extensive services to its members, and is the first place other taxi advocates turn for advice on building their local organizations (Ten Eyck 2010). Thus NYTWA anchored the negotiations to create the national taxi union charter with the AFL-CIO, discussed below.

But without formalized collective bargaining, can the taxi alliance live up to its bold billing as the newest union on the block? The NYTWA has demonstrated that its capacity for collective action can be wielded effectively, even as its work is guided by the moral appeals of a public-policy campaign and the urgencies of immigrant incorporation in an unforgiving climate bounded by race and religion. The fare rates and lease caps that the alliance negotiates with the city are legally enforceable, a point the alliance reinforces with periodic class-action lawsuits against garage owners who attempt to skirt the rules with fines, fees, and other illegal overcharges.

One crucial determinant is its ability to protect and expand the gains it has made, the essence of the "contractual" unionism that took root among U.S. unions in the 1940s (Lichtenstein 2002). Jenkins (2002) argues that worker centers, unlike unions, are inherently limited in what they can accomplish in flexible labor markets reordered by footloose global capital. Thus much of what they call "organizing" in fact involves appeals to elite institutions through advocacy with a worker's face. The gains worker centers make are often short-lived, because they cannot be defended against a chaotic and intensively competitive market.[11] Even more significant, most worker centers lack the leverage to bring pay and conditions above the minimum provided by law. Advocacy strategies have led to pathbreaking new legal protections for key groups of excluded and marginalized workers, particularly in New York (see Goldberg, McAlevey, this volume), although vexing difficulties of enforcement remain. The taxi alliance, on the other hand, given an existing enforcement agency—the TLC—has effectively negotiated a greater share of industry income through fare hikes. It has bargained as well to direct the city's disciplinary power against employers, as the large fines levied for illegal overcharges exemplify.

Other analysts (Early 2007; Fine 2007) suggest that the distinctive funding structures that support worker centers and unions explain much of the difference between the two. Foundation funding, they argue, drives many of the worker centers toward service delivery that may in fact hinder their organizing. That critique does not seem to apply to the taxi alliance, which stands out among worker centers for its robust dues structure. About two thousand of its members pay $100 a year to join, which gives them access to legal, insurance, and health services. Legal services are the major draw, helping drivers contest tickets for speeding or dropping off passengers too far from the curb, and offering referrals to NYTWA-affiliated lawyers for more complicated cases. NYTWA reports that 80 percent of its $450,000 budget in 2010 was derived from dues and other income generated from services provided to drivers. Its reliance on foundations has diminshed over time.

Through its years of action and well-honed moral suasion, the alliance gradually maneuvered its way into the formal labor movement. The NYTWA's relationship with New York's labor movement began almost from the organization's birth, when Desai reached out to Ed Ott at the city's Central Labor Council (CLC). Desai wanted help in quashing a city council bill in 1998 that would have returned taxi drivers to employee status. Ott recalls that the bill originated from "unions sniffing around the corpse of the deceased [SEIU] Local 3036."[12] Desai pleaded for more time to organize the drivers and Ott helped kill the bill, convinced that NYTWA was developing industry expertise and an authentic base among taxi workers.

When Ott became the CLC's interim director in 2006, he pressed to invite the taxi workers to become members of the council, warning affiliated unions that they ignored the city's "other working class," the hundreds of thousands of unorganized service workers, at their peril. Public sector workers, comprising the bulk of the city's unionized labor force (Milkman and Braslow 2011), could not expect to enjoy good wages and benefits for long on the backs of low-wage workers in the private sector, Ott argued.

In the eyes of many analysts (e.g., Moody 2007), the CLC's invitation to the taxi workers was a coming-of-age moment for worker centers nationally. The alliance's 2007 affiliation marked a rare openness in the world of CLCs, typically staid and unremarkable bodies that focus mostly on electoral work on behalf of Democratic politicians, although some (mostly on the West Coast) were reinvigorated in the 1990s (Dean and Reynolds 2009; Fletcher and Gapasin 2008). Although symbolically important, the practical effect of the Taxi Worker Alliance's entry into the official labor movement in New York was modest. At the peak of its 2007 campaign, the NYTWA had its strike headquarters at Transport Workers Local 100, the bus-and-subway workers' union whose power the alliance both envies and scorns.[13] The teachers' union president voiced support at an alliance press conference as the strike neared.

But after Ott's departure in 2009, the CLC dropped the taxi workers from its communications network and stopped inviting its representatives to meetings. The more significant legacy of the CLC's earlier decision to affiliate the NYTWA came in October 2011, when the alliance won a charter as an AFL-CIO union. The charter gives the Taxi Workers Alliance the status of a national union, with the capacity to affiliate other local taxi driver groups provided 10 percent of the drivers are paying dues. The AFL-CIO also committed financial and political support to NYTWA, which its leaders believe will aid their legislative program and end any questions about their legitimacy. Tariq pointed out that the alliance maintains control over its own agenda, since it affiliated to the AFL-CIO as an independent entity, rather than being merged into an existing national union. "We gain political power and more strength," Tariq said. "But we are still in charge of our movement."[14] The NYTWA received further confirmation of labor's commitment in 2013, when Desai became the first worker center leader on the AFL-CIO's executive board.

The new taxi workers' union dramatically challenges received wisdom about who is a union member in the twenty-first-century United States. This was clearly demonstrated by the driver-leaders of the alliance when they accepted their AFL-CIO charter at the federation's Washington, DC headquarters, overlooking the White House. After leaving a ceremony presided over by President Rich Trumka, a thick-chested former leader of the Mineworkers, several taxi workers retired to the bathroom to wash their feet in the federation's sinks. They reemerged, unrolled rugs, and knelt in silent prayer.

Mastering the Art of Politics

The city sees NYTWA as a counterweight to the brokers and fleet owners who have vigorously resisted the encroachment of regulation and public policy demands. The alliance's relentless lobbying and testimony at every TLC and city council hearing has won it respect not only at the TLC but also with the wider public, thanks in part to active coverage by the media, which identifies the NYTWA as the collective voice for drivers. Because the TLC answers to mayoral appointees, and because Mayor Michael Bloomberg has ruled as a strong executive in his three-term reign, the "city" for the taxi alliance has mostly meant the mayor's administration in the last decade, another aspect of the centralized system on which the NYTWA has learned to apply pressure.

The first demand that split the city from the owners was the imposition of higher fuel-efficiency (and higher cost) hybrid cabs, which the owners resisted (Irmas 2008). The alliance became an ally of the Bloomberg administration on this issue, isolating the owners after the city agreed that drivers should not bear an outsized portion of the vehicle's extra cost. The alliance's shaping of a significant industry restructuring during 2011, discussed below, is another example of its ability to strike deals with the city against the bosses' interests.

The NYTWA has claimed a seat at the bargaining table by showing its policy bona fides. Each fare and lease proposal from the garages is countered. Its representatives expertly interpret the city's regulatory language, shaping it into what might be called a de facto grievance process. Tickets and summonses are contested at "settlement conferences," winning fine reductions for groups of drivers facing the same ticket or sanction and identifying problematic trends within the industry. The best-known example comes from a scandal that broke in March 2010 when the outgoing TLC commissioner accused three-quarters of all drivers of overcharging passengers by a total of $8.6 million. Headlines screamed about thirty-six thousand crooked cabbies, but after the alliance challenged the TLC's data, the number of supposed scofflaws dropped to just three hundred. The alliance noted that the meter's design flaws caused thousands of cabbies to mistakenly punch the higher-fare button at the end of a ride—when it would earn them no additional money. As this example illustrates, NYTWA has established itself as an honest broker in an industry long accustomed to opaque accounting, off-the-meter fares, and an assortment of questionable operators.

Nowhere is the alliance's trusted role clearer than in its long campaign to win drivers a health care fund. According to the alliance's internal studies, 40 percent of drivers are uninsured—and 78 percent of drivers who do have insurance draw on a public plan (NYTWA 2011a). If anything, the NYTWA may be underestimating the number of uninsured drivers: Data from the 2010 Census ACS, similarly, indicate that 80 percent of all New York City taxi drivers have no employer-provided health insurance.

NYTWA negotiated with the city to set aside a percentage of the 2012 fare increase for a fund for drivers' health insurance. With unmet need so high, the alliance is confident that offering this key benefit to thousands of workers excluded from job-based benefits will cement its reputation among drivers and provide a basis for its fiscal independence. Like the organizations of informal sector workers in India that Rina Agarwala describes (2006), New York's taxi drivers have shifted their demands to the state to win benefits that their employers will not (or cannot) provide.

In June 2012, TLC commissioner Yassky agreed to earmark a portion of the 17 percent fare increase for a Voluntary Employee Beneficiary Association. The six-cent surcharge on each ride will provide a health care and disability fund for drivers (Goldenberg 2012). The city was in the process of selecting a vendor to administer the fund in late 2013. "We see it as part of the employment model we regulate to promote driver welfare, including doing what we can to ensure a taxi driver is a profession where somebody can earn a living, support a family, have good working conditions," Yassky explained. "Because when you have a driver who is earning a decent living and working conditions, you're going to have a better ride for the passenger."[15]

Leadership

Despite the alliance's embrace of collective action and mainstream unionism, drivers remain divided by language, culture, and the day-by-day competition for fares on the street, which can undermine these efforts. An "individualistic, privatized, corporate mentality seeps into the union," one leader said. NYTWA addresses this challenge by deliberately building a mass membership organization with careful attention to who represents the group publicly and how. The Organizing Committee, the alliance's leadership body, is exclusively composed of eighteen drivers or former drivers, who represent a broad array of nationalities. An executive committee of five forms the core leadership. Both groups are appointed by incumbent leaders, led by Desai. Their terms have no fixed length, but leadership rotates as new recruits are asked to step up and older ones step back. NYTWA leaders see this loose hierarchy as benefiting the group's internal decision making—although it also cloaks a less-visible power dynamic that is weighted toward the organization's staff. The staffers speak the major languages of the drivers, who by virtue of city licensing must all pass an English language proficiency test.

The alliance is driven by a belief that worker organizations are only as effective as their members, who rally to the alliance because they can access the levers of power inside the organization. Even though Desai, as executive director and de facto leader of NYTWA since the organization split from its parent group in 1998, is principally responsible for forming the alliance's plans, she consults drivers and Organizing Committee members at every step. Each plan is put to votes before the driver leadership and the membership in late-night mass meetings, the largest of which grew to five hundred during strike time. (A typical meeting during the day might attract forty, but the night meetings, held quarterly, usually bring out a few hundred.) The leadership's plans are sometimes amended by voices from the floor. "Our positions are worked out in a back and forth between leadership and drivers," Lindaeur said. "We don't want decisions handed down from on high."[16]

Desai is a powerful and respected force among city officials, reporters, and company owners. Members and officials alike praise her leadership, and industry representatives grumble about her closeness to city regulators. Although the bulk of the organizing at the airport lots and "member servicing" work in the office is carried on without her direct involvement, it's not clear the organization would have the same effectiveness without her articulate advocacy. An overreliance on charismatic leaders has hurt many labor organizations in the past, but Desai embraces worker leadership in the organization, and has hired as staff several drivers who first approached the alliance in their moment of need and were transformed by the encounter.

Although she shuns her media tag as the taxi driver's "confessor" (Widdicombe 2011), Desai's gender puts the taxi driving population—which is 97 percent male, according to 2010 Census ACS data—at ease. Desai, who immigrated from the Indian state of Gujarat when she was seven years old, says she sees one-on-one interactions with these men who feel voiceless as essential to base-building for a union that aims to shape drivers' collective consciousness.[17] Desai's mother was a Teamster member who worked the night shift at a New Jersey factory as she grew up. Desai was drawn to the taxi alliance from a belief in a bottom-up organizing culture shaped watching her mother fight battles at her job, and later by her days at Rutgers University, where she completed women's studies and history degrees. "Drivers appreciated that somebody gave a damn, that somebody recognized what the conditions were, and that they needed to change," she said (Nash and Rosenberg 2007).

When she was just starting out, Desai recalled, some taxi drivers, officers from the old union, and bosses told her that she could not embody worker power because she was an immigrant woman of color. Some went so far as to suggest that her only path to power was through sleeping her way to the top. "That was the expectation of what I should be doing," she said. But Desai sees her leadership as confronting racist and sexist legacies head-on. "In organizing the working class, the real beauty is transformation. The people you're organizing change because of you, and you change because of them," she explained (Nash and Rosenberg 2007).

The relationships built through that process of transformation can also challenge the dyanmics of power in the organization. NYTWA does not operate with the formality of mainstream unions; no sergeants-at-arms or parliamentarians are needed to assure Robert's Rules are followed to the letter. The internal culture of the alliance is a more rollicking and flexible affair. With the advent of the taxi alliance's union charter, the organization will amend its constitution and bylaws, however, which may lead to a more structured decision-making process as the NYTWA grows and matures.

The drivers' concerns directly shape the organization's imperatives in other ways. Up to fifty drivers drop by the office every day of the week, as late as 10 p.m., turning the headquarters into a constant hive of activity. The drivers seek out the NYTWA when they're in trouble with a ticket or summons, as word of mouth has drawn them toward the problem-solving mechanisms accorded to members. The organization, which started with half a desk at a community center, is fast outgrowing a Manhattan office housing its eight staffers.

The reputation of the alliance was built in the closest thing drivers have to a "break room," the restaurants and airport parking lots where the drivers gather. The NYTWA consciously approaches drivers with multiethnic delegations of organizers so drivers are pulled in across racial-ethnic divides. Desai would have groups of Pakistani drivers meet at Bangladeshi restaurants, and vice versa, until neither group saw themselves as predominant.

But racial divisions still vex the relationship between drivers and passengers. In May 2011 the mayor and city council increased penalties for drivers who refuse to take fares outside of Manhattan, with a third violation resulting in loss of the hack license. The stiff penalties result from a widespread belief that cabs refuse to pick up African American passengers hailing cabs in Manhattan because drivers are racist. In the aftermath of a widely publicized incident in 1999 when actor Danny Glover complained he was refused service, the alliance joined with sympathetic politicians and community groups to hold public hearings explaining the drivers' perspective: a fare refusal is a matter of economics, not race, because drivers face the risk of an hour-long ride back to Manhattan from black neighborhoods such as Brownsville or Bedford-Stuyvesant without a passenger, losing money with every minute and every drop of gas. By putting all the risk on the driver's back, the industry structure trains drivers to stick as close as possible to the densest fare-generating zones, the alliance argues.

Such a discourse, however, overlooks the ways that race has influenced the drivers' strategies. Drivers assume that black and brown passengers are heading to distant neighborhoods because a legacy of segregation, accelerated by the gentrification accompanying New York's swing toward the global city, has pushed people of color to the margins of the city. A cabbie's refusal to pick up people of color has as much to do with the passenger's skin color as the driver's fear of economic losses. Informal talk during an alliance meeting discussing the city's rules for refusals also suggests that drivers justify their refusal to pick up black passengers in safety terms, a reminder that even a majority people of color organization like NYTWA must confront pernicious stereotypes that mold behavior.

Drivers' fears for their safety are, however, very real. Taxi workers suffer extraordinary rates of violence on the job: According to the Bureau of Labor Statistics, taxi drivers are thirty-six times more likely to be killed while at work than the average employee (Sygnatur and Toscano 2000). On-the-job violence represents a critical workplace concern that has fed the alliance mobilizations. When a driver was stabbed with a knife during a religiously motivated hate crime in 2010, NYTWA blamed the crime on fear-mongering accompanying the potential building of a mosque in lower Manhattan (Grynbaum 2010a). But the organization quickly turned attention away from the driver's religion and toward industry conditions. NYTWA successfully lobbied for a law, approved almost unanimously by the state legislature just a month after the attack, that would have increased criminal penalties for passengers who assault drivers, only to see the governor veto it on a technicality (Grynbaum 2010b). The alliance continued to lobby for the bill and constantly discussed it in member meetings and newsletters, to no avail.

Drivers respond to the alliance's safety focus. When Mohammad Jamil Hussain was violently mugged while driving his cab, no news outlets covered the assault. His jaw was broken and he needed eighteen screws and two plates implanted to repair the damage. Sitting at home, unable to work, he sank into a deep depression. Desai heard about the attack on Hussain through the driver grapevine, tracked him down, and helped him secure workers' compensation—and therapy. Drivers like Hussain see Desai's emotional investment in their recovery as a powerful incentive to become more involved in the union. "I'm very much motivated because as a victim, it's a kind of moral obligation I have," Hussain said. "I'm totally convinced that I have to believe in taxi organizing, no matter what. I have to fight for the rights of taxi drivers."[18]

NYTWA cofounder Javaid Tariq says the education many cab drivers bring to the job benefits their organizing. His own story is a prime example. Tariq entered taxi driving accidentally: He was working odd jobs in the Bronx, after fleeing Pakistan under its military dictatorship, where his status as a student union leader was a liability. A photography student at the New School, he acquired a hack license to document the desperation and violence constantly surrounding cab drivers for a class project. Fourteen years later, he is at the center of the fight against the industry's exploitation. "The class background of drivers—it infuriates them and propels them to action," he said. "People think they'll leave the job and become professionals, but [because of] responsibilities here and back home—you get stuck."[19]

Interviews with members and organizational leaders highlight the shifting class position of drivers as they assume a new proletarian position in the United States. In 2010, 42.5 percent of the taxi driver population in New York City had some college education (either in their countries of birth or in the United States), while 21 percent had completed a bachelor's or advanced degree, according to the ACS. The alliance consistently argues for collective advancement of all drivers. But drivers' own self-conception can hinder organizing. With independent contracting came the promise of being one's own boss, and advancing from an unstable and precarious leasing arrangement into full participation in the "ownership society."

Among leaders of the alliance, the drivers' bid for economic independence is a complex issue. Some see the promise of entrepreneurship as a fiction to be challenged and overcome through organizing conversations, since the reality is that most drivers will not leave the industry, whatever their aspirations. They counter the entrepreneurial self-image by tracking which drivers respond negatively to the idea of unionism and collective action, and by challenging them in subsequent months and years when NYTWA organizers encounter them again, waiting for an airport fare despite confident promises that they were saving up enough to leave hacking behind them. Desai comments on the aspirations of the drivers:

> Drivers see [hacking] as a path of economic independence but not a path out of the industry. It's a path within the industry; they could be a medallion owner in the future, or a [driver-owned vehicle] operator and work less hours. But it's predominantly immigrants and they recognize this is their profession in this country. So they want to professionalize the working conditions.[20]

Another conception of entrepreneurialism exists within the NYTWA leadership, however. What is mistakenly read as "entrepreneurial" desires, others argue, is in fact a healthy appreciation of workplace control and autonomy. Drivers flocked to the industry even as conditions worsened because cab driving gave them a job where they could spend two hours in a restaurant on a slow night, or leave for a monthlong trip to visit the home country without seeking anyone's approval, or just switch on the "off duty" light for a while if a passenger had abused them and they wanted a break. In this telling of the story, the drivers' desire for control over their day overshadows ambitions of ownership. Their struggle for autonomy is part of a long tradition of resistance by U.S. workers to "management rights," from early twentieth century fights against Taylorist regimentation to the 1972 GM Lordstown strike, fueled by young workers' resentments over numbing work conditions (Gorz 1999; Aronowitz 1992).

In this case, however, the price of autonomy is stunted earning power, and the passive acceptance of a system that makes it well-nigh impossible to achieve economic independence, much less the promise of a secure retirement. "The extra money is not worth it if it means a loss of freedom," said Biju Mathew, a member of the alliance's executive committee.[21]

The issue of drivers' autonomy motivated the 2007 fight against GPS tracking systems in cabs, which provoked the strike that opened this chapter. Drivers resented not just the loss of privacy that the GPS represented but also the city's ability to monitor their worklife, which they understood to be the first step toward controlling it. The freedom accorded by the independent contractor status is particularly prized by the 60 percent of drivers who alliance leaders estimate are Muslim, though among that group they say only 15 percent might adhere to the ritual of five daily prayers.

The ownership status of drivers is a dividing line, too. Such concerns spelled the doom of previous organizing efforts among drivers in Los Angeles, as lease drivers and owner-operators saw their interests diverge (Leavitt and Blasi 2010). New York's taxi alliance attempts to manage the divisions by speaking to the needs of all segments of the workforce, who all share the same fare rates, for instance.

The divisions between the types of drivers is mirrored in larger segmentation between workers who drive yellow cabs and those driving "black cars," the livery cars that travel the "outer boroughs." The livery drivers have no effective organization; a nascent union effort undertaken by the Machinists in the 1990s sputtered in the atmosphere of fear provoked by the government crackdown on immigrants following 9/11 (Ness 2005). The other organization claiming livery drivers' allegiance is propped up by owners and led by an opportunistic livery-company operator who will claim to represent yellow cab drivers when convenient (Mathew 2008). Led by Fernando Mateo, the New York State Taxi Federation appears to have no base among drivers. It exists to provide "driver" support for owners' proposals in the media, pays drivers to participate in sporadic lobbying events, and periodically issues flyers denouncing the NYTWA. After launching a string of unprintable comments about Mateo, NYTWA executive council member Beresford Simmons said, "His job is to try to sow confusion among the drivers about our actions."[22]

The result is a relationship of mutual distrust. Whereas yellow cab drivers and their effective organizing and advocacy group can lead and win campaigns, livery drivers faced a historic crisis in 2011. When the mayor and the TLC proposed to place six thousand new taxis in the outer boroughs, they were met with furious opposition from livery owners who believed they would be swamped by new competition. Unwilling to surrender its policy prerogative, the city worked with the NYTWA on a plan to introduce two thousand new yellow taxis and establish a new permit exclusively for liveries' street-hail rights in the outer boroughs. The eighteen thousand new permits will be available to existing livery businesses, which must restrict their street pick-ups to areas underserved by yellow cabs. A lawsuit from livery-company owners halted the plan in June 2012, on the grounds that the city council, not the state legislature, is the proper forum for rule-making around city transportation issues (Flegenheimer 2012). But the suit failed to alter the legislation, and the city forced liveries to paint the cars an apple green to signal their special status to passengers. The city ensures they don't stray from their specially appointed zones through street enforcement, buttressed by GPS (Global Positioning System) data that the city gathers. Enforcement came swiftly, with the city reporting 1,869 summoneses and tickets and fifty-one cars impounded at the airports for illegal pickups in just one month (NYTWA 2011e).

The NYTWA's grand bargain with city leaders traded the alliance's blessing for expanded service in the outer boroughs in order to win TLC enforcement against garage overcharges and illegal pickups at the airports and throughout lower Manhattan. The taxi drivers also persuaded city regulators to freeze the credit-card processing fees charged to cab drivers at $10 a shift, another major economic win for the drivers. The alliance says the fees, which previously captured 5 percent of each transaction, cost drivers $55 million annually, and that a flat rate represents significant savings. "We just defeated the 1 percent," a tearful Desai told reporters as the TLC announced the lower fees for credit-card processing (Horan 2012). "We don't have their money, their lobbyists, or their P.R. people. Today is evidence that working people can still win in this society."

Desai notes that this is the first time taxi workers have intervened in the market-making arena dominated by industry players and city regulators, and forced them to make concessions to worker interests during a restructuring. The NYTWA knows the limit of its power, however. Alliance leaders agitated against the mayor's plans to expand service in the outer boroughs, insisting that putting more cabs on the road won't change the economics of an industry that shifts all risk to the driver. For months, the alliance publicly advocated for a zero-value medallion lottery—which would begin to uncouple the medallion from the financiers who control it—but acknowledged that a budget-strapped city was unlikely to pass up an opportunity to raise an estimated $1 billion in revenue from auctioning off the new medallions. Although tensions will run high between yellow and livery drivers over territory and enforcement of the new pickup rights, NYTWA leaders are pleased that the city's plan brings the new breed of livery cars closer to yellow cabs. Understanding that taxi and livery drivers share a common millstone around their necks is the first step toward breaking it, together, for everyone.

Bargaining Power

With the loss of employee status in 1979, cab drivers became a key category of misclassified workers: twenty-five thousand full-time cab drivers are told they are independent contractors although the majority own neither the tools of their trade (the car) nor the permit to operate it (the medallion). Yet the city, garage owners, and the broker groups engage in various forms of bargaining with NYTWA. Why has the alliance been able to "act like a union," and make it stick, when other worker centers have not? The organization has forced its way into these negotiations with its two strikes, in 1998 and 2007. Just as important, they have clear partners to bargain with, in the form of the employer associations and the city regulators, and an organizational leadership that has passed the credibility threshold by mastering the arcane details of the city's taxi regulatory policy.

In this regard, the NYTWA bears a significant resemblance to the labor organizations of the pre–Wagner Act era. It has antecedents among both the industrial and occupational union forms. In the industrial setting, many unions did not wait for an election or the state to recognize them as formal bargaining agents. Instead, these unions built a dues-paying membership among a minority of workers and achieved bargaining rights through the collective action of their members, commonly expressed through a strike. Even without formal collective bargaining rights, the early unions deployed stewards to argue in disciplinary hearings, and offered a "clearinghouse for information and action and an organizational link to an assortment of community activities" (Morris 2005).

Another mode of pre–Wagner Act collective bargaining, occupational unionism, sought to control the labor supply. The Teamsters in particular displayed this form of collective activity, using a "leapfrog" system of selective strikes among long-distance truck drivers and secondary boycotts at the hubs to take "labor out of competition" in over-the-road trucking. The strategy made major gains among an "unskilled" workforce that the union had shunned previously for its independent orientation and lack of intrinsic identification with the labor movement (Belzer 2000; Russell 2001). In this way New York's taxi organizing also finds a reference point among the many unionization campaigns conducted outside of the National Labor Relations Board framework in recent decades, particularly among immigrant workers who many unions had written off as "impossible to organize." Although the janitors and hotel workers in these campaigns are covered by labor law, unlike the taxi drivers, many unions returned to this type of organizing in the 1980s as a means to unionize workers without dragging them through an NLRB process, with its delays, weak remedies for employer abuse and threats, no guarantee of effective bargaining, and shop-by-shop focus that had become eclipsed by subcontracting in many industries (Milkman 2006; Tait 2005; Voss and Sherman 2000).

The Taxi Worker Alliance's success in achieving a bargaining relationship with the city and the capitalists who control the taxi market is still in the experimental phase. One thing is certain, however: with its AFL-CIO union charter secured, the alliance will brook no challengers from within organized labor for the right to represent taxi drivers. But neither enlightened leaders, nor advocacy techniques, nor an industry whose regulated structure could be exploited would have made much difference without the slow work that built the Taxi Worker Alliance's membership base and swung it into action. "Things have come together to the point where they have to contend with us," Desai said. "They contend with you when you bring them the drivers."[23]

13

"PREPARE TO WIN"

Domestic Workers United's Strategic Transition following Passage of the New York Domestic Workers' Bill of Rights

Harmony Goldberg

On August 31, 2010, Deloris Wright, a dignified middle-aged woman from Barbados who has worked as a nanny for twenty-two years, stood up in a small room in a community center in Harlem that was crowded with elected officials and news cameras. After nervously adjusting her bifocals, she took a deep breath, sighed and smiled broadly, and then began to speak. "I am a proud nanny and a member of Domestic Workers United [DWU]. Domestic workers have toiled for centuries in the shadow of slavery. Seventy-five years ago, when labor laws were written, legislators didn't think we were worthy of having rights. But today, after years of fighting for dignity and recognition, our day has finally come." After she spoke, the governor of New York State, David Paterson, signed the Domestic Workers' Bill of Rights, legislation that provided basic protections to domestic workers who have historically been excluded from many federal labor protections. The Bill of Rights was the product of a six year-long organizing campaign led by DWU, a grassroots organization of Caribbean and Latina nannies, housecleaners, and elderly care providers in New York City.

A year later, more than a hundred domestic workers gathered from around the metropolitan region to reflect on the impact of the Bill of Rights and to discuss new strategies moving forward. As the meeting opened, a petite Mexicana nanny stepped nervously to the microphone, gave an almost identical sigh to Deloris's of a year earlier, and introduced herself, speaking in Spanish, "My name is Sylvia, and I am a proud domestic worker and a member of Domestic Workers United." As her confidence grew, her words gathered steam and fire:

Before the Bill of Rights, the law didn't recognize us. We had to work behind closed doors, and we were all invisible. Now we have a Bill [of Rights], and we are not invisible anymore. We are not in a sector without laws anymore. So now we need a new vision for the industry. We have to grow if we want to raise the standards. We need to explore different ways to gain strength if we are going to go farther than the Bill of Rights. Today, we will plan together to change our working conditions, to make things better for us and for all domestic workers.

The passage of the Domestic Workers' Bill of Rights challenged decades of exclusion from basic labor protections and was an important turning point in the struggle for domestic workers' rights. As soon as DWU had finished its slow climb up the legislative mountain, a range of new political challenges came into view: the challenge of ensuring that domestic workers who are isolated in private homes across the state knew about their new rights, the challenge of enforcing the newly won rights given the private and decentralized nature of domestic workplaces, the challenge of raising standards above the Bill's minimal floor of protections, and the challenge of developing new models for collective bargaining. By overcoming the decades-long exclusion of domestic workers from basic labor protections, DWU profoundly shifted the terrain of its struggle from a legislative fight for equality and inclusion to a fight for enforcement of the newly won rights and for higher standards in the industry.

Building on previous literature (Boris and Nadasen 2008; Poo 2011), in this chapter I follow DWU in the first year after the passage of the Domestic Workers' Bill of Rights, exploring the new challenges that the organization faced in the wake of passage of the Bill of Rights and the strategies it developed to address those challenges. I highlight the ways in which the passage of the Bill of Rights changed the terrain of DWU's struggle, necessitating new approaches to power-building. Through this case study, I hope to demonstrate the importance of intentional preparation for strategic transitions after legislative victories or, in the words of Meches Rosales, a leading worker-organizer at DWU, the need to "prepare to win."

This analysis has implications that go beyond the experiences of DWU, pointing to the challenges facing many worker centers as they mature organizationally and politically. Many criticisms of the worker center model, particularly from within the traditional union movement, revolve around the emphasis on advocacy and legal or legislative strategies rather than workplace organizing and collectively bargained contracts. Some suggest that because worker centers focus on legislation rather than collective bargaining, they have a difficult time consolidating, enforcing, and building on their victories. Others argue that while advocacy and legal strategies can be effective in remedying inequalities in the law, and in securing enforcement of already-existing laws, they can rarely extend beyond the minimal standards embodied in those laws. Winning higher standards tends to require the deployment of more confrontational, power-based strategies targeting employers or legislators (Jenkins 2002). These critiques are most productively read not as dismissals of the worker center model but as pointing to the challenges that it must confront. Now that many worker centers have developed the capacity to deploy worker-led advocacy strategies to win significant legislative victories, they must begin to develop models for effective enforcement and for raising standards above legally established minimums, which in turn requires them to develop different power-building strategies.

DWU took on these challenges in the year after the Bill of Rights victory, and its successes and failures offer many important lessons to the broader worker center movement. DWU's experience suggests that worker centers would be well served to anticipate that the struggle to enforce legislative victories will be at least as difficult as the struggle to win those victories in the first place, and that this next stage of struggle requires the deployment of worker power and base-building on a much larger scale than was required to win legislative victories. It also suggests that the transition to these new organizing modalities requires significant strategic foresight and a reconfiguration of established organizational cultures and methodologies developed in the context of legislative and advocacy struggles. Successful campaigns for legal equality can create the conditions for the development of the struggle for higher standards, but clarity about the strategic transition between the two is essential.

This chapter begins with a brief description of the domestic work industry in New York City and a summary of DWU's historical model. I then describe the campaign for the Domestic Workers' Bill of Rights, reviewing both the technical provisions of the bill and the methods that DWU used to win its passage. Against that background, I explore the ways in which this victory shifted the political terrain on which DWU operates and argue that this new terrain has pushed the organization to develop a new strategic orientation and new organizing models. After documenting the organization's experimentation with grassroots enforcement efforts and its exploration of new strategic paths to win higher standards in the industry, I explore the new power-building approaches that DWU is developing and the challenges involved in implementing them. Finally, I conclude with a brief discussion of the lessons that other worker organizations can draw from these experiences so that they too can "prepare to win."

Domestic Work in New York City

After decades of decline, domestic work has reemerged as an urban growth industry over the last few decades, part of the broader expansion of low-wage urban service industries.[1] The rise of "global cities" (Sassen 1991; Castells and Mollkenkopf 1991) around the world with vast immigrant low-wage service working classes intersected with the widespread entrance of middle-class women into the labor market and the accompanying commodification of care work (see Hochschild and Machung 1989; Glenn 1992).

Although it is extremely difficult to specify the exact number of domestic workers, given the informal character of the work and the large presence of undocumented immigrants in the occupation, recent estimates indicate that there are between 120,000 and 240,000 domestic workers in New York City.[2] Between 1990 and 2000, a decade in which the overall job growth rate in New York City was 10 percent, the domestic work industry grew by an estimated 24 percent, although its growth later slowed under the impact of the Great Recession. Unlike other cities where domestic workers are primarily Latina or Asian, New York City's domestic workers are extremely diverse, including Caribbean, Latina, Asian, and eastern European immigrant women as well as a high-end tier of au pairs composed of middle-class western European and U.S.-born white women (Data Center 2006).

The category of domestic work includes several distinct occupations and employment forms. Nannies (sometimes called au pairs or babysitters), housecleaners, and privately paid eldercare providers are all "domestic workers." Most nannies and eldercare workers are employed on a full-time basis by a single employer, either on a "live in" or "live out" basis (living in the employer's home in the former case or maintaining a separate residence in the latter). By contrast, most housecleaners do "day work," working for many different employers in the course of a typical week or month.

Working conditions vary in this highly stratified industry: the elite tier of white au pairs in Manhattan work under strikingly different conditions from those of undocumented live-in workers in the outer reaches of Brooklyn. Even within a single neighborhood conditions often vary widely among employers, due the informal and highly personalistic nature of the industry (Rollins 1987). Individual employers have huge latitude in determining wages and working conditions, and domestic workers often endure arbitrary supervision, ranging from blatant forms of abuse to more liberal employers' discomfort and inexperience with being the "boss." Often workers are described as being "part of the family," a claim that may be intended to express the intimacy inherent in many types of domestic work but which can also lead to further informalization and increased exploitation (e.g., an expectation to work irregular hours to adapt to a family's changing schedule).[3]

Domestic work is further stratified along lines of race, nationality, and language. The upper tier of the industry is made up of young white au pairs from the United States and Europe, hired by employers seeking high-end education and cultural exposure for their children; these workers are often very well paid. The immigrant nannies, housecleaners, and eldercare providers from Asia, Latin America, the Caribbean, Africa, and eastern Europe are less fortunate, and many are subjected to extremely poor working conditions (see Colen 1995; Wrigley 1995; Burnham and Theodore 2012). Although some domestic workers earn a living wage and receive benefits such as health care and paid vacations, many others labor for long hours (sometimes around the clock) without such basic benefits as overtime pay or advance notice of termination. A 2012 report—*Home Economics*—written by Linda Burnham and Nik Theodore and released by the National Domestic Workers Alliance, estimates that 23 percent of domestic workers nationally are paid below the minimum wage, a figure that shoots up to 67 percent for live-in workers. Although most domestic workers have technically been covered by national minimum wage laws since 1974, weak government oversight means that many still receive wages far below the legal minimum. Some workers face verbal, physical, and sexual abuse as well, and they may be forced to live under inhumane conditions.

The industry's lower tiers are internally stratified by immigration status, recency of immigration, and English language capacities. Many newly arrived immigrants start off in live-in jobs, often working around the clock for subminimum wages, whether out of economic desperation, a need for a stable place to live, or due to lack of knowledge of their rights as workers. As they achieve a level of economic stability and learn the ropes of the industry by connecting with other domestic workers, many workers move on to better jobs. This often means shifting into better-waged live-out work, which offers greater autonomy and time to build strong ties with families and ethnic communities. Immigrant workers who have been in the United States for many years, who have legal status, and who are proficient in English have much greater capacity to negotiate for decent wages and working conditions. Because this hierarchy partly reflects the recency of immigration, the bottom tiers of the domestic work industry have undergone a continual process of ethnic succession. Live-in jobs were primarily inhabited by Caribbean workers two decades ago, but as Caribbean workers improved their conditions over time, they were replaced by Filipina and Central

American workers, who in turn were succeeded by Nepali, Mexican, and eastern European workers.

Domestic workers' low pay and poor working conditions reflect the societal devaluation of women's labor in the home, the racialized legacies of slavery and servitude that mark the domestic work industry, and the broader challenges facing low-wage immigrants of color. In addition, these conditions persist because domestic workers have historically been excluded from many federal employment protections and from the right to organize and collectively bargain, exclusions directly tied to the legacy of slavery. Thus when the 1935 National Labor Relations Act (NLRA) and the 1938 Fair Labor Standards Act (FLSA) were passed into law, domestic and agricultural workers were explicitly excluded. This was a concession to southern Democrats whose votes were necessary for the bills' passage. The overwhelming majority of African American workers in the South in the 1930s were either farm workers or domestic workers, so this concession effectively excluded African American workers in the South from the nation's bedrock labor laws—the NLRA-provided right to organize and to bargain collectively, as well as FLSA's minimum wage and overtime protections (Katznelson 2005). Some of these exclusions have been eradicated over time, but domestic workers are still excluded from the NLRA, and some categories of domestic workers remain excluded from the FLSA (live-in workers are excluded from its overtime protections and companions for the elderly are excluded from the minimum wage provisions). Other laws, such as the Occupational Safety and Health Act, the Family and Medical Leave Act, and Title VII of the Civil Rights Act (which prohibits race and sex discrimination in employment), are restricted to workplaces with a minimal number of employees, so that virtually all domestic workers are excluded from these protections as well.

Even when domestic workers are included under existing legislative protections, the decentralized character of their industry makes enforcement extremely difficult. Most employment laws, enforcement mechanisms, and models of unionization and collective bargaining reflect the conditions of the New Deal era, when large-scale industrial workplaces with high worker-to-employer ratios were widespread; they are at best a poor fit with the decentralized and informal nature of the domestic work industry (see Cobble 1991). This problem is exacerbated by the fact that many domestic workers are undocumented immigrants, which enables employers to take advantage of workers' fears of deportation as an intimidation strategy.[4] Undocumented status also limits the potential for effective government oversight to protect workers (see Gordon 2005; Fine 2006; Excluded Workers Congress 2010).

Enter Domestic Workers United

Recent organizing among immigrant domestic workers in New York City began in the 1990s when Pilipino and South Asian workers formed organizations such as the Women Workers' Project of the Committee Against Anti-Asian Violence (CAAAV) and Andolan, an organization of South Asian workers. Recognizing that they did not represent the majority of workers in the domestic work industry—who were Latino and Caribbean—CAAAV and Andolan began reaching out to those populations. In 2000, CAAAV helped to launch DWU as a membership organization for Caribbean, African, and Latina domestic workers. Caribbean workers have made up a large majority—about 80 percent—of DWU's membership since that time, with Latina workers comprising most of the balance. DWU was intentionally developed to serve the needs and represent the interests of the immigrant women of color in the lower tiers of the domestic work industry, reflecting a commitment to feminist and racial justice politics that differentiated DWU from the larger labor movement at the time (Fletcher and Gapasin 2008). DWU's multiracial and multinational composition also distinguishes it from other domestic worker support networks that have emerged in recent years, many of which are rooted in particular ethnic or nationality groups, reflecting the structure of support and recruitment networks in many immigrant communities. In this context, Eileen Boris and Premilla Nadasen (2008) highlighted the significance of DWU's multiracial composition, noting that "so much of labor history has been marred by racial and ethnic divisions."

Since 2000, DWU has grown into a nationally recognized organization with a significant base. It has approximately five thousand domestic workers in its database, although its formal membership of approximately three hundred is much smaller because to be counted as "members" workers must pay dues, actively participate in the organization's work, and attend the monthly general membership meetings. This reflects a broader pattern among worker centers to have a high bar for membership (see Jenkins 2002; Fine 2006). DWU does not, however, rely heavily on dues; more than 95 percent of its budget comes from private foundations.

The organization's staff includes both rank-and-file "worker-leaders" who have worked with the organization for several years and professional social justice organizers. The first director, Ai-jen Poo, helped to initiate DWU when she was working with CAAAV's Women Workers' Project. Poo later transitioned out of DWU in order to build the National Domestic Workers Alliance—a national federation of domestic workers organizations established in 2007 of which DWU was a founding member. She was replaced by Priscilla Gonzalez, who originally became involved in DWU when she was seeking resources to support her mother, who worked as a domestic worker. DWU's staff organizer, Joyce Gill-Campbell, worked as a nanny before joining DWU's staff.

Reflecting its commitment to worker participation and member leadership, DWU's members play a leading role in all of its core programs. In 2011, when the organization gained its status as a 501(c)3 organization, it changed its leadership from an all-worker Steering Committee made up of approximately twenty members to an all-worker Board of Directors made up of ten worker-leaders who are elected on an annual basis by the general membership. The board makes the bulk of the organization's decisions, meeting after work late into the night and struggling over decisions that range from major ("What strategies does the organization need to develop to reflect the new political conditions now that we've won the Bill of Rights?") to minor ("What color should the T-shirts be?"). In addition to the all-worker board, approximately thirty worker-leaders make up the core of DWU's informal active leadership. These worker-leaders coordinate the organization's working committees—including a Campaign Committee, a Base-Building Committee, a Leadership Development Committee, a Culture Committee, and a Fundraising Committee. Staff organizers serve as facilitators of these groups, with most of the actual work done by members, rather than as more traditional organizers.

Many DWU programs are similar to those of other worker centers (see Gordon 2005; Fine 2006; and Milkman 2010), including occupational training programs, leadership development with an emphasis on political education, legal clinics, and minicampaigns targeting abusive employers. DWU runs an annual Nanny Training Course that reaches about seventy-five domestic workers each year and incorporates practical skills trainings such as CPR certification to improve workers' prospects on the job market, as well as workshops on labor rights, negotiation trainings, and political education about the relationship between globalization and the U.S. domestic work industry. DWU also runs annual leadership training programs to deepen the organizing skills and the political analysis of its emergent leaders. These courses use popular education methodologies and offer opportunities for workers to share their experiences. They provide a space where workers can simultaneously build personal relationships and come to understand the broader forces shaping the domestic work industry and the political economy as a whole.

For many years, DWU has offered legal support and referral services to domestic workers who are victims of workplace violations such as wage theft, sexual harassment, and violence. The organization proudly reports that it has helped workers to win more than $500,000 in compensation for unpaid wages over the years. Since the passage of the Bill of Rights, DWU has established a monthly legal clinic in partnership with the Urban Justice Center to help domestic workers access their newly won rights by registering complaints with the state Department of Labor (DOL), and by filing lawsuits. Because legal strategies are not always sufficient to win justice from employers who withhold wages or use violence against domestic workers, DWU also uses direct action to publicly expose and pressure abusive employers.

The Fight for the Domestic Workers' Bill of Rights

DWU is best known for its groundbreaking campaign for the Domestic Workers' Bill of Rights, a six-year statewide legislative fight to win basic labor rights and protections for domestic workers in New York State. This was a landmark victory in the struggle of domestic workers to win inclusion under the labor protections forged in the 1930s. Building on earlier efforts of advocates for domestic workers, most importantly the African American led National Domestic Workers' Union's successful campaign that won coverage nationally for most domestic workers under FLSA's minimum wage and overtime provisions in 1974, the Domestic Workers' Bill of Rights was the first significant legislative victory won by the late twentieth- century generation of domestic worker organizations. In August 2012, a Domestic Workers' Bill of Rights passed through the California legislature, which would have established overtime pay, breaks, and meal breaks for domestic workers. This effort to replicate the DWU legislative model was blocked by a veto by California governor Jerry Brown, but he did sign a similar bill passed a year later.

The original vision for the New York bill emerged directly from the experiences and visions of domestic workers. Early in its history, in 2003, DWU convened the "Having Your Say" convention, a daylong gathering of hundreds of domestic workers from around the city. Marlene Champion, a Barbadian nanny and long-time DWU activist, described that day in a speech: "Hundreds of us gathered together from across the city for the first domestic workers convention to imagine a day when domestic workers will be valued equally."[5] Workers shared their stories across lines of nationality and language, and soon realized the commonalities in their working experiences. Those present at this convention identified a set of policy priorities to expand domestic workers' rights and protections on the job, including overtime pay, a minimum of one day of rest per week, an annual cost-of-living adjustment, health care, a living wage of $14 per hour, notice of termination, severance pay, paid holidays, paid leave, and protection from discrimination. These priorities were incorporated into the formal Domestic Workers' Bill of Rights, which was first introduced on the floor of the New York Legislature in 2004.

The Bill of Rights campaign relied on four basic organizing approaches:

(1) the efforts of a committed core of worker-leaders who persistently lobbied legislators and shared their stories in order to build a broad base of support for the Bill;

(2) a moral frame that emphasized care, interdependence, social justice, and—most centrally—rights;

(3) a formal alliance with an organization of domestic workers' employers; and

(4) the support of local and national labor leaders.

In this respect, the campaign reflected the standard worker center repertoire of legislative and advocacy campaigns: worker-led advocacy, cross-class alliances, moral framings, and support from organized labor (Fine 2006; Jenkins 2002).

DWU organized numerous lobbying visits to Albany, bringing domestic workers together with allies to testify to legislators about the need for these basic protections. In Albany and in the streets of New York City, DWU also deployed classical protest repertoires such as marches and speak-outs and cultural expressions such as the "Domestic Workers Calypso" and the "Domestic Workers Slide," songs and dance routines developed by DWU's Culture Committee. Worker-leaders also met regularly with employer allies and with labor leaders. They told their stories all over the state, speaking from church pulpits, university podiums, and at meetings of community-based organizations.

Although the Bill of Rights campaign was worker-led and enjoyed widespread support among domestic workers, it did not rely on large-scale base-building or mass mobilization. Instead, it was powered by the advocacy efforts of a cadre of worker-leaders and their alliance-building activities. This campaign fits comfortably into the "advocacy power" model described by Jenkins (2002), that is, power based on the ability of a group to persuade elite institutions to take action to change current injustices within the system. As Jenkins argues, advocacy power is often reliant on marshaling the "symbolic power" of a group to build support from broader allies. The Bill of Rights campaign did not rely on what Jenkins calls the "social power" of domestic workers, that is, "the power to force the institutions they are confronting to grant their demands," which in this case would have meant power to disrupt the workplace. DWU's advocacy-based approach was highly effective in winning core allies to support the Bill and ultimately convincing the legislature to pass it, using a strong moral frame for their arguments and sharing powerful personal stories.

DWU's lobbying efforts centered on story-sharing; lobby visits would always begin with a domestic worker recounting her experiences in the industry, weaving together the pride and love she feels for her work along with narratives of abuse and exploitation. The stories of workers' painful experiences in the industry demonstrated the need for the policy provisions contained in the Bill of Rights and lent emotional power to the campaign, helping to put to rest legislators' notions that domestic workers were warmly embraced and adequately cared for as "members of the family." DWU's lobbying also focused on the legal exclusions facing domestic workers, crafting a moral appeal that emphasized fairness and equality within the current system. The campaign's slogans also highlighted the living legacy of slavery in the contemporary domestic work industry—"Tell Dem Slavery Done!"—and invoked analogies to the civil rights movement—"We Have a Dream That, One Day, All Work Will Be Valued Equally." DWU's moral appeals emphasized the unrecognized importance of care work, drawing on the stories of workers, employers, and the children for whom they care. In addition to these moral claims, DWU also stressed the economic importance of domestic work, through slogans such as "We do the work that makes all other work possible."

The campaign was more than a simple legislative effort; DWU approached it as an opportunity for broad public education to make domestic workers' labor visible, demonstrating its importance on both the interpersonal and economic levels. The power of workers' stories and of the campaign's moral frame, in turn, allowed DWU to build alliances with two crucial allies: progressive employers of domestic workers and the labor movement.

Jews for Racial and Economic Justice, a progressive Jewish organization closely allied with DWU, built a network of employers called Shalom Bayit (a Hebrew phrase that means "peace in the home"), drawing on the labor organizing and social justice legacies in the Jewish community. Jews for Racial and Economic Justice used small living room gatherings, outreach in synagogues, and a Jewish communal meeting (similar to a town hall meeting) to educate employers about how to be responsible and respectful toward the domestic workers they hired and to encourage them to get engaged in the Bill of Rights campaign.[6] The active support of these employers played a crucial role in convincing key legislators to support the Bill of Rights, easing fears that they would alienate their upper middle class constituencies if they voted for it.

Organized labor also played a vital role in the Bill of Rights campaign. The support of high-level union leaders eased legislators' fears that labor would perceive the Bill of Rights as unfairly providing special protections for a particular workforce, and it helped to legitimate domestic workers as part of the wider labor community. DWU's first relationships with the labor movement in New York City developed through its participation in Jobs with Justice. In addition, key local labor leaders—particularly Ed Ott when he served as executive director of the New York City Central Labor Council—provided DWU with invaluable access to labor leaders across the state, including in districts where DWU needed local support to persuade particular legislators to support the Bill of Rights. In 2007, John Sweeney, president of the national AFL-CIO, also turned out in support of the Bill of Rights campaign. Sweeney's mother had been a domestic worker, and he invoked her memory when he spoke in support of the Bill of Rights in Albany. Sweeney's support helped to win wide support for the campaign, bringing the proposed law to the attention of many legislators and to that of the broader New York labor movement. Also in 2007, Ed Ott introduced DWU to an accomplished labor lobbyist, Richard Winsten, who volunteered his efforts in support of the campaign.

The support of organized labor was crucial for moving the Bill of Rights through the legislature, but that was not the only effect of labor's support. The relationship DWU built with the traditional trade union movement during this campaign also opened up space for the organization to see organized labor as an important site for learning and inspiration in the period of consolidation and reorientation that would follow the Bill of Rights' passage. Victory arrived in 2010, after six long years of organizing and alliance-building (Poo 2009). The final bill passed by the New York State legislature included:

- The right to overtime pay at time-and-a-half after forty hours of work in a week, or forty-four hours for workers who live in their employer's home;
- A day of rest (twenty-four hours) every seven days, or overtime pay if a worker agrees to work on that day;
- Three paid days of rest each year after one year of work for the same employer;
- Protection under New York State Human Rights Law, and the creation of a special cause of action for domestic workers who suffer sexual or racial harassment;
- A directive to the New York State Department of Labor to investigate the feasibility of including domestic workers in collective bargaining rights.[7]

Many other proposed provisions were cut from the Bill of Rights during legislative negotiations, including advance notice of termination, severance pay, a living wage, cost-of-living adjustments, health insurance, and paid vacations. Many legislators considered such provisions "special protections" for domestic workers that were not provided to other workers, and argued they should be obtained through organizing and collective bargaining, not through legislation. Extended debate over this "special protections" issue took place over the course of the campaign, with objections coming from both conservative legislators who were generally wary of expanding worker protections *and* from prolabor legislators who were resistant to providing state protections to which other workers were not legally entitled. DWU argued that it could not deploy the standard mechanisms that were available to other workers because domestic workers were explicitly excluded from the right to organize and collectively bargain through the NLRA. Rather than "special protections," they argued, domestic workers faced "special exclusions." Even if domestic workers were granted the standard right to organize without the threat of retaliation and the right to collectively bargain, the extremely decentralized nature of the industry would make it difficult to utilize these traditional mechanisms. On that basis, DWU argued that legislators should address the challenges facing domestic workers by establishing a higher floor of protection for workers in the industry.

Because legislators could not reach consensus on this issue, they ultimately included two different types of provisions in the Bill of Rights. The first mandated the provision of paid days of rest, raising the floor of direct state protections beyond the historic standard. The second called for an exploration of the implications of granting domestic workers the right to organize and collectively bargain so that they could win higher standards using standard trade union methods.

The final Bill of Rights included one "special protection" for domestic workers, namely the provision for three paid days of rest each year (for those who had been employed by the same employer for a full year). Provisions for paid days of rest have not typically been provided through legislation, but rather are normally the result of collective bargaining. Although this provision of the Bill of Rights scaled back the number of paid days of rest proposed in the original version of the legislation, that DWU was able to pressure legislators to agree to go beyond the historically established standard for state protections is highly significant. Although the three-day benefit is minimal, it suggests the ways in which employment law could address the dynamics of informal work in the service economy, which could benefit not only domestic workers but also other groups such as day laborers and restaurant workers.[8]

The State Employment Relations Act, first enacted in 1937, is New York State's supplement to the NLRA, designed to cover private employees who do not qualify for the right to organize and collectively bargain under the latter, particularly for workplaces that are "so small that they do not reach the NLRB thresholds" (New York State Employment Relations Board 2010). Because the State Employment Relations Act still explicitly excludes domestic workers from the right to organize and collectively bargain in New York State (New York State LRA 2010), the Domestic Workers' Bill of Rights included a provision requiring the New York State Department of Labor to conduct an internal assessment to determine whether traditional collective bargaining strategies could work for domestic workers. Alternatively, the state could move beyond its historically limited interventions in the labor market to provide basic protections to these vulnerable workers.

This state DOL completed its assessment in November 2010, issuing a report entitled *Feasibility of Domestic Worker Collective Bargaining* that highlighted the challenges of identifying an effective employer bargaining unit and of compelling private employers to participate in such units. It explored a number of possible options, including overseeing negotiations within single-employer units, establishing multiemployer bargaining units in specific locales (e.g., neighborhoods or apartment buildings), or legislation providing rights and protections and hiring halls that would facilitate collective agreements between workers and employers. After identifying structural challenges to each of these strategies, the report concluded with a recommendation that the New York State Employment Relations Act be amended to provide domestic workers collective bargaining rights.[9] The DOL's report argued that eliminating the exclusions of domestic workers would create space for workers' organizations and employers to develop new approaches that could eventually serve as the basis for future, more detailed legislation.

Because it overturned many of the explicit occupational exclusions of domestic workers from foundational labor rights and protections, the Domestic Workers' Bill of Rights has been widely hailed as a victory for equality. Indeed, the struggle for equality was a crucial frame throughout the campaign. But it is important to note that the original version of the Bill of Rights was a far more expansive proposal, reflecting the lived needs and hopes of domestic workers and going well beyond the historic limits of traditional labor law, calling for a living wage, health care, and other benefits. In the course of the legislative process, the proposed law was scaled back to a more limited measure establishing inclusion for domestic labor in existing employment laws such as minimum wage and overtime protections. This channeling illustrates Steve Jenkins's (2002) claim that "advocacy power" can be effective in convincing power-holders to correct injustices—in this case, convincing legislators to end the historic exclusions of domestic workers from established labor protections—but that it lacks the capacity to go beyond that minimal threshold by, for example, convincing legislators to establish a living wage for domestic workers or requiring employers to provide health insurance.

Moving Forward after the Bill of Rights Victory

After the Bill of Rights was passed, DWU began a process of strategic recalibration to promote enforcement of domestic workers' newly won inclusion in minimum standards and to build new forms of power to push beyond those standards. Having focused for years on a legislative struggle for equality and inclusion, DWU now realized it could no longer rely on the same strategic repertoire—moral framing around rights, advocacy by a core of worker-leaders, and coalition building with progressive employers and organized labor. The terrains of enforcement and the fight for higher standards were profoundly different and required new strategies and forms of organization.

After the Bill of Rights became law, DWU began a process of imagining the various long-term strategic trajectories that might be deployed to win higher standards in the industry: modified forms of collective bargaining, legislation to further expand existing employment rights, and mutual aid approaches to benefits provision. Although the organization's long-term strategic path is still at a formative stage, it has come to recognize that raising standards in the industry above the legal minimum will require a much higher level of mobilization, involving what Jenkins (2002, 62–63) calls "social power":

> Social power must be based in some capacity by the group itself to coerce the decision-maker to make the changes they seek. For example, workers have the power to disrupt the production of goods and/or services and interfere with profits. The social power of oppressed people can take many other forms, including the power of tenants to withhold rent; electoral power; and the power of disruption through riots, mass demonstrations, or civil disobedience.

It remains unclear what kinds of social power are available to domestic workers, given that traditional paradigms for worker mobilization and direct action (e.g., strikes) are predicated on the existence of large workplace units such as factories, rather than the isolated workplaces located in private homes. Adding to the challenge are the many vulnerabilities domestic workers face: economic instability, lack of legal status, and extremely low worker-to-employer ratios. Although one of DWU's favorite imaginaries is a "Day Without Nannies," when a domestic workers' strike would throw the lives of New York City's middle and upper classes into temporary chaos, the practical implementation of this kind of tactic is difficult to imagine. Developing alternative tactical repertoires that correspond to the unique dynamics of domestic work is a major challenge. Building and exercising this kind of collective power would require DWU to mobilize a much larger base of workers than it has been able to draw on in the past. Large-scale base-building in the industry is now a central priority for the organization.

DWU is also developing grassroots enforcement strategies to consolidate its victory in winning the 2010 Bill. "Winning the Bill of Rights was important, but it is not enough. The Bill of Rights doesn't mean anything unless we can enforce it," Priscilla Gonzalez declared at a "Know Your Rights" training for DWU leaders shortly after of the Bill of Rights victory. Given the structure of the industry and the limited reach of the DOL, the rights contained in the Bill will not become reality without ongoing pressure from below. Therefore DWU knew it would have to develop a much deeper and wider reach into the industry's workforce than it had needed to win the Bill of Rights.

The process began with a dialogue with the state DOL, whose staff were largely sympathetic to the concerns of domestic workers and welcomed DWU's input as it sought to identify effective strategies for education and enforcement among both workers and employers. Structural changes in the U.S. economy and decreased funding for labor inspections have compounded the challenges inherent in the decentralized domestic work industry (Fine and Gordon 2010). It would be impossible for the DOL to inspect the hundreds of thousands of workplaces in the industry in any case, but access is further complicated by the fact that these workplaces are located in private homes. The informal, cash-based payment practices that are typical of the industry make it difficult to track possible wage violations. In the absence of a more comprehensive plan, the DOL is working with DWU to identify representative cases for prosecution, which the department can publicize in order to educate the public about the Bill of Rights and its commitment to punishing violators.

To give enforcement efforts more reach and power, DWU is seeking an active role in grassroots education and the identification of violations and hopes to serve as a liaison between workers and the DOL.[10] DWU's active participation in enforcement efforts leverages the access to domestic workers that it can offer, access that is far more elusive for government officials. The similarities of racial, ethnic, gender, and class background that DWU members and staff share with domestic workers provide the ground for comfort and trust. "Workers feel more comfortable talking with you because you have been there as well," Joyce Gill-Campbell, a former nanny and current staff organizer at DWU, commented. "They feel more secure and at ease, telling their stories to another worker."[11] Worker-to-worker outreach is also far less intimidating to undocumented workers who are understandably wary of contact with government officials. DWU members and organizers have ready access to the informal ethnic and community networks that link domestic workers to one another, as well as to the neighborhood-based networks that nannies build in the city's parks and playgrounds. DWU aspires to take advantage of this access to use such networks to educate workers about the Bill of Rights and to gather information about violations.[12]

However, DWU must confront several internal structural and cultural challenges if it is to carry out this role. To date, the group's organizing model has relied on a core of worker-leaders who were trained as advocates and whose primary proficiencies are public speaking and sharing their personal stories with the broader public. In order to successfully carry out a grassroots enforcement strategy, DWU would need to be able reach thousands—or even tens of thousands—of workers. In its efforts to bring its work up to this scale, DWU recognized the need to shift its core leaders from public speaking to a focus on broad educational outreach to workers, and to develop new organizational structures to facilitate structured information gathering, along with a system for fielding workers' legal concerns and complaints. To this end, DWU has developed two new programs: the Ambassadors program, designed to train worker-leaders as neighborhood-based "Know Your Rights" educators, and a legal clinic developed in coordination with the Urban Justice Center to process workers' complaints about violations of the rights guaranteed by the Bill; this clinic would liaison with the DOL.

The Ambassadors program is intended to train a cadre of worker-leaders to organize in the neighborhoods where domestics work as well as those where they live. As Allison Julien Thompson, a youthful-looking Barbadian nanny and leading DWU member, said, "We need an army of us who are out there and who are recognized by workers and employers to make sure the Bill of Rights is being respected and upheld."[13]

A primary source of inspiration for the Ambassadors program was the "shop steward" model used by trade unions, in which a rank-and-file member serves as a liaison between the union leadership and workers on the shop floor.[14] "The role of the 'shop steward' is to be the representative of the union at the workplace," DWU director Priscilla Gonzalez explained. "We liked that concept, so we wanted to think about a similar model where domestic workers who are representatives of DWU are trained to support workers in the area where they're working or living."[15] Ambassadors are expected to educate workers about their rights and help those whose rights are violated to access DWU's legal clinic, whose lawyers are in regular contact with the DOL. Ambassadors are also expected to organize regular meetings in each neighborhood to provide workers with a space for mutual support and local organizing.

The pilot Ambassadors program provided four weeks of training to fifteen worker-leaders, focusing on developing skills in one-on-one outreach as well as knowledge of the technicalities of the Bill of Rights and other aspects of employment law. The ambassadors-to-be role-played scenarios designed to prepare them to navigate challenging situations: speaking to workers who were afraid that their employers would see them talking to an organizer, engaging with workers who believed that they were doing fine in their own jobs and didn't need to learn about the Bill of Rights, and connecting with workers who spoke a variety of languages. They coached each other on how to overcome their fears, and taught each other basic phrases in English and Spanish to facilitate multilingual outreach. At the end of the four-week training, each ambassador took responsibility for a specific neighborhood of New York City: Park Slope, the Upper East Side, Tribeca, and Brooklyn Heights, among others. Each ambassador was expected to talk with at least fifty workers and bring in five new members each month, using clipboards stocked with sign-up sheets, an ambassadors identification card to show their affiliation with DWU, and a pile of business-card-sized flyers that detailed the provisions of the Bill of Rights and provided contact information for workers who were victims of violations.

The results of the pilot program were highly variable. Myrna Alleyne, the Trinidadian baby-nurse who served as the DWU ambassador in Tribeca, was able to tap into her extensive social contacts in that neighborhood's parks and community centers and establish herself as a visible resource for both workers and employers on questions of workers' rights. She organized several social events at a local community center celebrating the labor of domestic workers and provided "Know Your Rights" information to many workers. But Myrna's success was an exception. Almost all of the other ambassadors who had volunteered to focus on neighborhoods where they worked found it difficult to balance their job responsibilities with these expanded outreach responsibilities. It became apparent that for this approach to work, staff organizers would need to take on some of the work, supporting the ambassadors while also holding them accountable. A more successful approach is illustrated by the success of Meches Rosales, a Guatemalan nanny who joined the organization in the year after the passage of the Bill of Rights. Rosales chose to focus on a neighborhood where many domestic workers live, namely the Sunset Park section of Brooklyn. She soon identified a base of Latina workers there who were excited to learn about their rights. Rosales organized a neighborhood group of domestic workers that meets on a monthly basis, combining education on employment rights with mutual support around both work and personal issues. For example, to address the fact that many of the women were struggling with unemployment, they collaborated to advertise their housecleaning services in nearby neighborhoods.

These experiences with the pilot Ambassadors program offered several insights to DWU leaders. First, while outreach in the parks and playgrounds of the city is important, base-building in neighborhoods where workers live can yield higher levels of connection. Second, although some workers may be able to do volunteer outreach while they are on the job (e.g., talking with other workers at the playground), such opportunities are likely to be highly constrained. Third, many longtime DWU members—particularly those who served as leaders and spokespeople—were uncomfortable with outreach and resistant to numerically based outreach goals. Instead, some of the most consistent outreach was done by members who had joined the organization after the Bill of Rights victory. This reflected the distinction between the organizing methods established during the campaign for the Bill (e.g., public speaking and legislative lobbying) and those required for grassroots education and enforcement (e.g., outreach and one-on-one support for workers whose rights had been violated), highlighting the need for deeper and more intentional work to help the organization make its transition into a new method of work. Finally, the success of the organizing efforts in the Sunset Park group demonstrated the need to expand the work of the ambassadors beyond Know Your Rights education to include group-building efforts.

Although the pilot Ambassadors program was not successful in accomplishing systematic citywide worker rights education or in establishing solid worker groups in a number of different neighborhoods, it did provide the organization with a much deeper sense of the conditions facing workers in different parts of the industry and specifically the differential patterns of employment rights violations in different neighborhoods. For example, many of the women who live in Sunset Park are undocumented and monolingual Latina housecleaners and nannies; many are also struggling with unemployment and minimum wage violations. The issues are different for Caribbean, Asian, and Latina nannies employed in Park Slope, who generally receive wages well above the minimum but face rampant overtime violations. They are regularly expected to work extra hours when their employers are running late or want to go out for the evening, but they typically receive no extra compensation or are paid at their regular hourly rate instead of the time-and-a-half rate that is legally required.

This type of geographically specific knowledge about the dynamics of the industry led DWU to initiate an experimental campaign in Park Slope in May 2012, in collaboration with Jews for Racial and Economic Justice, its longtime ally. The goal is to build awareness in Park Slope about the Bill of Rights' provision for time-and-a-half overtime pay, and to make Park Slope—a neighborhood with a large concentration of domestic workers and a long-standing reputation for progressive politics—a "Domestic Work Justice Zone," where the Bill of Rights is fully enforced. This effort has won support from local elected officials (e.g., City Councilmember Mark Lander), leaders from area synagogues, and the locally powerful Park Slope Parent Association. DWU hopes that the relationships and collaborations that it is building in Park Slope will also lay the groundwork for the development of a modified version of collective bargaining:

bringing together local associations of workers and employers to negotiate model standard contracts for their neighborhoods that go beyond the legally established minimum standards.

The DOL's recommendation that domestic workers should be included in the State Employment Relations Act has yet to be formally proposed and approved by the New York Legislature. In the meantime, DWU is grappling with the challenge of developing a model for collective bargaining that could work in this uniquely structured industry. "We want to try to negotiate with employers as a group. We want to sit at the table with employers and say that we have some bottom lines about how much we'll get paid and how much work we'll do," said Priscilla Gonzalez at the 2011 DWU Convention, which was held a year after the passage of the Bill of Rights. "We can take those negotiations out of the individual household and make them a collective community discussion."

There are several potential ways to configure collective bargaining in domestic work. One approach, implicit in the Park Slope Domestic Worker Justice Zone, is the neighborhood-based model of developing associations of workers and of employers in a given geographical space (e.g., a neighborhood or an apartment building) and then negotiating a standard contract for that area.[16] Another approach involves "hiring halls" through which employers could access workers who are certified as formally trained in specific job-related skills (e.g., CPR, medical procedures, early childhood development).[17] A third option relies on informal collective bargaining that builds on preexisting worker and employer networks to develop agreements establishing a higher floor for the industry, such as a mutually agreed on minimum wage.[18]

Priscilla Gonzalez promoted DWU's vision of collective bargaining at the 2011 "A New Day, A New Standard" Domestic Workers Convention:

> In order to build up the power that we need to change conditions in the industry, before we begin to have collective discussion with employers we need to be in dialogue with each other and support each other right where we are. Today, this convention is the beginning of that deeper neighborhood-based relationship-building. And we'll take it from here to the park and the playground, to the laundry rooms and the local libraries. This is a moment for us to really imagine and dream big. What if we got together in our neighborhoods and said, for example, that no domestic worker on the Upper West Side is going to work for less than $15 or $20 an hour, no matter what language you speak, no matter what your immigration status is. Can you imagine having a signed contract that actually contained benefits like health care?

After she spoke, those present at the convention divided into small groups with others who worked in the same neighborhoods to discuss the standards that they wanted to establish.

Yet many questions remain about the viability of collective bargaining in the domestic work industry. How would workers compel employers to agree to acceptable terms, through strong relationships and moral power, or through conflict and the use of workplace power? What would be the relationship between standard contracts and the long-standing practice of individual negotiation in the industry, an approach that has secured excellent pay and conditions for some individual workers while leaving others far behind? How would workers with decent working situations react to standard contracts? How would model contracts be enforced?

DWU leaders believe that these questions cannot be answered in the abstract but will be worked out in practice. The first step is developing structures through which collective agreements can be negotiated, that is, local associations of employers (like the one formed in the campaign to combat overtime violations in Park Slope) and local associations of workers (to be built through the Ambassadors program). Just as effective grassroots enforcement will require the DWU to develop a much larger base than was necessary to win the Bill of Rights, effective collective bargaining strategies will require it to build a deeper base in neighborhoods around the city and to develop new tactics to exert pressure on employers in order to win standards above the legally established minimum. Those are among the formidable tasks facing DWU in the aftermath of the Bill of Rights victory.

If DWU is able to win a decent contract in Park Slope, organizers believe, it could lay the groundwork for winning higher standards for the domestic industry in New York City as a whole. It could also serve as a pilot project to shape state policy on collective bargaining for domestic workers, and provide a prototype for innovations in collective bargaining for other informally structured low-wage industries as well.

Conclusion

In order to consolidate the Bill of Rights victory, DWU has begun to develop different ways to build power than those that helped them to win that historic legislation. This requires a break from the small-scale organizing model of the worker center movement and experimentation with new methods and new organizational forms. It may also require a shift from "advocacy power" to "social power."

The struggle to enforce the Bill of Rights creates an opportunity for the large-scale base-building that would be necessary to make that shift. DWU's challenge is to reach the thousands of domestic workers who are scattered throughout the city in order to educate them about their new rights, and to monitor violations. The expanded scale of organizing will also be necessary to build a base strong and coherent enough to effectively negotiate local collective bargaining agreements, or to pressure legislators to adopt policies that will raise the floor in the industry. DWU's underlying vision of bottom-up enforcement, geographically based worker-led base-building work, local worker organizations, and new forms of collective bargaining offers a starting point, but much more work remains to be done. In the meantime, DWU's experiments in the aftermath of winning the Bill of Rights can help other nontraditional worker organizations "prepare to win."

AFTERWORD

Lessons from the New Labor Movement for the Old

Ed Ott

I spent many years in the traditional labor movement. I went to work in an unorganized hospital at age nineteen, and soon became active in organizing a union there. Like many other people who were part of the "old" labor movement, I was often a heretic within. I was keenly aware of the movement's flaws, and when I had the opportunity I tried to do something about them. When I became political director of the New York Central Labor Council in 1996, I was in a position to not only advance the old labor movement but also to encourage the new one through collaborations with new types of organizations then taking shape among restaurant workers, taxi workers, domestic workers, and some of the other groups whose work is documented in this book. I consider this to be some of the most important work I've done in my career of over forty years in the labor movement. The collaboration continues, not least through the project that gave rise to this book, which generated unusually warm, respectful, and invigorating conversations about the labor movement, new and old.

The old labor movement missed a lot, especially as the world changed around it. One of the things that we missed, from the top of the unions on down, was that the day the National Labor Relations Act was passed—the culmination of decades of struggle—was also the beginning of a process that threatened to undo us again. The fact that farmworkers, domestic workers, and others were left out of this critical legislation opened the door to further exclusions from the standard definition of "worker." Today, we have a situation where not only domestic workers and farm workers but also temporary workers and those wrongly classified as managers or "independent contractors" are often unprotected by our basic labor and employment laws. And worst of all was something that most of the trade union movement accepted until recently, namely the dividing of workers into legal and "illegal." That helped set the tone for exclusion on a massive scale, and contributed to the isolation of the trade unions. It also set the stage for the creation of a political atmosphere in which we have members of an impoverished working class who subsist entirely apart from the standards that other workers in this country have attained over many decades of struggle.

In the past few years, the whole trade union movement has relearned something it should have known from its own history: immigrant workers are not helpless. If unions leave those workers with the impression that they are not welcome in our movement, they're going to organize on their own. And they have done that. Over and over again this city's immigrant workers have taught us that if they cannot get justice in the workplace, and if they cannot find their way into the mainstream unions, they will create new forms.

Years ago, Wing Lam of the Chinese Staff and Workers' Association and I were both in the same study group. I learned something very important from Wing, a view that he has insisted on from the first time I met him up until today: We must have one standard for all workers. As more and more union leaders now recognize, we need a new labor movement, but it should be *one* labor movement. That's what I learned from Wing.

The traditional American union movement has trailed behind the development of capitalism in recent decades. Love them or hate them, capitalists are always trying something new. As David Harvey has written, capital adjusts. It's like a heat-seeking missile, always looking for the next political opportunity. In contrast, most unions have been inflexible and tradition-bound. One reason for this is simply that the primary obligation of every union leadership is to its members, which can make it difficult to engage the new. Instead, we tend to circle the wagons and try to ward off anything that might impose change on us. And we tend to build structures like forts to defend what we have accomplished. But then the world changes around us.

The organizations described in this collection of case studies are different: they are experiments in new types of organizing that directly confront the changes in capitalism that have reshaped the world of working people in the last few decades.

Take the Restaurant Opportunities Center of New York (ROC-NY), which organizes to improve conditions for all restaurant workers, whether or not they are members of ROC. The strategy they have adopted is not that different from the struggle of the building trades to establish and defend prevailing wages in their industries. Like ROC, the building trades knew from the outset that they would never represent all the workers in their industry, which meant that the only way union contractors could compete was to bring up the standards for everyone.

When I was at the Central Labor Council, I actually got a call from the New York State Department of Labor about whether or not the "Freelancers" should be able to be called a union. And I said, "Yeah! They're allowed to call themselves whatever they want!" After all, the Knights of Labor weren't knights! Any group can declare itself to be a union if it decides to pursue certain goals. On the other hand, the Taxi Workers Alliance is an alliance; and although it does not call itself a union, it often acts like one.

Like ROC, the Freelancers' Union engages the economy the way it really is— and the way it seems to be heading for more and more workers. How can we organize to advance freelancers and contract workers? This is a challenge many unions face. I once had a conversation with a leader of Actors' Equity about this. I said, "You know, you're an organization that's used to dealing with unemployment. Ninety percent of your members are unemployed on any given day." He replied, "If we could get it down to 90 percent, this would be a very rich organization."

When Freelancers Union president Sara Horowitz chose the name "union," it was partially because she was inspired by unions like Sidney Hillman's Amalgamated Clothing Workers. Hillman had a strategy for making unions self-sustaining. He built a labor bank, an insurance company, printing companies—all because he understood that this was a movement that had to depend on itself. Similarly, the Freelancers Union's "new mutualism" is designed to engage a huge part of the new economy, and to develop self-sustaining structures that will allow the union to continue to organize and grow. It is also a work in progress. I remember a public meeting years ago where Sara challenged us to stop trying to put things out that are completely finished, but to learn something from the dot com people, and put out a 1.0 and then a 1.2 and 2.0.

She's right. Our goals are strategic, but the structures we create are tactical. And not all forms work all the time forever. *We need to be flexible in the forms, flexible in the tactics, and keep our eyes on the prize. In short, we need to change our conception of what a union is.*

The Freelancers Union also teaches us that *we need to expand our definition of the working class.* This union represents workers we might view as educated and middle class, but many of them are on the brink of poverty—or *in* poverty. There are a lot of poor freelancers in this country, and we've got to overcome the image of them as some kind of upper class elite. They are part of the new working class. They have work, but no jobs. Their relationship to employment is intermittent. But their commitment to survival is permanent.

As for the immigrant organizations, community-based organizations, the worker centers, they've taught us something equally important, namely that the struggle for social justice and respect is ongoing, and crosses all ethnic, racial, and class lines. In addition, they have reintroduced us to the word *struggle*. Back in 1970, I was taught by a Red trade unionist never to be optimistic or pessimistic, but just to struggle. People get out of bed every day and have to figure out strategies to survive. That's a struggle!

Every organization described in this book is struggling to combat the poverty of the workers they represent. There are hundreds of thousands of workers in this city, and millions of others across the country, who live in poverty. And this is something the traditional labor movement has to address directly. How was it possible for the United Federation of Teachers and teachers generally to become the bad guys in this country? How was it possible that during the last New York City transport workers' strike, the billionaire Republican mayor of the city could go before the microphones and call striking workers, who get out of bed every day to help run this city, "thugs"—while presenting himself as an advocate for the poor?

These things are possible because as a city worker, as difficult as the job may be, from the day someone is hired he or she gets paid vacations, sick time, holidays, as well as pension and health care benefits. To a nonunion worker who is paid $8 per hour or less, that can seem like too much for taxpayers to sustain. This was exactly the situation that Wisconsin governor Scott Walker exploited so successfully in his battle with public sector workers there.

What do we do about this? To begin with, *the established unions need to welcome low-wage organizers with open arms.* I remember when in the 1990s, under the Clinton administration's "welfare reform" law, welfare workers were sent to clean up the parks. A community-based organization leader came into my office at the Central Labor Council and said, "If we try to organize welfare workers in the park, will any of the unions take us in?" And I said, "Have you ever seen the movie *On the Waterfront*? Remember the last scene, when Marlon Brando picks up his bloody body after a fight on the docks, when the supervisor comes out and asks, 'Who leads these workers?'" Similarly, employers will deal with rank-and-file dealers who have genuine support from workers. As the new labor movement organizations build their base and gain the respect and trust of workers, the power structures, old and new, will learn to deal with them. One lesson of the new labor movement for the old is that if you're organizing workers, we have to welcome you. *We have to stand with you and demand justice.* If we do anything less than that, we can't call ourselves a movement.

Ai-Jen Poo of Domestic Workers United and I had a meeting a few years ago with the chief of staff of the Republicans in the New York State Senate to promote the Domestic Workers' Bill of Rights, which was later passed. The first words out of his mouth were, "I've got to do something here. My mother was a domestic worker." In the end, we're always dealing with human beings, and we all share the same essential need for dignity and respect.

Each of the case studies in this book profiles a slice of what the union movement is supposed to be about: that essential struggle for dignity and respect. It's a simple notion. But building organizations—and building a society—based on dignity and respect is extraordinarily difficult.

As we learned from the experience of Occupy Wall Street, it is possible to change the political conversation very quickly. But can we give that an organizational form? And a political expression, that resonates for people who go to work every day (if they're lucky)? That will require sustained effort.

As many organizers in the new labor movement know all too well, workers have no political instrument in this country that we can trust. We play a merry-go-round with the Democratic Party and the Republican Party, and they do have their uses. They have power in the legislature, and we have to deal with them. We also pour a lot of money into both of them. The labor movement put five hundred million dollars into the 2012 election process. The other guys put in six billion.

Ultimately, we need a political organization that advocates for working people. Whether we can come together to create such a thing is an open question. We have never had a labor party in this country, although I was part of two failed attempts to try to build one. The main reason the labor movement lacks such a political instrument is that we don't trust each other. What this new labor movement is about is creating a new foundation of trust and respect.

There is going to be a new labor movement. Which aspects of the traditional unions will continue? What forms will this new workers' movement take? These are not questions with easy answers. But the work of the organizations described in this book provides a basis for tremendous hope. Those of us in traditional unions need to work with these movements, fund them, and nurture them.

Notes

Introduction

Thanks to Dan Clawson, Dorothy Sue Cobble, Joshua Freeman, E. Tammy Kim, Penny Lewis, Stephanie Luce, and Ed Ott for helpful comments on an earlier version of this introduction.

1. These figures are for 2013 and were provided to the author by Janice Fine (personal correspondence). The preponderance of worker centers in New York City is is not simply because it is the nation's most populous metropolis; indeed, there are more worker centers in the New York City metropolitan area than in the entire state of California. The figure in the text (thirty-seven) includes worker centers in New York City and its suburbs and counts each location of organizations with multiple sites as a separate center. If such multiple sites are excluded, the figure declines to twenty-nine worker centers in the New York metropolitan area.

2. As many reviewers of Standing's provocative book have noted, the term "precariat" is problematic insofar as it collapses together many distinct groups of workers with widely varying income levels and working conditions, and ignores the fact that many workers (e.g., domestic servants) lacked job security and were excluded from labor protection even during the New Deal era. Nevertheless I adopt the term here as the best available to denote this growing segment of the U.S. workforce.

3. The union density data before and after 1973 are not strictly comparable due to changes in methodology. For a comprehensive review of the historical trends, see Mayer 2004.

4. Agriculture and domestic service originally were excluded from both statutes, and both these industries still have only partial coverage.

5. The ILGWU centers were established shortly after the passage of the 1986 Immigration Reform and Control Act, which offered amnesty to many formerly undocumented workers, so that immigration counseling was very much in demand.

6. The CIO also had a relatively small presence in Los Angeles, another example of what Yeselson calls "fortress unionism," and as I have documented elsewhere, one where organized labor weathered the era of deindustrialization relatively well (Milkman 2006).

7. Rina Agarwala (2013) has provocatively analyzed this state-oriented approach to organizing among precarious workers in the very different context of India.

8. Although New York City accounts for only 3 percent of the U.S. population, in 2008 it was home to 20 percent of the one hundred largest grant-making foundations and 16 percent of the fifty largest corporate foundations. See "History of Philanthropy in the U.S.," Philanthropy New York, http://www.philanthropynewyork.org/s_nyrag/sec_wide.asp?CID=167&DID=282. Data from 2012 on the number of lawyers per capita—with New York State ranked second only to Washington, DC—can be found at "Lawyers per Capita by State," *The Law School Tuition Bubble*, http://lawschooltuitionbubble.word press.com/original-research-updated/lawyers-per-capita-by-state/.

9. McAlevey, this volume, makes a similar point.

1. Taking Aim at Target

1. My field research consisted of about ten full days of participant observation over the course of the six-week campaign, alongside union organizers with UFCW Local 1500, as well as a few fruitless attempts to independently speak with Target "team members" in the store. Most days with Local 1500 organizers consisted of a morning group review session of the previous day, and then visits to the houses of Target employees, who more often than not were not at home. I also attended a union-organized cookout and two worker committee meetings, where I interviewed most of the workers present. I accompanied union organizers and worker committee members on two occasions to the store parking lot where they attempted to speak with Target workers. Over the course of these activities, I also conducted lengthy interviews, usually in cars, with both union organizers and the core members of the worker committee. There were two gaps in my fieldwork: I was unable to communicate with the workers who voted "no" in the union election, and the broad "no comment" policy of Target's Human Resources officials precluded any meaningful engagement with management. I'd like to thank the organizers from the UFCW International and Local 1500—particularly lead organizer Aly Waddy, Diana Robinson, and Brendan Sexton—who were always open and inviting, generously putting up with my constant questions and sharing various campaign documents with me.

2. With the exception of Tashawna Green, who was publicly identified with the campaign in many ways, the names of employees and Target supervisory personnel have been changed throughout this article.

3. As West Indian workers have come to disproportionately occupy these two fields in New York City, the unions have increasingly become significant social and political forces in these communities. Along with African Americans, Jamaican-, Haitian- and Guyanese-born workers are more unionized than any other ethnic groups in New York City. This reflects their concentration in the highly unionized health care and social assistance sectors (see Milkman and Braslow 2011). This close connection to the unions is also apparent at the annual West Indian Day Parade, held on Labor Day, at which 1199 and DC37 consistently have a major presence.

4. Local 1500 organizers and officials, including those with over a decade of experience, repeatedly called the campaign the most exciting project they have been a part of, citing the rarity of workers coming to the union rather than the other way around. Few Local 1500 staff had been part of successful organizing drives; recent campaigns had resulted in losses or withdrawal. Because union organizers typically move on to the stable work of servicing members, the organizing department tends to be younger and less experienced than the union staff as a whole.

5. In 2010, according to the American Community Survey, the mean wage for unionized "food and beverage retail workers" in New York City was $14.52, compared to $9.67 for nonunion shops (U.S. Census Bureau 2012). The wage gap is exaggerated for comparable stores in that this industry category includes many nonunion bodegas and other small grocery stores, which pay far lower wages than the larger chain stores.

6. Interview with Audra Makuch, special assistant to Region 1 director, United Food and Commercial Workers International Union, May 19, 2011. Makuch explained that the prevalence of part-time work has had a dramatic impact even in unionized stores, altering the dynamics among workers and creating a widening gap in union consciousness between full- and part-time workers. If the latter do not qualify for health coverage, for example, they will be less likely to appreciate the benefits of unionization. The high turnover associated with "flexible" scheduling also means that fewer workers interact personally with the union and understand its purpose. In stores with a functioning shop steward structure, active UFCW members come almost exclusively from the full-timers—although part-timers often make up a majority of the workforce. In turn, when union

leaders negotiate contracts, they tend to prioritize the needs of the active, full-time, better-paid, and older members who voted them in.

7. Interview with Charmaine Brown, June 17, 2011; Shapiro 2011; interview with several workers, June 14, 2011.

8. Interview with April, June 9, 2011; interview with Aaron, June 9, 2011; UFCW debrief meeting, May 19, 2011.

9. Interview with Aaron, June 9, 2011; interview with several workers, June 4, 2011.

10. Interview with Tashawna Green and Aaron, June 9, 2011.

11. Interview with UFCW organizers, May 11, 2011.

12. Interview with UFCW organizing team, June 28, 2011.

13. Observation from house visits with several union organizers; observation of May 11, 2011, organizers' briefing. See "Target's Turn to Be Targeted," *Crain's New York Business*, June 5, 2011.

14. Observed interaction, May 11, 2011; interview with UFCW organizer Diana Robinson, May 11, 2011.

15. Observation of worker committee meeting, June 9, 2011. The meeting was held in a Springfield Gardens Burger King (near the workers' homes, not the Target store) at 8 a.m.

16. UFCW Local 1500 generously supplied the individualized data they kept during the campaign, including their multiple evaluations of each worker's union proclivities.

17. According to the workers, around 2006 the store implemented a new overnight security policy that required closing the outside doors. Previously, these doors were left open and workers used them to catch fresh air or to go outside to get a snack during their breaks. Walmart has come under fire for similar "lock-in" policies. Interview with several workers, June 4, 2011.

18. Raw data supplied by UFCW Local 1500.

19. The Valley Stream workforce was nearly evenly split between men and women. The committee had a majority of women members, but outside the committee women were no more likely to vote for the union than men.

20. In UFCW debriefing meetings on May 19, May 23, and May 26, 2011, several organizers recounted parents of Target employees telling their children they would "be a fool" or "out of their mind" to vote no. In these cases, the parents were unionized public-sector or health care workers.

21. These attitudes of younger workers were a frequent subject of conversation in the union's morning debriefing sessions I attended on May 19, May 23, and May 26, 2011. Middle-aged workers Sophia, Aaron, and April brought up the issues of favoritism and age discrimination in interviews on June 4, June 9, and June 9, 2011, respectively.

22. Interview with Daniel, June 9, 2011.

23. Interview with Sophia, June 4, 2011; interview with Daniel, June 9, 2011.

24. The few house visits that I observed in more upscale Long Island neighborhoods were all with college-age workers, who were clearly not their households' primary breadwinners. This phenomenon of perceived class difference also played out interestingly with a Nigerian immigrant working the night shift in the Target stockroom; having earned a master's degree in his home country, he seemed to be offended by the prospect of needing union representation.

25. From the 11433 zip code of Jamaica, Queens, came four prounion employees (including two committee members) and eight predicted "no" votes.

26. Seven of the organizers came from Local 1500 and five from the UFCW International, along with the local's organizing director. The lead organizer, of Salvadoran descent, had been working with Local 1500 as an organizer for fifteen years after having been a unionized grocery store worker in her youth. The local organizers included three women who had recently graduated from college (two Latina, one white) and three men in their

thirties (two Latino, one white) who had previously been Local 1500 members in unionized grocery stores. From the international, there were two middle-aged Latino organizers who had experience in agricultural organizing and food processing plants and two younger white men who had participated in a variety of campaigns including Smithfield Foods in North Carolina. Audra Makuch, formerly an organizer with Service Employees International Union (SEIU) and then the Retail, Wholesale and Department Store Union (RWDSU)/UFCW, headed the international team. In the latter capacity, she had been the key organizer of the 2010 strike at Mott's applesauce factory in Williamson, New York.

27. Based on observations, raw data supplied by UFCW Local 1500 and June 28, 2011, interview with the local's organizing team.

28. Local 1500 organizers actually considered it easier to find workers at home in the residential Queens and Long Island areas compared to past campaigns in Manhattan and other areas dominated by apartment buildings, where downstairs access to the building often was a serious problem. How many people would buzz in an unexpected visitor? If an organizer finds another way to slip into the building, her visit is already tainted with illegality. During the Valley Stream campaign, for example, one worker who lived in an apartment building went from friendly to cold and skeptical after she realized the organizers had been improperly let in (although she still signed a union card).

29. I observed such interactions in the parking lot of Target on June 4 and June 12, 2011.

30. In *Lechmere, Inc. v. National Labor Relations Board* (1992), the Supreme Court ruled that companies may legally prohibit nonemployee union organizers from soliciting support on their property, including parking lots. The ruling overturned an NLRB ruling that such prohibitions violated employees' rights to organize without employer interference, as spelled out in the National Labor Relations Act. In *Lechmere* the court ruled that these rights only extended to the employees themselves; exceptions could be made for union organizers only in circumstances where no reasonable alternative to communicate with employees exist. The court turned down arguments that suburban shopping centers—as would be the case with Valley Stream mall—presented particular impediments to effective communication. A 1968 U.S. Supreme Court ruling had protected free speech activities, including labor union communications, in shopping centers because they represented the modern equivalents of town centers; through subsequent cases in the 1970s, the court repeatedly weakened and finally reversed this ruling.

31. Interview with UFCW Local 1500 lead organizer, June 9, 2011. On June 12, company representatives repeatedly informed me that I was "free to speak with team members" when they were off the clock and off company property.

32. Observation, June 4, 2011.

33. By law, the company must deliver this "excelsior" list with workers' names and addresses once the National Labor Relations Board certifies that the union has collected enough signatures to call for an election.

34. Interview with UFCW Local 1500 organizing team, June 28, 2011. Citing the NLRB rulings against Target, Local 1500 has called for a rerun of the election, and says it has not given up at the Valley Stream store.

35. The first Target store was opened in Minnesota in 1962 by the Dayton family, which played a powerful role in state Democratic politics, and was identified as a major benefactor of progressive causes and cultural institutions. In the early 1990s, as Target expanded nationwide, it came under new leadership, and turned in a more traditional corporate direction. Target funds free admission days at several major museums across the country; in New York City, this includes "Target Free Friday Nights" at the Museum of Modern Art and the popular "Target First Saturdays" at the Brooklyn Museum.

36. "Shop at Target? You're a Swing Voter," *Business Week*, September 25, 2006.

37. The "poverty line" definition was aired on *SNL*'s "Weekend Update" segment on December 17, 2011.

38. When called out by Walmart on the apparent double standard, Stringer responded that Walmart's size prevented any comparison between the two retailers (Durkin 2011).

39. There are two famous examples of union drives at Walmart. In 2000, the butchers at a Walmart store in Jacksonville, Florida voted for a union; in response, Walmart replaced their meat-cutting departments nationwide with prepackaged meats. In 2004, the UFCW successfully organized a Walmart in Jonquière, Québec. A few months later, Walmart closed the store. The closure was ruled illegal, and the corporation was required to pay compensation to the employees but it was not required to reopen. See Lichtenstein 2009.

40. Interview with UFCW Local 1500 field director, June 17, 2011.

41. Interview with Local 1500 spokesperson Patrick Purcell, April 19, 2011.

42. Interview with Patrick Purcell, April 19, 2011.

43. Letter, May 17, 2011. Copy in author's possession.

44. Interview with Local 1500 spokesperson Pat Purcell, June 16, 2012.

45. It is unclear how this video was leaked, but there were rumors that at least one team lead was quietly helping the union cause. The video went viral on the Internet, particularly after it was revealed that the actors hired to play the antiunion Target spokespersons were members of the Screen Actors Guild. Hamilton Nolan, "Here's the Cheesy Anti-Union Video All Target Employees Must Endure," *Gawker*, June 13, 2011. http://gawker.com/5811371/heres-the-cheesy-anti+union-video-all-target-employees-must-endure.

46. Interview with UFCW Local 1500 lead organizer, June 28, 2011.

47. April recounted this experience at the June 9, 2011 committee meeting.

48. Interview with UFCW Local 1500 lead organizer, May 19, 2011; the story of other team leads was related by several workers at the June 4, 2011, cookout and June 9, 2011, committee meeting.

49. UFCW Local 1500 debriefing, June 1, 2011.

50. Observation, June 14, 2011.

51. Interview with UFCW organizers Diana Robinson and UFCW Local 1500 lead organizer, June 16, 2011.

52. The irony here is that Target received extensive bad publicity in 2010 for donating some $150,000 to antigay politicians. Interview with Sophia, June 14, 2011; Brian Montopoli, "Target Boycott Movement Grows Following Donation to Support 'Antigay' Candidate," *CBSNews.com*, July 28, 2010, http://www.cbsnews.com/8301-503544_162-20011983-503544.html.

53. Interview with Tashawna Green, June 14, 2011. On her firing, see Daniel Massey, "Target Fires Pro-union Employee," *Crain's New York Business*, August 15, 2011. Citing insufficient evidence, the NLRB dismissed subsequent union charges that her firing came as reprisal for union activity.

54. House visit, June 1, 2011.

55. Although the company filed charges against the union as well, these were withdrawn after the election.

56. I was unable to confirm whether this was the result of overordering, the workers' conscious rejection of the company's food bribe, or simply bad pizza.

57. Interview with UFCW Local 1500 organizing team, June 28, 2011.

58. Still, Local 1500 believed a larger staff would have made the home-visiting process significantly easier.

59. Interview with UFCW Local 1500 organizing team, June 28, 2011.

60. Interview with Pat Purcell, June 16, 2012.

2. Organizing Immigrant Supermarket Workers in Brooklyn

1. "Miguel" is a pseudonym, as are the other workers' names in this chapter. Union and community organization staff, however, are quoted by their actual first and last names. Research for this chapter spanned the period from February 2011 to June 2012, inclusive, as well as a follow-up interview with two organizers in May 2013. I was a participant observer at meetings, rallies, and union representation elections and also conducted in-depth interviews with rank-and-file workers, NYCC staff, and union officials and staff.

2. Interview with Miguel, August 30, 2011.

3. "Latino" as used here is an umbrella term for immigrants from Mexico, Honduras, El Salvador, and Guatemala, who comprise the bulk of the workforce in Brooklyn's small grocery stores.

4. Interviews with Ed Ott, October 3, 2011, and John Durso, December 4, 2011.

5. Precise historical density data for this sector are not available, but by all accounts density and union bargaining power have been severely eroded in recent decades. Although small groceries, which had always been more prevalent in New York City than in other U.S. cities, were rarely unionized, the market strength of the larger unionized supermarket chains ensured high density in the past (Kevin Lynch interview, August 17, 2011).

6. When West African immigrant supermarket delivery workers organized and went on strike in 1999, according to Ness (2005), union staff repressed the voices of independent rank-and-file leaders.

7. Interview with Kevin Lynch, August 17, 2011.

8. Interview with John Durso, December 14, 2011.

9. Among other things, Lynch had worked with the International Association of Machinists to organize livery cab drivers in the 1990s and early 2000s.

10. For example, in 2003 about twenty-seven hundred workers at Duane Reade, a chain of New York City pharmacies, who had been members of the moribund Allied Trades Council, an independent union that had once been part of the Teamsters, voted to affiliate with Local 338 (Greenhouse 2003).

11. Interview with Kevin Lynch, August 17, 2011.

12. Ibid.

13. Interview with Jon Kest, April 25, 2011.

14. Interview with Jonathan Westin, December 14, 2011.

15. Ibid.

16. This campaign involved the RWDSU International office (which is located in New York), but not Local 338.

17. Interview with Ruben Traite, April 10, 2011.

18. Interview with Kevin Lynch, August 17, 2011.

19. Interview with Lucas Sánchez, April 10, 2011; interview with Kate Barut, March 7, 2011.

20. Interview with Kevin Lynch, August 17, 2011.

21. Interview with Jonathan Westin, April 10, 2011.

22. Interview with Ruben Traite, April 10, 2011.

23. Interview with Kevin Lynch, August 17, 2011.

24. Interview with Kate Barut, May 25, 2011.

25. Interview with Lucas Sánchez, April 10, 2011

26. According to 2010 American Community Survey data, 45 percent of grocery store workers in Brooklyn either speak English "not well" or "not at all."

27. ACORN had a long history of offering services such as tax and housing assistance as a component of its recruitment and organizing in low-income communities (Atlas 2010).

28. Interview with Kevin Lynch, August 17, 2011.

29. Mr. Cha did not wage an aggressive antiunion campaign, although workers reported that he did hold one-on-one meetings with some of them shortly before the election in an effort to dissuade them from voting for the union.

30. For example, the DOL charges at Golden Farm totaled $700,000.

31. Interviews with Kate Barut, May 25, 2011 and Lucas Sánchez, May 25, 2011.

32. Interview with Kate Barut, May 25, 2011.

33. Ideally union organizers want at least 70 to 80 percent of eligible employees to have signed union authorization cards prior to filing for an election because of drop-off from antiunion activity. Interview with Lucas Sánchez, November 22, 2011.

34. Interview with Kevin Lynch, August 17, 2011.

35. As Sánchez noted in an interview (November 22, 2011), this may have also reflected the passage of the New York Wage Theft Prevention Act, which went into effect on May 1, 2011.

36. In November 2011, Master Food workers ratified a contract that gave them small raises and sick and holiday pay, as well as a grievance procedure and—most important—stipulations that workers would maintain their current hours. This was a major issue for the workers, who would have earned far less money if their hours had been reduced to forty per week. As part of the agreement, the lawsuit was settled for around $300,000.

37. More specifically, they used eight of the ten tactics Bronfenbrenner and Hickey (2004) identify as increasing the likelihood of success in an NLRB election: adequate and appropriate staff and financial resources; an active and representative rank-and-file organizing committee; active participation of member volunteer organizers; person-to-person contact inside and outside the workplace; benchmarks and assessments to monitor union support and set thresholds for moving ahead with the campaign; issues that resonate in the workplace and community; creative, escalating external pressure tactics involving members outside the workplace, locally, nationally, and/or internationally; and building for the first contract before the election.

38. Two of the most important tactics, according to Bronfenbrenner and Hickey (2004)—having a representative rank-and-file committee and reaching the benchmark of 60 percent worker support before filing for elections—were conspicuously absent in these other stores, where at most five of the ten tactics Bronfenbrenner and Hickey identify as important were used: adequate and appropriate staff and financial resources; active participation of member volunteer organizers; issues that resonate in the workplace and community; person-to-person contact inside and outside the workplace; and creative, escalating external pressure tactics involving members outside the workplace, locally, nationally, and/or internationally.

39. At least some of the owners found out because of an article in *Crain's New York Business* in which Local 338 staff delineated their strategy (Lucas Sánchez interview, November 22, 2011).

40. Some commentators claim that immigrants are actually less fearful than native-born workers (see Delgado 1993; Milkman 2006). In the campaign discussed here, however, immigrant workers' fear was apparent. One activist, Manuel (interview, October 19,

2011), said that some workers were hesitant even to come to meetings because they did not want to reveal their phone number or address.

41. Interview with Miguel, August 30, 2011.

42. Interview with Lucas Sánchez, April 10, 2011.

43. Interview with Lucas Sánchez, May 25, 2011.

44. Hotel Employees and Restaurant Employees (HERE) organizer Vincent Sirabella once described the function of a committee, "the organizer organizes the committee, and the committee organizes the workers" (quoted in Getman 2010, 73).

45. Interview with Lucas Sánchez and Kate Barut, May 31, 2013.

46. Approximately three hundred workers at seven stores were under contract and one hundred at three stores were in contract negotiations. At another two stores disputes over union representation were pending resolution at the NLRB. Over the course of the campaign, three elections were lost outright (Interview with Lucas Sánchez and Kate Barut, May 31, 2013).

47. At Farm Country in particular a wide array of antiunion tactics were employed, including firings and threats of deportation (Lucas Sánchez interview, May 31, 2013).

48. Interview with Lucas Sánchez and Kate Barut, May 31, 2013.

49. On August 18, 2012, workers at Golden Farm voted for a permanent boycott of the store in response to the owners' refusal to settle a lawsuit. On September 17, 2012, Local 338 was certified by the NLRB as the collective bargaining representative for the workers after appeals from the owner failed. On March 18, 2013, the workers called off the boycott after the owner vowed to settle the lawsuit and negotiate a contract in good faith. But the owner also filed a lawsuit against NYCC, claiming that the boycott had cost him 20 percent of his business (Interview with Lucas Sánchez and Kate Barut, May 31, 2013).

50. Interview with Lucas Sánchez and Kate Barut, May 31, 2013.

51. Interview with Lucas Sánchez and Kate Barut, May 31, 2013.

52. By May 2013, all the contracts had been translated into Spanish, and according to Barut and Sánchez, the working relationship between Local 338 and NYCC was "infinitely better." Both sides viewed it as mutually beneficial: Local 338 because of the relatively large numbers of new members it had produced, and NYCC because the union had given the Workers' Committee more room to grow and develop new alliances with NYCC community chapters. Those alliances helped spark a new campaign called "Exploitation-Free Flatbush," in which NYCC community organizers worked hand-in-hand with NYCC grocery store organizers to produce a more cohesive labor–community coalition.

53. Interview with Lucas Sánchez and Kate Barut, May 31, 2013. NYCC organizers responded by setting up monthly meetings with workers from the contracted stores to discuss the union movement, the immigrant rights movement, and the Workers' Committee.

54. ILA Local 1964 played a role here similar to that in the recent NYCC-Local 338 campaign.

55. The campaign gained the support of New York attorney general Elliot Spitzer, however, and this led to a Greengrocers Code of Conduct that gave employers the option of granting specific benefits to workers in lieu of facing significant fines.

56. However, it is impossible to determine how successful the campaign could have been if other difficulties, including the transfer in jurisdiction to Local 1500, had not occurred.

57. Interview with Jon Kest, April 25, 2011.

58. Steve Kest and Jon Kest are brothers.

3. Faith, Community, and Labor

The authors are listed alphabetically to indicate their equal contributions to the research and writing of this chapter. We would like to thank the entire team from the Living Wage NYC for sharing their work with us. We are especially grateful to the many coalition members and allies who spent hours answering our questions, and to Ava Farkas and Jeff Eichler for their very helpful comments on earlier drafts. We would also like to thank Ed Ott and Stephanie Luce for their advice, and especially Ruth Milkman and the other chapter authors, each of whom read closely and commented in detail on multiple drafts of this chapter.

1. Field notes, January 13, 2011.

2. We studied the campaign for eighteen months starting in January 2011 as participant observers, attending the campaign's large public events, volunteering at the RWDSU office, and attending coalition meetings. We also conducted in-depth interviews with campaign staff members, volunteers, and policy experts and collected documents to supplement our ethnographic and interview data. Both of us began as campaign "outsiders": we had no affiliation with any of the participating labor, religious, or community-based organizations; both of us are also relative newcomers to New York. Being outsiders to this campaign had positive benefits for our research agenda, allowing us to observe, volunteer, and listen to many different stakeholders unencumbered by institutional obligations or preexisting commitments.

3. 2013 mayoral candidate comptroller John Liu took an early position in favor of the bill, as did Bronx borough president Ruben Diaz Jr. In addition, Bill de Blasio, then the city's public advocate, and Scott Stringer, then Manhattan borough president, expressed their support.

4. A policy preference for the Economic Development Corporation is not a legal mandate, but instead entails setting goals for living wage jobs with developers and encouraging them to collect and supply wage information from renters in their commercial real estate projects (Living Wage NYC campaign archive 2012).

5. Local Law 48 requires public disclosure of information regarding the city's Economic Development Corporation and Industrial Development Agency projects. As part of the living wage deal announced by Speaker Quinn, the law's overhaul includes more vigorous reporting of company-specific data, including developers' promises to create and retain jobs, wage rates, the value of subsidies, and the percentage of New York City employees (Good Jobs New York 2013).

6. San Francisco has the nation's strongest law in that its coverage is citywide, although the wage level it mandates is slightly below the Fair Wages for New Yorkers Act. More typical cases are cities such as Pittsburgh, with narrow coverage limited to businesses with city contracts and subsidized tenants.

7. This racial composition is roughly similar to New York City's population: 27 percent Latino, 25 percent black, and 12 percent Asian.

8. Paraphrasing a famous remark by the late Jack Newfield. Interview with Bettina Damiani, April 8, 2011.

9. For an elaboration of the Bloomberg administration's position, see the mayor's veto message, Michael R. Bloomberg to Michael McSweeney, city clerk, May 30, 2012.

10. District Council 9 Painters and Allied Trades and the New York City District Council of Carpenters both testified and lobbied against the FWNYA, arguing that it would slow development.

11. Field interview, July 14, 2011.

12. Field notes from January, April, and November 2011 rallies. These rallies featured a "call-and-response," where the audience cheered in response to the speakers asking who

they represented. "Retail workers" and specific congregations were named as well as other organizations. Volunteer and staff reports on turnout delivered during coalition meetings also confirmed these findings on the composition of the rally participants.

13. Resolutions passed by community boards are only advisory, but offer important institutional opportunities for public input.

14. Oyefeso left RWDSU in December 2012 to join Speaker Quinn's staff as director of member services for the Community Outreach Unit of the New York City Council in the run-up to her mayoral campaign (Bragg 2012).

15. "Speaker Quinn Storms Out of Living Wage Press Conference," YouTube, posted by Ava Farkas, April 30, 2012, http://youtu.be/2gxZX3NtwIA.

16. The *New York Times* and *Village Voice* cite a range of four hundred to five hundred workers covered by the Quinn compromise (Powell 2012; Surico 2012). The campaign is more optimistic, however, and estimates that at least nine hundred workers per year will be covered, based on a retrospective calculation of projects that would have been covered from 2002 to 2010 had the law already been in place. See "Living Wage Agreement with Speaker Quinn," Coalition Meeting, Local 1-S, February 6, 2012, Powerpoint Presentation, Slide 9. Copy in author's possession. The RWDSU report referred to in the text is: "Economic Impact of First Nine Months of Living Wage Legislation: New York City Local Law 37 of Year 2012," RWDSU Research Department, July 18, 2013.

4. United New York

1. This chapter is based on extensive participant observation at meetings, with canvassers and at rallies in the United New York campaign from spring 2011 through fall 2012, as well as primary documents obtained from campaign participants and interviews (cited below) with key leaders.

2. According to the U.S. Department of Labor, Labor Organization Annual Report (LM-2) for SEIU National Headquarters, the union disbursed $67,059,660 for political activities and lobbying in calendar year 2008. See http://www.dol.gov/olms/ or http://kcerds.dol-esa.gov/query/orgReport.do; this figure does not include campaign contributions from SEIU's local affiliates. See also Maher 2009.

3. Interview with Larry Bortoluzzi, 1199 SEIU special projects coordinator, May 20, 2011.

4. Interview with Maryann Collins, SEIU Local 32BJ deputy chief of staff, July 8, 2011.

5. Ibid.

6. United NY, "About," Facebook page, https://www.facebook.com/UnitedNY/info.

7. NYCC is an organization founded in part by leaders and staff people of the former New York City chapter of ACORN. See Shapiro, this volume.

8. Interviews with Lenore Friedlander, SEIU Local 32BJ member strength director and vice president, March 12, 2011, and Rob Hill, Local 32BJ organizing director and United NY board member, March 22, 2011. (Rob Hill later became a vice president of Local 32BJ.) "The Values, Principles & Responsibilities that Guide Us," a booklet produced by Fishman to accompany the discussions, affirms that the union's "mission extends beyond the workplace and it is our responsibility to build healthy communities as well as strong workplace organizations."

9. Interview with Rob Hill, March 22, 2011.

10. Labor Organization Annual Report (LM-2) for 1199 SEIU United Healthcare Workers East, 2011, http://www.dol.gov/olms/ or http://kcerds.dol-esa.gov/query/orgReport.do.

11. 1199 figures for membership in New York City and Long Island were obtained directly from the union; e-mail correspondence in author's possession.

12. Interview with Larry Bortoluzzi, May 20, 2011.

13. Ibid.

14. Ibid.

15. Interview with Mary Anne Collins, July 8, 2011.

16. Interview with Hector Figueroa, 32BJ secretary-treasurer and United NY board member, September 27, 2011.

17. Interview with Jon Kest, December 8, 2011.

18. Interview with Ana Maria Archila, August 16, 2011.

19. Interview with Working America staff member, September 20, 2011, http://www.workingamerica.org/index.cfm.

20. "Time for a Main Street Contract: Heal America/Tax Wall Street," "Campaigns," National Nurses United, http://www.nationalnursesunited.org/affiliates/entry/msc1.

21. E-mail correspondence with United NY staff member, in author's possession.

22. United NY printout from database on canvass results provided July 15, 2011.

23. Interview with Ana Maria Archila, August 16, 2011.

24. Interview with Hector Figueroa, September 27, 2011.

25. Interview with Larry Bortoluzzi, May 20, 2011.

26. Interview with Rob Hill, August 9, 2011.

27. Interview with Hector Figueroa, September 27, 2011.

28. Interview with Jon Kest, December 8, 2011.

29. Some initial staff were drawn from 1199 and 32BJ with others hired from outside the labor movement.

30. According to Hector Figueroa, the board made administrative decisions, including decisions about the allocation of funds, some of which were provided to the community partners to implement United NY's programs.

31. Interview with Jon Kest, December 8, 2011.

32. Interview with Camille Rivera, December 20, 2011.

33. Examples of these actions included a June 2011 Congressional Progressive Caucus speak-out at Hostos Community College in the Bronx, which attracted eight hundred participants, many of them from United NY partner organizations; a week of actions in August 2011, including a rally highlighting youth unemployment, pickets outside and "knit-ins" inside bank lobbies where seniors stitched together blankets saying "Save Medicare" that were to be delivered to members of Congress; and protests at a Queens branch of Chase Bank spotlighting high foreclosure rates and Chase's failure "to adequately invest in the local community."

34. Interview with Camille Rivera, August 9, 2011.

35. Ibid.

36. Interview with Florence Williams-Johnson, September 22, 2011; 1199 SEIU member education materials in author's possession; interview with Larry Bortoluzzi, December 14, 2011.

37. Demands included "Jobs not cuts," "Create jobs with revenues from corporations and the rich," and "No deficit reduction until employment goes up" (FFE PowerPoint presentation, copy in author's possession). There was also a "Work that Needs Doing" campaign focused on repair of the nation's infrastructure—especially bridges.

38. Conversation with United NY staff, September 22, 2011; United NY, "Unemployed Community Members Rally on Brooklyn Bridge in Support of President's Jobs Plan," press release, September 22, 2011.

39. Interview with Rob Hill, August 9, 2011.

40. On the Beyond May 12 website, event flyer, http://www.onmay12.org/sites/default /files/5.3%20may12flier%20english%20bw.pdf.

41. Beyond May 12 coalition leaflet distributed on October 11, 2011, copy in author's possession.

42. Leaflet for October 11, 2011, March on the Billionaires of Park Avenue, copy in author's possession.

43. #OCCUPYWALLSTREET Facebook event page, https://www.facebook.com /events/144937025580428/.

44. "1199SEIU Votes Support for Wall Street Occupation and October 5 NYC March," October 3, 2011, http://www.1199seiu.org/1199seiu_votes_support_for_wall_street_oc cupation_and_october_5th_nyc_march?recruiter_id=51.

45. Interview with Larry Bortoluzzi, December 14, 2011.

46. Beyond May 12 Facebook event invitation for October 5, 2011, "Community /Labor March to Wall Street," https://www.facebook.com/#!/events/282473051782707/.

47. Interview with Jon Kest, December 8, 2011.

48. Interview with Camille Rivera, October 20, 2011.

49. Interview with Larry Bortoluzzi, December 14, 2011.

50. Interview with Rob Hill, December 8, 2011.

51. Interview with Larry Bortoluzzi, December 14, 2011.

52. Mike Hall, "Union Movement Opens 'Arms and Hearts' to Occupy Wall Street Activists," Statement by Richard Trumka on Occupy Wall Street, October 5, 2011, http:// www.aflcio.org/Blog/Corporate-Greed/Union-Movement-Opens-Arms-and-Hearts-to -Occupy-Wall-Street-Activists.

53. Interview with Camille Rivera, October 20, 2011.

54. Interview with Larry Bortoluzzi, December 14, 2011.

55. Interview with Rob Hill, December 8, 2011.

56. Michael Kink, "Strong Economy for All Response to Albany Tax Deal," press statement, December 6, 2011, http://strongforall.org/strong-economy-for-all-response -to-albany-tax-deal/.

57. Interview with Camille Rivera, December 20, 2011.

58. These included a Bain Capital workers' bus tour with a video of the "Bain Capital Monster," and crashing a Romney fund-raiser at Trump Tower with the protest troupe, the Tax Dodgers. See Kosinksi 2012; "Bain Capital Monster" 2012.

59. Interview with Rob Hill, December 8, 2011.

60. Examples include a joint action with CWA held at Verizon headquarters on January 26, 2012, to protest the company's tax evasion; a research report produced with the Center for Working Families and the Strong Economy for All Coalition (Stewart 2011) on how Wall Street lending has served to defund the New York transit system; and a July 24, 2012, rally of low-wage workers, community organizations, and unions including Utility Workers Local 1–2 to support low-wage worker struggles, an increase in the minimum wage, and an end to the Con Ed workers lockout (Piazza 2012; Arkin 2012; Chinese 2012).

61. Interview with Camille Rivera, June 20, 2012; Chen 2012; Rivera 2012.

62. E-mail correspondence from United NY staff member to author, December 14, 2012.

5. Infusing Craft Identity into a Noncraft Industry

1. This is the acronym for the Retail, Wholesale and Department Store Union, part of the United Food and Commercial Workers (UFCW), the largest retail union in North America.

2. The names of all organizers and union staff are real; those of most members and retail workers have been changed for purposes of confidentiality.

3. All quotes in this section are from author's observations at an RAP meeting conducted on February 15, 2011.

4. Network membership has since risen to more than two thousand.

5. Retail Action Project website, http://retailactionproject.org/about/.

6. The other is the 2011-instituted Organization United for Respect at Walmart (OUR Walmart), a national nonprofit organization sponsored by the United Food and Commercial Workers and exclusively oriented toward Walmart workers.

7. Interview with Carrie Gleason, April 29, 2011.

8. Ibid.

9. Interview with Jeff Eichler, February 25, 2011.

10. Interview with Carrie Gleason, August 29, 2012.

11. Jenkins's formulation parallels concepts developed by other labor movement analysts. See, for example, Offe and Wiesenthal (1980), who distinguish "monological" from "dialogical" forms of collective action. Similarly, Ganz (2009) sharply differentiates between bureaucratically based staff-driven organizing and the development of rank-and-file "strategic capacity" in his study of the California farmworker movement. See also Piven and Cloward (1979). All these analysts claim that the trajectory of labor organizing is neither linear nor predetermined.

12. The account below draws on twenty-three interviews with RAP members, staff, and union officials; analysis of internal RAP documents and external media coverage; and approximately one hundred hours of participant observation at RAP events, meetings, and as a volunteer at its Midtown office.

13. The other four were the Teamsters, the Retail Clerks International Association, the Amalgamated Clothing Workers of America, and the Amalgamated Meat Cutters and Butcher Workmen.

14. For 1948, the nonrestaurant retail workforce in New York City was estimated at 302,147; for 1964, the corresponding figure was 304,385. Though there were likely ups and downs in the size of the retail workforce over this sixteen-year timeframe, it is reasonable to assume that it remained close to 300,000 in the mid-1950s.

15. However, the campaign's final and less successful phase was overseen by a UFCW local.

16. Interview with Jeff Eichler, June 30, 2011.

17. Ibid.

18. Interview with Demaris Reyes, April 12, 2011.

19. By "free" she refers to being paid insufficiently and working off the clock.

20. Member interview, November 1, 2011.

21. Ibid.

22. Interview with Carrie Gleason, August 29, 2012.

23. Interview with Sudatu Mamah-Trawill, June 30, 2011.

24. Managers had illegally refused to accept West African employees' valid work authorization forms, dismissing several because of this.

25. Staff interview, June 30, 2011.

26. Ibid.

27. Interview with Jeff Eichler, February 25, 2011.

28. In July 2012, Shoemania closed its Manhattan stores, citing financial difficulties (McCarty 2012; Grinspan 2012).

29. Interview with Carrie Gleason, April 29, 2011.

30. Member interview, November 1, 2011.

31. Member interview, November 14, 2011.

32. Interview with Carrie Gleason, January 19, 2011.

33. Interview with Carrie Gleason, April 29, 2011.

34. Interview with Jeff Eichler, June 30, 2011.

35. Staff interview, April 7, 2011.

36. Member interview, November 6, 2011.

37. Interview with Talisa Erazo, April 20, 2012.

38. Member interview, March 25, 2011.

39. Interview with Carrie Gleason, April 29, 2011.

40. Member interview, April 4, 2011.

41. Member interview, March 25, 2011.

42. Interview with Naoki Fujita, May 3, 2012.

43. RAP e-mail, May 30, 2012, in author's possession.

44. Interview with Naoki Fujita, May 3, 2012.

45. Interview with Yana Walton, April 26, 2012.

46. Interview with Talisa Erazo, April 20, 2012.

6. Street Vendors in and against the Global City

1. All street vendors' names mentioned in this chapter have been changed.

2. Interview with Virginia, August 2011.

3. These include the New York City Council; the New York Police Department; the New York Department of Consumer Affairs; the city Department of Health and Mental Hygiene (for food vendors); the Department of Sanitation; the Environmental Control Board; and the Parks Department, as well as the NYC Department of Transportation.

4. The most widely cited definition of informal work—legal economic activities that occur beyond the direct regulation of the state—comes from Portes, Castells, and Benton (1989).

5. As Gross (2005, 179) defines them, BIDs are "publicly authorized, legally sanctioned, privately administered institutions that provide services designed to enhance the local business environment." Property owners hold most of the votes within BIDs, while elected officials often serve as nonvoting members. Their funding comes from a tax on brick-and-mortar businesses located within each BID jurisdiction. BID services typically include street cleaning, security patrols, and public programming such as concerts and movie nights in parks. There are now sixty-four BIDs in New York City, more than in any other U.S. city.

6. Interview with Virginia, August 2011.

7. Interview with Juana, October 2011.

8. My data come from over a year of participant observation, including weekly volunteering at VAMOS's offices; semistructured interviews with twenty-two VAMOS members and six with the organization's staff and volunteers; and attendance at the group's monthly meetings, street actions, and fund-raising events. My fieldwork with VAMOS began in 2010, but I have also drawn here on background data obtained in the course of my dissertation research on New York City street vendors, which began in 2008.

9. The Parks Department runs a bidding system for food vending permits within their jurisdiction, the most expensive of which cost close to $160,000 for a two-year term. These permits are therefore usually purchased by corporations, not individual vendors; prices and goods offered are in turn regulated by the Parks Department. In 2009, the Revenue Division of the Parks Department collected $110 million from a wide range of leasing

agreements, including but not limited to food vending concessions. See "Concessions," "Business Opportunities," City of New York Parks and Recreation, nyc.gov, http://www.nycgovparks.org/opportunities/concessions.

10. Merchandise "helpers" may legally assist merchandise vendors (unloading or restocking goods, for example) as long as they do not take part in any sales transactions.

11. This is not a new phenomenon. As early as 1976, a study found that vendors cost the city $116 million in lost revenue, including $44 million in lost sales tax, $10 million in lost income tax, and $15 million in unpaid tickets from the police (Devlin 2010).

12. Interview with Rafael Samanez, June 2011.

13. Interview with Jennifer Arieta, June 2011.

14. Interview with Elena, October 2011.

15. Interview with Jennifer Arieta, June 2011.

16. Interview with Rafael Samanez, June 2011.

17. Fines for most other violations begin at $50 for the first violation and increase with each subsequent violation, to $100, $250, $500, $750, and then $1,000 for the sixth ticket and beyond.

18. VAMOS recently decided to change its legal representation program; instead of finding pro bono lawyers to represent vendors, they are training vendors to represent themselves at ticket appeals hearings.

19. Interview with Claudia and Marcellino, November 2011.

20. Interview with Rafael Samanez, December 2011.

21. Interview with Jennifer Arieta, June 2011.

22. Interview with Jennifer Arieta, June 2011.

23. As Celik (2011) argues in regard to vendor organizing in South Africa, street labor organizing can play a bridge-building role precisely because it blends community and labor demands, embodied in coalitions between squatters' and vendors' associations and traditional labor unions.

7. Protecting and Representing Workers in the New Gig Economy

Epigraph: This Freelancers Union subway advertisement can be found at http://www.3rdward.com/blog/2011/11/8/essential-event-profile-freelancers-unions-althea-erickson-d.html.

1. https://www.freelancersunion.org/about/history.html.

2. The Freelancers Union includes this as part of its timeline, which can be found at http://www.freelancersunion.org/about/history.html.

3. In New York State, an organization must be classified as an association if it is going to provide health insurance to members at a group rate level.

4. Eligibility is limited to people residing in thirty-four counties in New York State, but the union has plans to expand their insurance plans to include members in other states.

5. These information projects are increasing and include a Yelp-like site to write and read reviews of clients, a site where members write about why and how they live the freelance life, and another site where members can advertise their experience and services.

6. A 2005 Freelancers Union membership survey found that 100 percent of respondents had voted in a national election, 87 percent in a state election, and 83 percent in a local election (Horowitz, Erickson, and Wuolo 2005).

7. The Union does not collect racial and ethnic data on its members and has no plans to do so. These data on membership meetings are from my own participant observation.

8. The endorsement committee includes the current member representative on the board, another board member, the executive director, another Freelancers Union member, and a representative from an allied organization (in 2011, from Make the Road New York).

9. Similar workshops are offered on and offline by the Union for a fee.

10. Some worker organizing efforts in the past have challenged the misclassification of standard workers as independent workers. Companies have sought to do this to avoid delivering costly benefits to workers. However, the Freelancers Union wants to prevent the misclassification of all workers—including independent workers who have been misclassified as employees. In this scenario the worker cannot claim certain tax benefits or deductions associated with independent status.

11. The funds were eliminated from the final 2012 budget by Congress, but were again included in the president's 2013 budget request.

12. The 2010 Act is intended to cover full- and part-time workers.

13. The New York State Senate and Assembly introduced the legislation in March 2011. The Assembly passed it in June 2011 and June 2012; as of September 2013, the Senate has not yet voted the bill out of committee.

14. Of Union survey respondents 91 percent expressed interest in contributing $100 per month to a tax advantaged savings account for security during periods of unemployment.

15. Member interview, December 16, 2011.

16. From "Lobster or Mac & Cheese," *The Freelance Life* blog, a compilation of stories written by Union members. Posted by Jenny Troester, July 8, 2011. https://be.freelancer sunion.org/the-freelance-life/story/3_lobster-or-mac-cheese.

17. This finding can be contrasted with another survey, conducted in 1998, in which 59 percent of temps said that they would prefer a traditional job (Cohany 1998, 12).

18. However, freelancers often discount the time they invest in improving their skills, looking for work, and so on.

19. Staff interview, March 17, 2011.

20. Staff interview, March 10, 2011.

21. Interview with Sara Horowitz, December 20, 2011.

22. Monthly member meeting, March 15, 2011.

23. Member interview, December 16, 2011.

24. A 1099 is the income tax form that freelancers receive in lieu of the W-2 that wage and salary workers receive.

25. "I Can Work Whenever I Want," *The Freelance Life*, posted by Steve, November 16, 2011. https://be.freelancersunion.org/the-freelance-life/story/49_i-can-work-whenever-i -want.

26. Interview with Sara Horowitz, April 8, 2011.

27. Freelancers Union "Organizing Models" document, given to author by union staff on May 1, 2011.

28. In business accounting "the bottom line" refers to the sum of revenue minus expenses. The "triple bottom line" is a play on this phrase that refers to accounting for social and environmental or sustainability outcomes in addition to economic ones.

29. Interview with Sara Horowitz, March 8, 2011.

30. Interview with Sara Horowitz, April 8, 2011.

31. This list of advertisements and the one in the next paragraph is compiled from the author's observations of posters in the Freelancers Union's office, in NYC subways and other public places, and of Internet images.

32. "New Mutualism: Mutual Support for the Information Age," Freelancers Union website, http://www.freelancersunion.org/newmutualism.html?utm_source=homepage& utm_medium=new_mutualism&utm_campaign=mutualism.

33. This list is from Freelancers Union 2010 and author's correspondence with Free-lancers Union staff, February 23, 2012.

8. The High-Touch Model

1. The organization's name mirrors an article, a book, and a poem containing the same phrase: Jennifer Gordon's 1995 article in the *Harvard Civil Rights–Civil Law Review* "We Make the Road by Walking: Immigrant Workers and the Struggle for Social Change"; the book *We Make the Road by Walking: Conversations on Education and Social Change*, which includes the reflections of Myles Horton, a radical educator and the founder of the Highlander Research and Education Center, in conversation with Brazilian educator Paulo Freire; and a 1912 poem by Antonio Machado entitled "Proverbios y Cantares," which is the original source of these words.

2. Juan Bosch was the first democratically elected president of the Dominican Repub-lic. Exiled both before and after his brief presidency—which lasted only seven months in 1963—he was known for his plain words.

3. MRNY's budget combines dues revenue, service provision contracts, foundation grants, union donations, major donors, legal settlements, and fundraising events.

4. Youth members are not charged dues until they turn twenty-one. Adult members who cannot afford to pay $100 upfront can borrow that sum from a local credit union, which is then paid back in installments over the course of the following year.

5. "Eldridge & Co. w/ Andrew Friedman - 4/24/07 PART 1- Make the Road New York," posted by maketheroad, April 27, 2007, YouTube, http://www.youtube.com/watch ?v=07l4vy3yEc8.

6. Annual Report, 2006, We Make the Road by Walking. (Copy in author's possession.)

7. LAIC IRS form 990 for the tax year 2006.

8. The research for this chapter includes structured interviews with MRNY full-time staff and activist volunteer leaders; semistructured interviews with members; and partici-pant observation at MRNY during 2011 at leadership development trainings, fund-raising events, regular weekly meetings, get-out-the-vote door-knocking operations, and in the hallways of the bustling Bushwick and Jackson Heights offices. In addition, the leaders of MRNY were generous and open about sharing internal documents such as strategic plans, grant proposals, leadership development curricula, staff and leader devel-opment plans, campaign plans, and Board of Directors' reports. I also reviewed media coverage of MRNY activities over the past decade.

9. Ruth Milkman (2006) makes the case that successful contemporary union cam-paigns often combine top-down and bottom-up strategies.

10. MRNY annual reports 2007–10.

11. Interviews with Deborah Axt, April 7, 2011 and Andrew Friedman, March 17, 2011.

12. Interview with Javier Valdes, December 2, 2011.

13. The coalition included the American Civil Liberties Union; ACLU of New Jersey; American Friends Service Committee of New York; American Immigration Lawyers As-sociation of New York; Cardozo Immigration Justice Clinic; Center for Constitutional Rights; Families for Freedom; Immigrant Defense Project; Legal Aid Society; NYU Im-migrants Rights Clinic; New York Immigrants Rights Coalition; and Youth Ministries for Peace and Justice.

14. Steve Jenkins, 32BJ staffer, interview, April 11, 2011; remarks by 32BJ president Mike Fishman, November 16, 2011.

15. Friedman's grandparents were part of the early twentieth-century wave of Jewish immigration from eastern Europe.

16. The proposal also states, "Make the Road New York's members, Board of Directors, and staff are all representative of the low-income, communities of color within which we work. All of these bodies [listed in the table] are comprised of at least seventy-five percent people of color and fifty percent women. A majority of our staff, as well as our Board of Directors live in the communities within which we work. Having a constituency comprised of neighborhood residents enables Make the Road New York to address directly the community problems identified by the membership."

17. Additional documents available to members (all of which are regularly updated) include By-laws, an Employee Manual, Leadership Team Criteria and Responsibilities, Employee Evaluations, Leadership Development Plans, and a Board of Directors Goal Review. (Copies in author's possession.)

18. December 9, 2011, DREAM Act press conference at city hall. Groups in attendance included the Chinese Progressive Association, DREAM Scholars, Hispanic Federation, Make the Road New York, MinKwon Center for Community Action (see McQuade, this volume), the New York Immigration Coalition, New York State Youth Leadership Council, and the Professional Staff Congress (the union of City University of New York staff and faculty).

19. Steve Jenkins, author interview, April 4, 2012.

9. Bridging City Trenches

1. These figures are for Public Use Microdata Area 03801, which includes all of Washington Heights and Inwood, along with Marble Hill (with a 2010 population of eighty-five hundred) and one additional strip of Riverside Drive south of 155th Street).

2. Interview with Amy Sugimori, May 19, 2011.

3. Interview with Ann Bastian, May 3, 2011.

4. Interview with Gouri Sadhwani, March 10, 2011.

5. Interview with Amy Sugimori, May 19, 2011.

6. Interview with Gouri Sadhwani, March 10, 2011.

7. Interview with Amy Sugimori, May 19, 2011.

8. Ibid.

9. NYCPP defines "general members" as those who participated in at least one meeting or action in a given year, "active members" as those who attended more than five such activities in a given year, and "somewhat active members" as those who took part in three to five activities in a given year (interview with Angeline Echeverria, May 5, 2011).

10. Interview with Sussie Lozada, June 13, 2011.

11. Interview with Angeline Echeverria, May 5, 2011.

12. Ibid.

13. Interview with Gouri Sadhwani, March 10, 2011.

14. Interview with Amy Sugimori, May 19, 2011.

15. Interview with Gouri Sadhwani, March 10, 2011.

16. La Fuente internal documents in author's possession.

17. Interview with Hector Figueroa, January 23, 2012.

18. Interview with Andres Mares Muro, December 15, 2011

19. Ibid.

20. Between 1999 and 2004 the median price of a two-bedroom apartment in the neighborhood increased from $180,000 to $460,000 (Jackson 2004).

21. Interview with Andres Mares Muro, December 15, 2011

22. As Jordan (1997) explains, "Democratic Party 'district leaders,' who are elected—one male and one female—in every state-assembly district of New York City . . . are charged with overseeing all party financial and political business in a given assembly district, including the selection of poll watchers in local voting sites. Their most important function is to vote for the Democratic county chairman of each of the city's five boroughs."

23. Jane McAlevey, personal communication.

24. Interview with Hector Figueroa, January 23, 2012.

25. Ibid.

26. Interview with Amy Sugimori, May 19, 2011.

27. Ibid.

28. Interview with Sussie Lozada, June 13, 2011.

10. Creating "Open Space" to Promote Social Justice

1. Flushing's population in 2010 was 71 percent Asian American, up from 35 percent in 2000 (Asian American Federation of New York 2012).

2. California Proposition 187 aimed to prohibit undocumented immigrants from accessing health care and social services, including public school education for their children. Voters approved the proposed law in a referendum in November 1994; it was later challenged in federal court and struck down as unconstitutional.

3. Young Koreans United was founded by Yoon Han Bong, a well-known student activist in Korea. As a college student, his leadership of the "Youth and Student Coalition for Democracy" led to his expulsion from Jun Nam University. In the late 1970s, Yoon was imprisoned multiple times for opposing the military dictatorship and later was blacklisted due to his involvement in the May 18, 1980 Gwangju People's Uprising, a watershed event in the modern democracy movement in Korea in which as many as 165 people were killed. In April 1981, Yoon secretly escaped on a cargo ship and, after more than forty days, arrived in the United States where he won political asylum. He then focused on building an overseas solidarity movement to support the democracy movement in South Korea, founding YKU in 1984 and the Korean Alliance for Peace in 1987. YKU was an incubator for grassroots community-based organizations throughout the United States, including the Korean American Resource & Cultural Center in Chicago, YKASEC in New York City, and the National Korean American Service Education Consortium in Los Angeles (Korean Resource Center, http://krcla.org/en/Young _Koreans_United).

4. E-mail correspondence with Steven Choi, December 4, 2011.

5. Interview with Pyong Gap Min, May 20, 2011.

6. Ibid.

7. MinKwon annual report, 2009, http://www.minkwon.org/images/uploads/pdfs /2009_MinKwon_Annual_Report_(FINAL).pdf.

8. MinKwon 27th Anniversary Gala Program, October 2011. Copy in author's possession.

9. MinKwon website, Spring, 2011.

10. MinKwon 27th Anniversary Gala Program, 2011.

11. Interview with Yu Soung Mun, October 14, 2011.

12. The Skadden Fellowship Program, sometimes described as "a legal Peace Corps," provides two years of funding for graduating law students to allow them to pursue their interests in public interest work, http://www.skaddenfellowships.org/about-foundation.

13. Interview with Liz Chong Eun Rhee, March 21, 2011.

14. Interview with Liz Chong Eun Rhee, October 14, 2011.

15. Interview with Liz Chong Eun Rhee, March 21, 2011.

16. Interview with Steven Choi, August 11, 2011.

17. Ibid.

18. While Confucianism is a major spiritual value system among many Koreans, 60 percent of Korean Americans are Protestant and 15 percent are Catholic, the result of a large and continued presence of missionaries on the peninsula (Min 2011).

19. Interview with Pyong Gap Min, May 20, 2011.

20. Interview with Yu Soung Mun, October 14, 2011.

21. Interview with Steven Choi, August 11, 2011.

11. An Appetite for Justice

1. This figure is prorated based on the estimated $31.9 billion in restaurant sales in New York State in 2012. National Restaurant Association, 2012. http://restaurant.org /pdfs/research/state/newyork.pdf.

2. I conducted interviews with ROC-NY staff and also engaged in participant observation for several months in 2011. Unless otherwise indicated, all quotations in the text from staff members are from my interviews and in some cases follow-up e-mail correspondence with interviewees.

3. Many workers employed in New York's hotel restaurants are unionized, but they are affiliated with a different UNITE HERE local.

4. Emergent labor–community organizing partnershpis signal potential change in the fast-food segment that may positively impact the prospects of future unionism. Starting in late 2012 in New York City, and spreading nationwide in 2013, the fast-food worker campaigns launched a series of short strikes demanding increasing hourly pay to $15.

5. These data are from an analysis of the U.S. Current Population Survey, merging monthly files for the period from January 2003 through June 2011.

6. Interview with Daisy Chung, March 16, 2011.

7. Under New York State law, each hour worked beyond ten hours in one workday entitles the worker to double compensation.

8. Interview with Sekou Luke, March 28, 2011.

9. Interview with Daisy Chung, March 16, 2011.

10. Interview with Sekou Luke, March 28, 2011.

11. Interview with Sekou Siby, April 29, 2011.

12. Interview with Sekou Luke, March 28, 2011.

13. http://www.nyclu.org/case/arroyo-et-al-v-redeye-challenging-employment-prac tices-nyc-restaurant.

14. Interview with Sekou Luke, March 28, 2011.

15. Interview with Rekha Eanni-Rodriguez, February 16, 2011.

16. Interview with Virgilio Arán, March 21, 2011.

17. Interview with Eric Brown, March 22, 2011.

18. Ibid.

19. Interview with Kevin Scott, April 27, 2011.

20. http://rocny.org/high-road-organizing/nycrir/.

21. The High Road Code of Conduct includes the following elements: complies with city, state, and federal wage and overtime requirements, as well as requirements set forth by the NYC Department of Health and Mental Hygiene and the Occupational Safety and

Health Administration; creates a respectful work environment free from hostility and abuse; offers a regularly updated employee manual and establishes a neutral and clear grievance procedure; makes training, reference materials, and the opportunity to be promoted available to all staff members; utilizes documentation to improve business practices, including publicized discipline standards; offers health insurance to its employees, or at minimum helps employees obtain access to information on affordable health care in New York City; and works toward providing paid sick days for all staff. http://rocny.org /high-road-organizing/nycrir/.

22. This effort failed because the city insisted that labor standards can be enforced only at the state level.

12. Not Waiting for Permission

1. My understanding of the structure and history of New York's taxi industry was shaped by Biju Mathew's invaluable *Taxi! Cabs and Capitalism* (2008), which provides too many insights to offer a citation for each. This background has been buttressed by interviews with NYTWA leaders and members over a period of six months, review of organizational documents and an e-mail Listserv, and observation of the alliance's member meetings, office interactions, and partnerships.

2. Because New York did not limit the transferability of medallions, unlike other cities, they are subject to market forces that have driven the price of an individual medallion in the first decade of the twenty-first century near $1 million (Mathew 2008; Grynbaum 2011b).

3. Interview with David Yassky, October 21, 2011.

4. Interview with Bhairavi Desai, April 9, 2011.

5. Interview with Bill Lindauer, October 20, 2011.

6. Interview with Javaid Tariq, October 20, 2011.

7. Since 1937, the value of a New York taxi medallion has risen by 1,900 percent, beating the increases in value of the Dow Jones industrial average, gold, oil, and U.S. real estate (Grynbaum 2011b).

8. Interview with Zubin Soleimany, October 20, 2011.

9. The ACS data cited here and below includes not only drivers of yellow cabs but also those who operate "black cars," radio-dispatched livery vehicles that serve the "outer boroughs" of Queens, Brooklyn, Staten Island, and the Bronx, as well as those who operate limousine services, mostly in Manhattan. Both workforces have different traditions and ownership arrangements than yellow cab drivers.

10. Interview with Mohammad Jamil Hussain, October 20, 2011.

11. Jenkins's analysis is illustrated by the experience of day laborers in New York's shadows, who succeeded in pushing up the wage rate on some Long Island street corners from $45 to $60 during the boom years of the mid-2000s. After it became apparent that their gains on the corners would not hold, however, they settled on advocacy strategies to increase penalties for wage-thieving employers through legislation (Gordon 2005).

12. Interview with Ed Ott, October 24, 2011.

13. Insofar as taxi workers scorn transit workers, it is because they have a more powerful union, have higher status and better pay and benefits, and have won state protections against violent passengers, despite doing essentially comparable work to that of taxi workers.

14. Interview with Javaid Tariq, October 20, 2011.

15. Interview with David Yassky, October 21, 2011.

16. Interview with Bill Lindauer, October 20, 2011.

17. Interview with Bhairavi Desai, April 9, 2011.

18. Interview with Mohammad Jamil Hussain, October 20, 2011.

19. Interview with Javaid Tariq, October 20, 2011.

20. Interview with Bhairavi Desai, April 11, 2011.

21. Interview with Biju Mathew, April 11, 2011.

22. Interview with Beresford Simmons, October 20, 2011.

23. Interview with Bhairavi Desai, April 11, 2011.

13. "Prepare to Win"

1. There is a large literature on the domestic work industry, both in the United States and internationally, including Romero 1992, Colen 1995, Wrigley 1995, Chang 2000, Hondagneu-Sotelo 2001, Parreñas 2001, Sassen 2003, and Ehrenreich and Hochschild 2003.

2. In 2006, Domestic Workers United estimated that there were 200,000 domestic workers in New York City (Data Center 2006), based on the assumption that households with incomes of more than $100,000 that include either children under age eighteen or elderly people over age sixty-five were likely to be employers of domestic workers. A 2010 New York State Department of Labor report estimated that there were between 120,000 and 240,000 domestic workers in the city, based on a projection from unemployment insurance payments for workers in private household industries. U.S. government data, for example, the U.S. Census American Community Survey, suggest that the number is smaller, but these data do not include domestics hired by placement agencies and are likely to undercount undocumented workers as well (see Burnham and Theodore 2012, 10).

3. The dynamics of the U.S. domestic work industry have been documented in works such as Chang 2000 and Hondagneu-Sotelo 2001. The specific dynamics of New York City are captured statistically in Data Center 2006 and ethnographically in Wrigley 1995 and Brown 2011.

4. Although some scholars (e.g., Ness 2005) have argued that undocumented workers are more likely to support unionization than native-born workers, in practice fears around documentation status have been a challenge in DWU's organizing work.

5. Marlene Champion, speech delivered at the "A New Day, A New Standard" Domestic Workers Convention, December 3, 2011.

6. Although many worker centers build alliances across class lines, they typically do so to marshal support from students, religious leaders, and consumers in order to pressure employers and the government (Milkman 2010). DWU's model *does* involve cross-class alliances, but it broke from that pattern by organizing with employers themselves.

7. The bill's full text is available at http://www.labor.state.ny.us/sites/legal/laws/domestic-workers-bill-of-rights.page.

8. In a related development, several U.S. city and state jurisdictions have passed legislation mandating paid sick days in recent years. This suggests that DWU's advocacy for expanded labor protections may be part of a larger trend that is expanding the boundaries of state labor protections. These types of protective legislative strategies could indicate a withdrawal from attempts to raise standards through direct workplace action and collective bargaining, reflecting the current weakness of the labor movement. Seen from this angle, this trend recalls the history of protective legislation in the pre–New Deal era, when unions were also relatively weak.

9. The recommendations of this report closely paralleled the recommendations that DWU made in a 2010 report, *Domestic Workers and Collective Bargaining: A Proposal for the Immediate Inclusion of Domestic Workers in the New York State Labor Act*, developed with the Urban Justice Center in an effort to inform the DOL's recommendations.

10. A similar model of collaboration between the New York DOL and community organizations was established in 2009 through the Wage and Hour Watch program, when the department was under the leadership of Patricia Smith (now the solicitor at the federal Department of Labor). The Wage and Hour Watch program delegated educational programs (e.g., know-your-rights trainings for workers, education for employers) and monitoring to community organizations, and designated a DOL point person to receive and prioritize reports of workplace violations (New York State DOL 2009). Informal reports from participating organizations suggest the difficulty of implementing the Wage and Hour Watch program, given the lack of resources for education and monitoring efforts by those organizations. Similar challenges have already become apparent in DWU's early efforts at grassroots enforcement and monitoring of the Domestic Workers' Bill of Rights.

11. Joyce Gill-Campbell, speaking at a DWU meeting on November 9, 2011.

12. Other commentators have pointed out that ethnically and nationally based networks can serve as a basis for solidarity-building in industries where the traditional forms of relationship-building among workers on the "shop floor" are impractical (Milkman 2006; Ness 2005; Das Gupta 2006; Krinsky 2007).

13. Allison Julien Thompson, speaking at a DWU meeting on August 5, 2010.

14. DWU members were reluctant to use the term "shop steward" to describe these rank-and-file worker-organizers, however. Some were critical of the traditional trade unions and others felt that it would be presumptuous and technically inaccurate to describe DWU as a "union," given the exclusion of domestic workers from the right to collectively bargain and DWU's small scale. The term "DWU Ambassadors" was suggested by a member whose evangelical church had outreach volunteers called "Ambassadors for Christ," illustrating the varied political and cultural fields on which DWU's members draw.

15. Prisiclla Gonzalez, speaking at a DWU meeting on August 5, 2010.

16. In conceptualizing this approach, DWU has drawn on the home health care organizing model developed by SEIU Local 434B in Los Angeles. Home health care workers face some of the same organizing challenges as domestic workers, in that they labor in isolation in thousands of private homes and often lack a central employer with whom to bargain. In the late 1990s, SEIU overcame this obstacle by lobbying the county government to establish itself as an "employer of record" with whom workers could collectively bargain. This was only possible, however, because of public funding for home health care (Boris and Klein 2008). Since domestic work is usually privately funded, the government cannot serve as an employer of record in this manner. Nevertheless, the employer of record concept has been useful to DWU in its efforts to envision multiemployer collective bargaining in a decentralized industry.

17. The historical basis for this model is the hiring halls utilized by the "skilled trades" (such as carpenters and electricians), but the model of "occupational unionism" described by Cobble (1991a) is better suited to domestic workers. As Cobble details, early twentieth-century waitresses used job training and performance quality control through peer supervision to assert the "professionalism" of their skills in an industry in which they had previously been seen as "unskilled." They used this approach to gain control over the labor supply in their industry and thus to induce employers to rely on the union for hiring and training.

18. This model would reflect historical strategies deployed by African American domestic workers in Washington, DC and Atlanta in the nineteenth century, as described by Hunter (2004). Domestic workers established secret mutual aid societies through which they set informal policies in the industry (e.g., boycotting abusive employers), thereby "transforming individual grievances into collective dissent."

Bibliography

"1199SEIU Votes Support for Wall Street Occupation and October 5 NYC March." 2011. 1199 SEIU United Health Care Workers East, October 3. http://www.1199seiu.org /1199seiu_votes_support_for_wall_street_occupation_and_october_5th_nyc _march?recruiter_id=51.

Abel, Jaison R., and Richard Deitz. 2012. "Job Polarization and Rising Inequality in the Nation and the New York–Northern New Jersey Region." Federal Reserve Bank of New York. *Current Issues in Economics and Finance* 18 (7).

Abelman, Nancy, and John Lie. 1995. *Blue Dreams: Korean Americans and the Los Angeles Riots.* Cambridge, MA: Harvard University Press.

Agarwala, Rina. 2006. "From Work to Welfare: A New Class Movement in India." *Critical Asian Studies* 38 (4): 419–44.

——. 2013. *Informal Labor, Formal Politics and Dignified Discontent in India.* New York: Cambridge University Press.

Allen, Zita. 2007. "28,000 Child Care Providers Join UFT." *New York Amsterdam News*, November 22–28, 6.

Alterman, Eric. 2010. "Kabuki Democracy: Why a Progressive Presidency Is Impossible, for Now." *Nation*, August 30–September 6. http://www.thenation.com/article /154019/kabuki-democracy#.

Angotti, Tom. 2008. *New York for Sale: Community Planning Confronts Global Real Estate.* Cambridge, MA: MIT Press.

Arkin, James. 2012. "Mayor Hopefuls Join Rally for Minimum Wage Raise." *New York Daily News*, July 25. http://www.nydailynews.com/blogs/dailypolitics/2012/07 /mayor-hopefuls-join-rally-for-min-wage-raise.

Aronowitz, Stanley. 1992. *False Promises: The Shaping of American Working-Class Consciousness.* Durham, NC: Duke University.

Asian American Federation of New York. 2011. "New Census Data Show Increasing Diversity in New York City's Asian Community." Press release, July 14. http://www .aafny.org/press/pressrelease.asp?prid=126&y=2011.

——. 2012. *Asian Americans in New York City: A Decade of Dynamic Change 2000–2010.*

Associated Press. 2011. "Push to Limit Immigration Authorities in NYC Jails." *Wall Street Journal*, August 17.

Atlas, James. 2010. *Seeds of Change.* Nashville, TN: Vanderbilt University Press.

Axt, Deborah, and Andrew Friedman. 2010. "In Defense of Dignity." *Harvard Civil Rights–Civil Liberties Law Review* 45 (2): 577–99.

Bagli, Charles. 2010. "After 30 Years, Times Square Rebirth Is Complete." *New York Times*, December 3.

Bailey, Thomas. 1985. "A Case Study of Immigrants in the Restaurant Industry." *Industrial Relations* 24 (2).

"Bain Capital Monster: 'Ask Bain for Family Advice.'" Video, *Huffington Post*, October 18, 2012. http://www.huffingtonpost.com/2012/10/18/bain-capital-monster-fam ily-advice_n_1982506.html.

Barley, Stephen R. 2002. "Why Do Contractors Contract? The Experience of Highly Skilled Technical Professionals in a Contingent Labor Market." *Industrial & Labor Relations Review* 55: 234.

Bayona, Jose. 2011. "Immigrants Finding Financial Aid Available Right around Corner." *New York Daily News*, April 20.

Beekman, Daniel. 2012. "Labor Strikes Averted as Unionized Bronx Nurses, Office Building Workers Sign Deals before New Year's." *New York Daily News*, January 3. http://www.nydailynews.com/new-york/bronx/labor-strikes-averted-unionized-bronx-nurses-office-building-workers-sign-deals-new-year-article-1.999915.

Belzer, Michael. 2000. *Sweatshops on Wheels: Winners and Losers in Trucking Deregulation*. New York: Oxford University Press.

Bendick, Marc, Rekha Eanni-Rodriguez, and Saru Jayaraman. 2009. "Race-Ethnic Employment Discrimination in Upscale Restaurants: Evidence from Paired Comparison Testing." *Social Science Journal* 39 (10): 895–911.

Benson, Susan. 1986. *Counter Cultures: Saleswomen, Managers, and Customers in American Department Stores, 1890–1940*. Urbana: University of Illinois Press.

Bergad, Laird. 2008. "Washington Heights/Inwood Demographic, Economic, and Social Transformations 1990–2005 with a Special Focus on the Dominican Population." Center for Latin American, Caribbean, and Latino Studies, CUNY Graduate Center. Latino Data Project Report 18. http://web.gc.cuny.edu/lastudies/pages/latinodataprojectreports.html.

Bernhardt, Annette, Sioban McGrath, and James DeFelippis. 2007. *Unregulated Work in the Global City: Employment and Labor Law Violations in New York City*. New York: New York University, Brennan Center for Justice.

Bernhardt, Annette, Ruth Milkman, Nik Theodore, Douglas Heckathorn, Mirabai Auer, James DeFilippis, Ana Luz Gonzalez, Victor Narro, Jason Perelshteyn, Diana Polson, and Michael Spiller. 2009. *Broken Laws, Unprotected Workers: Violations of Employment and Labor Laws in America's Cities*. University of Illinois, UCLA, and the National Employment Law Project. http://www.unprotectedworkers.org.

Bernhardt, Annette, Diana Polson, and James DeFilippis. 2010. *Working without Laws: A Survey of Employment and Labor Law Violations in New York City*. National Employment Law Center. http://nelp.3cdn.net/990687e422dcf919d3_h6m6b f6ki.pdf.

Bernstein, Nina. 2009. "Immigration Officials Often Detain Foreign-Born Rikers Inmates for Deportation." *New York Times*, August 25.

Bloom, Joshua. 2010. "Ally to Win: Black Community Leaders and SEIU's Security Unionization Campaign." In *Working for Justice: The L.A. Model of Organizing and Advocacy*, edited by Ruth Milkman, Joshua Bloom, and Victor Narro, 167–90. Ithaca, NY: ILR Press.

Boris, Eileen, and Jennifer J. Klein. 2008. "Labor on the Home Front: Organizing Home-Based Care Workers." *New Labor Forum* 17 (2): 32–41.

Boris, Eileen, and Premilla Nadasen. 2008. "Domestic Workers Organize!" *WorkingUSA* 11 (4): 413–37.

Bragg, Chris. 2012. "Top Union Operative Headed to Quinn's Staff." *Crain's New York Business, Insider* blog. December 17. http://mycrains.crainsnewyork.com/blogs/insider/2012/12/top-union-operative-headed-to-quinns-staff/.

Brash, Julian. 2011. *Bloomberg's New York: Class and Governance in the Luxury City*. Athens: University of Georgia Press.

Braverman, Harry. 1974. *Labor and Monopoly Capital: The Degradation of Work in the Twentieth Century*. New York: Monthly Review Press.

Brody, David. 1964. *The Butcher Workmen: A Study of Unionization*. Cambridge, MA: Harvard University Press.

Bronfenbrenner, Kate. 2009. *No Holds Barred: The Intensification of Employer Opposition to Organizing*. Washington, DC: Economic Policy Institute and American Rights at Work, Briefing Paper 235, May 29. http://www.epi.org/publication /bp235/.

Bronfenbrenner, Kate, and Robert Hickey. 2004. "Changing to Organize: A National Assessment of Union Strategies." In *Rebuilding Labor: Organizing and Organizers in the New Union Movement*, edited by Ruth Milkman and Kim Voss, 17–61. Ithaca, NY: Cornell University Press.

Brown, Tamara Mose. 2011. *Raising Brooklyn: Nannies, Childcare, and Caribbeans Creating Community*. New York: New York University Press.

Buckley, Cara. 2011. "Complaints That Rent Is Illegally High Often Languish." *New York Times*, August 5.

Burnham, Linda, and Theodore, Nik. 2012. *Home Economics: The Invisible and Unregulated World of Domestic Work*. New York City: National Domestic Workers Alliance.

Burns, Joe. 2011. *Reviving the Strike: How Working People Can Regain Power and Transform America*. New York: IG Publishing.

Callegari, John. 2011. "N.J.-Based Great Atlantic and Pacific Tea Co. Reaches Agreement with Union Workers." *Long Island Business*, December 1.

Caro-Lopez, Howard, and Laura Limovic. 2010. "Dominicans in New York City, 1990–2008." Center for Latin American, Caribbean, and Latino Studies, CUNY Graduate Center. Latino Data Project-Report 31. http://web.gc.cuny.edu/lastudies/pages /latinodataprojectreports.html.

Carré, Françoise, and Chris Tilly. 2008. "America's Biggest Low-Wage Industry: Continuity and Change in Retail Jobs." Center for Social Policy, CSP Working Paper #2009-6, McCormack Graduate School at UMass Boston. http://scholarworks.umb.edu /csp_pubs/22/.

Castells, Manuel, and John H. Mollenkopf. 1991. *Dual City: Restructuring New York*. New York: Russell Sage Foundation.

Celik, Ercüment. 2011. "Rethinking Street Traders as a Promising Agent of Re-Empowering Labour Movement in Contemporary South Africa." Draft paper, Global Labour University Conference, September, South Africa.

Center for Responsive Politics. 2012. "Heavy Hitters: Top All-Time Donors, 1989–2012" and "Heavy Hitters: Independent Expenditures and Communication Costs, 1989–2012." *OpenSecrets.org* online campaign finance database, www .opensecrets.org.

Chaison, Gary N. 1996. *Union Mergers in Hard Times: The View from Five Countries*. Ithaca, NY: Cornell University Press.

Chang, Grace. 2000. *Disposable Domestics: Immigrant Women Workers in the Global Economy*. Cambridge, MA: South End Press.

Chant, Silvia, and Carolyn Pedwell. 2008. "Women, Gender, and the Informal Economy: An Assessment of ILO Research and Suggested Ways Forward." ILO Working Paper Series. Geneva: ILO.

Chen, Margaret. 2001. "Women in the Informal Economy: A Global Picture, the Global Movement." *SAIS Review* 21 (1): 71–82.

Chen, Michelle. 2012. "New York's Low-Wage Workers Rally for Rights and Stir Solidarity." *In These Times*, July 25. http://www.inthesetimes.com/working/entry/13573 /new_yorks_low-wage_workers_rally_for_rights_and_stir_solidarity/.

Chen, Pei Yao. 2003. "The 'Isolation' of New York City Chinatown: A Geo-historical Approach to a Chinese Community in the United States." PhD diss., City University of New York Graduate Center.

Chinese, Vera. 2012. "United NY, New York Communities for Change and Make the Road NY Visit Workers Looking to Unionize: Pro-Labor Coalition Calls Out Employers Who Discourage Organizing among Workers." *New York Daily News*, April 4. http://www.nydailynews.com/new-york/queens/unitedny-new-york-communi ties-change-road-ny-visit-workers-unionize-article-1.1056161.

Clawson, Dan. 2003. *The Next Upsurge: Labor and the New Social Movements*. Ithaca, NY: Cornell University Press.

Clines, Francis. 2008. "Regulating the 99-Cent Store." *New York Times*, October 21, 28.

Cobble, Dorothy Sue. 1991a. "Organizing the Postindustrial Workforce: Lessons from the History of Waitress Unionism." *Industrial Labor Relations Review* 44, no. 3 (April): 419–36.

———. 1991b. *Dishing It Out: Waitresses and Their Unions in the Twentieth Century*. Chicago: University of Illinois Press.

———. 1994. "Making Postindustrial Unionism Possible." In *Restoring the Promise of American Labor Law*, edited by Sheldon Friedman, Richard W. Hurd, Rudolph A. Oswald, and Ronald L. Seeber, 285–302. Ithaca, NY: ILR Press.

———. 1997. "Lost Ways of Organizing: Reviving the AFL's Direct Affiliate Strategy." *Industrial Relations* 36 (3): 278–301.

———. 2001. "Lost Ways of Unionism, Historical Perspectives on Reinventing the Labor Movement." In *Rekindling the Movement, Labor's Quest for Relevance in the Twenty-First Century*, edited by Lowell Turner, Harry Katz, and Rick Hurd, 82–98. Ithaca, NY: Cornell University Press.

———. 2005. "Kissing the Old Class Politics Goodbye." *International Labor and Working Class History* 67: 54–63.

Cohany, Sharon R. 1998. "Workers in Alternative Employment Arrangements: A Second Look." *Monthly Labor Review* 121 (11): 3–21.

Colen, Shellee. 1995. "'Like a Mother to Them': Stratified Reproduction and West Indian Childcare Workers and Employers in New York City." In *Conceiving the New World Order: The Global Politics of Reproduction*, edited by Faye D. Ginsburg and Rayna Rapp, 78–102. Berkeley: University of California Press.

Compa, Lance. 2000. *Unfair Advantage: Workers' Freedom of Association in the United States under International Human Rights Standards*. New York: Human Rights Watch.

Confessore, Nicholas, and Monica Davey. 2012. "Michigan Effort Shows G.O.P. Sway in State Contests." *New York Times*, December 17, A1.

Cordero-Guzmán, Héctor R. 2005. "Community-Based Organisations and Migration in New York City." *Journal of Ethnic and Migration Studies* 31 (2): 889–909.

———. 2011. "An Analysis of the Opinions of New York City Residents on Minimum Wage, Paid Sick Days, and Living Wages: Results from a Survey of 1200 New Yorkers." April–May. New York: Baruch College School of Public Affairs, City University of New York.

Cordero-Guzmán, Héctor R., Pamela A. Izvănariu, and Victor Narro. 2013. "The Development of Sectoral Worker Center Networks." *Annals of the American Academy of Political and Social Science* 647 (May): 102–23.

Corrigan, Katie, Jennifer Luff, and Joseph A. McCartin, with Seth Newton Patel. 2013. "Bargaining for the Future: Rethinking Labor's Past and Planning Strategically for Its Future." Discussion Paper, Kalmanovitz Initiative for Labor and the Working Poor, Georgetown University.

Costella, Ann Marie. 2011. "Protesters Surprise Meeks over Debt Vote." *Queens Chronicle*, August 25. http://www.qchron.com/editions/eastern/article_00010cdc-840c-5b43-b6c0-a5f486f647f6.html.

Cross, John. 1998. *Informal Politics: Street Vendors and the State in Mexico City*. Stanford, CA: Stanford University Press.

Cross, John, and Alfonso Morales, eds. 2007. *Street Entrepreneurs: People, Place and Politics in Local and Global Perspectives*. New York: Routledge.

Crossa, Veronica. 2009. "Resisting the Entrepreneurial City: Street Vendors' Struggle in Mexico City's Historic Center." *International Journal of Urban and Regional Research* 33 (1): 43–63.

Dark, Taylor E. 1999. *The Unions and the Democrats: An Enduring Alliance*. Ithaca, NY: Cornell University Press.

Dart, Raymond. 2004. "The Legitimacy of Social Enterprise." *Nonprofit Management & Leadership* 14 (4): 411–24.

Das Gupta, M. 2006. *Unruly Immigrants: Rights, Activism, and Transnational South Asian Politics in the United States*. Durham, NC: Duke University Press.

Data Center. 2006. *Home Is Where the Work Is: Inside New York's Domestic Work Industry*. New York: Data Center, DWU.

Davis, Mike. 1986. *Prisoners of the American Dream*. London: Verso.

———. 1992. *City of Quartz*. New York: Vintage Books.

De Genova, Nicholas. 2007. "The Production of Culprits: From Deportability to Detainability in the Aftermath of 'Homeland Security.'" *Citizenship Studies* 11 (5): 421–48.

Dean, Amy. 2012. "Mobilizing the Unorganized: Is 'Working America' the Way Forward?" *New Labor Forum* 21 (1): 61–69.

Dean, Amy, and David Reynolds. 2009. *A New New Deal*. Ithaca, NY: Cornell University Press.

DeFilippis, James, Nina Martin, Annette Bernhardt, and Siobhan McGrath. 2009. "On the Character and Organization of Unregulated Work in the Cities of the U.S." *Urban Geography* 30 (1): 63–90.

Delgado, Gary. 2009. "Reflections on Movement Building and Community Organizing." *Social Policy* (Summer): 6–14.

Delgado, Hector. 1993. *New Immigrants, Old Unions*. Philadelphia: Temple University Press.

Devenish, Annie, and Caroline Skinner. 2004. *Organizing Workers in the Informal Economy: The Experience of the Self-Employed Women's Union, 1994–2004*. WIEGO. http://wiego.org/publications/Devenish%20and%20Skinner%20Organizing%20Workers%20in%20the%20IE.pdf.

Devlin, Ryan. 2010. "Informal Urbanism: Legal Ambiguity, Uncertainty, and the Management of Street Vending in New York City." PhD diss., University of California, Berkeley.

Dolnick, Sam. 2011a. "Even Bloomberg Can't Escape Complexity of Immigration." *New York Times*, January 20.

———. 2011b. "Helping Immigrants Navigate Government." *New York Times*, April 10.

———. 2011c. "Council Bill Would Curb Assistance by Rikers to Immigration Officials." *New York Times*, August 1.

———. 2011d. "For Many Immigrants, Marriage Vote Resonates." *New York Times*, June 27.

———. 2011e. "In Change, Bloomberg Backs Obstacles to Deportation." *New York Times*, September 30.

Domestic Workers United, National Domestic Workers Alliance, and the Urban Justice Center. 2010. *Domestic Workers and Collective Bargaining: A Proposal for the*

Immediate Inclusion of Domestic Workers in the New York State Labor Act. http://www.domesticworkersunited.org/index.php/es/component/jdownloads/view download/3-reports/2-domestic-workers-and-collective-bargaining-full-report.

Duany, Jorge. 2008 [1994]. *Quisqueya on the Hudson: The Transnational Identity of Dominicans in Washington Heights.* 2nd ed. New York: CUNY Dominican Studies Institute Research Monograph.

Duneier, Mitchell. 1999. *Sidewalk.* New York: Farrar, Straus and Giroux.

Durkin, Erin. 2011. "Walmart in Harlem Would Put Other Food Stores Out of Business, Report Predicts." *New York Daily News*, December 14. http://www.nydailynews.com/new-york/uptown/walmart-harlem-put-food-stores-business-report-pre dicts-article-1.991697

Early, Steve. 2007. "Can Worker Centers Fill the Union Void?" *New Labor Forum* 16 (2): 120–21.

——. 2011. *The Civil Wars in U.S. Labor: Birth of a New Workers' Movement or Death Throes of the Old?* Chicago: Haymarket Books.

Edwards, Aaron. 2012. "Planning a March, and Envisioning a Movement, to Unite Low-Wage Workers." *New York Times*, July 18. http://www.nytimes.com/2012/07/19/nyregion/planning-a-march-and-envisioning-a-movement-to-unite-low-wage -workers.html?_r=0.

Ehrenreich, Barbara. 2001. *Nickel and Dimed: On (Not) Getting by in America.* New York: Owl Books.

Ehrenreich, Barbara, and Arlie Russell Hochschild. 2003. *Global Woman: Nannies, Maids, and Sex Workers in the New Economy.* New York: Metropolitan Books.

Eidelson, Josh. 2013. "Alt-Labor." *American Prospect* 24 (January–February): 15–18.

Elan, Elissa. 2007. "Advocacy Group Growth Push Could Put Industry between a ROC and a Hard Place." *Nation's Restaurant News*, August 13.

Employee Benefit Research Institute. 2011. *Employment-Based Retirement Plan Participation: Geographic Differences and Trends.* EBRI Issue Brief #363. Washington, DC: EBRI.

Estey, Marten S. 1955. "Patterns of Union Membership in the Retail Trades." *Industrial and Labor Relations Review* 8 (4): 557–64.

Excluded Workers Congress (with Harmony Goldberg and Rebecca Smith). 2010. *Unity for Dignity: Expanding the Right to Organize to Win Human Rights at Work.* New York: Excluded Workers Congress.

Fine, Janice. 2006. *Worker Centers: Organizing Communities at the Edge of the Dream.* Ithaca, NY: Cornell University Press.

——. 2007. "Marriage Made in Heaven? Mismatches and Misunderstandings between Worker Centres and Unions." *British Journal of Industrial Relations* 45 (2): 335–60.

——. 2011. "New Forms to Settle Old Scores: Updating the Worker Centre Story in the United States." *Relations Industrielles/Industrial Relations* 66 (4): 604–27.

Fine, Janice, and Jennifer Gordon. 2010. "Strengthening Labor Standards Enforcement through Partnerships with Workers' Organizations." *Politics & Society* 38 (4): 552–85.

Fink, Leon, and Brian Greenberg. 1989. *Upheaval in the Quiet Zone: 1199/SEIU and the Politics of Health Care.* Urbana: University of Illinois Press.

Fiscal Policy Institute. 2011. *Immigrant Small Businesses in New York City.* October 3.

——. 2012. *Pulling Apart: The Continuing Impact of Income Polarization in New York State.* http://fiscalpolicy.org/wp-content/uploads/2012/11/FPI-Pulling-Apart-Nov -15-20121.pdf.

Flegenheimer, Matt. 2012. "Judge Blocks City Plan for New Class of Livery Cabs." *New York Times*, June 2, A17.

Fletcher, Bill, and Fernando Gapasin. 2008. *Solidarity Divided: The Crisis in Organized Labor and a New Path toward Social Justice*. Berkeley: University of California Press.

Florida, Richard. 2002. *The Rise of the Creative Class*. New York: Basic Books.

Foerster, Amy. 2006. "'Isn't Anybody Here from Alabama?' Solidarity and Struggle in a 'Mighty, Mighty, Union.'" In *Becoming New Yorkers: Ethnographies of the New Second Generation*, edited by Philip Kasinitz, 197–226. New York: Russell Sage Foundation.

Foner, Nancy. 2001. *New Immigrants in New York*. New York: Columbia University Press.

——. 2002. "Second-Generation Transnationalism, Then and Now." In *The Changing Face of Home: The Transnational Lives of the Second Generation*, edited by Peggy Levitt and Mary Waters, 242–52. New York: Russell Sage Foundation.

Francia, Peter. 2006. *The Future of Organized Labor in American Politics*. New York: Columbia University Press.

——. 2010. "Assessing the Labor-Democratic Party Alliance: A One-Sided Relationship?" *Polity* 42 (3).

Frazier, Ian. 2011. "Dept. of Hoopla: Meals on Wheels." *New Yorker*, October 24.

Freelancers Union. 2010. "New Mutualism Conference Proposal for the Bellagio Center to the Rockefeller Foundation." Supplied by Caitlin Pearce, July 14.

——. 2011a. Member materials. Supplied by Gabriele Wuollo, February 1.

——. 2011b. Internal document. *Organizing Models*. Supplied by Althea Erickson, May 1.

——. 2011c. Internal document. *Unpaid Wages Campaign 2011 Campaign Plan*. Supplied by Althea Erickson, May 1.

Freelancers Union Online Forums. 2011. https://be.freelancersunion.org/forum. April 6.

Freeman, Joshua B. 1989. *In Transit: The Transport Workers Union in New York City, 1933–1966*. Philadelphia, PA: Temple University Press.

——. 2000. *Working-Class New York: Life and Labor since World War II*. New York: New Press.

Freeman, Richard B. 1998. "Spurts in Union Growth: Defining Moments and Social Processes." In *The Defining Moment: The Great Depression and the American Economy in the Twentieth Century*, edited by Michael D. Bordo, Claudia Goldin, and Eugene N. White, 265–96. Chicago: University of Chicago Press.

Frege, Carola, Edmund Heery, and Lowell Turner. 2004. "The New Solidarity? Trade Union Coalition-Building in Five Countries." In *Varieties of Unionism: Strategies for Union Revitalization in a Globalizing Economy*, edited by Carola M. Frege and John Kelly, 137–58. London: Oxford University Press.

Freire, Paulo. 1970. *Pedagogy of the Oppressed*. New York: Herder and Herder.

Friedman, Andrew. 2011. "Unfair to Immigrants, Costly for Taxpayers." *New York Times*, April 4.

Gallin, Dan. 2001. "Propositions on Trade Unions and Informal Employment in Times of Globalization." *Antipode* 33 (3): 531–49.

Ganz, Marshall. 2000. "Resources and Resourcefulness: Strategic Capacity in Unionization of California Agriculture, 1959–1966." *American Journal of Sociology* 105 (4): 1003–62.

——. 2009. *Why David Sometimes Wins: Leadership, Organization, and Strategy in the California Farm Worker Movement*. New York: Oxford University Press.

Getman, Julius G. 2010. *Restoring the Power of Unions: It Takes a Movement*. New Haven, CT: Yale University Press.

Gill, Rosalind, and Andy Pratt. 2008. "In the Social Factory? Immaterial Labour, Precariousness, and Cultural Work." *Theory, Culture & Society* 25: 1–30.

Giuffre, Patricia, and Christine Williams. 1994. "Boundary Lines: Labeling Sexual Harassment in Restaurants." *Gender and Society* 8, (3): 378–401.

Glenn, Evelyn Nakano. 1992. "From Servitude to Service Work: Historical Continuities in the Racial Division of Paid Reproductive Labor." *Signs* 18 (1): 1–43.

Goldenberg, Sally. 2012. "Cabbies Like Hike, But Want *More*." *New York Post*, June 13. www.nypost.com/p/news/local/cabbies_like_hike_but_want_more_sESSOu5Qy8Fzaylbh3rrKP.

Good Jobs New York. 2013. "Economic Development Glossary." http://goodjobsny.org/resources-tools/glossary-economic-development-terms/.

Goodwin, Jeff, and James Jasper. 2004. *Rethinking Social Movements: Structure, Meaning, and Emotion*. Lanham, MD: Rowman and Littlefield.

Gordon, Jennifer. 2005. *Suburban Sweatshops: The Fight for Immigrant Rights*. Cambridge, MA: Harvard University Press.

Gorz, André. 1999. *Reclaiming Work: Beyond the Wage-Based Society*. Malden, MA: Blackwell Publishers.

Greenberg, Miriam. 2008. *Branding New York: How a City in Crisis Was Sold to the World*. New York: Routledge.

Greenhouse, Steven. 1996. "Unions Push for Higher Minimum Wage on City Contracts." *New York Times*, January 2.

——. 2003. "Metro Briefing New York: Queens; Workers Vote on Affiliation." *New York Times*, June 3, B4.

——. 2006a. "In Modern Rarity, Workers Form Union at Small Chain." *New York Times*, February 5, 29.

——. 2006b. "Metro Briefing New York: Manhattan." *New York Times*, April 14, B5.

——. 2008a. "Judge Approves Deal to Settle Suit over Wage Violations." *New York Times*, June 19.

——. 2008b. "Labor Needs to Improve Conditions for Nonunion Workers, Official Warns." *New York Times*, June 23.

——. 2009. *The Big Squeeze: Tough Times for the American Worker*. New York: Anchor Books.

——. 2011. "Union Effort Turns Its Focus to Target." *New York Times*, May 24.

——. 2012a. "Challenging Owners to Raise Wages, Workers at a Second Carwash Vote to Unionize." *New York Times*, October 21.

——. 2012b. "With Day of Protests, Fast-Food Workers Seek More Pay." November 30, A29.

——. 2012c. "Drive to Unionize Fast-Food Workers Begins." *New York Times*, November 29.

——. 2013. "Going It Alone, Together." *New York Times*, March 24, B1.

Grinspan, Izzy. 2012. "Shoe Mania Abruptly Disappears, Sparking Lawsuit." *Racked NY*. http://ny.racked.com/archives/2012/07/27/shoe_mania_abruptly_disappears_sparking_lawsuit.php.

Gross, Susan. 2005. "Business Improvement Districts in New York's Low Income and High Income Neighborhoods." *Economic Development Quarterly* 19 (2): 174–89.

Grynbaum, Michael. 2010a. "Rider Asks Cabdriver if He Is Muslim, Then Stabs Him." *New York Times*, August 26, A19.

——. 2010b. "Technicality Is Cited in Veto of Bill to Protect Cabdrivers." *New York Times*, September 21, A24.

——. 2011a. "Plan for 6,000 Yellow Cabs Only Outside Manhattan." *New York Times,* May 17, A22.

——. 2011b. "2 Taxi Medallions Sell for $1 Million Each." *New York Times City Room Blog,* October 20. http://cityroom.blogs.nytimes.com/2011/10/20/2-taxi-medallions -sell-for-1-million-each/.

Hamilton, Shane. 2008. *Trucking Country: The Road to America's Wal-Mart Economy.* Princeton, NJ: Princeton University Press.

Harrington, Michael. 1962. *The Retail Clerks.* New York: Wiley and Sons.

Hartocollis, Anemona. 2011. "Hospitals in Brooklyn Defended at Hearing." *New York Times,* July 29.

Harvey, David. 2007. *A Brief History of Neoliberalism.* New York: Oxford University Press.

Hauptmeier, Marco, and Lowell Turner. 2007. "Political Insiders and Social Activists: Coalition Building in New York and Los Angeles." In *Labor in the New Urban Battlegrounds: Local Solidarity in a Global Economy,* edited by Lowell Turner and Daniel B. Cornfield. Ithaca, NY: Cornell University Press.

Hays, Elizabeth. 2004. "BJ's Out to Bust Us: Union Irate Over Firing of 2 Leaders." *New York Daily News,* July 21.

Heckscher, Charles. 1996. *The New Unionism.* Ithaca, NY: Cornell University Press.

——. 2001. "Living with Flexibility." In *Rekindling the Movement: Transforming the Labor Movement in the 1990s and Beyond,* edited by Richard Hurd, Harry Katz, and Lowell Turner, 59–81. Ithaca, NY: Cornell University Press.

Hekscher, Charles, and Francoise Carré. 2006. "Strength in Networks: Employment Rights, Organizations and the Problem of Coordination." *British Journal of Industrial Relations* 44 (4): 605–628.

Heckscher, Charles, Sara Horowitz, and Althea Erickson. 2010. "Civil Society and the Provision of Services: The Freelancers Union Experience." In *Civil Society and the Provision of Services,* edited by David Finegold, Mary Gatta, Hal Salzman, and Susan Schurman. Ithaca, NY: Cornell University Press.

Hermanson, Jeff. 1993. "Organizing for Justice: ILGWU Returns to Social Unionism to Organize Immigrant Workers." *Labor Research Review* 1 (20): 53–61.

Hernandez, Javier C. 2011. "Despite City Crackdown, Immigrants Still Are Often Cheated by Job Agencies." *New York Times,* May 15.

Hernandez, Ramona, and Pedro Ortega. 2010. "Estudio comparativo sobre la vida cotidiana de la población de descendencia Dominicana residente en los condados del Bronx y Manhattan en la ciudad de New York." CUNY Dominican Studies Institute.

Hernandez, Ramona, and Francisco Rivera-Batiz. 2003. "Dominicans in the United States: A Socioeconomic Profile." CUNY Dominican Studies Institute Research Monograph.

Herod, Andrew. 1997. "From a Geography of Labor to a Labor Geography: Labor's Spatial Fix and the Geography of Capitalism." *Antipode* 29 (1): 1–31.

Hetland, Gabriel. 2009. "Labor in Movement: Contradictory Articulations of Union, Community, and State in Neoliberal New York." Proceedings of the 2009 American Sociological Association Conference, Section on Labor and Labor Movements. http://asalabormovements.weebly.com/uploads/6/8/2/8/6828078/2009hetland.pdf.

Hirsch, Barry, and David Macpherson. 2003. "Union Membership and Coverage Database from the Current Population Survey: A Note." *Industrial and Labor Relations Review* 56: 349–54.

——. 2013. "Union Membership and Coverage Database from the CPS." http://union stats.com/.

Hochschild, Arlie. 1983. *The Managed Heart: Commercialization of Human Feeling.* Berkeley: University of California Press.

Hochschild, Arlie, and Anne Machung. 1989. *The Second Shift: Working Parents and the Revolution at Home.* New York: Viking.

Hodges, Graham Russell. 2007. *Taxi! A Social History of the New York City Cabdriver.* Baltimore, MD: Johns Hopkins University Press.

Hondagneu-Sotelo, Pierrette. 2001. *Doméstica: Immigrant Workers Cleaning and Caring in the Shadows of Affluence.* Berkeley: University of California Press.

Horan, Kathleen. 2012. "Taxi Commission Approves Fare Hike." *WNYC News Blog.* July 12. http://www.wnyc.org/blogs/wnyc-newsblog/2012/jul/12/taxi-commission-vote fare-hikes/.

Horowitz, Sara. 2011. "Memorandum of Support for S4129/A6698: An Act to Amend the Labor Law, in Relation to Independent Contractors." New York: Freelancers Union.

——. 2011a. "The Freelancer Surge Is the Industrial Revolution of Our Time." *Atlantic,* September 1. http://www.theatlantic.com/business/archive/2011/09/the-freelance -surge-is-the-industrial-revolution-of-our-time/244229/.

——. 2011b. "Welcome to Middle Class Poverty—Does Anybody Know the Way Out?" *Atlantic,* September 23. http://www.theatlantic.com/business/archive/2011/09/wel come-to-middle-class-poverty-does-anybody-know-the-way-out/245447/.

——. Various years. Blog posts on New Mutualism. https://be.freelancersunion.org /blog/?p=1188 and https://be.freelancersunion.org/blog/?p=1197.

Horowitz, Sara, Hollis Calhoun, Althea Erickson, and Gabrielle Wuolo. 2011. *America's Uncounted Workforce.* New York: Freelancers Union. http://fures.org/pdfs/advo cacy/2011_Counting_the_Independent_Workforce%20Policy_Brief.pdf.

Horowitz, Sara, Althea Erickson, and Gabrielle Wuolu. 2010. *Independent, Innovative, and Unprotected: How the Old Safety Net Is Failing America's New Workforce.* Free-lancer Union's Annual Survey Report. http://fures.org/0020091124/pdfs/advocacy /2009surveyreport.pdf.

Horowitz, Sara, and Gabrielle Wuolo. 2011. *Creating a 'New' New Deal: Evolving Worker Protections for the 21st Century.* http://fu-res.org/pdfs/advocacy/2011-the-new -new-deal.pdf.

Horowitz, Sara, et al. 2006. *2005 Report: The Rise of the Freelance Class; A New Constitu-ency of Workers Building a Social Safety Net.* New York: Freelancers Union.

Horowitz, Sara, et al. 2006. *New Unionism and the Next Social Safety Net.* New York: Free-lancers Union.

Horton, Myles, and Paulo Freire. 1990. *We Make the Road by Walking: Conversations on Education and Social Change,* edited by Brenda Bell, John Gaventa, and John Peters. Philadelphia: Temple University Press.

Hunt, Stacey. 2009. "Citizenship's Place: The State's Creation of Public Space and Street Vendors' Culture of Informality in Bogota, Colombia." *Environment and Planning D: Society and Space* 27: 331–51.

Hunter, Tera. 2004. "'The Brotherly Love for Which This City Is Proverbial Should Ex-tend to All': The Everyday Lives of Working-Class Women in Philadelphia and Atlanta in the 1890s." In *The African American Urban Experience,* edited by Joe W. Trotter, Earl Lewis, and Tera W. Hunter. New York: Palgrave Macmillan.

INCITE! Women of Color Against Violence, 2007. *The Revolution Will Not Be Funded.* Boston: South End Press.

Independent Budget Office (IBO), New York City. 2010. "Sidewalk Standoff: Street Vendor Regulations Are Costly, Confusing, and Leave Many Disgruntled." November Pol-icy Brief. www.ibo.nyc.ny.us/iboreports/peddlingnovember2010.pdf.

Informador.com. 2011. "Indignados presionan en Nueva York: Miles de personas de todo Estados Unidos se suman la lucha de los llamados 'anti-Wall Street.'" October 7. http://www.informador.com.mx/internacional/2011/327682/6/indignados-pre sionan-en-nueva-york.htm.

International Labor Office (ILO). 2002a. *Women and Men in the Informal Economy: A Statistical Picture.* Geneva: ILO.

———. 2002b. *Decent Work and the Informal Economy.* Report 6. Geneva: ILO.

Irmas, Jared. 2008. "Taxi Industry Questions Safety of Switching to Hybrid Vehicle." *New York Sun,* January 17, 3.

Itzigsohn, José. 1994. "The Informal Economy in Santo Domingo and San Jose: A Comparative Study." PhD diss., Department of Sociology, Johns Hopkins University.

Jackson, Nancy Beth. 2004. "Drawn by the Prices, Betting on the Neighborhood." *New York Times,* November 14.

Jaffe, Sarah. 2012. "McJobs Should Pay, Too: Inside Fast Food Workers' Historic Protest for Living Wages." *Atlantic,* November 29. http://www.theatlantic.com/business /archive/2012/11/mcjobs-should-pay-too-inside-fast-food-workers-historic-pro test-for-living-wages/265714/.

Jaramillo, Catalina. 2011a. "Activista revela su lucha personal, Ana María Archila ha peleado por los derechos de los inmigrantes." *Impre,* June 26.

———. 2011b. "Census 2010 New York: A State for all Hispanics." *Impre,* August 25.

Jayaraman, Saru. 2006. "Communities of Color and New Models of Organizing Labor." *Berkeley Journal of Employment and Labor Law* 27, (1): 223–25.

———. 2011. "From Triangle Shirtwaist to Windows on the World: Restaurants as the New Sweatshop." Special issue on Triangle Shirtwaist Fire. *New York University Journal of Legislation and Public Policy* (December).

———. 2011a. "Restaurants and Race." *Race, Poverty & the Environment: A Journal for Social & Environmental Justice* 18 (1): 6.

———. 2013. *Behind the Kitchen Door.* Ithaca, NY: Cornell University Press.

Jayaraman, Saru, Jonathan Dropkin, Sekou Siby, Laine Romero, and Steven Markowitz. 2011. "Dangerous Dining: Occupational Safety and Health of New York City Restaurant Workers." *Journal of Occupational & Environmental Medicine.* 53 (12): 1418–24.

Jayaraman, Saru, and Immanuel Ness. 2005. *The New Urban Immigrant Workforce: Innovative Models for Labor Organizing.* Armonk, NY: M. E. Sharpe.

Jenkins, Steve. 2002. "Organizing, Advocacy and Member Power: A Critical Reflection." *Working USA* 6 (2): 56–89.

Jones-Correa, Michael. 1998. *Between Two Nations: The Political Predicament of Latinos in New York City.* Ithaca, NY: Cornell University Press.

Jordan, Howard. 1997. "Dominicans in New York: Getting a Slice of the Apple." *NACLA Report on the Americas* 30.

Kalleberg, Arne L. 2000. "Nonstandard Employment Relations: Part-Time, Temporary, and Contract Work." *Annual Review of Sociology* 26: 341–65.

———. 2006. "Nonstandard Employment Relations and Labour Market Inequality Crossnational Patterns. In *Inequalities of the World,* edited by Goran Therborn, 36–61. New York: Verso.

———. 2009. "Precarious Work, Insecure Workers: Employment Relations in Transition." *American Sociological Review* 74: 1–22.

———. 2011. *Good Jobs, Bad Jobs: The Rise of Polarized and Precarious Employment Systems in the United States, 1970s to 2000s.* New York: Russell Sage Foundation.

Kalleberg, Arne L., Barbara F. Reskin, and Ken Hudson. 2000. "Bad Jobs in America: Standard and Nonstandard Employment Relations and Job Quality in the United States." *American Sociological Review* 65: 256–78.

Kang, Milann. 2010. *The Managed Hand: Face, Gender, and the Body in Beauty Service Work*. Berkeley: University of California Press.

Kaplan, Thomas. 2011. "Albany Tax Deal to Raise Rate for Highest Earners." *New York Times*, December 6. http://www.nytimes.com/2011/12/07/nyregion/cuomo-and -legislative-leaders-agree-on-tax-deal.html?ref=opinion.

Kasinitz, Philip, John Mollenkopf, and Mary Waters, eds. 2004. *Becoming New Yorkers: Ethnographies of the New Second Generation*. New York: Russell Sage Foundation.

Katznelson, Ira. 1981. *City Trenches: Urban Politics and the Patterning of Class in the United States*. New York: Pantheon.

——. 2005. *When Affirmative Action Was White: An Untold History of Racial Inequality in Twentieth-Century America*. New York: W. W. Norton.

Kelly, Sarah N., and Christine Tramantano. 2006. "Working Today." *New York Law School Law Review* 8 (14): 597–606.

Kest, Steve. 2003. "ACORN and Community-Labor Partnerships." *WorkingUSA* 6 (4): 84–100.

Kibria, Nazli. 2002a. *Becoming Asian American: Second-Generation Chinese and Korean American Identities*. Baltimore, MD: Johns Hopkins University Press.

——. 2002b. "Of Blood, Belonging, and Homeland Trips: Transnationalism and Identity among Second-Generation Chinese and Korean Americans." In *The Changing Face of Home: The Transnational Lives of the Second Generation*, edited by Peggy Levitt and Mary C. Waters, 295–311. New York: Russell Sage Foundation.

Kieffer, David, and Immanuel Ness. 1999. "Organizing Immigrant Workers in New York City: The LIUNA Asbestos Removal Workers Campaign." *Labor Studies Journal* 24 (1): 12–26.

Kim, Dae Young. 2004. "Leaving the Ethnic Economy: The Rapid Integration of Second-Generation Korean Americans in New York." In *Becoming New Yorkers: Ethnographies of the New Second Generation*, edited by Philip Kasinitz, John Mollenkopf, and Mary Waters, 154–88. New York: Russell Sage Foundation.

Kink, Michael. 2011. "Strong Economy for All Response to Albany Tax Deal." Press statement, December 6. http://strongforall.org/strong-economy-for-all-response-to-al bany-tax-deal/.

Kochan, Thomas A., Harry A. Katz, and Robert C. McKersie. 1987. *The Transformation of American Industrial Relations*. New York: Basic Books.

Korean Resource Center. n.d. "Yoon Han Bong." http://krcla.org/en/Yoon_Han_Bong.

Kosinski, T. J. 2012. "Mitt Romney's Trump Fundraiser Has a Few Elaborate Protesters." *New York Magazine*, April 17. http://nymag.com/daily/intelligencer/2012/04/mitt -romney-fundraiser-donald-trump-protesters.html.

Kothari, Uma. 2008. "Global Peddlers and Local Networks: Migrant Cosmopolitanisms." *Environment and Planning D: Society and Space* 26: 500–516.

Krinsky, John. 2007. "Constructing Workers: Working-Class Formation under Neoliberalism." *Qualitative Sociology* 30 (4): 343–60.

Krinsky, John, and Ellen Reese. 2006. "Forging and Sustaining Labor-Community Coalitions: The Workfare Justice Movement in Three Cities." *Sociological Forum* 21 (4): 623–58.

Kwon, Jon Bum. 2010. "The Koreatown Immigrant Workers Alliance: Spatializing Justice in an Ethnic 'Enclave.'" In *Working for Justice: The LA Model of Organizing and Advocacy*, edited by Ruth Milkman, Jonathan Bloom, and Victor Narro, 23–48, Ithaca, NY: Cornell University Press.

Kwong, Peter. 1994. "Chinese Staff and Workers' Association: A Model for Organizing in the Changing Economy?" *Social Policy* 25 (2): 30–38.

La Fuente. 2007. "Building Strong Labor/Community Partnerships." Unpublished Power-Point presentation.

Lafer, Gordon. 2005. *Free and Fair? How Labor Law Fails U.S. Democratic Standards.* Washington, DC: American Rights at Work.

——. 2007. *Neither Free nor Fair: The Subversion of Democracy under National Labor Relations Board Elections.* Washington, DC: American Rights at Work.

Lambert, Susan J. 2008. "Passing the Buck: Labor Flexibility Practices That Transfer Risk onto Hourly Workers." *Human Relations* 61 (9): 1203–27.

Lambert, Susan J., and Julia R. Henly. 2010. *Work Scheduling Study: Managers' Strategies for Balancing Business Requirements with Employee Needs.* University of Chicago School of Social Service Administration. http://ssascholars.uchicago.edu/work -scheduling-study/files/univ_of_chicago_work_scheduling_manager_report_6 _25.pdf.

Leavitt, Jacqueline, and Gary Blasi. 2010. "The Los Angeles Taxi Worker Alliance." In *Working for Justice: The L.A. Model of Organizing and Advocacy*, edited by Ruth Milkman, Joshua Bloom, and Victor Narro. Ithaca, NY: Cornell University Press.

Lee, Sara. 2004. "Class Matters: Racial, and Ethnic Identities of Working- and Middle-Class Second-Generation Korean Americans in New York City." In *Becoming New Yorkers: Ethnographies of the New Second Generation*, edited by Philip Kasinitz, John Mollenkopf, and Mary Waters, 313–38. New York: Russell Sage Foundation.

Lefebvre, Henri. 1968. *Le droit à la ville.* Paris: Anthropos.

Leidner, Robin. 1993. *Fast Food, Fast Talk: Service Work and the Routinization of Everyday Life.* Berkeley: University of California Press.

Lerner, Stephen. 2011a. "A New Insurgency Can Only Arise Outside the Progressive and Labor Establishment." *New Labor Forum* 20 (3): 9–13.

——. 2011b. "Organize and Occupy." *Nation*, October 19. http://www.thenation.com /article/164076/organize-and-occupy.

Lewis, Penny, and Stephanie Luce. 2012. "Labor and Occupy Wall Street: An Appraisal of the First Six Months." *New Labor Forum* 21 (3): 43–49.

Lichtenstein, Nelson. 2002. *State of the Union.* Princeton, NJ: Princeton University Press.

——. 2009. *The Retail Revolution: How Wal-Mart Created a Brave New World of Business.* New York: Metropolitan Books.

Light, Ivan, and Edna Bonacich.1988. *Immigrant Entrepreneurs: Koreans in Los Angeles, 1965–1982.* Berkeley: University of California Press.

Light, Joe. 2010. "More Freelancers Fight to Be Paid." *Wall Street Journal*, April 27.

Limonic, Laura. 2008. "Where Do Latinos Work? Occupational Structure and Mobility within New York City's Latino Population 1990–2006." Center for Latin American, Caribbean, and Latino Studies, CUNY Graduate Center. Latino Data Project Report 23.

Logan, John. 2006. "The Union Avoidance Industry in the United States." *British Journal of Industrial Relations* 44 (4): 651–75.

——. 2011. "New Data: NLRB Process Fails to Ensure a Fair Vote." UC Berkeley Center for Labor Research and Education, June.

Lopez, Elias. 2007. "City Cabdrivers Strike Again, But Protest Gets Little Notice." *New York Times*, October 23.

Lopez, Steven Henry. 2004. *Reorganizing the Rust Belt: An Inside Study of the American Labor Movement.* Berkeley: University of California Press.

Low, Setha, and Neil Smith, eds. 2006. *The Politics of Public Space.* New York: Routledge.

Luce, Stephanie. 2004. *Fighting for a Living Wage.* Ithaca, NY: ILR Press.

Luce, Stephanie, and Naoki Fujita. 2012. *Discounted Jobs: How Retailers Sell Workers Short.* Murphy Institute, City University of New York and Retail Action Project. http://retailactionproject.org/wp-content/uploads/2012/01/FINAL_RAP.pdf

Lund, Francis, and Caroline Skinner. 2004. "Integrating the Informal Economy in Urban Planning and Governance: A Case Study of the Process of Policy Development in Durban, South Africa." *International Development Planning Review* 26 (4): 431–56.

Maher, Kris. 2009. "SEIU Campaign Spending Pays Political Dividends." *Wall Street Journal*, March 16. http://online.wsj.com/article/SB124243785248026055.html.

Martinez-Novo, Carmen. 2003. "The 'Culture' of Exclusion: Representations of Indigenous Women Street Vendors in Tijuana, Mexico." *Bulletin of Latin American Research* 22 (3): 249–68.

Marwell, Nicole. 2004. "Privatizing the Welfare State: Nonprofit Community-Based Organizations as Political Actors." *American Sociological Review* 69 (2): 265–91.

Massey, Daniel. 2010. "Ugh: The Free in Freelance." *Crain's New York Business.com*, August 29. http://www.crainsnewyork.com/article/20100829/SMALLBIZ/308299994.

——. 2011a. "Veteran Agitators Flock to Occupy Wall Street." *Crain's New York Business .com*, September 29. http://www.crainsnewyork.com/article/20110929/FINANCE /110929865.

——. 2011b. "Big NY Voter Majority Favors 'Millionaire Tax,'" *Crain's New York Business. com*, October 17. http://www.crainsnewyork.com/article/20111017/POLITICS /111019892.

——. 2011c. "City Taxi Drivers' Organization Joins AFL-CIO." *Crain's New York Business*, October 20. http://www.crainsnewyork.com/article/20111020/LABOR_UNIONS /111029995.

——. 2011d. "NY Employers Must Get Wages Right—or It'll Cost; Employers Face More Paperwork, Bigger Penalties." *Crain's New York Business*, April 10. http://www .crainsnewyork.com/article/20110410/SMALLBIZ/304109973.

——. 2011e. "Target Fires Pro-Union Employee." *Crain's New York Business*, August 15. http://www.crainsnewyork.com/article/20110815/FREE/110819935.

——. 2011f. "Building Cleaners Launch Ads as Strike Deadline Nears." *Crain's New York Business.com*, December 27. http://www.crainsnewyork.com/article/20111227/LA BOR_UNIONS/111229920.

——. 2011g. "NLRB Alleges Target Violated Labor Laws." *Crain's New York Business*, August 25. http://www.crainsnewyork.com/article/20110826/FREE/110829928.

Massey, Douglas, Jorge Durand, and Nolan Malone. 2002. *Beyond Smoke and Mirrors: Mexican Immigration in an Era of Economic Integration.* New York: Russell Sage Foundation.

Mathew, Biju. 2008. *Taxi! Cabs and Capitalism in New York City.* Ithaca, NY: Cornell University Press.

Mayer, Gerald. 2004. "Union Membership Trends in the United States." Washington, DC: Congressional Research Service, US Library of Congress. http://digitalc ommons.ilr.cornell.edu/cgi/viewcontent.cgi?article=1176&context=key_work place.

McAlevey, Jane, and Bob Ostertag. 2012. *Raising Expectations (and Raising Hell).* New York: Verso Press.

McCarty, Dawn. 2012. "Shoe Mania Creditors Seek to Force It into Bankruptcy." *Bloomberg*, August 3. http://www.bloomberg.com/news/2012-08-03/shoe-mania-credi tors-seek-to-force-it-into-bankruptcy.html.

Mehta, Chirag, and Nik Theodore. 2005. *Undermining the Right to Organize: Employer Behavior during Union Representation Campaigns*. Washington, DC: American Rights at Work.

Meyerson, Harold. 2011. "Labor's Hail Mary Pass." *Washington Post*, May 24.

——. 2012. "If Labor Dies, What's Next?" *American Prospect* 23 (September–October): 19–29.

Middleton, Jennifer. 1996. "Contingent Workers in a Changing Economy: Endure, Adapt, or Organize?" *NYU Review of Labor and Social Change* 22: 557.

Milkman, Ruth, 2006. *L.A. Story: Immigrant Workers and the Future of the US Labor Movement*. New York: Russell Sage Foundation.

——. 2010. "Introduction." In *Working for Justice: The L.A. Model of Organizing and Advocacy*, edited by Ruth Milkman, Joshua Bloom, and Victor Narro, 1–19. Ithaca, NY: Cornell University Press.

Milkman, Ruth, Joshua Bloom, and Victor Narro, eds. 2010. *Working for Justice: The L.A. Model of Organizing and Advocacy*. Ithaca, NY: Cornell University Press.

Milkman, Ruth, and Laura Braslow. Various years, 2009–2012 *The State of the Unions: A Profile of Organized Labor in New York City, New York State, and the United States*. New York: Joseph S. Murphy Institute for Worker Education and Labor Studies, Center for Urban Research, and NYC Labor Market Information Service, CUNY. http://www.urbanresearch.org/about/docs/lmis_pubs/Union_Density2012_re7.pdf.

Milkman, Ruth, Stephanie Luce, and Penny Lewis. 2013. *Changing the Subject: A Bottom-Up Account of Occupy Wall Street in New York City*. New York: Joseph S. Murphy Institute for Worker Education and Labor Studies, City University of New York. http://sps.cuny.edu/filestore/1/5/7/1_a05051d2117901d/1571_92f562221b8041e.pdf.

Milton, Laurie P. 2003. "An Identity Perspective on the Propensity of High-Tech Talent to Unionize." *Journal of Labor Research* 24 (1): 31–53.

Min, Pyong Gap. 1987. "Filipino and Korean Immigrants in Small Business: A Comparative Analysis." *Amerasian Journal* 13 (1): 53–71.

——. 2008. *Ethnic Solidarity for Economic Survival: Korean Greengrocers in New York City*. New York: Russell Sage Foundation.

——. 2011. "Koreans' Immigration to the US: History and Contemporary Trends." Research Report No. 3, January 27. Research Center for Korean Community Queens College, CUNY.

MinKwon Center for Community Action. 2009. *Annual Report 2009: Celebrating Our History, Building a Movement for Action*.

——. 2011. "27th Anniversary Gala: Defining Our Future through Community Action," October 27.

Mitchell, Don. 2003. *The Right to the City: Social Justice and the Fight for Public Space*. New York: Guilford Press.

Mitra, Diditi. 2005. "Driving Taxis in New York City." In *The New Urban Immigrant Workforce: Innovative Models for Labor Organizing*, edited by Saru Jayaraman and Immanuel Ness, 33–56. Armonk, NY: M. E. Sharpe.

Mollenkopf, John. 1992. *A Phoenix in the Ashes: The Rise and Fall of the Koch Coalition in New York City Politics*. Princeton, NJ: Princeton University Press.

——. 2011. "Immigrants and the Precincts of Power in New York City." Unpublished manuscript, CUNY Graduate Center, Center for Urban Research.

Moody, Kim. 2007a. *From Welfare State to Real Estate: Regime Change in New York City, 1974–Present*. New York: New Press.

——. 2007b. *U.S. Labor in Trouble and Transition: The Failure of Reform from Above, the Promise of Revival from Below*. New York: Verso.

——. 2008. "Harvest of Empire: Immigrant Workers' Struggles in the USA." In *Socialist Register 2008: Global Flashpoints*, edited by Leo Panitch and Colin Leys, 315–344. New York: Monthly Review Press.

Moreton, Bethany. 2009. *To Serve God and Wal-Mart: The Making of Christian Free Enterprise*. Cambridge, MA: Harvard University Press.

Morris, Charles. 2005. *The Blue Eagle at Work: Reclaiming Democratic Rights in the American Workplace*. Ithaca, NY: Cornell University Press.

Morris, Keiko. 2011. "A&P Union Workers OK 'Concessionary' Pact." *Newsday*, December 1, A53.

Murrmann, Suzanne K., and Kent F. Murrmann 1990. "Union Membership Trends and Organizing Activities in the Hotel and Restaurant Industries." *Journal of Hospitality & Tourism Research Journal* 14: 491–504.

Nash, Ken, and Mimi Rosenberg. 2007. "Building Bridges." April 3. WBAI 99.5 FM, New York. http://www.radio4all.net/index.php/program/22724.

National Employment Law Project (NELP). 2011. "Local Living Wage Ordinances and Coverage." January 20. www.nelp.org.

National Nurses United. 2013. "Time for a Main Street Contract: Heal America/Tax Wall Street" campaign. http://www.nationalnursesunited.org/affiliates/entry/msc1.

National Restaurant Association. 2012. "New York Restaurant Industry at A Glance." http://www.restaurant.org/Downloads/PDFs/State-Statistics/newyork.

Needleman, Ruth. 1998. "Building Relationships for the Long Haul: Unions and Community-Based Groups Working Together to Organize Low-Wage Workers." In *Organizing to Win: New Research on Union Strategies*, edited by Kate Bronfenbrenner, Sheldon Friedman, Richard Hurd, Rudy Oswald, and Ronald Seeber, 71–86. Ithaca, NY: Cornell University Press.

Ness, Immanuel. 2005. *Immigrants, Unions and the New U.S. Labor Market*. Philadelphia: Temple University Press.

Newman, Andy. 2011. "Clashes and More Than 240 Arrests on Protest's Day of Action." *New York Times*, November 17, http://cityroom.blogs.nytimes.com/2011/11/17/protesters-and-officers-clash-near-wall-street/.

New York Chamber of Commerce. 1951. *New York State Business Facts: New York City*. On reserve at the New York Public Library.

——. 1966. *The New York City Economy: An Overview, Trends*. On reserve at the New York Public Library.

New York City Economic Development Corporation. 2010. "Snapshot of NYC Economy." December. New York: NYCEDC.

New York Civil Liberties Union. 2012. "*Arroyo et al. v. Redeye*: Challenging Employment Practices at NYC Restaurant." http://www.nyclu.org/case/arroyo-et-al-v-redeye-challenging-employment-practices-nyc-restaurant.

New York Post. 2011. "Public Joblessness Advocate." December 25. http://nypost.com/2011/12/26/public-joblessness-advocate/

New York State Department of Labor. 2009. "Labor Department Initiative Empowers Ordinary People to Join the Fight against Wage Theft." Press release. www.labor.ny.gov/pressreleases/2009/Jan26_2009.htm.

——. 2010. *Feasibility of Domestic Worker Collective Bargaining*. http://www.labor.ny.gov/legal/laws/pdf/domestic-workers/domestic-workers-feasibility-study.pdf.

New York State Employment Relations Board. 2010. *Representation Petitions*. http://www.labor.ny.gov/erb/representation.asp.

New York State Labor Relations Act. 2010. http://www.labor.ny.gov/erb/pdf/Article%252020%2520_2_.pdf+new+york+state+labor+relations+act&hl=en&gl=us&pid=bl&srcid=ADGEESiTIJLt5Irc0vG_a4PuvsBugmUjROY_MbKTv_krHJApC

ziaakG8QgqnT1FyLAtGBFgSmdVPGxE4kQ5nOEKZALxh0LdkZAm2DrPYNkx-
Euyd7qg3n3gQMtJ5uKf5s7mb9aLfNIYH_&sig=AHIEtbTIScpRNzOz7rWyZRW
nQrGxUzsL4A&pli=1.

Nichols, John. 2011. "ALEC Exposed." *Nation*, August 1–8. http://www.thenation.com
/article/161978/alec-exposed

Nissen, Bruce. 2004. "The Effectiveness and Limits of Labor-Community Coalitions: Evidence from South Florida." *Labor Studies Journal* 29 (1): 6789.

Nolan, Hamilton. 2011. "Here's the Cheesy Anti-Union Video All Target Employees Must
Endure." *Gawker*, June 13. http://gawker.com/5811371/heres-the-cheesy-anti+union
-video-all-target-employees-must-endure.

NYTWA 2010. Press release, March 23.

——. 2011a. Health Needs Assessment. May. (unpublished data).

——. 2011b. *Shift Change* newsletter 2, no. 1, August.

——. 2011c. *Shift Change* newsletter 2, no. 2, September.

——. 2011d. *Shift Change* newsletter 2, no. 3, October.

——. 2011e. *Shift Change* newsletter 2, no. 4, November.

——. 2011f. *Shift Change* newsletter 2, no. 5, December 2011–January 2012.

O'Brien, Erin. 2008. *The Politics of Identity: Solidarity Building among America's Working
Poor*. Albany, NY: SUNY Press.

Offe, Claus, and Helmut Wiesenthal. 1980. "Two Logics of Collective Action: Theoretical
Notes on Social Class and Organizational Form." *Political Power and Social Theory*
1: 67–115.

Opler, Daniel J. 2007. *For All White-Collar Workers: The Possibilities of Radicalism in New
York City's Department Store Unions, 1934–1953*. Columbus: University of Ohio
Press.

Organization for Economic Cooperation and Development. 2009. "Is Informal Normal?
Towards More and Better Jobs." *OECD Observer*, March. www.oecd.org/publica
tions/Policybriefs.

Osnowitz, Debra. 2007. "Individual Needs versus Collective Interests: Network Dynamics
in the Freelance Editorial Association." *Qualitative Sociology* 30: 459–79.

——. 2010. *Freelancing Expertise: Contract Professionals in the New Economy*. Ithaca, NY:
Cornell University.

Osterman, Paul. 1999. *Securing Prosperity: The American Labor Market: How It Has
Changed and What to Do about It*. Princeton, NJ: Princeton University Press.

Park, Keumjae. 2009. *Korean Immigrant Women and the Renegotiation of Identity: Class,
Gender and the Politics of Identity*. El Paso, TX: LFB Scholarly Publishing.

Parreñas, Rhacel Salazar. 2001. *Servants of Globalization: Women, Migration, and Domestic
Work*. Stanford, CA: Stanford University Press.

Parrott, James. 2008. *Low Wages, No Bargain: Retail Jobs in New York City*. December.
New York: Fiscal Policy Institute.

Pearson, Erica. 2012. "Another Car Wash Votes to Unionize." *New York Daily News*,
December 11. http://www.nydailynews.com/new-york/union-vote-bronx-car
-wash-article-1.1218123.

Petro, John. 2011. *Low-Wage Jobs Dominate City's Job Growth*. Drum Major Institute
for Public Policy. http://drummajorinstitute.org/low-wage-jobs-dominate-nyc
-job-growth.

Pew Research Center. 2012. "The Rise of Asian Americans: Political Party and Ideology."
www.pewsocialtrends.org.

Piazza, Jo. 2012. "Low Wage Workers Join Forces in New York City March." *Current TV*,
July 24. http://current.com/groups/news-blog/93852010_low-wage-workers-join
-forces-in-new-york-city-march.htm.

Piven, Frances Fox, and Richard A. Cloward. 1979. *Poor People's Movements: Why They Succeed, How They Fail.* New York: Vintage Books.

——. 2000. "Power Repertoires and Globalization," *Politics & Society* 38 (3): 413–30.

Pofeldt, Elaine. 2011. "Temporary Workers in Demand: Specialty Freelancers Calling the Shots." *Crain's New York Business,* August 7. http://www.crainsnewyork.com/arti cle/20110807/SMALLBIZ/308079991.

Polletta, Francesca. 2002. *Freedom Is an Endless Meeting: Democracy in American Social Movements.* Chicago: University of Chicago Press.

Poo, Ai-jen. 2009. "Organizing with Love." http://www.domesticworkersunited.org /media/files/287/OrganizingWithLoveFinal.pdf.

——. 2011. "A Twenty-First Century Organizing Model: Lessons from the New York Domestic Workers Bill of Rights Campaign." *New Labor Forum* 20 (1): 51–55.

Portes, Alejandro, Manuel Castells, and Lauren Benton, eds. 1989. *The Informal Economy: Studies in Advanced and Less Developed Countries.* Baltimore, MD: Johns Hopkins University Press.

Powell, Michael. 2012. "The Revolution Will Be Minimized." *New York Times,* April 30.

Preis, Art. 1972. *Labor's Giant Step: The First Twenty Years of the CIO: 1936–55.* 2nd ed. Princeton, NJ: Princeton University Press.

Putnam, Robert. 2000. *Bowling Alone: The Collapse and Revival of American Community.* New York: Simon & Schuster.

Quinnipiac University. 2011. "New Yorkers Nix Mayor on Occupy Wall Street, University Polls Finds; Voters Back Living Wage 4 to 1." December 14. http://www.quinnipiac .edu/institutes-and-centers/polling-institute/new-york-city/release-detail?Re leaseID=1680.

Reddy, Sumathi. 2011a. "Immigration Backers Cheer Cuomo Action," *Wall Street Journal,* June 2.

——. 2011b. "Prices for Food-Cart Permits Skyrocket." *Wall Street Journal,* March 9.

Reed, Adolph. 2010. "Why Labor's Soldiering for the Democrats Is a Losing Battle." *New Labor Forum,* 19 (3).

Retail Action Project website. http://retailactionproject.org.

Reynolds, David. 2004. *Partnering for Change: Unions and Community Groups Build Coalitions for Economic Justice.* Armonk, NY: M. E. Sharpe.

Reynoso, Julissa. 2003. "Dominican Immigrants and Social Capital in New York City: A Case Study." *Encrucijada/Crossroads: An Online Academic Journal* 1: 1. http:// journals.dartmouth.edu/cgi-bin/WebObjects/Journals.woa/2/xmlpage/2/article /104.

Rivera, Camille. 2012. "Workers Rising: A Unified Fight for New York's Workers." *Huffington Post,* July 27. http://www.huffingtonpost.com/camille-rivera/workers-rising -a-unified-_b_1706653.html.

ROC-NY. 2009a. "Burned: The High Risks and Low Benefits for Workers in New York City's Restaurant Industry." http://www.scribd.com/embeds/65092837/content ?start_page=1&view_mode=list&access_key=key-2ky5ky07juk3evgja8sv#.

——. 2009b. "The Great Service Divide: Occupational Segregation & Inequality in the New York City Restaurant Industry." http://rocunited.org/files/2013/04/reports _great-service-divide.pdf.

——. 2010. "Waiting on Equality: The Role and Impact of Gender on New York City's Restaurant Industry." http://www.scribd.com/doc/65092777/Waiting-on-Equality -The-Role-and-Impact-of-Gender-in-the-New-York-City-Restaurant-Industry.

ROC-NY and the New York Restaurant Industry Coalition. 2005. "Behind the Kitchen Door: Pervasive Inequality in New York City's Restaurant Industry." http://www .urbanjustice.org/pdf/publications/BKDFinalReport.pdf.

Rodgers, William. 2010. "The Threat of Nonpayment: Unpaid Wages and New York's Self-Employed." Heldrich Center for Workforce Development, Bloustein School of Planning and Public Policy. New Brunswick, NJ: Rutgers University.

Rollins, Judith. 1987. *Between Women: Domestics and Their Employers*. Philadelphia: Temple University Press.

Romero, Mary. 1992. *Maid in the U.S.A*. New York, Routledge.

RT. 2011. "OWS Day of Action: Police vs. People (PHOTO, VIDEO)." *RT.com*, November 18. http://rt.com/usa/news/occupy-wall-street-619/.

Rubinstein, Dana. 2012. "'Living Wage' Reminds Bloomberg of Soviet Communism; Say's He'll Stop It in Court If He Has To." *CapitalNewYork.com*, April 13. http://www.capitalnewyork.com/article/politics/2012/04/5689146/living-wage-reminds-bloomberg-soviet-communism-he-says-hell-stop-it.

Russell, Thaddeus. 2001. *Out of the Jungle: Jimmy Hoffa and the Remaking of the American Working Class*. New York: Alfred Knopf.

Rutkoff, Aaron. 2010. "New Bill Would Help Freelancers Fight Deadbeat Companies." *Wall Street Journal*, June 24.

Sadhwani, Gouri. 2007. "The New York Civic Participation Project: Case Study for the SEIU Community Strength Committee." Unpublished report.

Santos, Fernanda. 2011. "In Queens Neighborhood, Schools Are Bursting." *New York Times*, May 10.

Sassen, Saskia. 2001 [first published 1991]. *The Global City: New York, London, Tokyo*. Princeton, NJ: Princeton University Press.

——. 2003. "Global Cities and Survival Circuits." In *Global Woman: Nannies, Maids, and Sex Workers in the New Economy*, edited by Barbara Ehrenreich and Arlie Russell Hochschild, 254–274. New York: Metropolitan Books.

Schaller Consulting. 2003. *The New York City Taxicab Fact Book*. September.

Scheie, David, Craig McGarvey, TriciaVankerkooy, Stephanie J. Nawyn, and T. Wilson. 2009. "Renewing the Democracy: Findings from the 2009 Immigrant Civic Participation Survey Customized for New York Civic Participation Project (NYCPP)." Minneapolis: Touchstone Center for Collaborative Inquiry.

Semple, Kirk. 2012. "Queens Carwash's Employees Are First in City to Join Union." *New York Times*, September 9. http://www.nytimes.com/2012/09/10/nyregion/employees-at-a-queens-carwash-vote-to-unionize.html.

Semuels, Alana. 2011. "Labor Department Reveals More Americans Are Self-Employed." *Los Angeles Times*, February 4.

Sen, Rinku. 2006. "Changing the Menu." *New Labor Forum* 15, (1): 88–93.

Sen, Rinku, and Fekkak Mamdouh. 2008. *The Accidental American: Immigration and Citizenship in the Age of Globalization*. San Francisco: Berret-Koehler Press.

Shapiro, Lila. 2011. "Target Workers Reject Union, Union Cries Foul." *Huffington Post*, June 18. http://www.huffingtonpost.com/2011/06/18/target-union-vote-reject_n_879668.html.

"Shop at Target? You're a Swing Voter." 2006. *Business Week*, September 25. http://www.businessweek.com/stories/2006-09-24/shop-at-target-youre-a-swing-voter.

Skinner, Caroline. 2010. *Challenging City Imaginaries: Street Trader Struggles in Warwick Junction, Durban*. African Centre for Cities. http://africancentreforcities.net/papers/31/.

Slavnic, Zoltan. 2009. "Political Economy of Informalization." *European Societies* 12 (1): 3–23.

Smith, Andrea. 2007. "Introduction: The Revolution Will Not Be Funded." In *The Revolution Will Not Be Funded*, edited by INCITE! Women of Color Against Violence, 1–18. Boston: South End Press.

Snarr, C. Melissa. 2011. *All That You Labor: Religion and Ethics in the Living Wage Movement.* New York: New York University Press.

Sorkin, Michael, ed. 1992. *Variations on a Theme Park: The New American City and the End of Public Space.* New York: Hill and Wang.

Spencer, Jim. 2011. "Target Union Vote a Test for Industry." *Minneapolis Star-Tribune*, June 12.

Standing, Guy. 2011. *The Precariat: The New Dangerous Class.* New York: Bloomsbury Academic.

Staten Island Advance. 2011. "Demonstrators Rally Outside Rep. Michael Grimm's New Dorp Office." *Staten Island Advance*, August 8. http://www.silive.com/eastshore/index.ssf/2011/08/working_families_party_organiz.

Stewart, Michael. 2011. *Money for Nothing: How Interest Rate Swaps Have Become Golden Handcuffs for New Yorkers.* United New York report with Center for Working Families, and the Strong Economy for All Coalition, December 14. http://unitedny.org/files/2012/07/Money-For-Nothing-New-York-Interest-Rate-Swaps.pdf.

Stoller, Paul. 2002. *Money Has No Smell: The Africanization of New York.* Chicago: University of Chicago Press.

Strasser, Susan. 2006. "Woolworth to Wal-Mart: Mass Merchandising and the Changing Culture of Consumption." In *Wal-Mart: The Face of Twenty-First Century Capitalism*, edited by Nelson Lichtenstein, 31–56. New York: New Press.

Street Vendor Project (SVP). 2006. *Peddling Uphill: A Report on the Conditions of Street Vendors in New York City.* http://www.scribd.com/doc/18948529/Peddling-Uphill.

Surico. John. 2012. "NYC Living Wage Bill Heads to Court." *Village Voice*, July 28.

Surowiecki, James. 2002. "Fare Games." *New Yorker*, March 18.

Swanson, Katherine. 2007. "Revanchist Urbanism Heads South: The Regulation of Indigenous Beggars and Street Vendors in Ecuador." *Antipode* 39 (4): 708–28.

Sygnatur, Eric, and Guy Toscano. 2000. "Work-Related Homicides: The Facts." Bureau of Labor Statistics, *Compensation and Working Conditions* Statistics (Spring): 3–8.

Tait, Vanessa. 2005. *Poor Workers' Unions.* Cambridge, MA: South End Press.

Tannock, Stuart. 2001. *Youth at Work: The Unionized Fast-Food and Grocery Workplace.* Philadelphia: Temple University Press.

"Target's Turn to Be Targeted." 2011. *Crain's New York Business.* June 5. http://www.crainsnewyork.com/article/20110605/SUB/306059991.

Tattersall, Amanda. 2010. *Power in Coalition: Strategies for Strong Unions and Social Change.* Ithaca, NY: Cornell University Press.

Ten Eyck, Tiffany. 2010. "Taxi Groups Taking Multiple Routes to Organize." *Labor Notes*, August 24. http://labornotes.org/2010/08/taxi-driver-groups-taking-multiple-routes-organize.

Tilly, Chris. 1992. "Dualism in Part-Time Employment." *Industrial Relations* 31 (2): 330–47.

——. 1996. *Half a Job: Bad and Good Part-Time Jobs in a Changing Labor Market.* Philadelphia: Temple University Press.

Trepasso, Clare. 2011. "Classrooms Crowded in Corona: Parents Demand City Look into Formula." *New York Daily News*, May 11.

Troy, Leo. 1957. *Distribution of Union Membership Among the States, 1939 and 1953.* Cambridge, MA: National Bureau of Economic Research.

Trumka, Richard. 2013. "Remarks." Conference on New Models for Worker Representation, University of Illinois—Chicago (March 7). http://www.aflcio.org/Press-Room/Speeches/Remarks-by-AFL-CIO-President-Richard-L.-Trumka-2013-Conference-on-New-Models-for-Worker-Representation-Chicago.

"UFT Reaches Contract with State for Home Child Care Providers." 2009. UFT.org, July 31. http://www.uft.org/press-releases/uft-reaches-contract-state-home-child-care-providers.

United New York and ALIGN. 2012. *The Economic Low Road: New York Low-Wage Workers and the One-Percenters*. July 19. http://unitedny.org/files/2012/07/The-Economic-Low-Road-New-York-Low-Wage-Workers-and-the-One-Percenters.pdf.

United New York and the Center for Popular Democracy. 2013. *Workers Rising: Organizing Service Jobs for Shared Prosperity in New York City*. http://populardemocracy.org/wp-content/uploads/2013/02/CPD-Workers-Rising-Report-02132013.pdf.

U.S. Bureau of Labor Statistics. 2005. *Contingent and Alternative Employment Arrangements*. February 3. http://www.bls.gov/news.release/pdf/conemp.pdf.

——. Various years. *Current Employment Statistics*. http://bls.gov/ces/data.htm.

——. Various years. *Labor Productivity and Costs*. http://bls.gov/lpc/#data.

——. Various years. *Occupational Employment Statistics*. http://www.bls.gov/oes/.

U.S. Census Bureau. 2012. *Selected Population Profile in the United States. 2008–2010. American Community Survey 3-Year Estimate*. http://factfinder2.census.gov/faces/tableservices/jsf/pages/productview.xhtml?src=bkmk.

U.S. Government Accountability Office. 2006. *Employment Arrangements: Improved Outreach Could Help Ensure Proper Worker Classification*. GAO-06-656: Washington, DC: GAO.

Van Jaarsveld, Danielle D. 2004. "Collective Representation among High-Tech Workers at Microsoft and Beyond: Lessons from WashTech/CWA." *Industrial Relations* 43 (2): 364–85.

——. 2006. "Overcoming Obstacles to Worker Representation: Insights from the Temporary Agency Workforce." *New York Law School Law Review* 7 (56): 355–84.

Vosko, Leah F. 2010. *Managing the Margins: Gender, Citizenship, and the International Regulation of Precarious Employment*. New York: Oxford University Press.

Voss, Kim, and Rachel Sherman. 2000. "Breaking the Iron Law of Oligarchy: Union Revitalization in the American Labor Movement." *American Journal of Sociology* 106 (2): 303–49.

Waheed, Saba, and Laine Romero-Alston. 2003. *UNFARE: Taxi Drivers and the Cost of Moving the City*. New York: Community Development Project of the Urban Justice Center.

Waldinger, Roger. 1996. *Still the Promised City? African-Americans and New Immigrants in Post-Industrial New York*. Cambridge, MA: Harvard University Press.

Walsh, John P. 1993. *Supermarkets Transformed: Understanding Organizational and Technological Innovation*. New Brunswick, NJ: Rutgers University Press.

Warren, Dorian. 2005. "Wal-Mart Surrounded: Community Alliances and Labor Politics in Chicago." *New Labor Forum* 14 (3): 17–23.

Waters, Mary C. 2001. *Black Identities: West Indian Immigrant Dreams and American Realities*. Cambridge, MA: Harvard University Press.

Wei, William. 2004. "A Commentary on Young Asian American Activists from the 1960s to the Present." In *Korean American Youth: Culture, Identify and Ethnicity*, edited by Jennifer Lee and Min Zhou, 299–312. New York: Routledge.

Weinbaum, Eve S. 2004. *To Move a Mountain: Fighting the Global Economy in Appalachia*. New York: New Press.

Western, Bruce, and Jake Rosenfeld. 2011. "Unions, Norms and the Rise in U.S. Wage Inequality." *American Sociological Review* 76 (4): 513–37.

Widdicombe, Lizzie. 2011. "Thin Yellow Line; The Taxi-Driver's Advocate." *New Yorker*, April 18.

Wilkinson, Amy. 2009. "The Entrepreneurial Union: How the Freelancers Union Is Modernizing the Labor Movement for Independent Workers." *Stanford Social Innovation Review* (Fall): 59–60.

Wilson, Marianne. 2011. "Survey: Top 10 Discounters with the Best Consumer Perception." *Chain Store Age*, July 21.

Wolch, Jennifer R. 1990. *The Shadow State: Government and Voluntary Sector in Transition.* New York: Foundation Center.

Wong, Janelle. 2006. *Democracy's Promise: Immigrants and American Civic Institutions.* Ann Arbor: University of Michigan Press.

Wright, Erik Olin. 2000. "Working-Class Power, Capitalist-Class Interests, and Class Compromise." *American Journal of Sociology* 4 (2000): 957–1002.

Wrigley, Julia. 1995. *Other People's Children.* New York: Basic Books.

Yeselson, Rich. 2013. "Fortress Unionism." *Democracy: A Journal of Ideas* 29 (Summer): 68–81.

Zeiger, Henry. 1998. "Hailing Cab Drivers: Labor's Lost Opportunity." *Union Democracy Review* 120 (September).

Ziskind, Minna P. 2003. "Labor Conflict in the Suburbs: Organizing Retail in Metropolitan New York, 1954–1958." *International Labor and Working-Class History* 64 (2003): 55–73.

Zukin, Sharon. 1995. *The Cultures of Cities.* New York: Wiley-Blackwell.

——. 2004. *Point of Purchase: How Shopping Changed American Culture.* New York: Routledge.

About the Contributors

Benjamin Becker is a PhD candidate in History at the City University of New York Graduate Center. His research focus is on the labor movement, civil rights, and education. He is at work on a dissertation about the politics of immigration reform in the late twentieth century.

Marnie Brady is a PhD candidate in Sociology at the City University of New York Graduate Center. Her dissertation focuses on the relationship between labor and housing in the context of private equity investments. Marnie's research and teaching interests in urban politics and social movements developed out of more than a decade of work experience in public policy, participatory action research, and community organizing.

Jeffrey D. Broxmeyer is a PhD candidate in Political Science at the City University of New York Graduate Center. He has previously published in *New Political Science* and *Women's Studies Quarterly*. His dissertation examines the ways in which Gilded Age New York City politicians built financial wealth and the relationship of that process to their political careers.

Kathleen Dunn is an Assistant Professor of Sociology at Loyola University in Chicago. She received her PhD in Sociology from the City University of New York Graduate Center in 2013. She is at work on a book manuscript based on her ethnographic study of the street vending industry in New York City.

Mischa Gaus is the Staff Director of United Food and Commercial Workers Local 2013, a seventeen-thousand-member union based in Brooklyn, New York, that represents workers in the food processing, manufacturing, and warehousing industries. Previously employed as editor of the magazine *Labor Notes*, his work focuses on rank-and-file efforts to build power among low-wage immigrant workers. He received his MA in Labor Studies from CUNY's Murphy Institute, School of Professional Studies, in 2013.

Harmony Goldberg is a PhD candidate in Cultural Anthropology at the City University of New York Graduate Center. Her dissertation focuses on the organizing work of Domestic Workers United. A founder and former codirector of the School Of Unity and Liberation (SOUL), a social justice movement training center in Oakland, California, she has provided political education and writing support to the Right to the City Alliance, the National Domestic Workers Alliance, and the Excluded Workers Congress. She is a founding editor of the online journal *Organizing Upgrade*.

Peter Ikeler received his PhD in Sociology from the City University of New York Graduate Center in 2013 and is Assistant Professor of Sociology at SUNY College at Old Westbury. Previously trained in philosophy and with firsthand experience in the German labor movement, his current research focuses on workplace dynamics and organizing potential in the U.S. retail sector.

Martha W. King is a doctoral student in Sociology at the City University of New York Graduate Center. Her academic research investigates three areas: organizational behavior and change among civic groups; race, ethnicity, and discrimination; and consumerism. She is also a management and strategy consultant to nonprofit, philanthropic, and governmental organizations. She received her BA from Wesleyan University, and two master's degrees—in Public Affairs and in Urban and Regional Planning—from the Woodrow Wilson School for Public and International Affairs at Princeton University.

Jane McAlevey is a PhD candidate in Sociology at the City University of New York Graduate Center. Before entering academia, she worked for many years as an organizer in the labor and environmental justice movements. She is a regular contributor to the *Nation* magazine, which chose her book *Raising Expectations (and Raising Hell)* as the "most valuable book of 2012."

Stephen McFarland is a PhD candidate in Geography at the City University of New York Graduate Center. His dissertation is on the role of union halls, labor temples, and other interior spaces in the formation of the U.S. working class. He is active in the Adjunct Project, which organizes Graduate Center students around issues of precarious labor at CUNY.

Susan McQuade is a doctoral student in Public Health at the City University of New York Graduate Center. She is also a staff member of the New York Committee for Occupational Safety and Health (NYCOSH), where she provides training and technical assistance to workers, unions, and community-based organizations. Before joining NYCOSH, she worked for the Service Employees International Union as a safety and health specialist, a union organizer, a labor educator, and a contract administrator.

Erin Michaels is a doctoral student in Sociology at the City University of New York Graduate Center. She received her master's degree in Sociology from Portland State University. Her research focuses on the U.S. immigrant rights movement, specifically the role of labor and community-based organizations in the struggles of unauthorized immigrant youth for education rights.

Ruth Milkman is a sociologist of labor and labor movements who has written on a variety of topics involving work and organized labor in the United States, past and present. She helped lead a multicity team that produced a 2009 study documenting the prevalence of wage theft and violations of other workplace laws in Los Angeles, Chicago, and New York. Her most recent book is *Unfinished Business* (2013), coauthored with Eileen Appelbaum, a study of paid family leave in California. After twenty-one years as a sociology professor at UCLA, where she directed the Institute for Research on Labor and Employment from 2001 to 2008, she returned to New York City in 2010, where she is Professor of Sociology at the City University of New York Graduate Center and Professor and Academic Director at the Murphy Institute.

Ed Ott is a Distinguished Lecturer in Labor Studies at the Murphy Institute, in the City University of New York's School of Professional Studies. He spent over forty years in the New York City labor movement, as a union organizer, a local union officer, and a political director, and most recently as executive director of the New York City Central Labor Council, AFL-CIO, which includes unions representing over 1.3 million workers. In that position he helped to build relationships between traditional labor unions and worker centers, immigrant rights groups, and community-based organizations. During his tenure as executive director of the NYC Central Labor Council, the Taxi Workers Alliance became the first worker center organization in the United States to affiliate with an AFL-CIO central body.

Ben Shapiro received a BA from Goucher College and an MA in Labor Studies from the Murphy Institute, in the City University of New York's School of Professional Studies. He has experience organizing hotel workers with UNITE HERE and organizing fast food workers in New York with New York Communities for Change (NYCC). He is currently a community organizer with NYCC.

Lynne Turner is the organizing director of New Jersey Communities United. She holds a BA from Swarthmore Collage and received her MA in Labor Studies from the Murphy Institute in 2012. She previously spent two decades working as an organizing director, strategic researcher, and educator in several different organizations, including Jobs with Justice and the Justice for Janitors campaign, with a focus on organizing low-wage workers and working to build labor, community, and global partnerships for economic justice.

Index

Page numbers followed by f or t indicate figures or tables.

Street labor movement. *See* VAMOS Unidos
StreetNet International, 148
Street Vendor Project (SVP), 138–39, 141, 148
Stringer, Scott, 39–40, 303n3
Strong Economy for All coalition, 100, 105
Sugimori, Amy, 191, 192, 193, 196, 204–5
Sweeney, John, 7, 277

Taft-Hartley Act (1947), 4
Tannock, Stuart, 34
Target, union organizing efforts at Valley
    Stream store, 25–48
    age, shift, and gender issues in workers'
        committee, 26–27, 32–34
    anti-immigrant bias, 30–31
    election results, 25, 37
    generational and economic differences
        within immigrant population, 34–37, 36
    grievances, 28–30
    lessons of, 46–47
    management's anti-union strategies, 31,
        37–38, 41–45
    union's broader big-box strategies, 39–41
Tariq, Javaid, 249, 255, 261
Tattersall, Amanda, 97
Taxation issues, Freelancers Union and, 158
Taxi and Limousine Commission (TLC),
    248–49, 252, 254, 256–57, 263
Taxi Workers Alliance, 15, 18, 127
Taxi Workers Alliance Organizing Committee
    (TWAOC), 1, 15, 20, 21. *See also* New York
    Taxi Workers Alliance (NYTWA)
Theodore, Nik, 270
"Think Hard Before You Sign" video, 42–43
Thompson, Allison Julien, 282
Tilly, Chris, 153–54
Trabajadores en Accion (Workers in Action),
    173, 183
Transit Workers Union Local 100, 101
Transport Workers Union, 249
Trumka, Richard, 1, 9, 104, 255–56
Turner, Lowell, 22

Undocumented immigrants. *See* Grocery
    workers, organizing of immigrant
United Federation of Teachers (UFT), 53,
    74–75
United Food and Commercial Workers
    (UFCW), 15, 20, 49, 51, 76, 118
    Target campaign and, 25, 27, 31, 32, 38–41,
        47
United New York, 88–109
    coalition-building and, 92–96
    collaborations, 99–100

initial canvassing and organizing efforts,
    96–99
Occupy Wall Street movement and, 89,
    100–109
partner organizations, 90, 91f, 92
2012 elections and, 107–9
United Retail Employees of America–CIO,
    117–18
UNITE (Union of Needletrades, Industrial, and
    Textile Employees), 15, 66, 119
UNITE HERE, 191, 196, 230, 233
Unpaid Wages Campaign, 158–59

Vacca, James, 83
Valdes, Javier, 178–79, 180–81, 182, 183–84
VAMOS Unidos (Vendedoras Ambulantes
    Movilizando y Organizando en Solidari-
    dad), 134–49
    advantages of street vending, 137
    key areas of work, 146–49
    members' engagement with, 148–49
    regulatory and licensing issues, 135, 136–37,
        140–41, 141t, 145
    similar organizations, 138–40
    street labor movement and, 135–36
    structure, funding, and campaigns of, 142–46
Vendy Awards, 139
Viertel, Josh, 244
Voss, Kim, 14, 66

Wage and Hour Watch program, of New York
    Department of Labor, 317n10
Wage Theft Prevention Act (2010), MRNY and,
    177–78, 185
Walker, Scott, 292
Walmart
    Target contrasted, 39–40
    unions and, 41, 299n39
Walton, Yana, 131
Washington Heights. *See* New York Civic
    Participation Project
Waters, Mary, 34–35
Weinbaum, Eve, 76, 86
Welfare–minimum wage trap, 29–30
Westin, Jonathan, 59
West Indian immigrants. *See* Target, union
    organizing efforts at Valley Stream store
Wha-Hung, Chung, 217
Williams, Jesse T. Jr., 70
Williams-Johnson, Florence, 99
Windows on the World restaurant, 230–31,
    232
Winsten, Richard, 277
Wisconsin, 8, 292